ANALYTICAL AND CROSS-CULTURAL
STUDIES IN WORLD MUSIC

Analytical and Cross-Cultural Studies in World Music

Edited by Michael Tenzer and John Roeder

OXFORD
UNIVERSITY PRESS

OXFORD
UNIVERSITY PRESS

Oxford University Press, Inc., publishes works that further
Oxford University's objective of excellence
in research, scholarship, and education.

Oxford   New York
Auckland   Cape Town   Dar es Salaam   Hong Kong   Karachi
Kuala Lumpur   Madrid   Melbourne   Mexico City   Nairobi
New Delhi   Shanghai   Taipei   Toronto

With offices in
Argentina   Austria   Brazil   Chile   Czech Republic   France   Greece
Guatemala   Hungary   Italy   Japan   Poland   Portugal   Singapore
South Korea   Switzerland   Thailand   Turkey   Ukraine   Vietnam

Library of Congress Cataloging-in-Publication Data
Analytical and cross-cultural studies in world music / edited by Michael Tenzer and John Roeder.
    p.   cm.
Includes bibliographical references and index.
ISBN 978-0-19-538458-1 (alk. paper) — ISBN 978-0-19-538457-4 (alk. paper) 1. World music—History and criticism.
2. World music—Analysis, appreciation. I. Tenzer, Michael. II. Roeder, John.
ML3545.A53   2011
780.9—dc22   2010053120

1 3 5 7 9 8 6 4 2

Printed in the United States of America
on acid-free paper

➤➤　◅◅

for Mike and Kathleen,

and for Bernie and Marion

➤➤ CONTENTS ◄◄

⤙ ABOUT THE COMPANION WEBSITE ⤚
www.oup.com/us/accswm

To accompany *Analytical and Cross-Cultural Studies in World Music,* we have created a password-protected website where readers can access the recordings linked to the chapters. Throughout the text these are signaled with Oxford's symbol.◐ Most of them can be played directly on the site. We have provided links to eight more that can downloaded elsewhere at nominal cost. The remaining two (discussed in chapter 11 only) were unavailable when the book went to press. Also on the site is a complete transcription of the music discussed in chapter 6 and an innovative interactive video interface linked to chapter 3.

Access with username Music5 and password Book1745.

Introduction

John Roeder

The predecessor to this volume, *Analytical Studies in World Music* (Tenzer 2006), explored how diverse cultures organize sound into music. In each chapter, using terms and concepts familiar to most musically trained readers, a specialist identified the elements, processes, and form of a particular selection, represented by an audio recording and detailed transcriptions. Going beyond an inventory of generic technical features, the contributors highlighted the music's individuality, in many cases by focusing on its distinctive ways of shaping time. Hitherto such specifically analytical accounts could only be found dispersed throughout the academic research literature. Bringing them together was intended to satisfy the evident desire of music practitioners and students to appreciate others' music in these terms. To scholars it also exemplified how music theory broadly construed—not as a codification of Western harmonic practice, but as symbolic systems for conveying musical knowledge—can serve ethnomusicology's consideration of music in culture, by enabling the description and comparison of sound patterns, and of the cognitive schemas that shape how they are heard.

For many reasons this project deserved continuation. Building a knowledge base for comparison requires an appropriately diverse set of repertoires, both musically and geographically, but the constraints of a single volume forced the omission of whole continents and popular genres. The more that today's students gather music recordings from various places and times into their personal music libraries, the greater the need for an accessible consolidation of expert analyses that can help them appreciate its nature and contexts, whether as part of an expanded music pedagogy appropriate for our globalizing era or as models for further research. Not incidentally, the project has revived interconnected methodological questions about the purview of musical analysis and about the possibility of cross-cultural comparison; these concern the object of analysis, the cultural values it respects or violates, and the extent to which it connects listening and production and their respective systems of signification. Any contemplation of them would surely benefit from more case studies.

We are therefore pleased to present this second volume of analytical studies in world music.[1] While expanding the scope to many more cultures, it maintains a similar format and objectives. Each chapter treats a recording, accessible through a link on the companion website at www.oup.com/us/accswm. To encourage the most appropriate analysis, as well as a consideration of the questions mentioned above, we have not required the authors to conform to any particular theoretical approach, but only to be explicit about their methodology. Along with transcriptions, they provide explanations of instrumentation and of pertinent indigenous conceptions of the music, and they contextualize their findings with historical narratives, characterizations of the genre, and personal anecdotes. Again we have guided them to make each discussion accessible to a general readership without specialized knowledge beyond basic musical literacy. Naturally our coediting has reflected both our common interests and our individual specialties (in my case, theories of rhythm), so these studies, like those in the original collection, share a focus on musical time. But whereas the previous essays were grouped to highlight facets of musical periodicity—repetition and its role in musical form—the contributions to this volume seemed to invite the comparison of other temporal aspects, and also some explicit comparisons of music across different cultures.

To that end we have sequenced the chapters in part I, "Analytical Encounters with Music of Diverse Cultures," to juxtapose musics that originate in cultures widely separated in space or time but that share some reasonably objective features (such as type of performing ensemble, notation, or union with other media like text or dance) or technical properties (such as strophic form or meterless pulse). What is shared varies with the chapter pairings, so that each juxtaposition suggests different ways to compare and contrast cultures' musical systems, forms, and techniques, and to consider the validity and value

1. Support for the research and production of this book was provided, in part, by a research grant to the editors from the Social Sciences and Humanities Research Council of Canada.

of such an exercise. As I briefly summarize each essay below, I raise a few points of comparison with the essays next to it, hoping to encourage readers to consider others (and to consider mine critically).

Interwoven Patterns of Music and Culture

Although the specific points of correspondence and difference vary from pair to pair, several recurring threads of inquiry can be perceived to weave throughout all the essays. These range in scope from microscopic descriptions of local patterns to macroscopic observations about the musics' social functions:

- How does the distinctive character of a musical item arise from its particular sound patterns and their positions within a culturally constrained field of possibilities?
- How do certain categories of sound patterns (such as cadence formulas) play greater or lesser roles in various kinds of music?
- How does the organization of rhythm—its regularity, the interplay of voices in the texture, the sense of continuity—reflect the nature of the performing ensemble?
- How does the music's large-scale organization mediate the specific properties of its local materials and its social and performing contexts?
- How do musicians construct their social identities by their actions in relation to cultural convention and to the internal exigencies of their music?

The order of this list reflects a crucial assertion: that these questions are not incompatible, but form an interconnected continuum. The essays' more global concerns with human social behavior rely on their accurate and appropriate smaller-scale descriptions of musical minutiae. Analysis thus provides a basis for progressing from an appreciation of particular local patterns to a more general understanding of music in culture.

In chapter 1, Naoko Terauchi analyzes *Etenraku,* an example of Japanese imperial court music. This item poses several challenges to listeners unfamiliar with its conventions. The protracted, wavering tempo obscures continuity and phrasing; and while the ensemble texture appears to be an accompanied heterophony, the identity of melodic events is frequently blurred when several instruments play conflicting pitches. By reviewing the history of the genre, its systems of modes and rhythm, and its instruments' various notational schemes, she demonstrates that the music is indeed organized on several hierarchical levels as an embellished, memorable basic melody. The conflicting notes actually originated in unnotated variants of the same scale degree, but their clash is now heard as expressive, not wrong. Terauchi points out other unnotated features as well, such as the way that the players take turns leading the ensemble to the next beat. And she shows how the large repeated sections of the basic melody are measured by faster repeated accompaniment patterns that are understood to organize time cyclically even when (as in this recording) they cease sounding.

Although the subject of the next chapter, Machaut's fourteenth-century polyphonic balade *De petit po,* is a landmark in the development of Western art music, its context and conventions are unfamiliar to most modern listeners. So, as much as the other world music treated in this volume, it benefits from a culturally grounded analysis, here provided by Elizabeth Eva Leach. Like *Etenraku,* it is an ensemble piece intended for the delectation of a social elite, with each part's rhythm notated with reference to an underlying series of conceptually equal durations to which the performers synchronize, and with the pitches selected from a referential diatonic collection. Leach's discussion, like Terauchi's, considers the problems of interpreting scores whose realization is dependent on extranotational traditions, and of the meaning of old music to modern listeners. To determine which of the parts should play together and which pitches they may sound, she locates (as the original performers must have) repetitions of a basic "directed progression" of harmonic intervals, variously transposed and elaborated. This schema was understood by its audience to provide changing tension and cadence to music organized rhythmically in a continuous, noncyclical flow. As in *Etenraku,* form arises from the repetition then alternation of large, multiphrase sections, roughly equal in duration, that are distinguished by changes of content, range, and pitch focus. But *De petit po*'s formal divisions also match the organization of its poetic text into strophes with a recurring refrain. Musical events that satisfy or violate schema, along with quotations of well-known tunes, inflect the words' meaning, which engages the culture's intertwined concepts of gender, religion, and social status.

"Sorriso Aberto," analyzed in chapter 3 by Jason Stanyek and Fabio Oliveira, is also a song with ensemble accompaniment, but one that is sited as specifically and richly in the culture of modern-day Rio de Janeiro as are the previous musics in their respective ancient courts. The authors focus on the text (as witty and rich in its own way as Machaut's), on form, and especially on musical processes, the determination of which poses a special challenge since, like much world music, the performance realizes not a score, but an unnotated exemplar. They find that, although the song does realize a predetermined, metrically regular but asymmetrically grouped progression (analogous to *De petit po*), the essence of its processes resides more in the constantly varying "groove" of improvised and sometimes unsynchronized instrumental interactions, which they represent through innovative notation and interactive audiovisuals. Both through its own temporalities and as part of an hours-long social event, the song blurs the boundaries between performers and audience.

A regular succession of distinctive events also underlies a rather different music, Thelonius Monk's solo piano improvisation on the 1940s ballad "I Should Care," which is the subject of chapter 4. Through a concise summary of jazz theory, and with reference to the idioms of Monk's contemporaries, Evan Ziporyn and Michael Tenzer explain how the performed sounds both divulge and resist implicit structures. Essentially, Monk elaborates on a pre-composed continuity—the chord changes and melody of the source tune, analogous to the "deep melody" in *Etenraku,* and drawing upon a harmonic language related to that of "Sorriso Aberto"—in the context of an understood but elastic meter; as in *De petit po,* this underlying continuity involves variously elaborated directed progressions that are grouped to match the versification of a text. But, as the authors detail, he constantly diverges from the norm, creating discontinuity by dissonance and extreme tempo variation, while maintaining an instantly recognizable set of pianistic techniques that include (as do the instruments of "Sorriso Aberto") faintly audible sounds and special tone colors. A listener who knows the norm and attends carefully to all dimensions of sound can attribute to his playing a "quest for self-realization" that positions him distinctively within mid-twentieth-century American musical culture.

Chapter 5, by Richard Widdess, concerns another premeditated solo improvisation, an *ālāp* by North Indian sitarist Budhaditya Mukherjee. He finds that it engages not only culturally specific schemas—the characteristic patterns of its *rāga*—but also more general expectations of melodic discourse, possibly because it was intended as a recording, capable of repeated replay and study by listeners across the world. Its focal pitches are organized into a clear overall contour and are elaborated locally by a variety of inventive melodic phrases, often in nested recursive processes, also conforming to contextually established contour schemas. The analytical description focuses on basic musical techniques that create continuity within the phrases and that articulate their beginnings and endings, techniques that seem to apply to music of the preceding chapters as well. The temporality of the *ālāp* also bears more specific comparison with Monk's improvisation. Each creates a waning and ebbing temporal flow, within a free tempo only occasionally regulated by pulse, by raising and playing with knowledgeable listeners' expectations—about the melodic tendencies of tones within the *rāga,* or of the progress of the underlying chord changes of "I Should Care." By repeating, varying, and developing distinctive gestures, each artist not only creates a coherent and unified composition, but also calls attention to his unique and original vision, an indication of the value that these different cultures place on the individual.

The productive tension between individualism and group values is evident in the next chapter's analysis of an ensemble improvisation by the BSC, a performance collective situated in the artistic and intellectual milieu of the American Northeast. Unlike in all the other music discussed in this book, the performers eschew predetermined schemas of content and form. Yet there remain the basic cognitive mechanisms for grouping, shared by performer and listener alike, to which the preceding analyses have also referred. Lou Bunk, a composer and concert producer belonging to this community, explains how the performers take advantage of those mechanisms to articulate beginnings and endings, maintain continuity and gradual change, and create loose sectional forms by listening to and responding to each other's idiosyncratic contributions. These interactions, like those of "Sorriso Aberto," give a sense of shared leadership that resembles how the players of *Etenraku* alternate responsibility for driving toward the next beat, but is not so evident in the master-led ensemble musics discussed elsewhere in this volume. Undirected by any essential pitch or rhythmic regularity, the listener feels an intense focus on each event but also a sense of progress inculcated (as in *ālāp*) by the sustaining and incremental variation of activity. The performers seem able to enfold any sound—even the siren of a passing emergency vehicle—into the ongoing becoming. Their music thus strives toward a utopia of complete personal autonomy and a perfectly cooperative, environmentally responsive community, metaphorically linking the creators and their sounds. These ideals are thrown into relief by Bunk's history of their struggles to establish this music as a distinct genre, with its own specialists, venues, and audiences.

Chapter 7 demonstrates how very differently structured musics can serve similar social purposes. Whereas the BSC's music is variegating timbre, microtonally inflecting pitch, freely developing form, and intense listening to quiet, South Korean *p'ungmul* is percussive, pitchless, periodic, and brash. Yet Nathan Hesselink's close analysis shows how the latter also fosters community and a transcendent experience of time, even considered independently of the pageantry it normally accompanies. Although there are no melodies, the music, like *Etenraku*, heterophonically declaims a set succession of related patterns, each of which can be repeated *ad lib*. (To specify them, Hesselink avails himself of indigenous notation that emphasizes the cyclic processes.) The repetition promotes entrainment, enhanced by the social connotations of the particular patterns. One may perceive the succession of patterns as a sectional form, but they are so similar that for the performers it also becomes a gradual process toward total engagement rather than closure. The design draws amateur musicians from the community into the ensemble, increases their mastery, and eventually gives them some freedom of expression.

Music associated with community ceremonies is also the subject of the following discussion by Victoria Lindsay Levine and Bruno Nettl, which compares the form of songs from different North American Indian cultures. The topic raises some classic methodological questions about how to transcribe and compare music about which there is little verbal knowledge. Navigating these uncertainties, the authors locate in each song the basic units of musical grouping by observing how repetition occurs both very locally—in vocal pulsing, reiterated pitches, and brief motives—and over long time spans, as phrases and phrase sequences are repeated. Across all four examples, separated in time and geography, they find a principle of "asymmetric" (by which they mean inexact or varied) repetition governing the melodic process. (One can hear this principle operating also at levels of grouping structure both smaller and larger than the phrase and strophe.) The pervasiveness of the principle in this repertoire, and its comparative rarity in music elsewhere, suggests prehistorical diffusion across the continent.

A focus on cross-cultural musical influence is also evident in chapter 9, which employs analysis to expose not only similarity, but also culturally significant difference. Linda Barwick examines a whole range of musical features—phrase lengths, contour, text repetition, melodic variation, rhythm, instrumentation, and texture—in three examples of northwestern Australian Aboriginal music. By typologizing them, she is able to illuminate the defining characteristics of the songs' respective genres and to give a detailed confirmation of cross-repertory distinctions that inside authorities acknowledge. For example, one song is organized as a succession of repeated strophes, whereas in another the music and text recur cyclically at different rates. She also shows how certain features derive from the exigencies of the accompanying dances and ritual context, rather than from any purely musical schemas. Not only her transcription methods, but also her actual observations on grouping, melodic contours, and strophic form resemble those of Levine and Nettl, even though the respective aboriginal musical repertoires stem from opposite sides of the globe.

Daring to Compare

This last pairing, then, brings to the fore some methodological questions like those I broached above, which are addressed in part II, "Cross-Cultural Analytical Comparisons." How can analysis inform a comparison of the meaning and value that inhere to organized sound in different cultures? Do the structural properties exposed by analysis index the essential cultural meanings of different musics any more than a description of shape, color, and nutrient content accounts for the way one values apples and oranges? Or are the respective cultures' systems of musical signification so incommensurate that any technical similarities are misleading? One can contemplate such questions from the listener's perspective, considering how analysis may contribute to one's personal evaluations of various musics. Or one can look to see whether analysis captures the creative responses of musicians when they confront music outside their culture. The final two chapters approach the questions from these different angles.

Michael Tenzer describes a personal effort to achieve an inner reconciliation between two musics in terms of the values they signify. He establishes that Balinese musicians evaluate pieces in the contemporary *lelambatan* genre in terms of the quality of *bayu* (loosely, the rhythmic flow) that he can attribute to specific musical processes. The sensations that one gamelan passage elicits in him are similar to those he attributes to the beginning of a nineteenth-century Western chamber music movement by Robert Schumann, which similarity he explains by comparing their respective, culturally contingent "middleground levels." Ultimately this comparison enables him to determine, with personal integrity, which music he values the most. More generally, as formerly isolated traditions, under pressure from globalization, are fading into history, his essay argues for grasping the interconnections among cultural values through analysis.

In contrast, the final essay, by Simha Arom and Denis-Constant Martin, considers a public effort to mediate the values of different cultures by combining their artistic expressions, namely, the commercial venture marketed as "world music." The authors explore the various and sometimes inconsistent connotations of this term, attributing its origins to historical Western fascinations with exoticisms and the Other, but also identifying the contemporary values it connotes that appeal to its target audience. They show that there are actually several types of "world music" distinguished by the way they are produced. Focusing on the "synthetic" category, they use analysis to inquire whether the shared production method is reflected in any consistent traits. This requires deciding which theoretical concepts can be applied across the many different cultures represented by their world music exemplars. Suggestively, they decide to compare not pitch structures, such as scales or chords, but rhythmic form—grouping, meter, and repeated durational patterns— which are treated in all of the other essays in this book. This analysis informs a typology of synthetic world music they propose based on how it combines preexisting material simultaneously (within the texture) and successively (in sectional form).

Global Concerns

The ordering of chapters is not meant to restrict attention to sorts of contrasts and similarities I briefly mentioned above. Considered altogether, these eleven essays also engage perpetually vital questions about music representation, cognitive universals, and the purview of music analysis. A brief overview of them may be useful for the reader who wishes to analyze other music of the world, to extend or ponder more deeply the analyses given here, or to undertake further comparisons. To start, we must acknowledge that in many cultural contexts in which organized sound is inseparable from religious practice or dance, or where it results from a process regulated by certain principles rather than from the repetition of a fixed model, the Western notion of a musical work is inappropriate (Bohlman 2002: 6–9; Goehr 1995). This does not prohibit us from describing sound organization; indeed, analysis may help explain why music foreign to our experience can affect us as profoundly as did our contributors' first encounters with their eventual objects of study. But it affects how we regard the recordings and transcriptions upon which every essay concentrates, whose similar appearance may mislead us into assuming that all music is the same kind.

In seeking to describe and compare music, one naturally wants to concentrate on essential features, but, depending on the nature of the music, these may be represented with varying definiteness and fidelity. For *Etenraku* and *De petit po,* the music consists of distinctive sound sequences and combinations that are specified by a fixed score, to the extent that it can be interpreted in its proper historical, cultural, and performative context. Most of the other music discussed in this volume—Aboriginal songs, Brazilian *pagode,* gamelan, and "world music"—similarly consists of prescribed series of sounds or sound relations, but these are specified by an exemplar (such as a remembered performance) rather than in written notation (S. Davies 2003: 35). In contrast, the improvisations of Mukherjee and the BSC each constitute a unique act. The focus of study in those cases is not some stable underlying exemplar but rather particular audible features or processes that arise from the principles of its creation (D. Davies 2004), which may be evident in other improvisations of that performer or genre.

Comparisons are complicated not only by these different ontologies, but also by the subjectivity of transcription. The information on a score, representing the composer's performance instructions, does not comport readily with a notation of what an analyst hears, even if informed by the creators. On the one hand, unnotated performance practices may greatly affect how a score sounds (hence Leach and Terauchi renotate original scores as transcriptions of real or imagined performances). On the other hand, transcriptional accuracy may be limited by failing to discriminate significant differences, by imposing foreign conceptions of pitch and time, or by the limitations of the recording itself, which, as Levine and Nettl caution, can distort timbre and form. The authority with which an analyst's transcription seems to establish a music's essential facts is subject to poststructuralist objections that "facts are probably theory-laden—selected, organized, hierarchized, formalized, narrativized—and theories probably instantiate ethical values that are founded on political commitments" (Scherzinger 2004: 258). Readers may wish to ponder the values and commitments underlying the facts observed in the essays here, and the extent to which they reflect ethics and commitments of the music's creators as well as the authors as listeners.

Some of these difficulties are evident in the essays' transcriptions and other graphical representations. The Western staff notation that they share seems valid to the extent that it captures some essential distinctions and identities, such as the diatonic ways of categorizing pitch that seem to apply to music of Japan, India, and late-Medieval Europe, not to mention jazz and various popular musics that regularly employ it. But its rigid quantization makes it hard to transcribe Monk's time-warping performance, to express tempo change in *gagaku,* to distinguish the critical timbral subtleties of the *pagode* instruments, and to represent microtonal inflections in *ālāp* and timbre-and-form music. Indeed, nearly every author who employs Western notation resorts to modifications and extensive verbal commentary in order to describe essential features it omits. One alternative explored in several essays is proportional notation, which entails a spatial metaphor for time of which one must be critically aware; for music such as *p'ungmul,* which is specified only by attack times, not by duration or pitch, comprehensible indigenous notation seems more appropriate and concise. Still, appropriately adapted Western notation does provide a common, familiar symbol system to fix musical sound sequences for study.

Granting the ontological disparities and the potential for misrepresentation, it is nevertheless possible to discern some basis for comparing these musics in the similar observations and terminology the authors employ. They all endeavor, through transcription and description, to identify those aspects of the music that are both perceptible and essential, and to connect their hearing of the music to what is known about the creator's (often unsystematic or vaguely articulated) conceptions, and to the culture that embeds them. By thus synthesizing listening- and making-oriented discourses about music (Nattiez 1990), they assert that patterns are chosen and combined for specific purposes, not arbitrarily, and that those purposes do not solely satisfy conventions in the minds of the creators, but also engage features that are audible and relatively stable for most listeners.

All the most striking similarities involve rhythm, consistent with recent research suggesting that "some temporal processes may be universal, in the sense that they function in a similar manner irrespective of an individual's cultural exposure and experience" (Drake and Bertrand 2001: 17). Analysis of rhythm need not impose Western aesthetic concepts such as "structural unity," "organicism," "developing variation," or "absolute music." Rather, with a tightly controlled theoretical vocabulary, it can focus attention on what both insiders and outsiders can hear, as the essays in this collection do. This sort of analysis is thus not an etic imposition, but, as I argue below, an indispensable method of appreciating the individuality of a music, recognizing its similarities to other music, and understanding its dynamic relationship to its cultural contexts.

One fundamental cognitive process is the association of successive musical events into groups. Listeners sense the same sorts of temporal properties in groups—beginning, ending, continuation—as they do for the individual sounds that constitute them, and they understand them organized hierarchically, hearing shorter groups connected into larger ones, analogous to the way that one strings together successive gestures to play music or accomplish other tasks. Memory permits a comparison of present sensations with remembered experience, that is, to compare the quality and features of currently proceeding groups with those of past groups.

The description of grouping structure is one of the central concerns of every essay; for example, authoritative informants often focus on sectional design as critical to the music's identity. Attention to even such a basic property pays surprisingly rich dividends, not only in discovering shared procedures in different music, such as the few I mentioned in the chapter summaries above, but also in describing each music's particularity. Consider, for instance, the distinctive grouping structures of some of the music discussed here: the unequal durations of the groups in North American Indian songs, patched together from the most elemental motivic cells; the distinctive ways that the BSC starts and cadences its phrases; the role of unheard background melody in maintaining group continuity at the glacial tempos of *Etenraku* and "I Should Care"; the ways that the grouping of Machaut's music both supports and cuts across the syntax of his poetry; and the dialog of voices and instruments and the surprising variability of group length in *pagode* strophes. Some music is individuated by the ways it *blurs* grouping: the subtle and gradual variations of motivic content in *ālāp* that only retrospectively are understood to signal new sections; the conflict of textural discontinuity and harmonic continuity in m. 29 of "I Should Care"; and the ways that the Kiowa Peyote song simultaneously projects two- and three-phrase structure.

Another principle evident in nearly all the music is the repetition of patterns, ranging from specific sounding pitched rhythms to more abstract successions that are understood but not necessarily sounded. It entrains listeners, and it contributes to the perception of grouping by marking beginnings and endings. Music can be characterized according to the explicitness of the repetition, by the way that various periodicities combine or are arranged hierarchically, and by whether they are presented explicitly with repeated patterns or implicitly with underlying metrical cycles.

Like grouping analysis, such detailed characterization of periodicity provides a highly salient description of a music's individuality. For instance, in Monk's improvisation the informed listener senses the tension between his incredibly wavering tempo and the pervasive periodicity (regular tempo, quadruple meter, highly symmetrical melodic construction) of the source tune. Just at the moment when the tune's periodicity is most forceful—in the drive toward the final cadence—Monk is most free, slowing greatly, then breaking into an unprecedented world with different chords, scales, and a sudden bebop swing. As another example, in "Sorriso Aberto" different sorts of periodicities proceed at the same time, each articulated in distinctive ways by the different instruments and continually varying in such a way that every moment is unique.

Such individuality is often most apparent when comparing musics that are similar. For instance, the striking similarities between *Etenraku* and *De petit po,* mentioned above, also highlight their substantial differences. *Etenraku*'s beats are very slow and somewhat elastic, and the music involves a multibeat cycle of distinctive percussion events, which is constantly and exactly repeated. The contents of the cycle are strongly directed, through acceleration, toward certain moments, and the phrasing boundaries coincide with cycle boundaries. Even when the cycle is not explicit, as in latter half of the version studied here, these affects of periodicity persist, and we understand even fragmentary events as locked to the cycle. In contrast, *De petit po* constantly varies its rhythm; there is no repeated duration between the mensuration value and the length of the section. Direction is created by the repetition of formulaic contrapuntal progression, arranged irregularly. It has fewer parts, and they are not doubled. All these factors, together of course with the fact that it sets a personal and witty text about courtly love, prioritizes the individual will. In *Etenraku,* individuality is certainly apparent—in the local deviations from and embellishments of the melodic core tone, and in the way that different instruments take charge of the tempo at different moments in the cycle—but without detracting from the impressive ensemble conformity to the basic melody. These examples, as well as my comments about the essays above, show how rhythmically oriented analysis may serve one aspect of ethnomusicology's inquiry into the relation of music and culture: the role of music in defining the identity of the culture and the groups and individuals who comprise it.

Also like grouping analysis, analysis of periodicity permits recognizing similarities between music from different cultures, grounded on cognitive principles shared by creator and listener. An example from this collection is the process shared by the *djanba* song item and the Kiowa Peyote song, both of which establish a seven-beat pattern by repetition, then vary the length, and then return to it. *Analytical Studies in World Music* recognized the power of such comparisons by grouping the essays according to the sorts of periodicities present in the music they discussed. Michael Tenzer's afterword to this volume extends that scheme into a "topology of world musical temporalities" that sorts the music discussed here in both volumes into temporal categories, each featuring a particular mix of periodicity, grouping structure, and directed change. We invite readers to evaluate how this classification method applies to other music.

A coordinated consideration of grouping and periodicity (and change) can also expand our theoretical understanding of how these aspects of temporality affect and interact with each other. For instance, Mukherjee's *ālāp* can be heard as a study of the juxtaposition of measured and unmeasured time. Although his improvisation mostly floats untethered to an entraining pulse stream, the artist often initiates each fresh phrase with regular strumming on the sitar drone strings, and the resulting expectations of durational repetition permeate and shape the subsequent free rhythms. As another example, it is also interesting to observe, in the absence of an underlying rhythmic cycle, such as *De petit po,* the Arapaho Wolf Dance Song, or *Phoneme (3),* how group endings are much more definite and formulaic than in music where cycle endings regularly recur.

Thus, along with the specific insights the essays provide on their respective subjects, they collectively contribute to our understanding of universal aspects of musical production and cognition. We hope that readers will take from them the inspiration to extend this exploration of the nature of music, the specific ways it manifests itself in culture, and its centrality to human feeling, thought, and society. Musicians of the world—the ultimate experts in the shaping of time—have given us much to wonder at.

References

Bohlman, Philip V. 2002. *World Music: A Very Short Introduction.* Oxford: Oxford University Press.

Davies, David. 2004. *Art as Performance.* Oxford: Blackwell.

Davies, Stephen. 2003. *Themes in the Philosophy of Music.* New York: Oxford University Press.

Drake, Carolyn, and Daisy Bertrand. 2001. "The Quest for Universals in Temporal Processing in Music." *Annals of the New York Academy of Sciences* 930: 17–27.

Goehr, Lydia. 1995. *The Imaginary Museum of Musical Works.* Oxford: Oxford University Press.

Nattiez, Jean-Jacques. 1990. *Music and Discourse: Toward a Semiology of Music,* trans. Carolyn Abbate. Princeton, NJ: Princeton University Press.

Scherzinger, Martin. 2004. "The Return of the Aesthetic: Musical Formalism and Its Place in Political Critique." In *Beyond Structural Listening? Postmodern Modes of Hearing,* ed. Andrew dell'Antonio, 252–277. Berkeley and Los Angeles: University of California Press.

Tenzer, Michael, ed. 2006. *Analytical Studies in World Music.* New York: Oxford University Press.

PART I

*Analytical Encounters with Music
in Diverse Cultures*

CHAPTER I

Surface and Deep Structure in the Tôgaku Ensemble of Japanese Court Music (Gagaku)

Naoko Terauchi

Tôgaku 唐楽 (literally, "music of [the Chinese] Tang [dynasty]") comprises a large portion of Japanese court music *gagaku,* which has been passed down and strongly associated with imperial court cultures for more than 1,300 years. This essay clarifies how its melody and rhythm are organized on multiple structural levels. Ethnomusicologist John Blacking employs the

Photo: Kangen Ensemble of the Ono Gagaku Kai Society, 2006 in New York. Photo by James Ware Billett.

concepts of surface structure and deep structure respectively to analyze musical patterns and to interpret cognitive processes (Blacking 1971). His notion of deep structure comprises an especially wide and deep viewpoint from which to understand the nonmusical, cultural, and social background of human behaviors. Here, however, I would like to limit the connotations of these terms simply to the context of sonic form and process. Between the surface and deep structures in present-day *tôgaku* practice there is certainly a disjunction of musical idiom and mode. In other words, different principles govern each level of the music. Analysis of these levels in contemporary practice reveals stages of historical change. The disjunctions it identifies between surface melody and deep melody not only inform an understanding of contemporary *tôgaku* but also provide important clues that permit a reconstruction of features of this music as it is thought to have been in the past, closer to its Tang Chinese source.

Current *gagaku* tradition can be divided into three categories according to origin and style: (1) indigenous vocal and dance repertoires, which are primarily performed in Shinto (Japanese native religion) ceremonies accompanied by both indigenous and foreign instruments; (2) foreign instrumental music and dances, *tôgaku* and *komagaku* ("music of Korea") used in various court, Buddhist, and Shinto ceremonies, which feature instruments brought from the Asian mainland; and (3) vocalized Japanese or Chinese poetry, *saibara* and *rôei*, established in ninth-century Japan and enjoyed mainly by high-ranking noblemen in informal court ceremonies.

Tôgaku employs a characteristic ensemble of instruments introduced during the Tang era (618–907): *shô* (mouth organ), *hichiriki* (reed pipe), *ryûteki* (transverse flute), *biwa* (lute), *koto* (zither), *taiko* (big drum), *shôko* (small gong), and *kakko* (barrel-shaped drum). The music is *heterophonic* in that every melodic instrument plays a unique realization of a single, shared basic skeletal melody. But these realizations sometimes sound "contradictory" to one another. The inconsistencies are especially evident in the surface melodic patterns of the *ryûteki* and *hichiriki* parts, which lost some of their original Chinese modal features over the course of the long history since their introduction into Japan. On the other hand, the original Chinese modal principles are preserved well in the basic melody.[1]

---

1. The article on *tôgaku* in *The New Grove Dictionary of Music and Musicians* claims that *ryûteki* and *hichiriki* melodies, at least their surface structure, are "not part of the legacy from China" and have developed independently since the fourteenth century or earlier (Marett 2001). This perspective summarizes the work of a considerable body of scholarship by Laurence Picken, Allan Marett, and others in the so-called

Here, focusing on a short but well-made (and the most popular) piece, *Etenraku* in *hyô-jô* mode, I examine (1) musical idioms of each instrument, conversation among the instruments, and melodic patterns associated with the registers of each instrument in the surface structure; (2) the original characteristics of the mode according to Chinese theory, which are clear in the basic melody, and the structure of the melodic patterns therein; (3) different principles of modulation and transposition between modes in the surface and deep structures; and I demonstrate that (4) it is possible to reconstruct ancient *tôgaku* melodies by reading and interpreting current and historical sources of music notation with a full understanding of the relationship between the current surface realization and the deep basic melody.

Surface Structure of Etenraku

Rhythmic Structure, Tempo, and Form

There are two categories of rhythm in *tôgaku*, nonmetrical and metrical. Short introductory pieces (preludes) and closing patterns are often nonmetrical, whereas the main body of a piece is metrical. A significant aspect of the metrical rhythm is a cyclic principle in which the last beat of a unit is of primary importance.[2] Traditionally, it is marked by a stroke of the big drum known as *taiko*. The *taiko* stroke is called *hyôshi*, a term also indicating the measurement of a rhythmic cycle. The rhythmic unit consists of four, six, or eight parts, called *kobyôshi* ("small" *hyôshi*) that can be thought of as "measures" in Western notation. The unit made of four *kobyôshi* is referred to as *yo-hyôshi* (*yo* = four), six as *mu-hyôshi* (*mu* = six), and eight as *ya-hyôshi* (*ya* = eight). If each *kobyôshi* includes four beats, it is categorized as *haya* ("fast"), while it is labeled *nobe* ("extended") if it contains eight beats. For example, *Etenraku* is considered *haya yo-hyôshi*, wherein one unit of the cycle consists of four measures and every measure includes four beats (figure 1.1). Other types of metrical structure include *tada-byôshi* and *yatara-byôshi*. The former has alternating two- and four-beat measures (2 + 4), whereas the latter alternates two- and three-beat measures (2 + 3).

Cambridge School. The present analysis complements the Cambridge perspective by emphasizing the pitches falling on the first beat of every measure, which still mostly match those of *shô, biwa,* and *koto* and keep the outline of the original Chinese melody (discussed in detail later).

2. This is similar to Chinese *nanguan* and Indonesian gamelan, in which *paiban* or *gong* punctuate cycle endings.

haya-yo-hyôshi
1 · · · 2 · · · 3 · · · ● · · ·
haya-mu-hyôshi
1 · · · 2 · · · 3 · · · 4 · · · 5 · · · ● · · ·
haya-ya-hyôshi
1 · · · 2 · · · 3 · · · 4 · · · 5 · · · 6 · · · 7 · · · ● · · ·

Figure 1.1.   Rhythmic structure of *haya-byôshi* (● = *taiko*).

Thus, the *taiko* is struck with strict regularity once every four measures in *Etenraku* (every six or eight measures in other pieces) and is anticipated as the moment when all instruments converge. However, the rhythmic cycles and melodic phrases do not begin or end together. In *Etenraku,* melodic phrases start with the second measure of the rhythmic cycle. If we analyze a *tôgaku* piece prioritizing melody, the *taiko* beat falls in the middle of each melodic phrase (figure 1.2).

Beats in contemporary *tôgaku* performance are actually not equal in duration but rather elastic. In particular, often the last beat of a measure is extended and the original tempo recovered on the first beat of the next measure. Over the larger scale, the tempo also changes, often beginning slowly ($\jmath$= 40 or so), then gradually accelerating toward the end.[3]

In this slow tempo, two measures make one unit of melody. In figure 1.2, the first two measures (comprising the rhythm that is specified by the mnemonic syllables *to – ra – ro o ru ro*) make a unit, and the next two measures (*ta – a ro ra a a –*) make another unit, which *ryûteki* and *hichiriki* can play with a single breath. In the current standard notation of *gagaku* (*Meiji-senteifu*[4]), each such unit is punctuated by intercolumnal dots.[5]

3. The final tempo differs among pieces. However, music for dance accompaniment *(bugaku)* often ends at $\jmath$ = 80–100, while music without dance *(kangen)* can end as slow as $\jmath$ = 50–60. The tempo was much faster, both in *kangen* and *bugaku,* at the beginning of the twentieth century (Terauchi 2002).

4. *Meiji-senteifu* was compiled in 1876 and 1888 by Gagakukyoku, a predecessor of the present-day Kunaichô gakubu, or the Department of Music, Imperial Household Agency, which has been the highest authority of the *gagaku* tradition since the Meiji era.

5. Sukehiro Shiba (1898–1982), a court musician who, in the *Meiji-senteifu,* completed a great work of transcription of the whole *gagaku* repertoire into Western notation, refers to a two-measure unit as *gakushi* ("musical word"), and to a melody lasting one rhythmic cycle (*hyôshi*) as *gakku* ("musical phrase") (Shiba 1968, 1969, 1971, 1972). Garfias also analyzes *tôgaku* melodies in terms of two-measure units (Garfias 1975).

↓ melody begins

1		2			3			4			(measures counted by melody)
to	*ra*	*ro*	*o*	*ru*	*ro*	*ta*	*a*	*ro*	*ra*	*a a*	(*ryūteki* mnemonic syllables)
2		3			●4 = *taiko*			1			(measures counted by percussion)

↑ rhythmic pattern starts

Figure 1.2. Rhythmic cycle of *Etenraku*.

These two-measure melodic patterns, reflecting each instrument's function, are combined into larger, repeating segments. The basic melody underlying these units is not obvious in the surface structure, but is organized into larger units of four or eight measures. The full *Etenraku* consists of three such eight-measure sections (section 1: mm. 1–8; section 2: mm. 9–16; section 3: mm. 17–24). In most performances each section is immediately repeated.

There are three accepted ways of ordering *Etenraku's* three sections in performance. In the standard version, after the repeat of section 3, sections 1 and 2 are each played twice more (so the form is 112233 1122). A short version, omitting section 3 and playing sections 1 and 2 twice each, is acceptable when time is constrained. The *Nokorigaku-sanben* version (*nokorigaku*, "remaining music"; and *sanben*, "three times"), which is used for the present analysis, organizes the sections as follows: 112233 112233 1122.[6] ◐ As the music unfolds, percussion and winds drop out one by one until only the lead *hichiriki*, the *biwa*, and the *koto* remain. Here the *koto* plays unusually complex figures called *rinzetsu*, accompanied by *hichiriki* phrases cut into fragments and separated by sporadic pauses in the third repetition (figure 1.3).[7]

Musical Idiom and Notation of Each Instrument

In contemporary *tōgaku*, three winds (*shō, hichiriki,* and *ryūteki*), two strings (*biwa* and *koto*), and three percussion instruments (*taiko, shōko, kakko*) make up the ensemble. However, there are two styles of performance: one without dance, called *kangen* (literally "pipes and strings"), and one that accompanies dance, referred to as *bugaku* ("dance music"), in which only

6. In the recording linked to this volume's website, the last repetition of sections 1 and 2 is omitted, making the form 112233 112233 12.

7. *Nokorigaku* is assumed to have been created to feature *koto* and *biwa*, which were relegated to amateur musicians, often higher ranked noblemen. The special arrangement of *koto* and *hichiriki* parts used to be improvised, and is partly so even today.

	Ryūteki	*Shō*	*Hichiriki*	*Biwa*	*Koto*	*Kakko*	*Shōko*	*Taiko*
Section 1	leader starts, tutti from first *taiko*	joins in at the first *taiko*	join in at the first *taiko*	joins in after the first *taiko*	joins in after *biwa*	enters with *ryūteki*	joins in at the first *taiko*	joins in at the first *taiko*
Section 1 repetition	→	→	→	→	→	→	→	→
Section 2	→	→	→	→	→	*kuwae–byōshi*, quits at the end	*kuwae–byōshi*, quits at the end	*kuwae–byōshi*, quits at the end
Section 2 repetition	→	→	→	→	→			
Section 3	leader only	leader only	leader only	→	→			
Section 3 repetition	→	→	→	→	→			
Section 1	→	→	→	→	→			
Section 1 repetition	→	→	→	→	→			
Section 2	→	→	→	→	→			
Section 2 repetition	quits in the latter half	→	→	→	→			
Section 3		quits in the latter half	fragmentary	→	*rinzetsu*			
Section 3 repetition			→	→	→			
Section 1			→	→	→			
Section 1 repetition			quits in the latter half	→	→			
Section 2				→	→			
Section 2 repetition				→	→			

Figure 1.3. Sectional form of *Etenraku: nokorigaku-sanben* version.

24

winds and percussion are used. In *kangen,* there are three players for each wind instrument, two for each string instrument, and one for each percussion instrument, making a total of sixteen musicians. *Bugaku* performances feature five or more musicians on each wind instrument, and one on each percussion instrument.

SHŌ (MOUTH ORGAN)[8]

The *shō* is thought to have originated in the Yunnan province of China and in the surrounding areas in Vietnam, Thailand, and Laos, where one can find various types of this instrument. It has seventeen thin bamboo pipes, arranged into a circle (figure 1.4) and fixed onto a wooden chamber. Fifteen of them have a single metal reed at the bottom, above which there is a small finger hole. When the hole is covered the pipe sounds, both when exhaling and inhaling through the wooden chamber. Chords or clusters of five or six notes, called *aitake* (literally, "combining bamboos"), are commonly used in *tōgaku,* whereas in *saibara* or *rōei* songs the *shō* accompanies the melody only with single notes. Each *aitake* (figure 1.5) is named after the lowest pitch of the bamboo pipes played in the chord, although there are a few exceptions. (In the notation, the name of the *aitake,* or single pipe, is indicated by Chinese characters together with rhythmic signs.) Figure 1.6 shows all the possible lowest pitches. The series of lowest pitches presented by the series of *aitake* is actually the basic melody of the ensemble.

Shifting from one chord to another requires changing both fingering and the direction and pressure of breath, which varies the dynamics. Usually finger changes (*te-utsuri;* literally "moving of chord or hand") come first, followed by a change (*ki-gae;* literally "change of breath") from inhaling to exhaling or vice versa, starting on the first beat of the next measure. The breath pressure, and so the loudness, is minimal on the first beat, but it gradually increases, culminating at the last beat (figure 1.7).

HICHIRIKI (REED PIPE)

Hichiriki is a small vertical bamboo pipe 18 centimeters long, inserted with a large, flattened, shaved double reed that can produce a very loud sound. The main body has seven finger holes in the front and two in the back; its inside is lacquered, and its outside is wrapped with thin strings made of cherry bark. This instrument's sound is distinguished by its pitch-gliding technique, called

---

8. The following information about instrumental and ensemble techniques comes from my personal experience of *gagaku* practice with master musician Shiba Sukeyasu (1935–), a former court musician, leading *ryūteki* player, composer, and instructor.

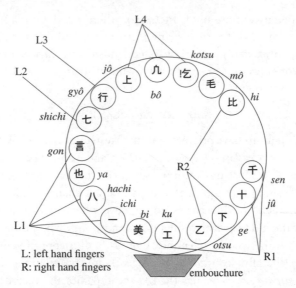

Figure 1.4. Structure and fingering of the *shô*.

Figure 1.5. *Aitake* chords of the *shô*.

Figure 1.6. Bamboo (and lowest *aitake*) pitches of the *shô*.

embai (literally, "salted plum seasoning"), which is attained with subtle adjustment of the lips, breath, and fingers. *Hichiriki* is so popular that it is used not only in *tôgaku* and *komagaku* ensembles, but also to accompany *saibara, rôei,* and other Japanese indigenous songs.

In *hichiriki* notation, finger positions are indicated by tablature signs derived from Chinese characters (figure 1.8). However, wind melodies are mainly learned with mnemonics (*shôga*) indicating pitch, rhythm, breath

Figure 1.7. Timing of *te-utsuri* and *ki-gae* for the *shô aitake* succession *bô–ichi–otsu*.

cuts, and other detailed information. Each wind instrument employs its own system of *shôga*. Present-day *hichiriki* and *ryûteki* notation, such as shown in figure 1.9, is presented in columns, each showing *shôga* syllables in the center, finger positions (tablature) on the left, and rhythmic signs on the right.

Shôga were already in use very early in the history of *tôgaku*, certainly before the end of the twelfth century, but only relatively recently, in the seventeenth century, did they begin to be actually written down in musical scores. The premedieval notation for *hichiriki* and *ryûteki* contained only tablature signs, as few as one or two per *kobyôshi* (measure), and thus seem to conform to the ancient basic melody.[9] In contemporary practice the *shôga* syllables prescribe the ornamentations that are associated with the separately shown tablature signs.

RYÛTEKI (TRANSVERSE FLUTE)

Ryûteki is a transverse flute 40 centimeters long, with seven finger holes. Its body is finished like the *hichiriki*'s. Finger positions are likewise indicated by tablature signs based on Chinese characters. The same finger position can produce the lower register *(fukura;* "soft") and the one an octave higher *(seme;* "tight")* (figure 1.10). The *ryûteki* adds a colorful ornamentation to the *hichiriki* melody, frequently switching from one register to another. It is used also in *saibara* and other few indigenous vocal genres such as *ô-uta, ônaobi-uta* and *kume-uta*.

9. In the oldest extant large-scale wind score, *Hakuga no fue-fu*, compiled in 966 by the noble musician Minamoto no Hiromasa (918–980), only tablature signs and *taiko* beats are written. Hayashi Kenzô (1899–1976), focusing on number and distribution of tablature signs and the periodicity of the rhythm, tried to restore the basic melody as early as in 1960 (Hayashi 1960/1969). Allan Marett also worked on early *ryûteki* notations and interpreted them as a legacy of Chinese tradition (Marett 1977, 1985, 1988, 2006).

Figure 1.8.   Tablature symbols and names for *hichiriki* finger positions.

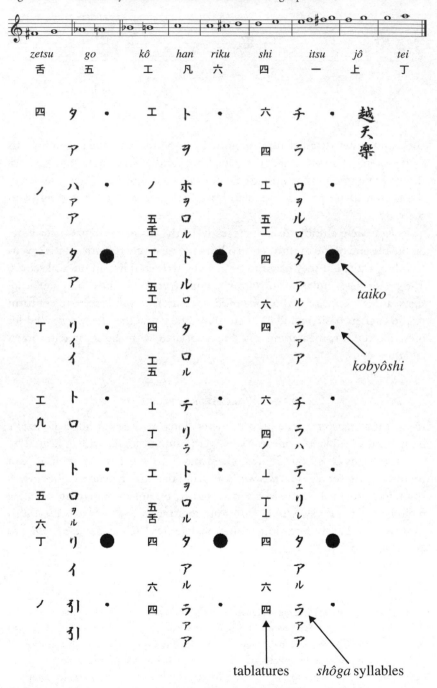

Figure 1.9.   Traditional columnar notation for the *hichiriki* ("Etenraku").

Figure 1.10.   Tablature symbols and names for *ryûteki* finger positions.

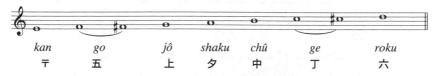

kan	go	jô	shaku	chû	ge	roku
〒	五	上	夕	中	丁	六

BIWA (LUTE)

Biwa is a pear-shaped, four-string lute with four frets attached to the neck, which is angled back sharply. Twenty left-hand finger positions, including open strings, are indicated by signs made from Chinese characters (figure 1.11). The interval between the second, third, and fourth frets is equivalent to a semitone, whereas that between an open string and the first fret is a whole tone. There are six kinds of tuning, each corresponding to one of the six modes used in *tôgaku* (see below). The instrument's role is mainly rhythmic. The strings are plucked downward from lowest to highest with a boxwood plectrum, creating arpeggios. The notated pitch sounds on the first beat of its measure and is the last (and highest) of each arpeggio pattern (figure 1.12). The primary left-hand action is to hold fingers on frets. Sometimes a finger is released and replaced to produce a lower neighbor-note figure, but this technique may be almost inaudible. The notes played by the plectrum are indicated by large symbols, while those produced by left-hand finger motions are indicated by small ones (and are transcribed as small notes in figure 1.12).

KOTO (LONG ZITHER)

Koto, also known as *sô* or *gakusô,* is a thirteen-string-long zither plucked with bamboo artificial nails worn on the thumb, index, and middle fingers. Each string is tuned with a movable wooden bridge to one of the six modal tunings. Notational signs are either single or in combinations of two. A pair of signs indicates two strings of the same pitch or at an octave, but they are realized as *hayagaki* or *shizugaki* patterns in the actual ensemble. For example, in figure 1.13, the actual notation on the left specifies only the seventh and twelfth strings, but when it is realized as *hayagaki* or *shizugaki* as shown on the staff, the eighth, ninth, and tenth strings are also plucked. The *koto*'s idiom strongly articulates the quarter-note beats on which it plays. In Heian times (794–1185/1192), left-hand techniques of pressing or pulling strings were used that are now lost, with consequences for music analysis to be discussed below.

	Open	Fret 1	Fret 2	Fret 3	Fret 4
IV	⊥ *jô*	八 *hachi*	Ⅰ *boku*	厶 *sen*	也 *ya*
III	ク *gyô*	七 *shichi*	ヒ *hi*	ʠ *gon*	之 *shi*
II	L *otsu*	下 *ge*	十 *jû*	乙 *bi*	コ *ko*
I	— *ichi*	エ *ku*	几母 *bo*	フ *shû*	斗 *to*

Figure 1.11. Tablature symbols and names for *biwa* finger positions.

Figure 1.12. Timing of arpeggio patterns in the *biwa*.

也 厶 也　　　　八
IV4 3 4　　　　IV1

Figure 1.13. *Shizugaki* and *hayagaki* patterns that realize a *koto* notation.

TAIKO (BIG DRUM)

There are three types of *taiko*, a large double-headed barrel-shaped drum. The *dadaiko* has the largest diameter skin and an elaborate ornamental sculpture attached to its body; it is usually used outdoors for *bugaku* performances. The *ninai-daiko* is small enough to carry and play in processions. The most common type is *tsuri-daiko*, used in ordinary indoor *kangen* performances. All these *taiko*, however, have the same musical function: a strong right-hand stroke (*o-bachi*, "male stroke") preceded by a weaker left-hand stroke (*me-bachi*, "female stroke") articulates the end of each *hyôshi* rhythmic cycle.

SHÔKO (GONG)

The flat gong *shôko* also has three types: the largest one, *ô-shôko*, is used for outdoor *bugaku* performance; *ninai shôko* is for processions; and *tsuri-shôko* for indoor *kangen*. *Shôko*'s concave side is struck with two thin wooden sticks. Combinations of right-hand, left-hand, and double strokes by both hands produce distinctive rhythmic patterns.

KAKKO (CYLINDRICAL DRUM)

Kakko is a double-headed cylindrical drum playing one of three basic patterns with two long, thin sticks. The solid single stroke *sei* is played with the right stick. Two kinds of gradually accelerating rolling patterns—*rai*, with one stick on either side, and the double roll *mororai*—are combined into larger patterns that span the rhythmic cycle. In *tôgaku*, all the percussion repeat a specific pattern throughout the first half of a piece (figure 1.14a), then in the standard version they often replace it with another pattern called *kuwae-byôshi* ("added pattern") (figure 1.14b).

Conversation among the Instruments: Who Leads the Ensemble?

There is no conductor in *gagaku*, but the ensemble is maintained even with the elastic beat and gradual acceleration. It is commonly held that the *kakko*, usually relegated to the eldest musician, acts as conductor, but the situation is actually more complicated. Smooth performances of *tôgaku* are possible due to a stylized "conversation" among the instruments. Undoubtedly, the *hichiriki* and *ryûteki* carry the most important melodic lines, but the percussion and

Figure 1.14. Standard percussion patterns for *haya yo hyôshi*.

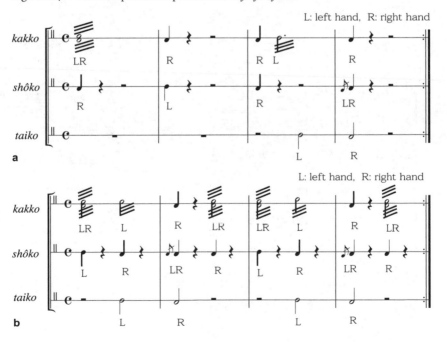

strings also help to determine the subtle tempo changes within each quarter-note beat and from measure to measure.

Figure 1.15 is a transcription of section 1 of *Etenraku* in *hyô-jô* mode (with the tonic equivalent to the Western *E*), *nokorigaku-sanben* version, and its slightly varied initial repetition. Like other *tôgaku* pieces it opens with a *ryûteki* solo, whose first two half notes define the tempo. Percussion enters in m. 2, where the focus shifts to a *kakko* stroke on the first beat and a tremolo on the

Figure 1.15.   *Etenraku* in *hyô-jô* mode, *nokorigaku-sanben* version, section 1.

Section 1 (measures 1–8), first statement

Figure 1.15.   (Continued)

Measures 9–16: Section 1(mm. 1–8) repeated

second, then to a weak *taiko* stroke on the third beat, which announces the coming of the most important stroke in the cycle at m. 3. The *shô* begins to play on the fourth beat of m. 2, just before the *hichiriki* begins. Measure 3, where all the winds have entered, is called *tsuke-dokoro* ("joining place").[10]

10. In the standard version, *tsuke-dokoro* is on the next *taiko* beat in measure 7.

After *tsuke-dokoro,* the texture thickens with the addition of *biwa* and *koto. Biwa* arpeggios start after the *shô*'s change of fingering at the end of m. 4, helping the ensemble to synchronize at the next downbeat. Two measures later, *koto* eighth notes on the second beat help reestablish the original tempo after a *ritardando* on the fourth beat of the preceding measure.

Thus, *hichiriki, ryûteki, kakko,* strings and *shô* are each focused on at specific spots and lead the ensemble at those moments. Figure 1.16 shows this shifting of focus: *shô* and *biwa* lead from the ritardando at beat 4 of every measure to beat 1 of the next. *Koto* leads on beats 2–3 every two measures, where the tempo is faster. Every four measures the *kakko* leads on beats 2–3–4–1, and *taiko* on beats 3–4–1.[11] The *kakko* and *taiko* also establish and maintain the periodicity of the four-measure rhythmic cycle, but this larger cycle regulates the more active conversation among winds and strings.

In the standard version, a piece closes with the last *taiko,* briefly suffixed by an ending pattern in free rhythm played by *shô, hichiriki, ryûteki, kakko, biwa,* and *koto.* However, *nokorigaku* employs a quite different and more complex procedure (figure 1.3). First, the percussion quits at the end of the repetition of section 2. The *shô* quits at the second repetition of section 2. After the *ryûteki* quits at section 3, the *hichiriki* plays fragmentary phrases to focus attention on the *koto*'s own intricate patterns. Through this, the *biwa* continues normally.

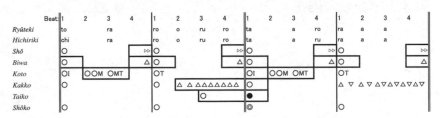

Notes:

(1) Ryûteki and *hichiriki: shôga* syllables are shown
(2) *Shô* O = usual chord, ▷▷ = preceding finger change (*te-utsuri*)
(3) *Biwa* O = last note of arpeggio, △ = preceding notes of arpeggio
(4) *Koto* O = pluck, I = index finger, M = middle finger, T = thumb
(5) *Kakko* O = single stroke by the right stick, △ = tremolo by the left stick, △▽△▽ = tremolo by both sticks
(6) *Taiko* O = weak stroke by the left hand, ● = strong stroke by the right hand
(7) *Shôko* O = stroke by a stick, ◎ = stroke by both sticks

Figure 1.16.   Instrumental focus, beat by beat (after *tsuke-dokoro*). The part in focus is outlined in bold.

11. This account is based on my own experience. Shiba Sukeyasu has also pointed out the existence of multiple leaders in the ensemble, and describes as "listening" what I here call "conversation" (see Shôno 1987).

Patchwork Structure, Repeating Melodic Patterns, and Shared Patterns

As stated above, two measures constitute a melodic unit. In twenty-four measures of music (sections 1, 2, and 3), twelve such units are heard, but in *Etenraku* only ten are distinct because some are repeated. If we label each pattern alphabetically (A, B, C, . . ., J), the structure, including all sectional repeats, can be represented by figure 1.17.

Sections 1 and 2 (ABCB DEFB) conclude with B (mm. 7–8, 15–16), which insists strongly on the prime note *E,* whereas section 3 changes to another mode (*ôshiki-chô*) that stresses the note *A.* Patterns H and J also end on *A.* Sections 1 and 2 especially emphasize pattern B's closing function (underlined). Counting all repetitions in the standard version, out of ten pattern types (A–J), patterns A and C through F are heard four times each and G through J twice each, but pattern B is played a full twelve times.

Etenraku is a rather short piece of *tôgaku.* In other larger pieces, several patterns also appear repeatedly. In not a few cases, three or four consecutive units are repeated in the latter half of a piece. The proportion of iterating patterns ranges from less than 10 to about 60 percent for pieces in *hyô-jô* mode. For example, figure 1.18 shows melodic structure in *Funan,* a piece also in *hyô-jô* mode and *haya-yo-hyôshi* rhythm. There are twenty kinds of different melodic patterns, from A to T. Out of them, only patterns J, O, S, and T are unique to *Funan.* The rest can also be found in other pieces.

		*		*		
Section 1 (repeated)	A	B	C	B	Measure 1–8	
Section 2 (repeated)	D	E	F	B	Measure 9–16	Short version ends
Section 3 (repeated)	G	H	I	J	Measure 17–24	
Section 1 (repeated)	A	B	C	B	Measure 1–8	
Section 2 (repeated)	D	E	F	B	Measure 9–16	Standard version ends
Section 3 (repeated)	G'	H'	I'	J'	Measure 17–24	
Section 1 (repeated)	A'	B'	C'	B'	Measure 1–8	
Section 2 (repeated)	D'	E'	F'	B'	Measure 9–16	*Nokorigaku* ends

Figure 1.17. Melodic patterns of *Etenraku* (italicized sections are repeated in *nokorigaku* only; * = *taiko*).

A	B	C	D
E	F	G	H
I	J	K	L
A	B	M	H
N	O	P	Q
R	S	G	H
K	T	P	Q

Figure 1.18. Common patterns (underlined) employed in *Funan.*

Examining all patterns found in pieces in *hyô-jô* mode and *haya-byôshi* rhythm in the current *Meiji-senteifu*[12] repertoire, we find some thirty-five patterns that are used in more than two pieces. Each piece includes at least one of the patterns in common use. Figure 1.19 shows the total number of unique and common patterns included in each piece. *Yûjô no kyû, Funan, Yahanraku, Korôji, Ôshôkun, Ôjô no kyû,* and *Shun'yôryû* each contain more than ten common patterns.

The more a piece employs common patterns, the more it gives the impression that it is similar to others and therefore its melody's distinctiveness is minimized. Conversely, the fewer such patterns, the more it carries a flavor of originality. In this regard *Etenraku* (together with the piece *Ringa*) is rather exceptional for music in *hyô-jô* mode and *haya byôshi* rhythm, since it uses only one common pattern, while most other pieces employ many. This is one reason why *Etenraku* makes such a strong impression, despite its small scale.

Deep Structure

Tang Dynasty Modal Theory

To grasp the relationship of the surface melody to the deep structure articulated by the basic melody, a brief review of the Chinese modal theory brought to Japan around the eighth century will be helpful. The ancient Chinese

Title	Number of Patterns	Common Patterns
Ôjô no kyû	16	11
Goshôraku no kyû	18	7
Sandai no kyû	26	9
Shun'yôryû	34	11
Ringa	32	1
Rôkunshi	12	8
Keitoku	16	5
Yûjô no kyû	30	14
Funan	20	16
Yahanraku	31	14
Korôji	25	13
Ôshôkun	14	12
Etenraku	10	1

Figure 1.19. Number of distinct patterns, and of patterns used in more than one piece, in the current *Meiji-senteifu* repertoire.

12. Pieces with *nobe byôshi* and *tada byôshi* rhythm are omitted here, because their melodic units are differently composed and derive from different rhythmic structures.

devised a mathematical method of calculating pitches called *sanbun son'eki* ("dividing into three segments and subtracting or adding one"), which is comparable to proceeding along the Pythagorean circle of fifths. If we divide a sounding length of string or pipe into three equal segments and subtract a segment (that is, take two-thirds of its length), the resulting pitch is a perfect fifth above the original. Adding a segment (taking four-thirds) gives the pitch a perfect fourth below. The left side of figure 1.20 shows how this process can be continued. Beginning from a given fundamental tone and proceeding by this method (alternately up by fifth and down by fourth) twelve times generates a pitch collection, which, collapsed into the range of a single octave, creates the analog of a Western chromatic scale. The first five of these make a pentatonic scale. These scale tones are referred to as the prime (*gong* in Chinese; *kyû* in Japanese), the second (*shang; shô*), the third (*jiao; kaku*), the fifth (*zhi; chi*), and the sixth (*yu; u*). Adding the next two pitches, flat-*chi* (*bian-zhi; hen-chi*) and flat-*kyû* (*bian-gong; hen-kyû*), creates a heptatonic collection equivalent to the Western Lydian mode (figure 1.20, right). In Chinese theory, this fundamental scale, consisting of the first seven pitches in the circle of fifths, is called *gong diao* (the mode of *gong*; in Japanese, *kyû-chô*, the mode of *kyû*). Shifting the prime note up a step to *shang/shô*, one obtains *shang-diao/shô-chô* (the mode of *shang/shô*). In this way, we can produce seven modes (figure 1.21). Transposing each of the seven to all twelve notes results in eighty-four distinct combinations of mode and prime note.

This theory was certainly introduced into Japan. However, only a small number of the eighty-four possibilities were actually used. Until the late Heian period (the end of the twelfth century), ten were known.[13] Only six, called *chôshi*, survive in current *tôgaku* practice. These comprise two types, *ryo* and *ritsu*, equivalent to the Western Mixolydian and Dorian modes, respectively (figure 1.22). *Ichikotsu-chô* (prime note = *D*), *sô-jô* (prime note = *G*), and *taishiki-chô* (prime note = *E*) fall in the former category, and *hyô-jô* (prime

Figure 1.20.   *Sanbun son'eki* and the fundamental mode *kyû-chô* (*gong-diao*).

sanbun son'eki process   fundamental scale = *gong-diao* (*kyû-chô*)

13. In the *biwa* score *Sango yôroku* and in the *koto* score *Jinchi yôroku*, both compiled by aristocrat and musician Fujiwara no Moronaga (1138–1192), *ichikotsu-chô* (prime note *D*), *sada-chô* (*D*), *hyô-jô* (*E*), *taishiki-chô* (*E*), *kotsujiki-chô* (*E*), *sei-chô* (*E*), *sô-jô* (*G*), *ôshiki-chô* (*A*), *sui-chô* (*A*), and *banshiki-chô* (*B*) can be found.

Figure 1.21.   Seven modes of *tôgaku,* according to theory.

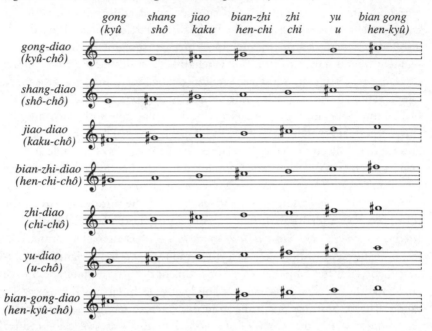

Figure 1.22.   Six current modes of *tôgaku.*

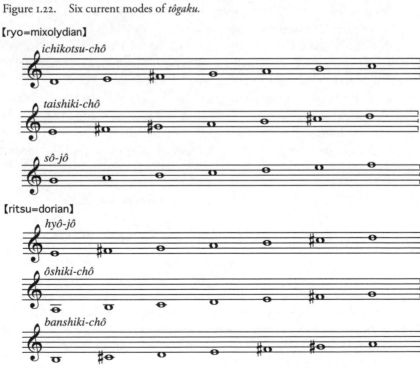

note = *E*), *ôshiki-chô* (prime note = *A*), and *banshiki-chô* (prime note = *B*) in the latter.

However, some notes used in present-day *tôgaku*, notably those produced on the *ryuteki* and *hichiriki* with certain fingerings, deviate from the "correct" pitches in modal theory, whereas the *shô, biwa,* and *koto* retain them. In *Etenraku* (such as in mm. 6 and 14 of figure 1.15), the *ryûteki* and *hichiriki* frequently use *F* (and *C*, particularly on the *hichiriki*), which is not supposed to occur in *hyô-jô* mode. This deviation was possibly due to the influence of Edo period (1603–1868) music in general[14] and was facilitated by the instruments' inherent capabilities, as players of these two instruments can easily produce various pitches or slides between standard tablature positions by applying lip, breathing, and fingering techniques. The other instruments, and especially the *shô,* produce only pretuned fixed pitches. The *biwa* and *koto* mimicked the *shô* and have kept the original pitches.

Basic Melody in the Deep Structure

In current practice, the *shô, biwa,* and *koto* play idiomatic figures not directly deducible from the tablature. However, if we disregard present-day embellishment practice and simply take the pitches that the tablature signs indicate, we obtain the skeletal basic melody underlying the surface melodies played in the current ensemble. Figure 1.23 shows *Etenraku* extracted from the *shô, biwa,* and *koto* tablatures; each tablature sign in a *kobyôshi,* worth a full measure at the surface level, is shown as a quarter note,[15] and each rhythmic cycle (*haya-yo-hyôshi*) is shown as a measure.

Occasionally there is a clash between the parts, for example on the very first note. As we shall soon discuss, this may be explained by considering that *C♯* and *F♯* on the *koto* used to be *D* and *G* in the Heian period.[16] Otherwise, the *shô* and *biwa*, especially, share almost the same melody, consisting entirely of notes from the authentic *hyô-jô* mode, *E–F♯–G–A–B–C♯–D*. Indeed, for some instances of *tôgaku* it is only at this level that modality may be clear. For instance, current *ryûteki* or *hichiriki* practice uses not only the

---

14. Vocal genres in *gagaku* have also experienced pitch changes. *Kagura-uta, azuma-asobi, saibara, rôei,* and the like all employ scales similar to the *koto's* popular *miyako-bushi* scale, or *shamisen* music of the Edo period.

15. If two signs are included in a *kobyôshi,* they are represented by two eighth notes.

16. In Heian times there was a left-hand technique of pressing strings. The pitch *D* was produced if the left hand pressed the string tuned *C♯*. *G* was similarly produced on the eighth and thirteenth strings, tuned *F♯*. Current technique and notation do not continue this tradition (see below).

Figure 1.23.   Basic melody of *Etenraku* (*shô, biwa, koto*).

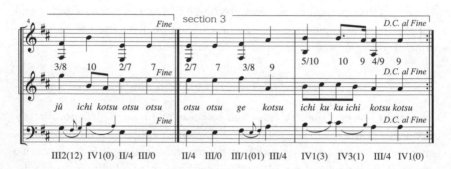

prime note *E* but also many of the same melodic patterns for the modes *hyô-jô* and *taishiki-chô* (*E–F♯–G♯–A–B–C♯–D*), so the difference between pieces, or sections of pieces, attributed to these modes is evident only in the different modalities of their respective basic melodies.

Figure 1.23 shows how *Etenraku*'s basic melody is organized into four-measure units, each corresponding to a rhythmic cycle. In current practice, however, the winds play the opening two measures (*to – ra – ro o ru ro*) (figure 1.15, mm. 1–2) on a single breath as if they were a complete phrase, even though these measures correspond to only two notes, *D* and *B,* in the basic melody. This discrepancy between surface-level and deep-level grouping structure is explained by taking into account the likelihood that the tempo was much faster in ancient times.[17] Played faster than they are today, the

17. *Gagaku* was played at a much faster tempo even as late as the beginning of the twentieth century, as 1903 recordings by F. Gaisberg demonstrate (Terauchi 2002). In addition, old documents describing Buddhist rituals in the Heian (794–1185/1192) and Kamakura (1192–1333/1363) eras indicate that many *bugaku* dances were staged in a single day, which would have been impossible if the dances were performed at today's slow tempi.

units *D–B–E–E* (figure 1.23, m. 1) or *D–G–F♯–E–E* (m. 2) could be managed on a single breath.

Differences of Modulation and Transposition in Surface and Deep Structures

Some *tôgaku* pieces contain modulation, or change of mode. Although *Etenraku* is fairly short, it includes such modulating phrases in section 3, where the melody moves into *ôshiki-chô* mode. This change is clearly audible in both the surface and deep melodies due to the relatively large distance of a perfect fourth between the prime tones *E* and *A* of *hyô-jô* and *ôshiki-chô*. However, it arrives at different moments in the surface and deep melodies.

In the current *hyô-jô* surface melody (the top staff of figure 1.24, which shows three different modal versions of this melody), the *ryûteki* part announces the beginning of the modulation in m. 18 by introducing a *C♯*. This note, not used before, sounds unfamiliar and therefore initiates the change. The next ascending phrase from *F* to *A* (mm. 19–20) completes the modulation, and the long repeated *A* at the end of the section (mm. 23–24) confirms it. In the deep structure, the phrase moving from *F♯* to *A* traces the same modal shift (figure 1.25), but the *C♯* is not evident until m. 21, three bars later than in the surface melody.

In Heian times, at the height of court culture and the *gagaku* tradition, it was popular to arrange a tune in different modes. This transformed repertoire is called *watashi-mono*, which literally means "things carried across." Such modal transformation is usually done within the same *ryo* or *ritsu* modal group. Most *sô-jô* (in *G*) pieces were transposed from the originals in *ichikotsu-chô* (in *D;* both *ryo*). Likewise, many *ôshiki-chô* (in *A*) pieces were transposed from *banshiki-chô* (in *B;* both *ritsu*). Currently, as indicated in figure 1.24, *Etenraku* is played in *hyô-jô*, *ôshiki-chô*, and *banshiki-chô*.[18] In making *watashi-mono*, quite different principles govern the modal transformation of the deep structure and the surface melody.

---

18. In the *koto* score, *Jinchi-yôroku*, compiled in the late Heian period (twelfth century), only *banshiki-chô Etenraku* can be found. However, based on the description in the musical treatise *Kyôkun-shô* compiled by *gagaku* musician Koma no Chikazane in 1233 (Koma 1233/1973), Shiba Sukeyasu claimed that the *hyô-jô* version is the original (Shôno 1987: 32).

Figure 1.24.   *Etenraku* in three modal versions, *ryûteki* part.

Most of the intervals of the deep structure are preserved exactly across a change in mode. For instance, the three *Etenraku shô* parts compared in figure 1.25 are intervallically identical (ignoring changes of octave). The only exceptions are in mm. 12 and 21–22. The latter shows greater discrepancies, due to the change of mode in section 3, mentioned above.

Figure 1.25. *Etenraku* in three modal versions, basic melody.

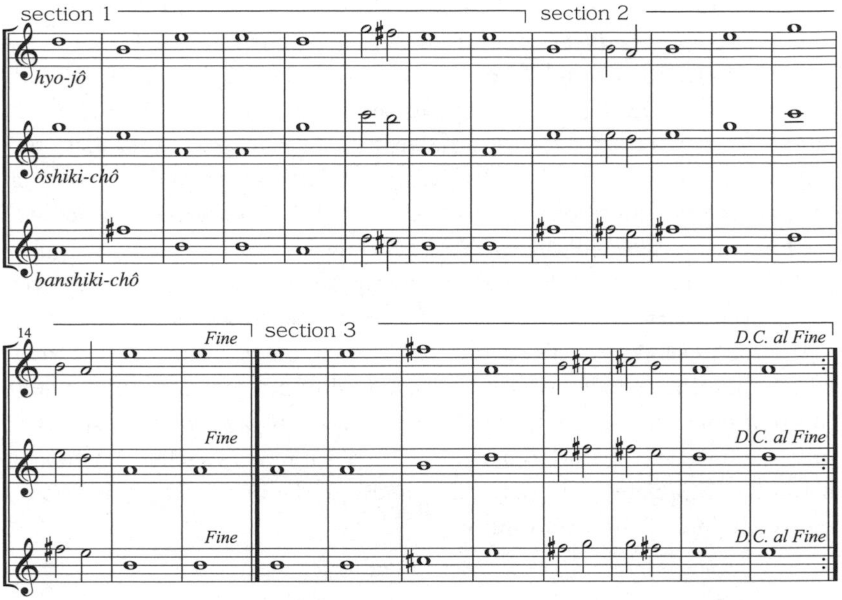

In the versions shown on the upper two staves, which begin respectively in *hyô-jô* and *ôshiki-chô* modes, the modulation involving transposition by fourth (to *ôshiki-chô*[19] and *ichikotsu-chô*, respectively) results in the same melodic interval, a whole tone, at this point. However, the third version, involving a modulation from *banshiki-chô*, requires a different interval at this spot—a semitone—to be consistent with the mode, *hyô-jô* (*E–F♯–G–A–B–C♯–D*), that is the fourth transposition of *banshiki-chô* within the *ritsu* group.[20]

For the present-day surface melodies of the *ryûteki* and *hichiriki*, *watashi-mono* is not transposition at all, but a substitution of certain idiomatic patterns for others. These patterns are often associated with particular registers.

19. Shiba Sukeyasu interprets the modulation in section 3 in *hyô-jô* mode from *hyô-jô* to *sui-chô*. *Sui-chô* existed in Heian times as a *ryo* mode *A–B–C♯–D–E–F♯–G*, since there is no *C♯* in *ôshiki-chô* mode (Shôno 1987: 28).

20. There seems to be confusion about the transposition in section 3. In the old *shô* score *Kofu ryoritsu no maki*, compiled in the thirteenth century by the Toyohara family of court musicians, the phrase in question (*banshiki-chô*, section 3) is *F♯–G–G–F♯–E–E*, but the *biwa* score *Sango yôroku*, compiled in the late twelfth century by Fujiwara no Moronaga, shows *F♯–G♯–G♯–F♯–E–E*.

Consider, for example, the pattern *F–G–A–F–G* found both in m. 6 of the *hyô-jô* version and in m. 1 of the *ôshiki-chô* version (figure 1.24); it is also idiomatic in pieces in *taishiki-chô* mode. In *hyô-jô* (and in *taishiki-chô*) it is often used, as here, to descend from the second scale degree, via structurally subsidiary third and fourth degrees, to the prime note of the scale, but in *ôshiki-chô* it goes from the sixth scale degree, via structurally subsidiary seventh and eighth (upper prime) degrees, to the fifth degree. This suggests that the pattern does not belong to a particular mode but is associated more with the fingering positions of the *ryûteki* around the specific register of *kan, go, jô,* and *shaku* (figure 1.10). Although the nature of the instruments would certainly make exact transposition possible, court musicians preferred to replace a particular melodic pattern suitable for a certain range in the original mode with a different melodic pattern associated with the corresponding range in the transposed mode. To arrange *watashi-mono* in *gagaku,* then, is not so much to transpose the surface melody exactly but rather to select the melodic patterns appropriate to the particular ranges of the instruments and coordinate them into a longer continuity.

Reconstructing Past Practice through Information Hidden in Tablature Signs

Tôgaku notation often provides clues allowing us to recover past practices. As shown above, current *ryûteki* and *hichiriki* melodies changed certain pitches, mostly flattening them, thereby creating discrepancies with *shô, biwa,* and *koto* pitches. In current practice, *shô, biwa,* and *koto* realizations featuring chords, arpeggios, and *hayagaki* and *shizugaki* patterns cannot be read from the simple tablature signs. But by stripping away present-day idioms and returning to the tablature we may recover what is shared by all melodic instruments. Analyzing *hichiriki* and *koto* tablature, in particular, suggests some possibilities for reconstruction of the music's past features.

History of Tôgaku Notation, and Inconsistency in the Hichiriki Part

Shô, biwa, and *koto* notation has been stable since the Nara and Heian periods (710–1185/1192). The Chinese characters of *shô* notation indicate the pitches of single bamboo pipes or chords; *biwa* signs indicate fret positions (including open strings); and those of *koto* indicate strings. Particularly for the scores completed after the twelfth century, small and large dots indicating rhythmic cycles are attached to these signs.

At the beginning of the Meiji period, when the standard collection of *gagaku* scores, *Meiji senteifu,* was compiled (1876, 1888), *hichiriki* and *ryūteki* notation changed drastically.[21] Until the late Edo period, it consisted of tablature signs and dots indicating measures. Most of these are too simple and imprecise to specify all the melodic nuances, so the *shōga* (mnemonics), transmitted orally, played an important role in the pedagogy of the genre. The *Meiji senteifu* (as in figure 1.9) shows them in the main column attached to tablature signs on the left side and rhythmic signs on the right.[22] Its introduction of *shōga* syllables into notation enabled the melodic movements of the *hichiriki* and *ryūteki* to be described with much more rhythmic detail than before.

Despite what we know about the history of *tōgaku* notation, there remains some uncertainty about the correspondence of signs and pitches. For instance, some tablature signs actually denote several pitches, the choice of which is relegated to oral tradition. Though we cannot trace the precise source of this confusion, Heian notational practice seems to have been more consistent, and examination of some old sources supports this view.

Figure 1.26 shows a transcription of *Etenraku's* current *hichiriki* melody along with its *shōga* syllables and tablature signs, respectively, on the upper and lower rows of symbols below the staff. (The traditional notation of this tune is given in figure 1.9.) One apparent inconsistency involves the notation of the events played as the note *F,* for which different tablature signs are given: *jō* ⊥ (上), in mm. 6 and 13; and *itsu* ―, in mm. 13 and 19. Recall that the *hichiriki* can produce a wide range of pitches from a single position using fingering and lip techniques, and that currently (as shown in figure 1.8) the position *jō* covers the notes *F–G,* and the position *itsu* covers *E–F–F♯–G.* *Jō* is originally the higher position on the instrument. Considering modal theory and the basic melody of *Etenraku* extracted from *shō* and the strings, it seems plausible that *jō* originally indicated *G* and *itsu F♯.* The large-scale musical treatise *Gakkaroku,* written in the late seventeenth century, provides interesting support for this conjecture. The author, Suehisa Abe (1622–1708),[23]

---

21. In the late nineteenth century, a new department of royal court music, Gagaku-kyoku, was established in Tokyo based on the traditions of three different *gagaku* groups in the Kansai area. The new department needed to unify tradition and to compile standard scores.

22. *Shōga* and fingering signs for *ryūteki* and *hichiriki* are similar but different in places.

23. Abe was a Kyoto court musician. The description of *hichiriki* is found in volume 11 (Abe 1690/1935/1977).

Figure 1.26. *Etenraku's* current *hichiriki* melody, with its *shôga* syllables and tablature signs.

Figure 1.27. Interpretation of *hichiriki* tablature currently, and according to *Gakkaroku* (1690 CE).

Current	Tablature signs		*Gakkaroku*
A, G	丁	*tei*	A
G, F	⊥(上)	*jô*	G
G, F♯, F, E	—	*itsu*	F♯
E, D	四	*shi*	E
D, C♯, C	六	*riku*	D
C	乁(凡)	*han*	C
B, A♯	工	*ku*	B
A, G♯	五	*go*	A
G, F♯	舌	*zetsu*	F♯

included a figure (transcribed here as figure 1.27) showing the structure of the *hichiriki* with finger holes and pitches as an example of old practice, corroborating the production of *jô* as *G* and *itsu* as *F♯*. I suggest, therefore, that the relationship of signs and pitches in *hichiriki* 300 years ago or earlier was more consistent and that pitches in *hyô-jô Etenraku* retained the original characteristics of Chinese modal theory.

Koto left-hand techniques

Let us return to figure 1.23, which juxtaposes the versions of the basic melody extracted from the notation of the *shô, biwa,* and *koto* parts. The melodies of *shô* and *biwa* are nearly identical, but that of *koto* diverges at certain moments, specifically:

Measure 1, beat 1	*Shô, biwa: D*	*Koto: C♯*
Measure 2, beat 1	*Shô, biwa: D*	*Koto: C♯*
Measure 2, beat 2	*Shô, biwa: G–F♯*	*Koto: F♯*
Measure 3, beat 2	*Shô: B–A, biwa: B*	*Koto: A*
Measure 3, beat 4	*Shô: E, biwa: D*	*Koto: C♯*
Measure 4, beat 1	*Shô, biwa: G*	*Koto: F♯*
Measure 4, beat 2	*Shô: B-A, biwa: B*	*Koto: B*
Measure 6, beat 2	*Shô: C♯–B, biwa C♯*	*Koto B–A*

Some of these differences can be reconciled if we reconsider *koto* tuning and revive lost left-hand techniques, based on an analysis of a late twelfth-century source of *koto* notation.

This source, called *Jinchi-yôroku* (*JCYR* hereafter) is a twelve-volume collection of *koto* scores edited by Fujiwara no Moronaga (1138–1192), a Heian aristocrat.[24] In the first volume he introduces a tuning for *hyô-jô* that is different from the one in use today (figure 1.28).

In present-day tuning, strings 3 and 8, as well as 6 and 11, are tuned an octave apart, but in *JCYR*'s tuning they are not. When ancient performers wanted to produce the octave, they used left-hand pressing or pulling techniques, which *JCYR* specifies, to bend the tones up or down. Each such action is indicated by dot(s) or scratch-like lines modifying the tablature (figure 1.29).

The score of *Etenraku* in *JCYR* specifies the following:[25]

- Technique 3 on string 6/11 (m. 1), 6/11 (m. 2), 11 (m.3)
- Technique 2 on string 13 (m. 2), 5/10 (m. 6)
- Technique 1 on string 3/8 (m. 4)
- Technique 4 on string 9 (m. 3)

To take one example, technique 3 applied on string 11 in m. 1, beat 1 will produce *D* instead of *C♯* with additional ornamentation (another *D* after

---

24. Several copies of handwritten manuscript have survived, among which the copy preserved in the library of Kyoto University (a former property of the noble clan Kikutei) is in relatively good condition, and its contents, on which this study is based, are considered reliable.

25. Unfortunately, *JCYR* does not contain *Etenraku* in *hyô-jô* but in *banshiki-chô*. However, as the tuning of *banshiki-chô* is an exact transposition of *hyô-jô*, the latter part can be derived from the former.

	1	2	3	4	5	6	7	8	9	10	11	12	13
Current	B	E	F#	A	B	C#	E'	F#'	A'	B'	C#'	E"	F#"
JCYR	B	E	G	A	B	D	E'	F#'	A'	B'	C#'	E"	F#"

Figure 1.28. *Koto* tuning for *hyô-jô* mode, according to *Jinchi-yôroku* (twelfth century CE).

Technique	Performance Action	Notation
(1) *Oshi-ire* ("press-in")	Press and pluck (keep pressing)	A dot at the foot of a tablature sign
(2) *Oshi-hanachi* ("press and release")	Press and pluck (then release)	A dot on the shoulder of the tablature sign
(3) *Nido oshi-ire* ("press-in twice")	Press and pluck, then release, and press again	Two dots on the shoulder and the foot of the tablature sign
(4) *Toriyu* ("take away")	Pluck, then pull once	Indicated by a scratch on the shoulder of the tablature sign
(5) *Toru tabitabi* ("take away several times")	Pluck, then pull several times	Double scratch on the shoulder of the tablature sign

Figure 1.29.   Left-hand pitch-bending techniques for the *koto,* according to *Jinchi-yôroku.*

the C#). If we implement all the left-hand techniques that *JCYR* specifies, the *koto* melody resembles *shô* and/or *biwa* melodies more closely, as follows:

Measure 1, beat 1   *Shô, biwa: D*   Koto: C# D–c#–d[26]
                                                        (technique 3)

Measure 2, beat 1   *Shô, biwa: D*   Koto: C# D–c#–d
                                                        (technique 3)

Measure 2, beat 2   *Shô, biwa: G–F#*   Koto: F# G–f#
                                                        (technique 2)

Measure 3, beat 2   *Shô: B–A, biwa: B*   Koto: A A–g
                                                        (technique 4)

Measure 3, beat 4   *Shô: E, biwa: D*   Koto: C# D–c#–d
                                                        (technique 3)

Measure 4, beat 1   *Shô, biwa: G*   Koto: F# G
                                                        (technique 1)

Measure 4, beat 2   *Shô: B–A, biwa: B*   Koto: B–A–G[27]
Measure 6, beat 2   *Shô: C#–B, biwa C#*   Koto: B–A C#–b–A
                                                        (technique 2)

26. Small letters indicate that these pitches are produced not by right-hand plucking but only by left-hand pressing or pulling, which is almost inaudible in the actual ensemble.

27. Exceptionally here, *JCYR* shows a glissando-like pattern on *B–A–G* called *ren.*

Thus, by considering the notation in light of the tuning system and forgotten techniques, we can interpret it more consistently, and distill features of the basic melody that seem to be closer to authentic Heian practice.

Conclusion

Encountering *gagaku* for the first time, some listeners are struck by its dissonant sound. This dissonance exists largely because of the ways that the *ryūteki* and *hichiriki* melodies have changed during the long history of the genre, creating conflicts with the melodies of the *shō, biwa,* and *koto,* which have changed less. However, at the level of the basic melody underlying the current heterophonic ensemble, the discordance cannot be found.

Research to revive the lost melodies of Heian times or reinterpret even the surviving repertoire of *tōgaku* in the context of Tang modal theory has been repeatedly carried out since the 1940s.[28] In addition, some reconstructed pieces, on reconstructed instruments, have actually been performed in a series of *gagaku* concerts at *Kokuritsu gekijō* (the National Theatre of Japan in Tokyo) since the 1970s,[29] showcasing the older modal and timbral practice.[30]

I do not place any lesser value on present-day practice just because it contains "deviated" pitches and dissonance. Rather, I appreciate it as a highly elaborated music in which each instrument's unique style of expression is refined almost to perfection. Once one becomes accustomed to the modern *gagaku* sound, one is attuned to its distinctive and striking features: the process of increasing tension caused by the dissonance among instruments, and the point of release where all instruments converge to a single pitch, both

---

28. Hayashi Kenzō was a great pioneer in this research (Hayashi 1964, 1969, 1973), followed by the post-1980 generation, including the author. Also, researchers outside Japan such as Laurence Picken and his group have worked on the reconstruction project of Tang music by analyzing Japanese manuscripts (Picken et al. 1981–2007; see also footnote 1).

29. Revival of melodies are based on such old handwritten manuscripts as *Hakuga no fue-fu* (966), *Sango yōroku, Jinchi yōroku, Motomasa fue-fu* (late twelfth century), *Kaichū-fu* (early thirteenth century), and the like. The reconstruction has been mostly done by Shiba Sukeyasu. *Kokuritsu gekijō* is also eager to reconstruct old instruments of the Nara period (710–794; most of them are designated as national treasures), which had been preserved in *Shōsō-in* of Tōdaiji temple, and are now under the supervision of Kunaichō (the Imperial Household Agency).

30. For more information on the forty years of *gagaku* activities at *Kokuritsu gekijō,* see Terauchi 2008.

heightened in effect by the elastic tempo and acceleration—a complex texture woven by a deliberate reciprocation among the instruments.

Recent developments in *gagaku* performance exhibit such diverse tendencies as preserving classical style, reviving ancient features, bringing out traditional expression in contemporary avant-garde art music,[31] and combining *gagaku* elements with pop music.[32] If it continues to diversify along with the global tide of music, we will certainly need to develop new ways to analyze and understand it. Paradoxically, however, change makes it even more important to understand the classical tradition at *gagaku*'s base. Not to be satisfied with a superficial impression, but to cultivate a deep insight into the tradition, will surely enable us to clearly distinguish features of *gagaku* in contemporary practice and imagine way to develop this music in the future.

Glossary

Abe Suehisa 安倍季尚
aitake 合竹
azuma-asobi 東遊
banshiki-chô 盤渉調
biwa 琵琶
bugaku 舞楽
chi (*zhi*) 徴
dadaiko 大太鼓
Edo 江戸
embai 塩梅
Etenraku 越殿（天）楽
Fujiwara no Moronaga 藤原師長
fukura 和
Funan 扶南
gagaku 雅楽
Gagakukyoku 雅楽局
Gakkaroku 楽家録

31. For instance, Takemitsu Tôru (1930–1996) is one of the few excellent composers who succeeded in grasping the essence of *gagaku* instruments (see De Ferranti and Narazaki 2002).

32. A former court musician, Tôgi Hideki (1959–), achieved popular success by making an easy-listening fusion music with *gagaku* instruments. Several essays analyze his music (for instance, Bürkner 2004 and Lancashire 2003).

gakushi 楽詞
gakusô 楽箏
gakku 楽句
Hakuga no fue-fu 博雅笛譜
haya 早
hayagaki 早搔
haya-mu-hyôshi 早六拍子
Hayashi Kenzô 林謙三
haya-ya-hyôshi 早八拍子
haya-yo-hyôshi 早四拍子
Heian 平安
hen-chi 変徴
hen-kyû 変宮
hichiriki 篳篥
hyô-jô 平調
hyôshi 拍子
ichikotsu-chô 壱越調
Jinchi yôroku 仁智要録
kagura-uta 神楽歌
Kaichû-fu 懐中譜
kakko 鞨鼓
kaku (jiao) 角
Kamakura 鎌倉
kangen 管絃
Keitoku 慶（鶏）徳
ki-gae 気替
Kikutei 菊亭
kobyôshi 小拍子
Kofu ryoritsu no maki 古譜呂律巻
Kokuritsu gekijô 国立劇場
komagaku 高麗楽
Koma no Chikazane 狛近真
Korôji 小娘子
koto (sô) 箏
kotsujiki-chô 乞食調
kume-uta 久米歌
kuwae-byôshi 加拍子
Kyôkun-shô 教訓抄
kyû (gong) 宮
kyû-chô (gong diao) 宮調
me-bachi 雌桴

Meiji-senteifu 明治撰定譜
miyako-bushi 都節
mororai 諸来
Motomasa fue-fu 基政笛譜
nido oshi-ire 二度推入
ninai-daiko 荷太鼓
nobe 延
o-bachi 雄桴
Ôjô no kyû 皇　急
ônaobi-uta 大直日歌
oshi-hanachi 推放
oshi-ire 推入
ôshiki-chô 黄鐘調
Ôshôkun 　王昭君
ô-uta 大歌
rai 来
Ringa 　林歌
ritsu 律
rôei 朗詠
Rôkunshi 老君子
ryo 呂
ryûteki 龍笛
sada-chô 沙陀調
saibara 催馬楽
sanbun son'eki 三分損益
Sandai no kyû 三台急
Sango yôroku 三五要録
sei 正
sei-chô 性調
seme 責
shamisen 三味線
Shiba Sukehiro 芝祐泰
Shiba Sukeyasu　芝祐靖
Shinto 神道
shizugaki 閑掻
shô 笙
shô (shang) 商
shô-chô (shang diao) 商調
shôga 唱歌
shôko 鉦鼓

Shôno Susumu 庄野進
Shôsô-in 正倉院
Shun'yôryû 春楊柳
sô-jô 双調
sui-chô 水調
tada-byôshi 只拍子
taiko 太鼓
taishiki-chô 太食調
Takemistu Tôru 武満徹
te-utsuri 手移
Tôdaiji 東大寺
tôgaku 唐楽
Tôgi Hidegi 東儀秀樹
toriyu 取由
toru tabitabi 取度々
Toyohara 豊原
tsuke-dokoro 付所
tsuri-daiko 釣太鼓　渡物
u (yu) 羽
watashi-mono 渡物
Yahanraku 夜半楽
yatara-byôshi 夜多羅拍子
Yûjô no kyû 勇勝急

References

Abe, Suehisa. [1690, 1935] 1977. *Gakkaroku*. Reprinted 1935 in *Nihon Koten Zenhshû*, ed. A. Masamune. Reprint, Tokyo: Gendai shichô-sha.

Blacking, John. 1971. "Deep and Surface Structures in Venda Music." *ICTM Yearbook for Traditional Music* 3: 91–108.

Bürkner, Yukie. 2004. "Togism: die Musik Tôgi Hidekis im Zeichen der japanischen Postmoderne." In *Stüdien zur traditionellen Musik Japans*. Vol. 10. Wilhelmshaven: Florian Noetzel.

De Ferranti, Hugh, and Yôko Narazaki, eds. 2002 *A Way a Lone: Writings on Tôru Takemitsu*. Tokyo: Academia Music.

Garfias, Robert. 1975. *Music of a Thousand Autumns: The Tôgaku Style of Japanese Court Music*. Berkeley and Los Angeles: University of California Press.

Hayashi, Kenzô. 1960. "Hakuga no fue-fu kou." *Nara gakugei daigaku kiyou, jinbun-shakaikagaku*. 19(1): 285–308. Reprinted in Hayashi 1969.

———. 1964. *Shôsô-in gakki no kenkyû*. Tokyo: Kazama shoin.

———. 1969. *Gagaku: kogakufu no kaidoku*. Ed. Tôyô ongaku gakkai. Tokyo: Ongaku no tomosha.

————. 1973. *Higashi ajia Gakki-kô*. Tokyo: Kawai gakufu.

Koma, Chikazane. 1233. *Kyôkun-shô*. Reprinted 1973 in *Nihon Koten Shisô Taikei* 23, ed. Ueki Yukinobu. Tokyo: Iwanami shoten.

Lancashire, Terence. 2003. "World Music in Japanese: the *Gagaku* of Tôgi Hideki." *Popular Music* 22(1): 21–39.

Marett, Allan. 1977. "Tunes Notated in Flute Tablature from a Japanese Source of the Tenth Century." *Musica Asiatica* 1:1–59.

————. 1985. "*Tôgaku*: Where Have the Tang Melodies Gone, and Where Have the New Melodies Come From?" *Ethnomusicology* 29(3): 409–431.

————. 1988. "An Investigation of Sources for *Chû Ôga Ryûteki Yôroku-fu*, a Japanese Flute Score of the 14th Century." *Musica Asiatica* 5: 210–267.

————. 2001. "Japan, §V. Court Music, 4. Performing Practice and Historical Change." In *The New Grove Dictionary of Music and Musicians*, 2nd ed., ed. Stanley Sadie, vol. 12, 859–861. London: Macmillan.

————. 2006. "Research on Early Notations for the History of *Tôgaku* and Points of Scholarly Contention in Their Interpretation." *ICTM Yearbook for Traditional Music* 38: 79–95.

Picken, Laurence E. R., with Rembrandt Wolpert, Allan J. Marett, Jonathan Condit, Elizabeth Markham, and Yoko Mitani. 1981. *Music from the Tang Court*. Vol. 1. London: Oxford University Press.

————. 1985. *Music from the Tang Court*. Vol. 2. Cambridge: Cambridge University Press.

Picken, Laurence E. R., with Rembrandt Wolpert, Allan J. Marett, Jonathan Condit, Elizabeth Markham, Yoko Mitani, and Noël J. Nickson. 1986. *Music from the Tang Court*. Vol. 3. Cambridge: Cambridge University Press.

————. 1987. *Music from the Tang Court*. Vol. 4. Cambridge: Cambridge University Press.

Picken, Laurence E. R., and Noël J. Nickson; with Rembrandt Wolpert, Allan J. Marett, Jonathan Condit, Elizabeth Markham, Yoko Mitani, and Stephen Jones. 1990. *Music from the Tang Court*. Vol. 5. Cambridge: Cambridge University Press.

————. 1997. *Music from the Tang Court*. Vol. 6. Cambridge: Cambridge University Press.

Picken, Laurence E. R., and Noel Nickson. 2000. *Music from the Tang Court*. Vol. 7. Cambridge: Cambridge University Press.

Shiba, Sukehiro. 1968. *Gosen-fu ni yoru gagaku sôfu: maki ichi kakyoku hen*. Tokyo: Kawai gakufu.

————. 1969. *Gosen-fu ni yoru gagaku sôfu: maki ni kangenkyoku hayagaku hen*. Tokyo: Kawai gakufu.

————. 1971. *Gosen-fu ni yoru gagaku sôfu: maki san kangenkyoku nobegaku, taikyoku hen*. Tokyo: Kawai gakufu.

————. 1972. *Gosen-fu ni yoru gagaku sôfu: maki yon komagaku, bugakukyokuhen*. Tokyo: Kawai gakufu.

Shôno, Susumu. 1987. "The Role of Listening in *Gagaku*." *Contemporary Music Review* 1(2): 19–43.

Terauchi, Naoko. 2002. "Nijusseiki ni okeru gagaku no tempo to furêzingu no henyou: Gaisberg rokuon to Hôgaku chôsa gagari no gosenfu." *Kokusai Bunkagaku Kenkyu* 17: 85–11.

———. 2008. "Beyond the Court: a Challenge to the *Gagaku* Tradition in the 'Reconstruction' Project of National Theatre." In *Performing Japan: Contemporary Expressions of Cultural Identity*, ed. J. Jaffe and H. Johnson, 93–125. Poole: Global Oriental.

⇥ CHAPTER 2 ⇥

Form, Counterpoint, and Meaning in a Fourteenth-Century French Courtly Song

Elizabeth Eva Leach

Photo: Guillaume de Machaut: the Ferrell-Vogué MS, f.1r. On loan to the Parker Library, Corpus Christi, Cambridge. Reproduced by kind permission of Elizabeth J. and James E. Ferrell. Digital imaging by DIAMM (www.diamm.ac.uk).

Background

The fourteenth-century French balade *De petit po* (hereafter B18) is one of the most widely transmitted examples of its genre, in terms both of the number of surviving manuscript copies and their geographical distribution.[1] Both text and music were written by one of the century's most important Western European poets and composers, Guillaume de Machaut (ca. 1300–1377), who was a Christian cleric in minor orders employed by the royal houses of Bohemia and Navarre (see Earp 1995: 3–51 and the revisions in Bowers 2004).[2] This song emanates from a time well before the emergence of the modern nation state, when the realm was governed by the person of the King and effected by his extended entourage, the court (see Vale 2001; Clanchy 1993). During this period in the later Middle Ages, courts grew in size and thus began to pay employees also in coin rather than merely in kind (courtiers typically received commons at table, transport in the form of horses and grooms, heat in the form of firewood, and light in the form of candles). Keeping records of such monetary payments required written accounts and literate administrators, of whom Machaut was one. The diverse body of individuals at these larger late-medieval courts supported an elite culture.

However, because of the functional nature of these records, they do not tell us everything about the art produced for and by courts. We do not know, for example, exactly when B18 was written, although it is copied in a manuscript that dates from the early 1350s. We also do not know exactly where Machaut was working after 1346; before this time he was almoner, notary, and then secretary to John of Luxembourg, King of Bohemia (Leach 2010a).

Machaut's output is unusual for its time and place in that he brought his highly learned interests to bear on music, using the latest notational technology to record his songs in writing with greater precision than had been seen before and—most important—arranging for his complete works to be copied into large parchment manuscripts, several of which have survived. B18 is contained in all seven of the principal "Machaut manuscripts," all but one of which have musical notation (for details of these sources, see Earp

---

1. The designation B18 represents the number in the standard ordering established by Machaut's earliest editor, Friedrich Ludwig (see Earp 1995: xvii–xviii). The spelling of "po" will be used here when referring to the song because this orthography is that used in the standard editions and thus the scholarly literature. However, as both collected editions predate the correct identification of the earliest surviving source (on which my text and translation are based), the spelling used in figure 2.5 will be different.

2. A religious in minor orders, Machaut had taken a vow not to marry but was not ordained as a priest.

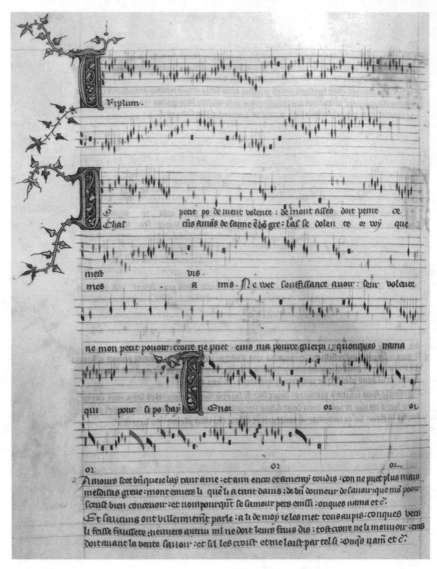

Photo: B18 in Guillaume de Machaut: the Ferrell-Vogué MS, f.305v. On loan to the Parker Library, Corpus Christi, Cambridge. Reproduced by kind permission of Elizabeth J. and James E. Ferrell. Digital imaging by DIAMM (www.diamm.ac.uk).

1995: 310–311 and ch. 3 passim). Unlike most of Machaut's large musical output, however, the song additionally survives in ten other sources with musical notation, sources that form part of the more usual transmission of music in this period. These sources—usually referred to as the "repertory manuscripts"—are musical miscellanies containing works that are only very patchily ascribed to any poet or composer: the greater proportion of the fourteenth-century song repertoire not by Machaut is transmitted anonymously.[3] The text without any musical notation survives copied into two manuscript lyric miscellanies and was also included in a printed lyric anthology, *Le Jardin de Plaisance,* published in Paris in 1501.

The sixteen surviving notations present several different versions of the song, showing the extent (and limitations) of the newly emerging author-centered work concept at this period. In the Machaut sources with music it is always copied in three contrapuntally related parts with each part written out separately: first, a part labeled "triplum," that is "third part" (Tr), which occupies the highest pitch range; second, the cantus part (Ca), which is not labeled, but which has the text of the first stanza of the poem underlaid to it; and finally the "tenor" (T), which has the lowest pitch range. In most of the repertory manuscripts, however, the cantus and tenor are joined instead by a "contratenor" (Ct), a part in the same range as the tenor but lying above it at major cadences. Some of the repertory manuscripts copy all four parts (Earp 1995: 310).

It is only through these manuscripts that this music has come down to us. My transcription of it into modern notation (modern clefs, note values quartered, and bar lines added) is based on the earliest source (*F-Pn* fr. 1586, manuscript **C**) but takes into account the other Machaut manuscripts as well. Its contemporary notation, however, is underprescriptive compared to the staff notation of our own time, so there are specific problems in recovering this music for modern performer and listener. For example, scholars and performers attempting to render Machaut's music in modern sounding or written versions have long debated the issue of when and how the size of interval steps might have been changed to give a semitone's approach to certain pitches in certain situations. Current staff notation clearly distinguishes an F and an F-sharp, but in medieval notation a note head on an F line or in an F space indicates only "some kind of F" and the singer must decide on the basis of his or her training as to whether it is a tone or a semitone away from the G that might follow it. In the present chapter, therefore, suggestions for the realization of semitones at cadence points are given above the staff line in question. Those that are chosen on the basis of linear factors are given in parentheses, while those that represent semitones necessary to the counterpoint, as explained below, are given without.

3. One of these ten notated sources *does* in fact ascribe the song to "G. de Machaut"—one of only three correct attributions to Machaut made outside the Machaut manuscripts.

It will be noticed from comparing the score with the recorded performance on this book's website (and, indeed, with any available recorded performance) that the modern performers make rather different choices, probably responding to the different accidentals indicated in one of the published editions. The editorial principles in common operation when the Machaut editions were made in the 1920s and 1950s (and operating, in fact, until the 1990s) encouraged "clean" copies with the minimal "addition" of accidentals. In the early '90s however, Margaret Bent drew attention to the somewhat different relation between notation, singers, and sonic product in the Middle Ages, and stressed how the transliteration into modern notation already intervened far more in the prescription of pitch than any so-called addition of accidentals. In arguing that singers had greater analytical intervention to mark their lines with semitonal adjustments made in accord with their understanding of the counterpoint, she made a case for viewing such modern clarification as a kind of realization rather than an addition and pointed out the fundamentally analytical nature of the edition-making enterprise itself.

Analytical Method

Counterpoint in its literal sense (from "[punctus] contra punctus" = "[note] against note") denotes the placement of one tone against another. In modern usages it is often used, sometimes loosely, to denote the presence of imitative melodic entries or contrary motion and independence of part writing. However, in its medieval usage it simply refers to the presence of more than one note sounding simultaneously and to the rules by which these various parts were organized and controlled. In effect, it means what we might today call harmony (although scholars avoid that term because it has rather different and specific meanings in the Middle Ages). *Simple* counterpoint in the Middle Ages is always dyadic (involving two parts), single-note-against-single-note, consonant, and without a fixed rhythm (that it, it is a theoretical construct). The contrapuntal texture of actual pieces is sometimes called *diminished* or *florid* counterpoint, since it involves specific relative rhythms, dissonance, many notes against a single note, and more than two parts.

The analytical framework employed here uses a modern understanding of fourteenth-century counterpoint treatises, singing practices, composition, and notational norms to identify the tonal organization of the simple counterpoint between the two fundamental voices, cantus and tenor (for more detail, see Leach, 2000a, 2000b, 2001). It then employs a modern extension of this historical perspective to look at the way in which the sonorities of this basic framework are enriched by the addition of a third voice. For reasons of space only, the focus will be on the three-part version with triplum, which seems likely to have been Machaut's original texture. This focus is in no way meant to suggest that the contratenor is not worthy of analysis—on the contrary, it might give a rare insight into singing practices outside Machaut's immediate sphere and provide a valuable record of the early reception history of this song. However, the present analysis should help modern listeners develop a sense for what Bent has termed the music's basic "grammar" so as to identify what its contemporary listeners would have heard as its moments of tension and expectation, and their fulfillment or evasion.

Since the 1990s in particular, a method of analyzing the counterpoint of fourteenth-century music has been employed that takes its starting point in medieval theory but extends this through an examination of the practice.[4] This has been controversial and is not the only system that has been proposed, but it is powerfully descriptive. The relevance of medieval treatises to medieval music is not universally accepted, but will be taken as axiomatic here; the voices of those who argue otherwise will be referred to in footnote references so that any interested reader may follow up the lively—and sometimes heated—debate to decide for him- or herself (see, for example, the varied perspectives found in the essays in Leach 2003). Medieval treatises classify two-note (dyadic) sonorities into those that are consonant and those that are dissonant (for a fuller exposition, see Leach 2000a). Only consonances are proper to strict counterpoint, such that the surfaces of actual musical pieces—which of course contain dissonances—are to be understood to be the ornamentation of underlying counterpoint proper, sometimes known as florid or diminished counterpoint (Berger 2005: 151–158 relates this to the fundamental training of singers). The elements that form Machaut's balade style, such as dissonance treatment, rhythmic practices, and text setting, can be pinpointed through an examination of how the rhythmic and frequently dissonant foreground relates to this notional, nonrhythmicized, and consonant background counterpoint.

4. The use of medieval counterpoint theory in analyzing Machaut's songs was not new in the 1990s. For earlier examples of its use, see especially Dömling 1970 and Arlt 1982. The groundwork for these approaches can be found in studies of the theoretical tradition, also in German, such as Sachs 1974 and Apfel 1982. Leech-Wilkinson's 1984 conference paper linking counterpoint teaching, composed music, and analysis has been web-mounted (1998): see www.kcl.ac.uk/kis/schools/hums/music/dlw/cdp.htm [accessed 03/30/09].

The consonances are classified as perfect (unisons, fifths, octaves, and their compounds) or imperfect (thirds, sixths, and their compounds).[5] Imperfect consonances were so called because in their medieval tuning they were more dissonant than the same intervals are today and required resolution to perfect consonances, which were the only types of consonance suitable for ending pieces. A basic sense of movement is achieved by an imperfect consonance (the "tension" sonority, in modern terminology) followed by a perfect consonance (the "resolution"), where one of the tones in the latter is a semitone away from one of the tones in the former. This progression of two dyads was called a cadence (*cadentia*) but is not syntactically confined to being merely closural, since it often opens or connects passages and is one of the fundamental ways in which musical phrases proceed.[6] Sarah Fuller has termed this "the directed progression" because of its sense of tension-resolution or movement. This feature was clearly perceived by contemporaries, some of whom found it a rather worrying projection of desire and satisfaction, others of whom rationalized it as exemplifying Aristotelian physics (see Cohen 2001 and Leach 2006). I will refer to this progression as a cadence when it *is* used closurally; as shall be seen in B18, in such clearly cadential uses, the tension sonority often forms the last of a succession of two or three imperfect consonances that extends and heightens the sense of tension.

The "directed progression" was so central to contemporary conceptions of contrapuntal motion that it was a fundamental part of singers' training, and thus helped bridge the interpretative gap between the underprescriptive notation and the sounding result of the performance (see the essays in Bent 2002). Thus contrapuntal "analysis" had to be performed, in the process of rehearsal, before the song could itself be "translated" into sounding performance (Leach 2010b). Today such analysis has to precede the translation of the medieval notational trace into the modern notation that its medieval notation so seductively (and erroneously) resembles. If contrapuntal analysis is a necessary stage in the realization of the text itself, the processes of analysis and of editing (of "fixing" a particular manuscript version for performance or analysis) are not

5. The exact designation of thirds and sixths varies, with some theorists referring to them as a type of dissonance rather than an imperfect consonance; see Sachs 1984: 81–103. As they are nevertheless proper to counterpoint (in a way that genuine dissonances— seconds, fourths, sevenths, and their compounds—are not) but not stable enough for the ends of pieces I shall refer to them as imperfect consonances.

6. See Fuller 1992. Fuller's derivation of terms for three-part sonorities by extrapolation from those pertaining to two-part sonorities in fourteenth-century treatises will not, however, be adopted here, where the basic focus remains on the overlay of essentially dyadic counterpoint.

fully distinct. The circularity of allowing counterpoint analysis both to pre-cede *and* drive the analysis of tonal process has been grist for the mill of those who deny the relevance of medieval counterpoint treatises and value the "unchanged" transcription of the medieval text, as if all its signs meant what similar-looking signs mean today. However, it seems unavoidable. Inevitably, those emphases of line and sonority that seem important in any explanation of tonal process will be those provided by the realization of semitones resulting from the basic contrapuntal analysis required for making the edition or perfor-mance of the piece in the first place. The "edition" of the music will perforce support and enhance the analysis. In acknowledging and accepting this her-meneutic circle I like to think that I am sharing—imaginatively—the likely approaches of a fourteenth-century singer, while being very self-consciously a modern analyst.

Overview of Form and Rhythmic Organization

De petit po (B18) is a balade, one of three highly formalized poetic and music forms in this period (the full text and translation are given in figure 2.5).[7] Poet-ically, the three stanzas share a single pattern of rhyme sounds, syllable count, and refrain. Each eight-line stanza rhymes ababccdD, where the rhyme types are *-é, -is, -oir,* and *-i*. The fifth line (the first c-rhyme) is a so-called cut line (*vers coupé*) and has only seven syllables, but all other lines have ten. The final line is a refrain, whose text is unchanging in each stanza (hence its rhyme type being given a capital letter): *Onques n'ama qui pour si po haÿ* (literally, "No one loved who for so little hates"—the sense being that someone who stops loving for a minor reason, cannot really have loved in the first place). Only the first stanza is underlaid in the sources; the second and third are copied underneath as text often arranged as if prose, rather than being laid out in lines.[8] As a musico-poetic form, B18 is similar to most of Machaut's other balades in all these respects.

The song is sectionally periodic in the sense that the music of the first stanza is repeated exactly for the other two stanzas. There is also some repeated material within the stanza itself, the sections of which are organized by the way in which they deliver the syllable-counted verse structure of the poem. The first two lines are set to the first section of music (the A section) with an

7. Together with the rondeau and virelai, these are the so-called *formes fixes;* see "Ballade," "Rondeau," and "Virelai" in *Grove Online.* For the prehistory of the balade, see Page 1998.

8. This space-saving layout for poetry is common in this period. In some sources various punctuation marks are used to signal poetic line ends.

ouvert (open) ending that cadences to *D/d* in the T–Ca duet.[9] This entire section is directly repeated for lines 3–4 (which share the same versification as lines 1–2), but with a second ending, the *clos* (closed) cadence to *C/c*. The B section, setting lines 5–7, follows directly. In many balades of this period, a marked break separates the end of the B section from the refrain line, which is set to a section of its own (R), offset from the rest of the song.[10] In B18, however, there is no notated section break between the refrain and the B section. Instead, there are measured rests in the cantus part following a cadence, and a connective figure in the tenor that leads direct into the refrain.[11]

The rhythm of the balade is conceived in terms of a hierarchical system of duration known as *mensuration*. The largest functional unit is the *breve* (transcribed here as a dotted half-note), which is called *perfect* because it is subdivided into three semibreves (quarter notes). These are subdivided duply, so that each *perfection* comprises three pairs of the smallest note value (the minim, transcribed here as an eighth note). Although the relation between mensuration and metrical stress patterns has been little investigated in this repertoire, it seems from the counterpoint of this piece that the onset of the first semibreve in a perfection group is metrically the strongest and the onset of the second is the weakest, much as in modern 3/4 time.

Analysis of Counterpoint and Tonal Structure

The analysis of counterpoint will start with an examination of the dyadic core of the piece—the sonorities created by the tenor and cantus parts. Evidence from music-theoretical sources suggests that this dyadic counterpoint was

9. Pitches throughout are given in italics using the Guidonian gamut in which lowercase letters *a–g* are the pitches that include middle C (*c*); the octave below these are shown by uppercase letters and the octave above by doubled letters. Pitch classes are designated using uppercase letters in roman type. Simultaneous pitches are separated with a forward slash (/) and successive pitches by a short dash (–).

10. The indication of this unmeasured break resembles measured rests in the original notation, occurring in all parts. These are ignored in the Machaut edition of Schrade and transcribed as measured rests in that of Ludwig. My favored method is to mark them as a double bar.

11. A measured rest is also present in the triplum part. In the versions with contratenor, the contratenor participates in the connecting measure (m. 31). Machaut uses the other parts to connect the B section and refrain in B13, B21, B33, and B42. B42, like B12, has a notated section break a line before the refrain line. B20, B29, B30, and B32 have no marked section break and that in B16 is arguably measured.

the basis for larger textures, and the varied transmission of this particular song supports that assumption, given that it survives in a two-part version as well as in two different three-part versions. Although some sources transmit four parts, evidence from the counterpoint of the piece suggests that they record two alternative three-part performance possibilities rather than true four-part versions.

While the triplum and contratenor on many occasions closely replicate each other's underlying basic counterpoint (with octave transposition in some cases), at the surface level they ornament the cadences present in the contrapuntally core T–Ca duet so differently as to create some sustained dissonances between these two third parts. This can be seen by comparing the two systems in figure 2.1. Points of divergence include the four most important cadences of the piece: the two *clos*-type cadences (the *clos* cadence itself in mm. 17–18, second time, and the final cadence in mm. 37–38) and the two *ouvert*-type cadences (the *ouvert* cadence itself in mm. 17–18, first time, and the similar cadence at the end of the B section before the start of the refrain in mm. 29–31). In all four of these cadences the contratenor delays its note of resolution between the imperfect sonority and perfect sonority of the T–Ct duet of each, by striking the note a tone above and holding it for two-thirds of a perfection (measure) before descending to the awaited note of resolution.[12] By contrast, at the same points, the triplum proceeds immediately to the note of resolution. Between the contratenor and triplum, this gives the relationship of a seventh, held for the initial two thirds of a perfection. The *ouvert* and *clos* cadences are shown in figure 2.1, with these dissonances between triplum and contratenor marked. An examination of theoretical rules and actual practice with respect to dissonance treatment in this period suggest that this combination of metrical placement and duration is not acceptable, leading to the conclusion that these two voices are mutually exclusive alternatives (for the fuller reasoning of these points, see Leach 2001: 67, 69–71, and Leach 2000a: 49–50).

Marie Louise Martinez (1963: 112) has commented that when an alternative third voice is added to a preexisting three-voice structure, "the piece is usually transmitted as a two-part piece in some of the sources," something that is indeed the case for this song, which exists in a two-part version in one source now in Prague.[13] Together with the evidence that the triplum and

12. This is a figure similar to that which is a consistent cadential feature of *Helas! tant* (B2), where, however, it appears in the mensural guise of major prolation; Leach 2002: 479–482.

13. On the Prague MS, *CS-Pu* XI E 9 (**Pg**), see Earp 1995: 127–128, MS [72]. See also Dömling 1969: 194.

Figure 2.1.   *Ouvert* and *clos* cadences in B18, comparing the triplum and contratenor versions.

contratenor are mutually exclusive, the existence of two-part and two different three-part versions suggests that the manuscripts that transmit all four parts contain a compendium of possibilities for performances, not a four-part piece (Leach 2001: 67, 69–71).[14] And since the three-part versions contain the same duet, a text-carrying cantus melody harmonized by the tenor, the song's basic musical identity may reasonably be regarded as that two-part structure, whose dyadic harmonies can be enriched by either a triplum—which seems to have been Machaut's own compositional contribution—or, slightly differently, by a contratenor.[15]

The variations in transmission also bear upon how we understand the relation between music and words. Machaut's own manuscripts present this

14. The manuscript **CaB** also contains all four voices and a fifth voice that has been identified as a second triplum in. Fallows 1976: 279. See http://www.diamm.ac.uk/jsp/DisplayImage.jsp?imageKey=79, which has a color image.

15. A three-voice texture with triplum seems to have been the preferred texture in the first half of the fourteenth century, a three-part texture with contratenor in the latter half. See Leach 2001: 70–71. Although I view the counterpoint somewhat differently, Memelsdorff 2003, which treats contratenors added to works by Ciconia, argues persuasively for a full consideration of nonauthorial voice parts as part of the historical context of a piece.

song only with the music and poetry together. However, the existence of sources transmitting both the poetry without its musical notation and the musical notation without full text might point to the separability of the two media. Perhaps, once the song was known to its audience, the verbal text alone, in conjunction with human memory, could effectively notate its music (just as stand-alone verbal texts in a hymnbook, especially in a stanzaic form, can cue singing when the readers already know the tune).[16] And conversely it might be the case that the bald cues "De petit peu" or "De petit" in the musical sources would have been enough to cue the entire text to those that knew the song.[17] Songs in this period would have had a multifaceted rather than unitary presence in the heads of listeners, who would have known them variously—well and badly, orally and written— and would have been adding to their knowledge and mental sound-trace of such songs (which seem to have been "current" for decades) through the course of their lives.

Thus although ultimately I would rather not separate the musical and poetic parts of this song, I will start by giving an outline sketch of the musical aspect—especially in terms of its counterpoint—before covering the musical delivery of the text, and finally the text's broader contexts. Figure 2.2 shows the music of the complete song underlaid with the poem's first stanza, together with three levels of analysis of the fundamental contrapuntal duet of the cantus and tenor on single staves beneath and a final stave that summarizes the contribution of the triplum, which will be treated in a separate subsection below.

The first stage of contrapuntal analysis is one of simple parsing. The smallest temporal unit used in the piece is the minim (transcribed as an eighth note in the example) and each minim moment may be classified as either dissonant (shown with crossed note heads), imperfectly consonant (filled note heads) or

16. In assuming that the contratenor is not by Machaut scholars have generally disregarded it: Earp (1995: 311, 399) deems it "unauthentic" and thinks it "should be suppressed" in modern recordings. Although for reasons of space the contratenor cannot be considered here, I would instead urge attention to this voice part, which offers a reflection of the more mixed oral-literate tradition of performance in this period. It is possible that by the time of the *Jardin de plaisance* (1501), the tune was no longer known, as this version of the poem is updated by restoring the *vers coupé* to a full decasyllabic line through the addition of three syllables to line 5 in each stanza. While it is not impossible to sing to Machaut's music for this line to the greater syllable count, it seems an unlikely change to make if the music were implied.

17. **Pg** and **Pit** have three words, **FP** has only two; **CaB** seems to lack the second and third stanzas. See the notes in Ludwig 1926–1954, I: 19.

Figure 2.2. B18 in three parts with triplum, with three-level analysis of tenor-cantus and analysis of tenor-triplum.

Figure 2.2. (Continued)

*cantus note acting as tenor here

69

Figure 2.2. (Continued)

Figure 2.2. (Continued)

Figure 2.2. (Continued)

perfectly consonant (open note heads).[18] The composite rhythmic profile of the piece when the parts are aggregated is to project almost constant minim movement, even in its two-part version, giving a high density of ornamental rhythmic and motivic interest, much of it dissonant. The next stage of analysis is to exclude those things, according to contemporary theorists, not proper to simple counterpoint, such as dissonances, repeated sonorities (including those repeated once dissonant ornamentation is removed), single notes, and sonorities that make a succession of parallel perfect consonances (for more detail, see Leach 2000a).[19] For example, removing one of at least two consonant cantus tones above a given tenor tone, as between syllables 5 and 7 of line 6 (mm. 24–25), which views the d setting syllable 6 ("mon") as ornamental, shows that one of a pair of parallel fifths heard at the surface level can easily be excluded from the underlying counterpoint even if the parallel fifths are perceptible on the audible surface and, as here, involve a tone at the start of a perfection group. (It is, in fact, typical of Machaut's style that where a stressed tone infringes contrapuntal rules, whether by being dissonant or by perpetrating a parallel perfect movement, it is, in compensation, of short duration; see Leach 2000a.)

An analytical sketch (shown on the penultimate staff of figure 2.2) then identifies broader contrapuntal and tonal progressions, in which the presence of directed progressions or potential directed progressions in the simple counterpoint is recognized. These "directed progressions" are shown by arrowed brackets above the staff and require the analytical realization of a semitone approach in one part to one tone of the ensuing perfect sonority. These accidentals are realized on this staff and were then added above the stave in the score where not present in the manuscript sources.[20] As mentioned

18. As in Schenkerian notation, the greater visual weight is thus given to those sonorities with greater contrapuntal weight using the basic way of signaling temporal weight in ordinary notation.

19. As a rule of thumb, the "weaker" of the two parallel perfect consonances should be excluded from the basic counterpoint, with relative strength being assessed on contrapuntal factors before rhythmic and metrical factors (because the *contrapunctus* is theoretically arrhythmic). In mm. 26–27 (as in mm. 1–2), the first consonance is the resolution of a directed progression and is therefore retained. In the example in Leach 2000a, example 6, p. 58, neither consonance of the two perfect ones in parallel is involved in a directed progression, so the consonance at the start of the perfection is retained.

20. I do not consider these inflections "optional" but part of the singers' response to the basic premises of the style. As the original notation uses only two accidental signs I have interpreted the "*mi* signs" of the source as either a natural or a sharp depending on their meaning in the context of modern pitch representation. Although in the original

above, the backward or forward extent of these accidentals is sometimes open to more choice, leading to the addition of parentheses to the accidentals above the staff.[21]

In other places the analysis of the underlying counterpoint has to supply expected elements of directed progressions that are only partially provided at the musical surface level. This can mean gathering together notes that do not in fact sound simultaneously but that conceptually precede sounding resolution sonorities. For example, at the caesura of line 6, (syllable 4) in m. 24 the tenor rests as the cantus sings *b* and then the cantus rests as the tenor sings *G,* yet the next dyad is the resolution of these two tones combined, *F/c.* Although the properly preceding dyad *G/b* never actually sounds, it is arguably implied by this brief hocket and thus appears in the analysis in curly brackets. Conversely, sometimes both notes of the tension sonority are present at the level of the musical surface but the resolution happens only in one voice. Examples of this can be seen in m. 10 and m. 14, where the expected resolutions (to unison *F/F* and the octave *C/c,* respectively) both lack the tenor tone as the tenor rests.

Sometimes a resolution is strongly implied by a tension sonority but is avoided, partially avoided, or weakened in some way. This feinting maneuver is rife in the opening melisma, which is arguably the most complex moment in the piece (discussed further below), but the most evident avoidance of an implied resolution occurs in the final melisma of the piece (syllable 5 of the refrain line 8, m. 35). The cantus outlines a strongly cadential directed progression from a chain of three descending parallel sixths as if cadencing to *D/d,* as does the *ouvert* in m. 18. But the tenor continues in parallel motion, rising to *F* in m. 36 rather than falling to *D.* The position of the expected but avoided sonority is marked with an X above the staff. This sixth rises again in m. 37 to *G/eb* (which had been the initial starting point in m. 35), delivering the remaining text syllables to a *clos*-type cadence of parallel sixths,

---

accidentals are often placed earlier, accidentals in the transcription are placed directly in front of the note that I consider they affect. The interested reader is urged to remain aware of the many levels of interpretation that a modern score requires and to have recourse to the original sources, microfilms or facsimiles where possible.

21. In addition, the argument for singing Ebs in the tenor in m. 20, the cantus and tenor in mm. 26 and 37, and the cantus in m. 29, is based on the similarity of these cadences to those in the *ouvert* and *clos* rather than on contrapuntal necessity. The flat may thus be considered a matter of taste. The same could be said for the tenor Eb in m. 35, although without the flat, the perception of the avoidance of the *D/d* resolution in this bar would be weakened.

which descend through the sixth *Eb/c* to the tension sonority *D/b♮* whose resolution is the final *C/c*. The effect of the irresolution in m. 36 is to increase the number of successive sixths to seven (the longest in the entire song), which strengthens the strong expectation of closure and so intensifies the final cadence of the song.

Cadences and Tonal Orientation

The overall tonal orientation of songs in the mid-fourteenth century is usually (but not always) governed as here by the open and closed endings of the repeated first section of music, the A section. In B18, the *ouvert* and *clos* endings both have directed progressions in which a sixth resolves to an octave. Both directed progressions are made more closurally cadential in that the sixth from which they resolve is the third in a chain of parallel sixths, a formulation that tends to be reserved for strong cadences. The relative priority of these two cadences can be seen in two features that differentiate them. First, the open ending is reached by a falling semitone and the closed cadence by a rising one, a difference that Bain (2005) has shown to exist more generally in this repertoire, indicative of the perception that rising semitones provide stronger tonal motion than falling ones. Second, the sixths that precede the closed sonority are ornamented with dissonant suspensions as opposed to the consonant suspensions that feature in the *ouvert*. A close identity between the surface consonances and the underlying counterpoint in the *clos* (resulting from the ornamentation of the basic counterpoint only by dissonances and not by other kinds of consonances) also seems to be a way of making a cadence stronger, since these dissonances are more clearly ornamental, not at all stable, and thus propel forward motion more than ornamental consonance.

The cadences of the *ouvert* and *clos* types feature in the second part of the balade, as has already been seen in the refrain section, where they occur immediately in succession, although the first avoids the resolution to the *ouvert*-type sonority *D/d*. The B section also presents them in close proximity to bring about closure, although (typically for this repertoire) it states them in reverse order, with the *clos* type in mm. 25–27 and the *ouvert* type in mm. 29–30 as the pre-refrain cadence. The very opening phrase in the B section also has a strong cadence to the *clos*-type sonority, whose resolution is preceded by three successive imperfect consonances (mm. 20–22).

Directed progressions to pitches other than D and C are usually more local in being only from a single imperfect consonance, often metrically weaker and temporally unsustained. The directed progression from the first to second minim of m. 20 is so weak (short in duration and metrically unstressed) that it is excluded from the analytical sketch (a fact confirmed by the triplum's disregard for it; see below). In effect it serves only to harmonize the notes *f* and *e* in the cantus's stepwise descent from *g* in m. 19 to its eventual cadence point on *c* in m. 22.

However, two other pitches are subject to direct progressions that have more surface weight: *F* and *G*. The resolutions to F, since their earlier appearances (mm. 12–15) represent a different tenor harmonization of the *b♮–c* movement in the cantus's *clos*-type progressions, may be seen to strengthen the *clos* tone C, although in the second part of the balade they are expanded to octave resolutions on *F/f*, approached either from *E♮/g* or from *G/e♮*. Resolutions to *G* may conversely be associated with a strengthening of the *ouvert* tone *d*, since they approach it not by the weaker *falling* semitone (from *e♭*) but strongly by *rising* semitone (from *c♯*) as in mm. 34–35. This latter tonal goal is further from the *clos* area not only because it "tonicizes" *d* with a rising semitone, but also because this involves the semitonal adjustment of the *clos* tone itself (from *c* to *c♯*). Similarly, the expanded *F* resolutions (to *F/f*) are the furthest from the *ouvert* tone because they involve the naturalization of the tone necessary for *its* tension sonority (E♮ instead of E♭). These relationships are sketched in figure 2.3.

Tonal Narrative

It is worth clarifying, given the later tonal organization of music in Western Europe, that these relationships are not, in my view at least, precompositional features of a thoroughgoing tonal system as they are in major-minor

Figure 2.3.   Tonal interrelations of *ouvert* and *clos* "areas."

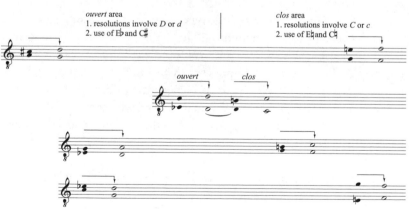

tonality.[22] Instead, the selection from a range of possible interrelations is made and justified by the course of the piece itself, in a quasi-narrative fashion. The relationship between dyadic harmony and fourteenth-century tonality appears far more flexible and less prescriptive than the relationship between triadic harmony and later European classical major-minor tonality in this regard. One hesitates, then, to posit a revised large-scale (or "deep-level") background structure deriving from the basic dyadic cadence structures of the pieces that could then be viewed as being "prolonged," much as a tonal *Ursatz* is prolonged in Schenkerian analyses of tonal music.[23] An account of the tonal "narrative" of the piece as it unfolds thus follows here.

SECTION A

The piece starts from a unison *c/c* sonority, with the two voices moving apart in contrary motion, initially in a metrically weak directed progression to *a/e* within m. 1. The rest of the opening musical phrase, setting the first syllable of text melismatically, refuses to make any clear tonal resolution until its end in m. 8. The cantus in this phrase introduces many of the minim-rich motivic figures that will feature in the rest of the piece. The second measure, however, presents a surface mixture of dissonances and parallel perfect consonances. Except for the final dyad of the measure (*F/a*), the underlying counterpoint must thus be viewed as having been rhythmically displaced. *F/a* could potentially resolve to *E/b* or, with *F♯*, to unison *G/G*, but the cantus rests as the tenor moves to *G* in m. 3 and then noodles around, retaking its descent from the high *e* that it had first reached at the summit of its opening measure (the goal of the first directed progression in m. 1). While the cantus shakes, the tenor holds its *G*, repeating the two minim approach to it at the end of m. 4 to finally sound the unison *G/G* sonority with cantus (which has by then completed its descent) in m. 5, the end of the initial melisma and the beginning of the rest of the text. However, the *F♯/a* that ought to precede unison *G/G* for

---

22. A systematization of the tonality of fourteenth-century song based on an empirical survey of range and key signatures has been proposed in Lefferts 1995 and given lengthy exposition in Plumley 1996. Lefferts's conclusions, which rely on the signatures given in modern editions (on the interpretation of such manuscript signs as "default" markings rather than signatures proper, see Bent 2002, 3–11 and passim) have been criticized by Fuller 1998a. Fuller's commitment to tonal process over tonal system has also led to her rejection of the alternative systematic view—a modal one—of Berger 1992; see Fuller 1998b.

23. See, however, Leach 2000a: 59–61 and 76n51 and, on the possibility of employing Schenkerian notions of prolongation without necessarily adopting the *Ursatz*, see, for example, Harper-Scott 2006.

this sonority to represent a contrapuntal resolution is hidden, nonsimultane-ously in the figuration of the two voices, which have parallel fourth disso-nances at the end of m. 4. Either one must posit rhythmic displacement at the surface level or imagine that the true antecedent tension sonority is the last minim in m. 2, such that the tenor singer could choose to sharpen his or her *F*s to play with a sustained tonal expectation of *G* resolution in this passage. A further *G* unison is present briefly and weakly (at the fourth minim) in m. 6, this time directly preceded by *a/F* (with the voices crossed) so that the cantus—the voice part of the fundamental duet in which sharpening for directed pro-gressions most commonly occurs—could easily decide to sharpen the *F* (especially as the tenor reaches the *a* first, giving perhaps enough time for this response to be made in performance).[24] But the other resolution of *F/a*—that is, *E/b*—follows at the start of m. 7, where the metrical stress makes the di-rected progression much more prominent, especially as it follows two measures of displacement caused by syncopation in the cantus. In retrospect, the whole phrase from m. 2 to m. 7 represents a tonally and rhythmically unclear passage in which the voices are so close together that they cross, obscuring their usual function and the overall tonal flow until mm. 7–8, in which the *E/b* resolution concatenates to a *D/b* tension chord that resolves the opening phrase (and text line) to *C/c,* the sonority that will form the eventual *clos* and final cadences. Figure 2.2 offers no concrete analysis of this section, since it would be possible for the singers to take (and vary) decisions, either after rehearsal discussions or on the fly in performance, that would project different levels of play with expectation in this phrase.

The end of the first line and musical phrase is held only the briefest of minims before the second line and musical phrase start, returning to close-position thirds that resolve to *F* at the text line's caesura (syllable 4, m. 10), although the tenor rests at the resolution, slightly weakening its status as a full phrase ending. When the (foiled) cantus then also rests, the tenor leaps above the level of the cantus resolution. The hocketed tones *F* (cantus) and *c* (tenor) resolve the dyad *E/G* in m. 9, but split the necessary semitone movement *E–F*

24. It is possible to envisage some play with these details, with the tenor not sharp-ening its *F*s in mm. 2 and 6 and the cantus having to descend below in order to empha-size the "correct" sharpening; the tenor arriving fractionally late on its *G* resolution note in m. 6 and immediately using *F♮* as the correct approach to *E/b.* The opening phrase then seems like a mutual working out of an area of tonal focus and contrapuntal function between the two voices. At the repeat of the A section and/or in subsequent stanzas, it would be possible to reconsider these options and play even further with the inchoate presentation of the opening phrase.

between the two voice parts. The cantus then reclaims the top of the texture by making a leap of its own, a minor seventh very unusual in this repertory, that introduces a new kind of tone—an *eb*—which augurs the tonal area that will form the secondary focus of the piece. These events take place free of the otherwise pervasive minim-rich ornamentation figures, which makes this setting of the opening of line 2 aurally striking.

The rest of the second phrase (starting from the upbeat to m. 11) is rich in directed progressions and links together virtually all the tones that will play an important role in the rest of the piece. The *c/eb* of m. 10 resolves in m. 12 to *G/d*, which concatenates by cantus movement to the imperfect sonority, *G/b*. This resolves to *F/c* before concatenation (by tenor movement this time) gives *Eb/c*, which resolves in turn to *D/d*, the eventual *ouvert* sonority. The cantus drops to *b*, and the resulting tension sonority *D/b* very nearly resolves to the eventual *clos* sonority, *C/c*. In fact, the tenor rests rather than descending to *C*, and then leaps up to *b*, which resolves above the cantus *G* to *F/c* (with the voices in inverted position). This progression is rerun with the voices in their usual registral positions within m. 16, but its resolution is metrically weak, especially compared to the *ouvert* chain of parallel sixths leading to *D/d* that ensues in mm. 17–18.

Thus far—after the first presentation of the A section of the music—it is clear that the rising semitone *b–c* is of great importance and will be set in contrast to the falling semitone *eb–d* or *Eb–D*. The falling semitone has been part of a directed progression to *G/d*, but the *ouvert* ending suggests that *D/d* will be more centrally the secondary sonority. However, it is still unclear as to whether the *b–c* rising semitone is to be set in an F context (as it is in mm. 10, 12, 15, and 16) or in a C context (as in mm. 8 and 14). This comment is not meant to reflect an uncertainty for the listener, although when the piece is heard for the very first time this might be the case, but rather to stress the point that the eventual tonal hierarchy that the piece projects has not yet been established at this point in the work. If we assume the longevity of these songs in the courtly repertoire, then statistically, the vast majority of listeners who have heard this piece were not, in any particular given hearing, hearing it for the first time. And even for most of the very first time a listener heard this piece, he or she would know what kind of *b–c* semitone context to expect, because once the *clos* cadence (mm. 17–18, second time) clarifies that *D* is to be the secondary focal tone to *C* rather than to *F*, the matter is settled.

B SECTION AND REFRAIN

The B section of the song opens with the widest interval between the voices yet heard, in fact the widest one that will occur in the piece, with both voices at the limit of their ranges: *C/g*. The section ends, as often in balades, with the *ouvert*-type sonority, reached, as in the *ouvert* itself, from a descending chain of parallel imperfect sixths, although the surface figuration and rhythm in both voices is somewhat different (cf. mm. 29–30 and mm. 17–18, first time). The final phrase of the B section is preceded by two phrases that both cadence to *C/c*—the first at the end of the short poetic line (1.5, with only seven syllables) in m. 22 and the second in m. 27. The latter is the only place in the song where a cadence falls so strongly on a syllable that is not important within the verse structure; rather than to the verse structure, the music responds instead to the grammatical syntax. Both of these *C/c* cadences are preceded by three consecutive imperfect sonorities, although the resolution at m. 22—a rare moment of stasis in the minim-rich movement of the song, lasting an entire perfect breve (a single measure in the transcription)—is reached not from *D/b* but from *G/b*. The *C/c* cadence at m. 27 follows the exact succession of sixths found in the *clos* cadence, although the exact pitch sequence in the cantus differs slightly and the text delivery is here syllabic (cf. mm. 26–27 and mm. 17–18, second time). This central phrase in the B section (mm. 23–27) contains directed progressions to *D/a* (within m. 23), *F/c* (within m. 24 where the *G/b* tension sonority is not presented simultaneously, but hocketed between the voices) and to *F/f* (m. 25). Another resolution to *F/f* occurs within m. 28. The E♮s that both *F/f* resolutions necessitate in their tension sonorities contrast certainly with the E♭ that approaches *D* in the final cadence of the B section and perhaps also with m. 26, because it is modeled on the *clos* cadence.

The refrain opens with the *F/f* sonority, implying e♮s in m. 33's descent, and the directed progression to *G/d* in bars 34–35 requires a c♯. The first part of the refrain thus collects together the two sonorities whose contrapuntal preparation requires the accidental inflection of the very pitches needed for both the *ouvert*-type cadences (where the resolution to *D* uses E♭) and the *clos*-type cadences (which resolve to C♮). This point of maximal tonal waywardness is immediately "rescued" by the bringing together of the *ouvert*-type cadence in mm. 35–36 (whose resolution is avoided; see above) and the *clos*-type cadence, that serves as the final cadence of the song.

Interim Summary

It seems, therefore that the song articulates a clear contrast between a primary and terminal tonal focus on C, which is reached by a rising semitone *b–c* and secondary tonal focus on D, reached by a falling semitone E♭–D. Within this scheme F resolutions stem from an alternative harmonization of the *ouvert*-type cadence and often use E♮, a tone farthest from the secondary tonal area (which uses E♭). The *a/c♯* preparing the G resolution implies a "tonicization" of D via the rising semitone common in directed progressions to primary tonal goals, and is thus the directed progression farthest from the primary tonal area, whose "tonic" is the same letter-name note in its uninflected guise. Figure 2.3's sketch of these relations may be taken as a key to these interrelations, which are established during the course of the song and confirmed by the reiteration of the music for the subsequent text stanzas.

Triplum Part

Thus far the focus has been on the cantus-tenor duet that forms the contrapuntal core of the work, but the song was often performed with three parts, using either the triplum found in all the Machaut sources or the contratenor that features in several other sources. The spacing of the core duet with all its major cadences at the octave and most progressing from a sixth to the octave makes it possible for either type of voice to be fitted in readily: the contratenor can sing a third resolving to a fifth above the tenor, and the triplum can sing this up an octave. Space prevents consideration of the contratenor's response to the T–Ca core, but an interested reader might want to examine the T–Ct duet in the light of the T–Ca analysis presented above and in comparison to the T–Tr's response to that T–Ca duet, discussion of which follows below.

At the most important cadences, the triplum part supports the fundamental duet, cadencing with the tenor at the same time that the cantus does. For example, in the series of sixths that form the *ouvert* and *clos* cadences, the triplum forms an octave and then two tenths, cadencing to the twelfth. It fittingly presents the *clos* cadence more strongly than the *ouvert* because the *f*♯ of the tension sonority sounds simultaneously with the tenor tone; in the *ouvert*, as figure 2.2, m. 17 shows with curly brackets, the two notes of the T–Tr tension sonority are rhythmically offset from each other.

In other places, rather than merely conforming to the counterpoint of the core duet, the triplum clarifies it. For instance, after supporting the T–Ca duet's initial progression from a third to a fifth within m. 1 with its own progression from a sixth to an octave, it fails to support any of the potential resolutions to *G/G* in the rest of the first phrase. It augurs instead the eventual *E* resolution, with m. 5 presenting the first progression to *E/e* in T–Tr, although the cantus still harps on *G*. The triplum then supports the T–Ca duet's resolution to *E/b* in m. 7 with an *e*, as well as the T–Ca duet's resolution to *C/c* in m. 8 with the tone *g*. The caesura in m. 10 is marked by a progression to *F/c* in the usually nonfunctional Ca–Tr duet, coincident with the partially fulfilled progression to *F* in the T–Ca core. This overall sounding progression is not only weakened by the tenor rest at the start of m. 10 but also by the triplum's own minim (eighth-note) rest and its swift leap away from the *c* of resolution to *g*, dismissing the F sonority of the contrapuntally messy cadence.

In mm. 12–13 the triplum movement from *g* to *aa* strengthens the resolution to *D/d/aa,* which initiates the terminal melisma of this section. The triplum also participates in the concatenation of other directed progressions (m. 12), which locally prepare that resolution, and effectively prolong the initial tension sonority of the phrase at the upbeat to m. 11 (*c/e* ♭). From the *g* to which the triplum so readily leaped after its delayed and short resolution to *c* for the *F* cadence at the caesura of line 2 (the downbeat of m. 10; see above), it proceeds immediately to the *aa* that would provide the right note of resolution for a progressions of *c/e* ♭/*g* to *D/d/aa,* although such a progression would necessitate a strange leap of a seventh in the tenor (and would thus resemble, in reverse, the odd cantus leap in m. 10). Instead, the tenor moves only by step down to *b,* making a compelling T–Tr dissonance of a seventh—metrically stressed by occurring at the beginning of a perfection (measure), and lasting a whole semibreve (quarter note)—which helps to connect this moment aurally to the actual resolution to *D/d/aa* in m. 13.[25] For the rest of the A section, the triplum is in an interesting position. It weakens the progressions into m. 14 and within m. 16, since it forms a perfect consonance with the tenor in each case. In between, in the progression into m. 15, it forms parallel fourths (*b/e* and *c/f*) with the tenor and a directed progression with the cantus, which is at this point below the tenor in pitch and—for the triplum at least—has assumed tenor function in the counterpoint.[26]

The B section's more limpid counterpoint (needed, perhaps, because the text setting is rather convoluted here) is almost entirely supported by the triplum. The full (modified) *clos*-type cadence in mm. 20–22 is present in the T–Tr duet, which unusually forms thirds in m. 20, allowing the cantus to sound at the top of the texture, and again in m. 21, where it directly duplicates the tension and resolution sonorities of the T–Ca duet at the end of the full cadence. However, a glance at this bar of duplicated underlying counterpoint shows how differently the same basic counterpoint can be projected at the surface level. The triplum and cantus in m. 21 seem unalike: the triplum has the contrapuntally essential note, *b–mi* at the outset before performing an upward flourish that intervenes between this note and the resolution to *c* in the next measure. The cantus, by contrast, does not reach its *b* until the last minim in the bar, fussing instead with a perfectly consonant *d* and a dissonant *c.* The two parts have complementary rhythms (trochaic in

25. In the first A section this marks the poetic "turn" with the surprising presentation of the verb "to take" (*prendre*) rather than the verb expected by the reference to the proverb at the point ("to give"); see below.

26. This is irrelevant in the two-part setting. Other parts do not always take on tenor function when lowest in pitch in the texture, but this can happen; see Leach 2001.

the triplum, iambic in the cantus) and move in contrary motion, further obscuring their contrapuntal duplication. Their effective movement in parallel unison is contrapuntally permissible, since these two parts are not ordinarily in counterpoint with each other, but rather each is in counterpoint with the tenor, but the disparity in their surface figuration hints that disguising of such parallels at the surface level might nonetheless have been a compositional concern.

The dissonant triplum *a* at the second minim in m. 20 confirms that the brief and metrically weak directed progression to *E/e* in the T–Ca duet is of passing importance only. The directed progressions to *F/f* in m. 25 and m. 28 are similarly weakened by the triplum's failure to create tension with the tenor, although the clear (if brief) tension sonority for the *F* resolution within m. 24 supports the analytical reading of an implied *G–b* in the T–Ca duet in the same measure. Another complex interaction of the parts is the brief chain of directed progressions, in m. 23, of a kind Machaut exploits more fully in other works: the T–Ca resolution to *D/a* is imperfected by *f♯* in the triplum, with the T–Tr duet resolving its *D/f♯* to *C/g* only on the last minim (eighth note) of the bar.[27]

The full cadences that dominate the second half of the B section (that to C in m. 27 and that to D at the end of the section) are also present in the T–Tr duet, and the exact intervals it supports preserve the hierarchy between these two tonal goals. At the T–Ca's resolution to *C/c* in m. 27 the triplum occupies its normative position at the top of the texture, with tenths supporting the cantus sixths, and with a twelfth for the cantus's octave resolution. For the resolution to *D/d* in m. 30, however, the triplum occupies the normative contratenor space, between the other two voices, singing in thirds with the tenor during the T–Ca duet's sixths and making a fifth at its octave resolution.

The refrain section is a fine example of what the diminished counterpoint of the surface adds to the fundamental contrapuntal duets with the tenor. The pace of the core T–Ca duet in this section is particularly clear, with one sonority per perfection except in the penultimate bar (which prepares the final cadence) and in m. 35 (which prepares an avoided cadence to *D*). The triplum similarly has one note of simple counterpoint except in those bars. In mm. 32 and 33, the sonority on the first minim of the perfection presents the contrapuntally essential notes of each part. In m. 34, the cantus has an accented dissonance, *d*, before introducing the *c♯* that is its contrapuntally essential tone. On the first minim, the triplum could be contrapuntally essential, but this would necessitate not only singing *f♯* there

27. On this kind of chaining, see Leach 2000a: 64–69.

but also (because of the difficulty of the chromatic movement from *mi* to *fa* on the same letter-name pitch), probably sharpening the *f* at the end of m. 33. This is perfectly possible (and is what I have indicated using bracketed signs above the staff), but it would also be possible for the triplum to withhold the sharpening of the leading tone until its final approach to the resolution tone in the last minim of the perfection.

Summary of the Analysis

The overall effect of the three-part whole, then, is of a piece whose sounding cadences are fewer than the number of directed progressions in the T–Ca core suggests, in a manner that clarifies the tonal shaping of the song. The opening phrase is the only one lacking strong tonal definition, and in this it seems to illustrate the process of establishing such definition. Upon first listening, the opening resolution to *a/e/aa* might have implied a future *ouvert* A and *clos* G focus, which the cantus indeed seems to attempt in the opening phrase, especially while the tenor uncharacteristically dwells on the tone *G* in mm. 3–4.[28] (In the original notation, its note shape is a *longa,* which is uncommon in balades, except at the end of pieces, and would have been visually striking to the reader.[29]) After this initial struggle to define the tonal world of the song (during which the tenor and cantus sing in rather similar ranges, crossing at times), the sudden strange leap of a seventh at m. 10 in the cantus introduces a new tone, E♭, that will define the *ouvert* sonority approach. This initiates a series of directed progressions that increasingly define the tonal aspect of the piece's pitch space, until this is partially clarified by the *ouvert* cadence and then, in the repeat, fully by the *clos.* The two subsequent stanzas will replay this initial struggle with increasingly less force as the listener's anticipation of what's to come, and memory of the closing measures of the song's stanza inflect the listening experience.

For most of its hearings, though, the piece's tonal orientation would be well known to the listener from the outset, making the opening phrase seem odd, even churlish, and highlighting the strange change in tonal orientation and rhythmic pace around mm. 8–11. What reasons might there be for this and what meanings might it imply? It is my view that the text of the song offers some assistance in interpreting these features.

28. A *G/d* resolution is reached, from a somewhat surprising sonority in the context, in the refrain.

29. On similar notational meanings of longs in Machaut's songs, see Stone 2003.

Text and Context

The text delivery of the musical setting is shaped variously by the versification of the poem and the syntactical sense of the poetic text. Figure 2.4 shows the text's pacing in all three stanzas (that is, assuming, as many scholars do today, that the second and third stanzas would be placed syllable-for-syllable where those of the first stanza are underlaid to the music).[30] This sketch clearly shows how the syllables are paced with respect to the meter (the succession of perfections) and the principal cadences. In the A section, the longest melismas are on the initial and penultimate syllables of the section, with a clear cadence marking the end of line 1 (= 3) and the caesura (fourth syllable) of line 2 (= 4). In the refrain, the first five syllables receive short melismas, and the "punch line" ("[he] who hates for so little") comes out in a confessionally syllabic rush at the very end, differentiating the final phrase from the tonally similar *clos* phrase, which merely prolongs a melisma on the penultimate syllable of the line.[31]

The only decoupling of verse lines and musical phrases is found in the B section, where the decasyllabic poetic phrase "ne mon petit pooir / Croire ne puet" (nor my little power / Can he believe) is set to a single musical phrase as if it were a bona fide line of poetry, with a full *clos*-type cadence at its end in m. 27. This allows the shocking conclusion "but rather has broken up with me for this" to occupy its own musical phrase at the end of the B section, increasing its rhetorical weight. Moreover, the way in which this pseudo-line is set up is that despite the strong *clos*-type cadence at the end of line 5 in m. 22, the expectation of a decasyllabic line, strongly established in the A section, allows the precaesural text of line 6, "Seur volenté," to appear, uncertainly, as if it might be the completion of a full line 5. In fact, it is a syllable too long; but there is a (weak) resolution to *F* within m. 24, and the caesural word of line 6 is "volenté" and thus a "pseudo-rhyme," identical to the a-rhyme (and the first rhyme word). This assessment of the verse structure seems to be confirmed by the following musical phrase, which, as noted above, proceeds exactly as if it were the start of a line, with the next cadence point—to the *clos*-type C cadence—a full ten syllables later at the caesura of line 7 (m. 27).

The pseudo-rhyme game in line 6 recurs in the second stanza, whose caesural word in line 2.6 shares the c-rhyme ("-oir") that is actually then in

---

30. For critiques of this rather large assumption see Maw 1999; 2002; Upton 2001: ch.4 and Earp 2005.

31. Withholding text like this in the refrain seems to be a trait of Machaut's earlier balades and can be found in balades 1, 2, 4, 5, 13, 16, 22, and 28 (of which only the last probably postdates the earliest source, ca. 1356).

A Section

Cadential (and opening) dyads (c/c)

Cadential labels: **C/c** (meas. 8) · **F/F** (meas. 10) · **D/d (ouvert)** (meas. 18) · **C/c (clos)** (meas. 18 bis)

Lines	1	2	3	4	5	6	7	8	9	10	11	12	13	14	15	16	17	18	18 bis
	1.1 De				petit peu,	de nient	volen-	-té, 1.2 De	mout as-	-sez	doit	prendre, ce	m'est———					vis,	
	1.3 Chas———				-cuns amans	de s'amie	en bon	gré. 1.4 Lasse! dolen-		-te,	or	voi que mes	a———						-mis.
	2.1 A———				-mours scet bien que je l'ai		tant a-	-mé 2.2 Et	aim en-	-cor,	et	amer- -ai	tou-					-dis,	
	2.3 C'on———				ne puet plus;	mes mesdi-	-sans gre-	-vé 2.4 M'ont envers	li,		qu'en li a	tant	d'a-						-vis,
	3.1 Et———				s'aucuns ont	vilaine-	-ment par-	-lé 3.2 A	lui de	moy,	je	les met tous	au-					pis,	
	3.3 Qu'on———				-ques vers li	feïsse	fausse-	-té 3.4 N'en-	vers au-	-trui,	n'il	ne doit	leur faux———						dis

B Section

Cadential labels: **(C/g)** · **C/c** (meas. 22) · **D/d** (meas. 31)

Lines	19	20	21	22	23	24	25	26	27	28	29	30	31
	1.5 Ne vuet souffis-	-sance a-		-voir	1.6 Seur volen-	-té,	ne mon petit po-	-oir	1.7 Croire ne puet,	ains m'a pour	ce guer-	-pi:	
	2.5 De bien, d'onnour,	de sa-		-voir	2.6 Que mon po-	-oir	sce- -üst bien conce-	-voir,	2.7 Et nonpour- quant	se	m'amour pers ein-	-si,	
	3.5 Tost croi- re ne	lui mou-		-voir,	3.6 Ains doit a-	-vant	la verité sa-	-voir.	3.7 Et s'ils les croit	et me laist	par tel	si,	

Refrain

Cadential labels: **(F/f)** · **[D/d avoided]** (meas. 35–37) · **C/c** (meas. 38)

Lines	32	33	34	35	36	37	38
R. On-	-ques n'a-	-ma		qui———————————			pour si pou ha- ý.

Figure 2.4. Text pacing.

86

play. This feint with the verse-phrase structure was to be exploited in a more thoroughgoing way in Machaut's later verse forms that have a shorter fifth line at the opening of the B section, the quintessential example being that of *De toutes flours* (B31; see Leach 2000b). Here, the strong cadence at the end of line 5 (lacking, for example, in B31) helps keep an attentive listener oriented, as would awareness that both A and B sections have caesural F resolutions after the C resolutions that close their opening phrase. Despite the offsetting of the poetic line and musical phrase structures, the overall effect is that the B section reprises tonally much of what was presented in the A section (opening C sonority, C cadence at the end of its first phrase and F cadence (weakened by a nonsimultaneous presentation in the T–Ca duet) at its caesura.

The first-person speaker of B18 starts in a clerkly sententious fashion uttering a proverbial statement found in works by younger contemporary poets John Gower and Philippe de Mézières, where it refers to largesse (text and translation of B18 are given in figure 2.5).[32] In these authors, the received wisdom is that somebody who has only a little should give a little, somebody who has a lot should give "enough," and the person who has nothing should give good will (*volonté*). The narrator of B18 seems to be about to provide the verb "to give" to complete the presentation of this proverb, but utters instead the verb "to take" (*prendre*). At this point the music reflects the unexpected verbal turn with one of its own: an upward leap of a seventh in the cantus to introduce *eb*, a pitch that shifts the tonal feel of the piece from a C-based "*ut*-tonality" (with E♮ and cadences to C achieved through the use of *b♮*) to a D-based "*mi*-tonality" (with cadences to D achieved through the use of E♭), which represents the secondary emphasis in the song.

The opening clerkly register—gendered masculine in medieval thought—is interrupted by the revelation that the speaker is in fact an emotionally involved female lover-protagonist. She complains "Lasse! dolente," and the feminine ending of the first word is audible because it is sung to a separate pitch in the setting at m. 9.[33] This makes the singing voice here an uneasy hybrid, swinging between the opening masculine objectivity and feminine

32. See Welker 2008, who cites Hassell 1982: 198, no. P139. The proverb appears in Philippe de Mézières, *Le songe du vieil pélerin*, II, 1.358, "Selon le proverbe qui dit: De pou, pou, et de nyent, bonne voulenté" (According to the proverb which says from a little [give] little, and from nothing, good will), and John Gower, *Mirour de l'omme*, II.15817–II.15818, "Du petit poy serra donné, / Du nient l'en dorra volenté" (From little, a little should be given; from nothing, good will should be given). Gower's usage illustrates the third daughter of Generosity, Almsgiving. Given Machaut's early post as almoner, such concerns would at one time have been uppermost among his duties. See Leach 2010a.

33. See also the music example in Welker 2008.

De petit peu, de nient volenté,
De mout assez doit prendre, ce m'est vis,
Chascuns amans de s'amie en bon gré.
Lasse! dolente, or voi que mes amis
Ne vuet souffissance avoir
Seur volenté, ne mon petit pooir
Croire ne puet, ains m'a pour ce guerpi:
Onques n'ama qui pour si pou haÿ.

In my opinion every lover should take
from his beloved in good faith from a small
amount a little, from nothing good will,
from much enough. Alas! [I am a]
sorrowful [woman], now I see that my
friend does not wish to have enough
[*souffisance*] in good will, nor can he believe
my little power but rather has ditched
me: *no one who hates so readily loved in the
first place.*

Amours scet bien que je l'ai tant amé
Et aim encor, et amerai toudis,
C'on ne puet plus; mes mesdisans grevé
M'ont envers li, qu'en li a tant d'avis,
De bien, d'onnour, de savoir
Que mon pooir sceüst bien concevoir,
Et nonpourquant, se m'amour pers einsi,
Onques [n'ama qui pour si pou haÿ].

Love knows well that I have loved him so
much and love him still and shall love him
ever [and] that one could not [love] more; but
gossips [*mesdisans*] have slandered me to
him, who has so much counsel, goodness,
honor, and knowledge that my power
might not well know how to conceive
of it; but nevertheless, if I lose my love
like this: *no one who hates so readily loved in the
first place.*

Et s'aucuns ont vilainement parlé
A lui de moy, je les met tous au pis,
Qu'onques vers li feïsse faussetë
N'envers autrui, n'il ne doit leur faux dis
Tost croire ne lui mouvoir,
Ains doit avant la verité savoir.
Et s'il les croit et me laist par tel si,
Onques n'ama qui pour si pou haÿ.

And if some people have spoken
villainously of me to him I place them all
beneath me for I have never been false to
him or to anyone, and he ought not so
readily believe their false words nor be
moved by them but rather ought to find
out the truth first. And if he believes them
and leaves me like this, *no one who hates so
readily loved in the first place.*

Figure 2.5. Text and translation.

lament. She laments because her lover has not taken only the little that he was offered and consoled himself with proverbial wisdom, but has instead left her, suspecting that her coldness is the fruit not of honorable loving but of lack of interest.[34] In the second stanza, the lady reveals more specifically that her lover has abandoned her because he has believed the "mesdisans" (gossips), who have told him that she has stopped loving him. The third stanza contrasts her lover's credulity with her own disbelief of those who have spoken basely of him to her. The refrain, like the opening, cites proverbial wisdom—"no one who

34. The relation between largesse and honor is highly gendered in Machaut's courtly doctrine. For women in private amorous contexts, keeping good one's honor involves being "large en refus"; for men in public political contexts, giving freely of gifts, land, money represents honorable largesse. The paired advice balades *Honte, paour* (B25) and *Donnez, signeurs* (B26) contrast these kinds of largesse most thoroughly. See Leach 2010a.

hates so readily loved in the first place"—but now accuses her lover of never having loved her. This makes her earlier praises of his goodness, honor, and understanding ring somewhat hollow.

The proverbial statement in B18's refrain appears in the middle of an earlier motet text (Badel 1995: 198–201) by Machaut's illustrious champenois forerunner, the poet-composer Adam de la Halle, but in Adam's motet the gender of the protagonists is reversed. A male lover, whose lady's belief in gossip about him has caused her to reject him, dreams of the hour when he will be able to see her and defend himself from the rumors: "Very dear beloved," he says, "have pity on me, for God's sake have *merci*—no one who hates so readily loved in the first place.[35] B18's female *je* and Adam's male *je* are in identical situations, and both fall back on the same piece of proverbial wisdom, suggesting that Fortune exercises her power equally over men and women.[36] This equation is furthered by the unstable staging of gender in B18's text: this feminine-voiced poem is a skin-deep simulacrum of a woman concealing the interior of a cleric; like the medieval personification of the pagan goddess Fortune—a figure often featured in Machaut's works—she is an "idol of false portraiture," not quite what she seems.[37] Even if Machaut did not take the proverb directly from Adam's use of it, the opening and closing use of the sententious, clerkly register undermines the central feminine lament in B18, perhaps thereby emphasizing the point the lady herself makes—that one should not believe everything one hears. Such intertextual play was a way of integrating individual lyrics into larger quasi-narrative thematic nexuses, in this case, the theme of the dishonorable woman. Ultimately, despite her protests to the contrary, the lady's doubts about her lover's lack of faith in her—for which she relies similarly on

35. He ends his text with another refrain bidding the gatekeeper give him way. The entire text forms the motetus of a three-part motet. The triplum is voiced by a lady who is also keen to find a way to go to her lover. She initially says she will send her belt in her place, but it retains the scent of her beloved and she cannot do without it. Instead she sends her song to go to him because she cannot, informing him that he should come to her at nightfall and will hear her song when the time is right for him to come and take his pleasure. As this motet's texts are full of grafted refrains, the one that forms Machaut's refrain in B18 might simply be another (albeit one that has not been considered as such by modern refrain commentators); if this is so, Machaut might conceivably know it from a third source. See Butterfield 2003: 89–90.

36. This is hinted at more thoroughly in the *Voir dit*, where both protagonists are assimilated to the figure of Fortune; see Attwood 1999.

37. This phrase is from Machaut's motet *Qui es / Ha! fortune / Et non est* (M8), and according to medieval usage, false portraiture would be a "contrefait." See Perkinson 2004. On Fortune in Machaut, see Leach 2000c.

gossip—betray a similar lack of faith in him, paradoxically justifying his (if indeed the allegation of his loss of faith is true).

Broader Contexts

We have no contemporary testimony of how this or other songs like it were performed, when or where they were heard, or what the listener made of them. However, the discussion of the text has already involved a number of broader contexts that point to the contemporary positioning of a song like this, which would have been used in the context of a more-or-less feudal court for the edifying entertainment of the nobility. The song's sociocultural context can reveal more aspects of meaning. The collection of literary topoi usually grouped under the modern heading of "courtly love" includes a large number of didactic texts, and those of Machaut are no exception. His courtly doctrine extols in particular the role of hope, usually personified as a beautiful lady with whom the man and woman engaged in "refined loving" have their primary relationship. Hope's mediation avoids both the disappointments that might come were the man's love to be rejected by the real lady who is its object and the opprobrium that might fall on the lady were she actually to reciprocate. Since the culture of refined loving was specifically nonmarital and normally thought proper to the very onset of sexual maturity, the engendering of illegitimate children who would disrupt noble bloodlines was avoided by diverting strong feeling into musical and literary activity, such as the singing and reading aloud of lyric poetry. As these cultural pursuits were group social activities, the poet, who is also a high-ranking court administrator and royal intimate, effectively instructs those governing to govern themselves (Huot 2002).[38]

Failure to trust in Hope places the lover instead in the demesne of Fortune, whose constant inconstancy will cause pain, potentially resulting in madness (usually for men) or death (usually for women). The chief mechanism of such inconstancy is the oral report of the "mesdisans" and this must have related to a real-life situation in which the circulation of knowledge moved at least as much orally with people as it did by letter. Evidence from the period shows that such rumors, particularly when connected to affairs of the heart, could be quite literally lethal.[39]

38. Reading in this period was almost always performed to a group; see Coleman 1996.

39. See Brown 1989.

The meaning of the song is further inflected by the identification of its tenor as a paraphrase of a piece of plainsong—the final verse of *Alma redemptoris mater*.[40] This chant was one of the most popular of the Middle Ages and was sung in praise of the Virgin Mary, the mother of the Christian God. Setting aside for present purposes the issue of whether this identification can be justified and would have been understood by the original audience for the song, the juxtaposition of Marian and secular love lyrics is common in this period and has been recently subject to analogical interpretations by Huot (1997), Robertson (2002), Clark (2007), and Rothenberg (2006). Using praise of Mary as the musical underpinning of a song whose feminine voice berates belief in gossip and praises constancy, but is herself inconstant because of her own belief in gossip, might be thought to imply the comparison of two feminine exemplars and, by extension, two personifications of Fortune: a woman subject to a predetermined fate in the shape of the pagan goddess Fortune, and a woman subject to a Christianized Fortune as divine intervention—the Virgin Mary.[41]

B18 Today

The performance history of this piece today, as least as reflected in its recordings, does not suggest that this song is as popular today as it was in the Middle Ages. Listing the three then-available recordings, Earp (1995: 399) commented, "It is unfortunate that Machaut's most popular work has not yet received a recording worthy of it," although at least two CD recordings have been made since that time.[42] Two of the three recorded versions listed by Earp offer the four-part performance that the modern editions seem to suggest and that I have argued above was probably not a medieval possibility. Only the recording by the Schola Cantorum of Basel (conducted by August Wenzinger) presents the piece in three parts with the triplum and is, for Earp, "a bit

---

40. Welker 2008 points out that the tenor rhythmicizes this in a way similar to that found at the opening of the upper parts in the motet *Rex Karole, Johannis genite / Leticie, pacis, concordie / [Virgo prius ac posterius]*. The upper parts of this motet are here paraphrasing this tenor chant, which comes from the final strophe of the *Alma Redemptoris Mater*.

41. This is related to the situation in B23, which also has been identified as having a Marian tenor. See Welker 2008.

42. The web page www.medieval.org/emfaq/composers/machaut/b18.html [accessed 03/30/09] has a more up-to-date discography than that in Earp 1995: 399.

slow" (the relative timings and scoring of the available recordings are given in figure 2.6). The post-Earp version on the website that accompanies the present book also contains the three-part version with triplum throughout, and their performance is even slower than that of the Basel group. In my opinion, however, this pacing works and it contrasts markedly with that of the other CD recording available, the group Ars Cameralis. This Czech ensemble performs the song at the rate of nearly a stanza per minute, whereas the Ferrara Ensemble's pace is almost half this, at nearly two minutes per stanza. The timings of these modern performances and their instrumentation show how little we know about the performance practice for this music. The difference between the very quick Ars Cameralis rendering and that of the other groups cannot be a result of historical change in modern performance practice (as, for example, in Baroque music's performance practice, which gets progressively quicker through the twentieth century), since the two CD recordings are almost contemporary. Instead, they project different "readings" of the poem as a song. The jaunty, staccato delivery of the rhythmic figuration in the melismas of the Ars Cameralis track is in stark contrast to the resonant sonorities of the Ferrara Ensemble. I know which one I prefer, which is why I have chosen it for inclusion here, and I think the text's sorrowful content (with its sententious start) lends itself to just such a delivery. While a text-based rationale for the quicker interpretation would not be impossible to cook up, this kind of pace seems to have more to do with the group's own style, since it can be found in most of the other tracks on the disk, rather than being a response to this particular text.

The Ars Cameralis performance also presents different scorings for each of its three stanzas: the first is given in three parts with triplum, the second in three parts with contratenor, and the third in all four parts

Recording	T	Ct	Ca	Tr	*Voices* and Instrumentation	Stanzas	Track Timing (seconds)	Stanza Average (seconds)
Ensemble Ricercare, Zurich, 1966	X	X	X	X	*Tenor*, fiddle, recorder, crumhorn, viol	1, 2	240	120
Ferrara Ensemble, 1998	X	—	X	X	*Contralto, tenor*, harp	1, 2, 3	339	113
Schola Cantorum Basiliensis, 1969	X	—	X	X	*Tenor*, lute, organ	1	105	105
New York Pro Musica, 1967	X	X	X	X	Flute, harpsichord, crumhorn, bass viol, organetto	1	88	88
Ars Cameralis, 1995	X	—	X	-	Organ, fiddle	1	66	66
Ars Cameralis, 1995	1:X 2:X 3:X	— X X	X X X	X — X	*Countertenor*, organ, douçaine, fiddle	1, 2, 3	191	63.67

Figure 2.6. Modern recordings compared.

simultaneously.[43] The presentation of all four voices in score in the modern editions of this piece has led many contemporary performers to present all four parts, with the presentation of harmonies incompatible in fourteenth-century terms but pleasantly scrunchy to twentieth-century ears. It is a truism to say that there is no history of some real Middle Ages but only the discursive traces of the Middle Ages that survive in our present. However, in the context of university teaching, the métier in which I practice music, certain kinds of performance are to be preferred because of their support for scholarly deductions about likely medieval performance practices. As a trait of reception, I would read the keenness of performers to sing all four parts (even though there seems, to me, good evidence that this was not an option in the Middle Ages itself) as indicative of contemporary interest in full sonorities, dissonance, and the picture of a magically "other" Middle Ages. This wondrous otherness is also pictured in the instrumentation of the recordings, although again in this the Ferrara Ensemble most nearly reflects contemporary scholarly understandings of medieval priorities. Their recording is of the three-part version with triplum and presents the contrapuntal core of cantus and tenor vocally, with single singers on each part—a woman singing the cantus and a man singing the tenor. The triplum is plucked on a harp, making it sound rather subsidiary since its timbrally differentiated tones do not sustain and are not prominent in the overall balance, especially when the triplum has pitches at the lower end of its range. As we have no unequivocal contemporary evidence for instrumentation, this rendering is a good as any and partakes of the history of the performance practice of Machaut's music in the modern period, since its first performances in the early twentieth century (see Earp 1995: 389–392 and Leech-Wilkinson 2002).

Of especial interest is the fact that, of the available recorded performances, only that of the Ferrara ensemble performance uses a woman's voice to sing this feminine voiced poem. While this level of prosopopoeiac "realism" is not strictly necessary given the Western song tradition's toleration of cross-gendered song performance, it is indicative of the informed care that this group has taken (and possibly also shows that its members understand the poem they are singing—they collaborate with the text specialist Nicoletta Gossen).[44] What is lost from these songs is the historical situation of performance with performers always present, of music as part of a special and

---

43. The succeeding track on the disc presents one stanza of the two-part instrumental version of the song as found in the Prague source.

44. See the brief biography of the group at www.goldbergweb.com/en/interpreters/orchestras/7801.php [accessed 03/30/09].

wonderful (if everyday) occurrence, and of culture as something emanating directly from living court functionaries, who can explain and guide. This vital use of a song like B18 is no longer of relevance to modern life, and the playing of these notes on a CD or streamed from the web—the same at each "performance" and without sight of any live human presence—is an entirely deracinated experience. That a song like this can nevertheless survive is a remarkable testimony to the modern appreciation of its sonorous beauty. B18 is born again in the present, not perhaps as a meaningful song but instead as beautiful, incomprehensible singing.

References

Apfel, Ernst. 1982. *Diskant und Kontrapunkt in der Musiktheorie des 12. bis 15. Jahrhunderts.* Wilhelmshaven, Germany: Heinrichshofen's Verlag.

Arlt, Wulf. 1982. "Aspekte der Chronologie und des Stilwandels im französischen Lied des 14. Jahrhunderts." In *Aktuelle Fragen der musikbezogenen Mittelalterforschung: Texte zu einem Basler Kolloquium des Jahres 1975,* ed. Hans Oesch and Wulf Arlt, 193–280. Winterthur, Switzerland: Amadeus.

Attwood, Catherine. 1999. "The Image in the Fountain: Fortune, Fiction and Femininity in the *Livre du Voir Dit* of Guillaume de Machaut." *Nottingham French Studies* 38: 137–149.

Badel, Pierre-Yves, ed. 1995. *Adam de la Halle: Oeuvres Complètes.* Paris: Brodard et Taupin.

Bain, Jennifer. 2005. "Tonal Structure and the Melodic Role of Chromatic Inflections in the Music of Machaut." *Plainsong and Medieval Music* 14(2): 59–88.

Bent, Margaret. 1994. "Editing Early Music: The Dilemma of Translation." *Early Music* 22(3): 373–92.

———. 2002. *Counterpoint, Composition, and Musica Ficta.* London: Routledge.

Berger, Anna Maria Busse. 2005. *Medieval Music and the Art of Memory.* Berkeley: University of California Press.

Berger, Christian. 1992. *Hexachord, Mensur und Textstruktur: Studien zum französischen Lied im 14. Jahrhundert.* Vol. 35, *Beihefte zum Archiv für Musikwissenschaft.* Stuttgart: Steiner.

Bowers, Roger. 2004. "Guillaume de Machaut and His Canonry of Reims, 1338–1377." *Early Music History* 23: 1–48.

Brown, Elizabeth A. R. 1989. "Diplomacy, Adultery, and Domestic Politics at the Court of Philip the Fair: Queen Isabella's Mission to France in 1314." In *Documenting the Past: Essays in Medieval History Presented to George Peddy Cuttino,* ed. J. S. Hamilton and P. J. Bradley, 53–83. Woodbridge, UK: Boydell.

Butterfield, Ardis. 2003. "*Enté:* A Survey and Re-Assessment of the Term in Thirteenth and Fourteenth-Century Music and Poetry." *Early Music History* 22: 67–101.

Clanchy, M. T. 1993. *From Memory to Written Record: England 1066–1307,* 2nd ed. Oxford: Blackwell.

Clark, Suzannah. 2007. "'S'en dirai chançonete:' Hearing Text and Music in a Medieval Motet." *Plainsong and Medieval Music* 16(1): 31–59.

Cohen, David E. 2001. "'The Imperfect Seeks its Perfection': Harmonic Progression, Directed Motion, and Aristotelian Physics." *Music Theory Spectrum* 23(2): 139–169.

Coleman, Joyce. 1996. *Public Reading and the Reading Public in Late Medieval England and France.* Cambridge: Cambridge University Press.

Dömling, Wolfgang. 1969. "Zur Überlieferung der musikalischen Werke Machauts." *Die Musikforschung* 22: 189–95.

———. 1970. *Die mehrstimmigen Balladen, Rondeaux und Virelais von Guillaume de Machaut: Untersuchungen zum musikalischen Satz.* Tutzing: Schneider.

Earp, Lawrence. 1995. *Guillaume de Machaut: A Guide to Research.* Vol. 36, *Garland Composer Resource Manuals.* New York: Garland.

———. 2005. "Declamatory Dissonance in Machaut." In *Citation and Authority in Medieval and Renaissance Music: Learning from the Learned,* ed. Suzannah Clark and Elizabeth Eva Leach, 102–122. Woodbridge, UK: Boydell and Brewer.

Fallows, David. 1976. "L'origine du Ms. 1328 de Cambrai: Note au sujet de quelques nouveux feuillets, et de quelques informations supplémentaires." *Revue de Musicologie* 62: 275–279.

Fuller, Sarah. 1992. "Tendencies and Resolutions: The Directed Progression in *Ars Nova* music." *Journal of Music Theory* 36(2): 229–257.

———. 1998a. "Exploring Tonal Structure in French Polyphonic Song of the Fourteenth Century." In *Tonal Structures in Early Music,* vol. 1, ed. Cristle Collins Judd, 61–86. New York and London: Garland.

———. 1998b. "Modal Discourse and Fourteenth-Century French Song: A 'Medieval' Perspective Recovered?" *Early Music History* 17: 61–108.

Harper-Scott, J. P. E. 2006. *Edward Elgar, Modernist.* Cambridge: Cambridge University Press.

Hassell, James Woodrow. 1982. *Middle French Proverbs, Sentences, and Proverbial Phrases.* Toronto and Leiden, The Netherlands: Pontifical Institute of Mediaeval Studies and Brill.

Huot, Sylvia. 1997. *Allegorical Play in the Old French Motet: The Sacred and Profane in Thirteenth-Century Polyphony, Figurae: Readings in Medieval Culture.* Stanford, CA: Stanford University Press.

———. 2002. "Guillaume de Machaut and the Consolation of Poetry." *Modern Philology* 100: 169–195.

Leach, Elizabeth Eva. 2000a. "Counterpoint and Analysis in Fourteenth-Century Song." *Journal of Music Theory* 44(2): 45–79.

———. 2000b. "Counterpoint as an Interpretative Tool: the Case of Guillaume de Machaut's *De toutes flours* (B31)." *Music Analysis* 19(2): 321–51.

———. 2000c. "Fortune's Demesne: the Interrelation of Text and Music in Machaut's *Il mest avis* (B22), *De fortune* (B23), and Two Related Anonymous Balades." *Early Music History* 19: 47–79.

————. 2001. "Machaut's Balades with Four Voices." *Plainsong and Medieval Music* 10(2): 47–79.

————. 2002. "Death of a Lover and the Birth of the Polyphonic Balade: Machaut's Notated Balades 1–5." *Journal of Musicology* 19(3): 461–502.

————, ed. 2003. *Machaut's Music: New Interpretations.* Woodbridge, UK: Boydell and Brewer.

————. 2006. "Gendering the Semitone, Sexing the Leading Tone: Fourteenth-Century Music Theory and the Directed Progression." *Music Theory Spectrum* 28(1): 1–21.

————. 2010a. "Guillaume de Machaut, Royal Almoner: *Honte, paour* (B25) and *Donnez, signeurs* (B26) in Context." *Early Music* 38(1): 21–42.

————. 2010b. "Nature's Forge and Mechanical Production: Writing, Reading, and Performing Song." In *Rhetoric Beyond Words,* ed. Mary Carruthers, 72–95. Cambridge: Cambridge University Press.

Leech-Wilkinson, Daniel. 2002. *The Modern Invention of Medieval Music: Scholarship, Ideology, Performance.* Cambridge: Cambridge University Press.

Lefferts, Peter. 1995. "Signature Systems and Tonal Types in the Fourteenth-Century French Chanson." *Plainsong and Medieval Music* 4(2): 117–147.

Ludwig, Friedrich, ed. 1926–1954. *Guillaume de Machaut: Musikalische Werke, Publikationen älterer Musik.* Leipzig, Germany: Breitkopf & Härtel.

Martinez, Marie Louise. 1963. *Die Musik des frühen Trecento.* Tutzing, Germany: Schneider.

Maw, David. 1999. "Words and Music in the Secular Songs of Guillaume de Machaut." Ph.D. dissertation, University of Oxford.

————. 2002. "Meter and Word Setting: Revising Machaut's Monophonic Virelais." *Current Musicology* 74(2): 69–102.

Memelsdorff, Pedro. 2003. "*Lizadra donna:* Ciconia, Matteo da Perugia, and the Late Medieval *Ars contratenor.*" In *Johannes Ciconia: musicien de la transition,* ed. Philippe Vendrix, 233–278. Turnhout, Belgium: Brepols.

Page, Christopher. 1998. "Tradition and Innovation in BN fr. 146: The Background to the Ballades." In *Fauvel Studies: Allegory, Chronicle, Music, and Image in Paris, Bibliothèque Nationale de France, MS français 146,* ed. Margaret Bent and Andrew Wathey, 353–394. Oxford: Oxford University Press.

Perkinson, Stephen. 2004. "Portraits and Counterfeits: Villard de Honnecourt and Thirteenth-Century Theories of Representation." In *Excavating the Medieval Image: Manuscripts, Artists, Audiences: Essays in Honor of Sandra Hindman,* ed. Nina A. Rowe and David S. Areford, 13–36. Aldershot, UK: Ashgate.

Plumley, Yolanda. 1996. *The Grammar of 14th Century Melody: Tonal Organization and Compositional Process in the Chansons of Guillaume de Machaut and the Ars Subtilior.* New York and London: Garland.

Robertson, Anne Walters. 2002. *Guillaume de Machaut and Reims: Context and Meaning in his Musical Works.* Cambridge: Cambridge University Press.

Rothenberg, David J. 2006. "The Marian Symbolism of Spring, ca. 1200–ca. 1500: Two Case Studies." *Journal of the American Musicological Society* 59(2): 319–398.

Sachs, Klaus-Jürgen. 1974. *Der Contrapunctus im 14. und 15. Jahrhundert: Untersuchungen zum Terminus, zur Lehre und zu den Quellen.* Ed. Hans Heinrich Eggebrecht, Walter Gerstenberg, Kurt von Fischer, Wolfgang Osthoff and Arnold Schmitz. Wiesbaden, Germany: Franz Steiner.

———. 1984. "Die Contrapunctus-Lehre im 14. und 15. Jahrhundert." In *Die mittelalterliche Lehre von der Mehrstimmigkeit,* vol. 5, ed. Hans Heinrich Eggebrecht, F. Alberto Gallo, Max Haas, and Klaus-Jürgen Sachs, 161–256. Darmstadt: Wissenschaftliche Buchgesellschaft.

Stone, Anne. 2003. "Music Writing and Poetic Voice in Machaut: Some Remarks on B12 and B14." In *Machaut's Music: New Interpretations,* ed. Elizabeth Eva Leach, 125–138. Woodbridge, UK: Boydell and Brewer.

Upton, Elizabeth Randell. 2001. "The Chantilly Codex (F-Ch 564): The Manuscript, Its Music, Its Scholarly Reception." Ph.D. dissertation, University of North Carolina at Chapel Hill.

Vale, Malcolm. 2001. *The Princely Court: Medieval Courts and Culture in North-West Europe 1270–1380.* Oxford: Oxford University Press.

Welker, Lorenz. 2008. "Guillaume de Machaut, das romantische Lied und die Jungfrau Maria." In *Annäherungen: Festschrift für Jürg Stenzl zum 65 Geburtstag,* ed. Ulrich Mosch, Matthias Schmidt, and Silvia Wälli. Saarbrücken, Germany: Pfau.

CHAPTER 3

Nuances of Continual Variation in the Brazilian Pagode Song "Sorriso Aberto"

JASON STANYEK AND FABIO OLIVEIRA

At the center, there's a table. Covered in yellow plastic, and strewn with half-filled glasses of beer and *cachaça,* cell phones, a guitar tuner, direct boxes, car keys, and plates of barbecued meat, it occupies the middle of the

Photo: The Pagode da Tia Doca, Rio de Janeiro, August 8, 2010. Photograph by Jason Stanyek.

space like an altar, or a beacon. The table is a rectangle, yes, but it really marks off a circle, a *roda,* and this one is in Tia ("Aunt") Doca's "big yard," her *terreirão,* a partially covered building that is located just along the train tracks, on the border of the neighborhoods of Madureira and Oswaldo Cruz, in Zona Norte, Rio de Janeiro. Although the table lies far from the entrance, it is still the first thing you notice as you enter the space. There's a large tree to your right. Its branches partially reach over the musicians, who are seated around the table's hard edges, peering at each other as they perform song after song until the hour becomes wet with the *sereno*—the late-night dampness—that was the subject of a song, just now.

Each performer can see not only the other musicians, but also some of the 200 people who have moved, for this moment, into the arc of the circle that connects them with the others at the event, into the *roda* with its efferent and afferent forces, spinning out to Rio's broader environs, and spinning into the very center of the circle that collects all sound and all movement. The audience members dance, and sing, and clap, and gossip, and try to hook up, and drink, and eat. If there's an anatomy to the event, they're part of it. And, of course, the musicians are too. You notice their instruments: *banjo, pandeiro, violão de 7 cordas, repique de mão, tantã, cavaquinho, surdo, violão de 6 cordas.* Each one is amplified, and you see the sound guy in front of a sixteen-channel board, off to the side of the table, just under the tree. Mostly, you can't stop noticing the musicians' hands. The sound comes from their touch, their gestures. Sometimes it's just a finger, sometimes a palm or a whole hand, or, sometimes, a hand holding a pick, or a mallet—coaxing all manner of audible residues from these instruments fashioned from wood, metal, plastic, and skin. Sounds from all frequency ranges come at you and hit your whole body, from your toes up to your head, "no pé e nos agudos."[1]

What you do *with* this sound world, what you do *in* this sound world, varies. *You might be clapping.* Now the sounds are in your hands; they create a rhythm that sends out a missive to the musicians, to all of the participants: "this is one of the ways that my body can be audible." *You might be dancing.* Your movements are tight, nothing flamboyant, ever so slight; you barely step out of the spot where your right foot first started its pulsed relationship with the floor. You can't help it—now your heel is a *surdo,* your hips a *pandeiro,* and

---

1. The phrase "no pé e nos agudos" (Salles 2000) is a difficult one to translate, evoking, as it does, both the corporeal (*pé,* "feet") and the sonic (*agudos,* "high tones"). It depicts the bodies that dance (the "feet", moving down on the ground) and that sing (the "highs," perhaps alluding to the vocal sounds resonating out of and among the audience participants).

your sly grin has spread into a smile. *You might be listening.* You can't follow all of the sounds, but they're all there, the sonic fabric so integrated that it's difficult to parse it into component parts. You hear the largest drum, the *surdo,* the only one played with a mallet, marking off the basic rhythmic structure with a frequency so low that you need your entire body to reckon with it, your ears don't suffice; you hear the other percussion instruments—*repique de mão, tantã, pandeiro* (all played only with the hands)—and the intricacy of their multilayered patterns is beguiling; you hear the string instruments laying down the harmonic palette but also melodically interacting with the vocals and percussively fusing with the drums; you hear the voices—almost everyone is singing, and those who are not are talking (and speech is part of the sonic fabric too). *You might be singing.* Now the sounds are in your mouth; there's a melody, a song you've heard and sung many times before, and it emerges fluently from deep in you. The lyrics are at turns funny and poetic, and they resonate with your experiences of the world.

The leader of the group has now called out "*Fa menor*" (F minor) and, without stopping (they seem never to stop), the musicians shift to a new key. The *cavaquinho* plays a melody on its upper strings, and, as it ends, the lead singer intones the beginning of the new song's melody. It takes only a single syllable—the vocable "lá," perched a perfect fifth above the song's tonic—for you to recognize it. You're singing again, everyone is singing again, and the song says what you're feeling: yeah, life is hard, but the samba is good tonight. We're smiling. Each with a big, open smile: *Sorriso aberto.*

All these sounds and all these movements saturate your dreams for days after, until you find yourself in the *roda* again, until your next *pagode.*

The Analytics of Live Pagode *Performance*

In the late 1970s, in the neighborhood of Ramos in Rio de Janeiro's Zona Norte ("north zone"), a group of musicians created a radical reformulation of samba, a genre which, by that time, had become stabilized as Brazil's "national music" through its articulation with various kinds of media sponsorship, the tourism industry, governmental patronage, and discourses of authenticity that emerged in the 1930s under the auspices of the vast nationalization project carried out during the Estado Novo.[2] Congregating on Wednesday evenings under a tamarind tree that has since taken on an almost mystical status in samba lore, they formulated a sound that, while rooted in traditional samba,

2. See McCann (2004) and Vianna (1999) on the emergence of samba as a national music in Brazil.

was something quite new. It was an experimental moment, one that the scholar, composer, and musician Nei Lopes called "the most important after bossa nova."[3] Employing a word that for over a century had been used to designate a festive occasion involving music, food and dance, these informal gatherings spearheaded a movement that became known simply as *pagode* (pah-GOH-gee).[4]

Dissatisfied with the commercialization of samba and the corruption of carnival, musicians in Ramos developed new instruments; they composed a repertoire of songs that has since become integrated into the national musical imaginary; they fashioned a rhythmic language that grew out of traditional samba but had its own groove; they rejuvenated certain forms of samba practice that had fallen out of fashion; and they invented a unique, and rather experimental, timbral world. The group Fundo de Quintal ("Backyard Group") was formed, inaugurating a distinct era in the history of samba. They performed on Beth Carvalho's seminal 1978 album *De Pé no Chão,* and in 1980 they released *Samba É no Fundo de Quintal,* their first record as a collective.

The rise of the *pagode* movement marks a crucial juncture in the history of Brazilian music. Since the mid-1980s *pagode* has spread out from Rio to become one of Brazil's best-known musical forms. It has been both celebrated and reviled, and has morphed into various subgenres, from the roots version to the saccharine, almost "boy band" form that inundated Brazilian airwaves in the 1990s. Thirty years after *pagode*'s emergence, artists such as Zeca Pagodinho, Beth Carvalho, Arlindo Cruz, and Jorge Aragão, and groups such as Fundo de Quintal and Revelação still sell hundreds of thousands of recordings, give shows at Brazil's most famous venues, and appear with great frequency on Brazilian television. At the heart of *pagode,* however, are the live performances that take place all over Brazil—and increasingly, all over the Brazilian diaspora. These events are called *pagodes,* and, in Rio de Janeiro—their birthplace—there are literally dozens every day. These informal gatherings do not stand in opposition to the more corporate manifestations of the genre; rather, there's a feedback loop between these two worlds. Even before songs are recorded by famous artists, they often have their first hearings at informal *rodas;* and once the songs are released on CD, they almost immediately find their way into the repertoire of local groups.

This chapter focuses on a live recording made at Tia Doca's *terreirão,* the site of one of Rio's most famous and long-standing live *pagode* events. We use the iconic song "Sorriso Aberto" (Open Smile), by the late composer Guará,

3. The quote from Nei Lopes comes from the documentary "Isto é o Fundo de Quintal," on the DVD *Fundo de Quintal: Ao Vivo Convida.* Indie Records, 2004.

4. See Pereira (2003) for a history of Caçique de Ramos.

to tease out some of *pagode*'s principal sonic characteristics.[5] ⬤ Unlike most studies of *pagode* (and studies of samba in general), we avoid a definitional approach; that is, we do not presume that *pagode* performance is reducible to a set of characteristic patterns from which a primary understanding of the genre might be gleaned. Rather, our analysis has at its core the notion that *pagode* is a set of practices that subsists on the micro-nuances of continual variation. In our understanding, patterns are the transitory effects of variation, not the other way around.

The Tia Doca recording of "Sorriso Aberto" compellingly brings the listener into the *roda*. But this digital representation of *pagode*'s "liveness" comes with an especially opaque sonic profile—instruments blend together, subtle sounds are covered over, and the sonic detail of individual instruments takes a backseat to the overall cohesion of the ensemble. This denseness raises questions about how to analyze sonic textures that resist disambiguation. Would disarticulating each instrument from the whole be a valid way to analyze *pagode*? Or could one proceed along a different line, perhaps with sound *types* rather than individual instruments orienting our critical listening? And how does one reckon with the barely audible micro-gestures—a click against the side of a drum shell, a choked sound on a string instrument—that are at once central but generally go unheard in the course of live performance? What role does the *almost inaudible* play in musical analysis?

This chapter responds to these questions. We begin with an introduction to Tia Doca's *roda* at her famous *terreirão*. The subsequent section provides an overview of the history of "Sorriso Aberto." We then proceed to analyze its lyrics and its melodic and harmonic structure. The final part of the chapter analyzes studio "rerecordings" of the instrumental accompaniment parts that we made at the Estúdio Copacabana in January 2009 with *pagodeiros* who regularly perform at Tia Doca's.[6] The chapter thus proceeds from the general

5. There are numerous recorded versions of "Sorriso Aberto." The first, by Jovelina Pérola Negra (discussed below), is the most famous, but others have recorded the song. As of July 2010, iTunes had five different versions available. Of these, the one that most closely approximates the sound of a live *roda* is found on the disc *Samba de Raiz—Ao Vivo,* a recording of an informal *pagode* event led by members of Revelação, one of Brazil's most popular *pagode* groups of the 2000s.

6. The video and audio recordings at the Estúdio Copacabana were made by Jason Stanyek on January 10, 2009. Jadir Florindo was the audio engineer, and Antônio Valdevino and Gabriel Damasceno provided invaluable assistance. Special thanks are extended to Tia Doca's son Nem, who graciously agreed to have the musicians from his weekly *pagode* event participate on the recording. Research funding was generously provided by the Center for Latin American and Caribbean Studies at New York University.

to the particular, from a broad sketch of Tia Doca's place in the history of samba to an analysis of the micro-level sonic details of a single performance.

Tia Doca

On January 25, 2009, Jilçária Cruz Costa—known affectionately in the world of samba as Tia Doca (Aunt Doca)—passed away at age 76. She was a *pastora* of the "old guard" (Velha Guarda) of Portela, one of Rio's longest standing *escolas de samba*.[7] She was also known as one of Rio's main patrons of samba. In the mid-1970s, outside her apartment building on Rua Antônio Badajós, between Madureira and Oswaldo Cruz—two of the most storied neighborhoods in the history of Zona Norte samba—the Velha Guarda da Portela congregated for their rehearsals. By the early 1980s, the rehearsals moved to another location but the gatherings at Doca's continued, and these "monumental *pagodes*" (Vargens 1987: 127)—known simply as the "Pagode da Tia Doca"—were "one of the first of the wave in the middle of the 1980s that led to the creation of the *pagode* genre" (Vianna 2004: 69). In the mid-1990s the *pagode* moved a mile or so to its current site on Rua João Vicente, the road along which Rio's main train line runs.[8] Attracting crowds of 200–300 people, it officially begins at around 6 p.m. on Sunday evenings and goes well into the predawn *madrugada,* ending around 3 a.m. The MC of the events is Nem (Jalmir de Araujo Costa), Tia Doca's son, who serves as the lead singer and generally calls the tunes.[9]

The version of "Sorriso Aberto" analyzed in this chapter was recorded at Tia Doca's *terreirão* on Mother's Day in 2000 and celebrated the twenty-year anniversary of the Tia Doca *roda.* It appears on the CD *Pagode da Tia Doca,* a remarkable collection of well-known *pagode* songs recorded to emphasize

---

7. Information on Tia Doca's life is drawn from Medeiros (2004).

8. Its location, Rua João Vicente, 219, is on the border of Oswaldo Cruz and Madureira in Zona Norte of Rio de Janeiro, about 12.5 miles northwest from the center of the city and 16.5 miles northwest of Ipanema. Madureira is the home of two of Rio's major samba schools (Império Serrano and Portela) and is frequently invoked in the *pagode* songs.

9. Other regular musicians (as of March 2009) include: Luiz Carlos, aka "Amendoim SP" (music director and *violão de 6 cordas*); Carlinhos da Cuíca (*cuíca*); Wando Silva de Azevedo, aka "Blackout" (*surdo*); Edson Roni Ferreira Reis, aka "Tuta" (*cavaquinho*); Diogo (*violão de 7 cordas*); Flávio Santos (*banjo*); Wallace Porto (*tantã*); Ronaldo Camilo Ferreira, aka "Ronaldinho do Pandeiro" (*pandeiro*); Juninho (*repique de mão* and *repique de anel*); Wagner Zaparolli Siqueira (*chique-balde* and *bateria*).

the liveness of the *pagode* event. Songs run into one another without any break, sounds of the audience are heard, and everyone sings (not just a lead singer and a select chorus).[10] In the liner notes, producer Marcos Salles writes, "In her *pagode,* where the instruments converse within the intimacy of every beat and the *pastoras* play 'no pé e nos agudos,' a true samba happens" (Salles 2000). This intimate, micro-level "conversation" is the primary focus of the second half of this chapter.

"Sorriso Aberto"

"Sorriso Aberto" is performed with great frequency at *rodas,* often at moments of heightened intensity. While the song was already heard at informal samba gatherings in the mid-1980s,[11] it was first recorded in 1988 by Jovelina Pérola Negra (Jovelina Faria Belfort, 1944–1998),[12] a core participant in the early *pagode* movement and later one of Brazil's most famous *sambistas.* She possessed one of the most remarkable voices in Brazilian popular music: a rich and gravelly alto, with a touch of nasality perfectly suited to cut through *pagode*'s percussive textures. The composer of "Sorriso Aberto," Guará (1955–1988; his birth name is Guaraci Sant'anna),[13] is generally (and undeservedly) unheralded in the world of Brazilian popular music. Though he died just months before the release of Jovelina's *Sorriso Aberto* album, his music's impact was formidable, and he composed or co-composed some gems of the repertoire.

But "Sorriso Aberto" is his classic song, and Jovelina's recording set the stage for its emergence as one of the most widely played compositions in the *pagode* repertoire. *Veja,* Brazil's major newsweekly, had this to say about the eponymous album upon which the track appeared:

> For those who prefer the controlled rhythm of samba-*pagode* and *partido alto* to the frenetic pulse of the samba schools' drum section, the LP of Jovelina Pérola Negra is highly recommended. On the twelve tracks of *Sorriso Aberto,* Jovelina gives a lesson on samba alongside a chorus of thirteen singers and with the support of a true

10. Yet, curiously, despite the CD's effectiveness at conveying the energy of live *pagode,* only the basic tracks were done live; after the recording session at the terreirão, the choral parts were augmented in the studio. To get to the live, it seems, one must go beyond it.

11. Information about the early history of "Sorriso Aberto" was provided by Jadir Florindo in a personal interview with Jason Stanyek in January 2009.

12. "Pérola Negra" means "Black Pearl" in Portuguese.

13. Information on Guará's life was provided by his daughter Iara Sant'anna in an interview with the authors in Bangu, Rio de Janeiro, on August 7, 2010.

orchestra. In addition to the traditional instruments of *samba de terreiro*—*cavaquinho, bandolim,* guitars and drums—alto saxophone, clarinet and trombone also make an appearance. The singer acknowledges the soloists and dialogues with the chorus, facilitating the integration of singers and instrumentalists. Jovelina's performance recaptures the original spirit of *pagode*—that of a party in which musicians improvise and recollect old sambas—and gives the disc a casual atmosphere, of carnavalistic joy. (Veja 1989: 93)

This commentary makes a complex appeal to authenticity. It suggests that the album simultaneously serves as a kind of recuperation of a lost essence ("recaptures the original spirit of *pagode*") but also pushes what was taken to be the standard *pagode* instrumentation beyond its traditional forces ("a true orchestra"). A key term in the review is "*samba de terreiro*" (yard samba), a designation for a type of samba that arose in Rio's *escolas de samba* in the 1930s as a complement to the *enredos* (theme sambas) that samba schools paraded to during carnival. The evocation of the genre (which, by the late 1980s had all but vanished), places Jovelina's record into what the reviewer clearly sees as a "traditional" frame, away from commercialized carnival samba, with its parades at the *sambadrome,* and back into the *place* where samba putatively belongs: the backyard. The distinction, therefore, between "the controlled rhythm" of *pagode* and "the frenetic pulse" of the samba schools is not simply a sonic one. It also calls upon samba's geographies and their imbrications with class and racial politics. As Nei Lopes has pointed out, "*terreiro* is a word connected with the Afro-Brazilian symbolic universe; and the *terreiro* of the samba schools always reproduced, in various aspects, the religious communities of African origin" (2003: 90).

We're back at Tia Doca's *terreirão.*[14] And we're reminded that *pagode* is not just a style, or a genre, or a set of precepts for musical performance; nor is it merely a "competence," as Luiz Fernando Nascimento de Lima provocatively and accurately calls it (2001: 265–272); *pagode* is also an *event* that is intimately linked to particular spaces. One might say that its spaces are simultaneously sonic, physical, symbolic, and political and that, in the case of Tia Doca's performance of "Sorriso Aberto," the space is the *terreiro* and the location is Zona Norte, a working class, mostly Afro-Brazilian neighborhood far from the glittering beaches of Copacabana and Ipanema. Importantly, before "Sorriso Aberto" was first recorded in 1988, it was already well known in the informal *rodas* of Zona Norte, and it persists there in the backyard samba events of the early twenty-first century.

14. *Terreirão* is the augmentative of *terreiro.*

Lyrics

The words of the song (figure 3.1) begin "Yeah, it *was* really bad," alluding to an unspecified past event that caused the song's narrator to become depressed.[15] We sense that the narrator is alone, using the guitar to work out a "solution" to a messy life moment. At first the process seems almost solipsistic, a barely registered externalization of a tumultuous inner state. By the second verse, however, other instruments besides the guitar are present—the *pandeiro,* the *ganzá,* and the *tamborim*—all helping to "keep the beat," manage life, maintain some kind of positive flow. By the third, it's clear that no matter how bad things are, they're going to get better. But there's no arrival, no definitive transcendence of the narrator's sadness, only a feeling of hopefulness and promise.[16]

"Sorriso Aberto" is through-composed, with three verses plus a vocalise section that serves as both introduction and ending, framing the verses. There is no refrain, although, as we discuss below, each verse finishes with repeated lines—what might be called "quasi-refrains"—that add parallelism to an otherwise unrepetitive form. Some semblance of symmetry is achieved through the tripartite structure of each verse (figure 3.2). Yet each verse has a different length and rhyme scheme. "Sorriso Aberto" succeeds in rendering rather disjunctive poetic subsections into a coherent whole.

Verse 1 is twenty-four measures long and principally structured around rhyming couplets and tercets (with a repetition on line 11).[17] Counting, as is customary in Brazilian scansion, until the last stressed syllable of each line, the first nine lines of the song each conform to the same five-syllable structure, reminiscent of the *redondilha menor,* a traditional metric scheme inherited from Portugal and commonly found in many Brazilian poetic genres.[18] The nine-syllable structure of the quasi-refrain in lines 10-11 ("Quase que sofri desilusão") can be broken into two parts (5+4), revealing another instance of the

---

15. In a personal interview with Fabio Oliveira conducted in October 2009, Xande de Pilares (Alexandre Silva de Assis), lead vocalist of the popular *pagode* group Revelação, spoke emotionally of his close relationship with Guará, his older cousin. Xande provided recollections of Guará's unexpected and violent death in the late 1980s and recounted the story surrounding the composition of "Sorriso Aberto." According to Xande, Guará was motivated to compose the song after the tragic death of his former lover.

16. It is interesting to note, however, that on Tia Doca's recording of "Sorriso Aberto," "perto" (near) is replaced with "certo" (certain), putting a particular kind of positive gloss on the lyrics that is not present in the original.

17. The "É" (Yeah) that starts the first verse functions as a kind of anacrusis, both semantically and metrically, and is not treated in this analysis of the verse's metric structure.

18. An example of this type of syllable counting as applied to an analysis of Brazilian popular music can be found in Lopes (2005: 153).

(Pois é)	(That's right)
É, foi ruim a beça	Yeah, it was really bad
Mas pensei depressa	But I quickly thought
Numa solução	Of a solution
Para a depressão	For depression
Fui ao violão	I went to the guitar
Fiz alguns acordes	Played some chords
Mas pela desordem	But given the mess
Do meu coração	That my heart was in
Não foi mole não	It really wasn't easy
Quase que sofri desilusão	I was almost stricken by disillusionment
Quase que sofri desilusão	I was almost stricken by disillusionment
(Tristeza)	(Sadness)
Tristeza foi assim	Sadness was, like that
Se aproveitando pra tentar	Taking advantage to try
Se aproximar	To get close to me
Ai de mim	Oh, poor me
Se não fosse o pandeiro e o ganzá	If it hadn't been for the *pandeiro*, and the *ganzá*
E o tamborim	And the *tamborim*
Pra ajudar a marcar	To help keep the beat
Meu tamborim	My *tamborim*
Pra ajudar a marcar	To help keep the beat
Logo eu	Even me
Com meu sorriso aberto	With my open smile
E o paraíso perto	And paradise near
Pra vida melhorar	For life to get better
Malandro desse tipo	Malandro of the type
Que balança mas não cai	That wavers but doesn't fall
De qualquer jeito vai	No matter what, will
Ficar bem mais legal	Get way better
Pra nivelar a vida em alto astral	To even out life into good vibes
Pra nivelar a vida em alto astral	To even out life into good vibes
Pra nivelar a vida em alto astral	To even out life into good vibes
(Samba aqui, samba ali, samba lá)	(Samba here, samba right over there, samba way over there)

Figure 3.1. The lyrics to "Sorriso Aberto" ("Open Smile"). Words and Music by Guará. © 1992 EDIÇÕES MUSICAIS TAPAJOS LTDA. This arrangement © EDIÇÕES MUSICAIS TAPAJOS LTDA. All Rights Controlled and Administered by EMI APRIL MUSIC INC. All Rights Reserved. International Copyright Secured. Used by Permission. *Reprinted by permission of Hal Leonard Corporation.*

five-syllable *redondilha menor* meter. At eighteen measures in length, verse 2 is the shortest and most compact. Its nine lines end, mostly alternately, with either "im" (pronounced "een") or "ar." Unlike verse 1, it has no rhyming couplets or overarching, semi-regular metric structure. Verse 3 is the longest of the song, and its twenty-eight measures are also arranged into three subsections. Much like verse 1, the metric structure of the majority of its lines is constant; until the quasi-refrain (and with the exception of line 6—"Que balança mas não cai"), each line has six syllables. And interestingly, the structure of the quasi-refrain mimics that of verse 1. Here, the verse's dominant line length (six

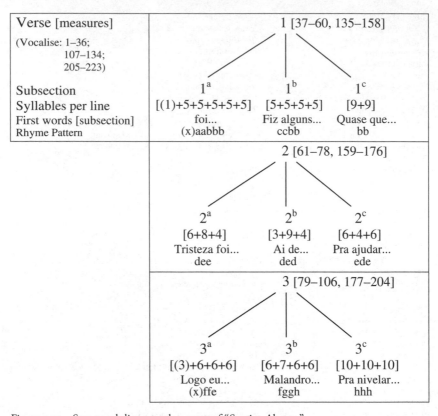

Verse [measures]	1 [37–60, 135–158]		
(Vocalise: 1–36; 107–134; 205–223)			
Subsection	1ª	1ᵇ	1ᶜ
Syllables per line	[(1)+5+5+5+5+5]	[5+5+5+5]	[9+9]
First words [subsection]	foi...	Fiz alguns...	Quase que...
Rhyme Pattern	(x)aabbb	ccbb	bb

Subsection · 1ª [(1)+5+5+5+5+5] foi... (x)aabbb · 1ᵇ [5+5+5+5] Fiz alguns... ccbb · 1ᶜ [9+9] Quase que... bb

2 [61–78, 159–176]

2ª [6+8+4] Tristeza foi... dee — 2ᵇ [3+9+4] Ai de... ded — 2ᶜ [6+4+6] Pra ajudar... ede

3 [79–106, 177–204]

3ª [(3)+6+6+6] Logo eu... (x)ffe — 3ᵇ [6+7+6+6] Malandro... fggh — 3ᶜ [10+10+10] Pra nivelar... hhh

Figure 3.2.   Structural diagram: the verses of "Sorriso Aberto."

syllables) has a four syllable "tag" added to it, resulting in the 6+4 syllable structure of "Pra nivelar a vida em alto astral."[19]

Subtle paronomastic touches—such as the play between "a beça" in the song's first line and "aberto" found in the song's title (and in verse 3)—indicate attentiveness to many kinds of relations between phonemes, not merely whether they rhyme. Such relations reveal Guará's poetic ingenuity and flair for creating micro-textual nuances. In verse 1, for example, the emphasis on "de" (in *carioca* Portuguese pronounced, in most cases, like the English letter *g*) in the words "**de**pressa," "**de**sordem," "acordes," and "**de**silusão," and the emphasis on *s* (in Portuguese the *ç, s, z,* and *ss*) in all of

19. In counting the syllables of the quasi-refrain of verse 3, note that the "a" at the end of "vida" is elided with the "e" in "em."

the previous "de" words, as well as "beça," "pensei," "solução," "fiz," "alguns," "mas," and "coração," provides a line through the three subsections. Alliteration ("paraíso perto, pra" in verse 3) and front rhymes ("aproveitando" and "aproximar," in verse 2) also highlight Guará's concern with the fine sonic gradations of his poetry.

The text is also full of rhymes embedded within words ("acordes," "desordem," and "coração" in the first verse, for example, all contain "or") or dispersed across words as elisions (for example, the rather sly—yet perceptible—rhyme on the sound "za" in "Fiz alguns acordes"). The word "ao" and the first syllable of "alguns" form near rhymes (on a kind of phonetic continuum) with "ão," the prominent rhyme in verse 1. In verse 2, "malandro" and "balança" rhyme "alan" internally, and also echo the aforementioned "al" sound from verse 1 (which also reappears in close proximity at the end of verse 3 in the words "qualquer," "legal," "alto," and "astral"). In the second verse, the sound associated with *e* and *i* (in these cases, both pronounced as in the English letter *e*) is used for end-of-line rhymes ("assim," "mim," "tamborim") but also at the start of lines and internally ("Se," "aproximar," "fosse," all of which sound like the English letter *c*). In verse 2, every line except the quasi-refrain "Pra ajudar a marcar" has the *e* sound, and the effect is both corporeal and sonic: to produce the *e*, the mouth needs to open ever so slightly, a nascent smile on the lips.

Each of the refrains that occupy the final lines of the three verses is built upon repetition of a few core vowel and consonant sounds. In the first verse, "Quase que sofri desilusão" focuses in on the vowels *i* and *e* (again, both pronounced identically, like the English vowel *e*) and, with less intensity, on a few near related sounds associated with the consonant *s* (in these words pronounced, variously, on a continuum between the English *s* and *z*). In the second verse, the line "Pra ajudar a marcar" weaves together the vowel sound *a* ("ah") and a few renderings of the consonant *r*. When sung, the line consists of a mere six syllables (the *a* in "pra" and the first *a* in "ajudar" are elided); but, remarkably, there are five instances of the open *a* sound and four uses of *r* (the *r* is rendered in two different manners: as a trilled *r* in "pra," and as a velar—or rough—*r* at the end of "ajudar" and for both *r*'s in "marcar"). The effect here is sharp and rhythmic, and seems to vocalize the sounds of the percussion instruments named earlier; in particular, the phrase evokes an emphatic *tamborim* rhythmic interjection that is typical in the *escolas de samba*. The refrain at the end of verse 3—"Pra nivelar a vida em alto astral"—is heard three times (in contrast to the single repetition of the refrains at the end of verses 1 and 2). Here we find a combination of the three sounds presented in the previous refrains—*a* (seven times), *i* (twice), and *r* (twice)—and a subtle repetition of a sequence of four vowel sounds *a-i-e* (like the *a* in the English "hay")-*a*: "Pra nivelar a vida em alto astral" (the *a* at the end of "vida" is elided with the *e* in "em").

"Sorriso Aberto" opens with a vocalise that more or less follows the melodic and rhythmic contour of verse 3. Only two sounds are used: "la" and "iá" (sounds like "ee-yah," with a stress on the second syllable). Rhythmic variety is achieved solely through conjunctive repetitions of "la" (there are no instances of two "iá's" in a row). While the "laiá" vocalise is widespread in all forms of samba, its origins are murky.[20] Its participatory function is clear, however, as it enables the audience to sing along with songs for which they don't know the complete lyrics. In the case of the opening of "Sorriso Aberto" it provides a pre-echo of the final verse.

The lyrical economy of "Sorriso Aberto" has one other layer: the *chamadas,* or "calls," that serve as audible cues for different sections of the text (these are placed within parentheses in figure 3.1).[21] These also induce participation, and remind the audience of what is about to be sung. In essence, it's a form of lining out. "Pois é" leading into verse 1 and the "tristeza" that cues the beginning of verse 2 are straightforward examples of this ubiquitous practice. The function of "Samba aqui, samba ali, samba lá" is slightly more oblique; it's more of an interjection than a call, its words not an exact pre-echo of the verse to come (although at the end of verse 3 the "lá" does subtly introduce the nonsemantic "la" of the vocalise section). This phrase functions more as a reminder of the song's primary injunction: "samba," both as noun and as imperative verb.

Harmonic and Melodic Features

Figure 3.3 is a transcription ("lead sheet") of the basic harmonic/melodic/rhythmic fabric of Tia Doca's "Sorriso Aberto." It represents the song *as* song, a fundamental, definitional depiction that, for example, might be

20. In an email conversation with Jason Stanyek, anthropologist Jonathan Shannon suggested that "Sorriso Aberto" has elements reminiscent of Eastern Arabian vocal music. According to Shannon, "In Levantine Arab song (and to a degree in North African forms such as Andalusian music/al-Ala) singers use the form yâ layl and or yâ ʿayn (literally meaning O night, O eye) as fillers, as vehicles for exhibiting skill in vocal improvisation. . . ." The "laía" of Brazilian samba might have some of its roots in the "yâ layl" and "yâ ʿayn" of Eastern Arabian song.

21. In theory, *chamada*s are improvised at the moment, but often, in practice, they are taken from the first (or most well-known) recording of a particular song; in other words, what was the meta-textual call of a soloist becomes so iconic that it literally becomes part of the text of the song. (This reflects a point made earlier regarding the interpenetration of live and recorded *pagode.*) Jovelina's recorded performance of "Sorriso Aberto" is a case in point; her *chamada*s—as melodic and rhythmic figurations—are often reproduced verbatim not just by the lead singer, but also by members of the audience.

Figure 3.3.   Lead sheet, with lyrics.

submitted under certain legal regimes to secure copyright. Lead sheets are not typically used in most live *pagode* performances and, in Brazil, it's very rare to see musicians at a *roda* not playing from memory; if a performer on a harmony instrument doesn't know the progression, extemporaneous comping is the norm. It bears emphasizing that such a transcription is contingent; in practice, there are several types of variability. For instance, we notate "Sorriso Aberto" in F minor (the key of the Tia Doca recording); its first recorded performance by Jovelina, however, was in D minor. Also, at

III

Figure 3.3. (Continued)

some moments, conflicting versions of a song's harmonic progression are performed simultaneously; the asterisks in mm. 68 and 98 indicate these.[22] Finally, the lead sheet provides a deceptive representation of harmonic rhythm. For some instruments, chord changes frequently occur on the final sixteenth note of the 2/4 measure, yet, as a rule, chords are notated above the beginning of measures, visually dislocating the symbol from the change.

The song is characterized by three principal types of harmonic motion:[23] (1) a tonic ii–V–i progression (Gm7/♭5–C7–Fm), (2) a modulatory ii–V–I progression leading to the relative major (B♭m–E♭7–A♭) and, most crucially, (3) a descending tetrachord progression (Fm–E♭7–D♭7–C7). While the ii–V–I sequence is often used in *pagode,* the tetrachord progression is found in only a few popular *pagode* songs;[24] it thus provides "Sorriso Aberto" with one of its most distinctive traits.[25] In the vocalise section and in verses 1 and 3, the descending tetrachord is matched by descending sequential patterns in the melody. The descending sequence is not the harmonic ballast for verse 2, however; rather, diatonic harmony dominates, with a modulation from the relative major back to the tonic. The ii–V–i progression is the principal mechanism for emphasizing the tonic here (although, as the lead sheet shows, different harmonic renderings, such as VI–V–I, can achieve this emphasis). Melodically, verse 2 is also distinct from the vocalise and verses 1 and 3; its melodic material contains no sequences and its contours do not follow those of the harmonic framework.

As with much of the *pagode* repertoire, the melody of "Sorriso Aberto" has a narrow range, covering only an octave in the version heard on the Tia Doca recording.[26] All of the pitches are drawn strictly from the F natural minor scale. There appears not a single leading tone (E♮) in the melody, although it is prominently heard in the dominant chord (C7) and it is used in the melodic figures of the seven-string guitar part (as can be gleaned from figure 3.4, the

----

22. See figure 3.web on the website for a transcription and recording of the contrasting harmonies present in the performance of mm. 99–102 by the two guitars, *cavaquinho* and *banjo*.

23. The chord nomenclature system used here is that used in jazz harmony. For a brief summary, see p. 156–159 of this volume.

24. Guará seems to have had a particular affection for the progression and, beyond "Sorriso Aberto," employed it in three of his other best-known compositions ("Viola em bandoleira," "Catatau," and "Sonho juvenil").

25. Lest there be any confusion, it should be pointed out that while the tetrachordal progression used in "Sorriso Aberto" is nominally identical to the Phrygian "Andalusian cadence" found in flamenco, it rests upon a different tonality (an Fm–E♭–D♭–C progression in flamenco would have C as its tonic; here Fm is decidedly the home key). To call Sorriso Aberto's descending tetrachord "Phrygian" would therefore be problematic; essentially, it's a slightly chromaticized and sequential harmonization of the upper tetrachord of the natural minor scale. For a discussion of the "Andalusian cadence" see Manuel (2006: 96–97).

26. On Jovelina's recording, the melody extends down another perfect fourth below the tonic, in mm. 70 and 74.

Figure 3.4.   "Sorriso Aberto" full score, mm. 9–36. Words and Music by Guará. © 1992 EDIÇÕES MUSICAIS TAPAJOS LTDA. This arrangement © EDIÇÕES MUSICAIS TAPAJOS LTDA. All Rights Controlled and Administered by EMI APRIL MUSIC INC. All Rights Reserved. International Copyright Secured. Used by Permission. *Reprinted by permission of Hal Leonard Corporation.*

full score that appears in the following section of this chapter). The melodic succession is smooth: motion is almost always stepwise or in thirds, and, with the exception of a few perfect fifths (in mm. 65–66, 81–82, and 104–105), the largest melodic leap is a major third.

Figure 3.4. (Continued)

At times, harmony and melody in "Sorriso Aberto" simultaneously utilize different logics. Although the melody stays within the natural minor scale, the descending tetrachord progression uses chromatic harmonies whose notes clash with that scale. During m. 13 these logics coexist. Harmony and melody are both organized primarily around a descending sequence in the first eight-measure phrase of the vocalise section (mm. 9–16), but the C♮ in the melody (first beat/second sixteenth of m. 13) disrupts the correspondence with the harmony, which at that moment implies the C♭ that is the seventh of the D♭7

Figure 3.4. (Continued)

chord. Guará's choice of the melodic C♮ suggests that the modal logic of the natural minor scale took precedence.[27]

Guará's use of melodic sequences is interestingly not typical of *pagode*. In mm. 9–16 (and its reiterations), we can see the sequential nature of the composition: the initial two-measure melodic figure is followed by two iterations down a full step, and one down a half step. Another interesting feature of the phrase construction is the interface between melody and text structure. To cite one example, the end of each line of text is typically marked by a rhythmic

Figure 3.4.   (Continued)

27. In a personal interview with Fabio Oliveira conducted in October 2009, Xande de Pilares recounted that Guará didn't know how to read music and only had very rudimentary skills on guitar. According to Xande, melodies were often composed first and full harmonizations were done later by arrangers. The presence of the contrasting logics of the descending tetrachord and the natural minor scale could suggest that the song's melody was composed before it was completely harmonized.

Figure 3.4. (Continued)

deceleration in the melody, providing a kind of release. This reflects a general tendency in *pagode* music.

The Virtual Roda *and the Full Score*

Pagode's instrumental accompaniment is extremely rich, and, as mentioned, its timbral profile distinguishes it from other forms of samba. Given the density of texture, it was not easy to disarticulate the live recording into individual

Figure 3.4. (Continued)

instrumental parts. In the end, we decided to follow Simha Arom, who famously employed the technique of "rerecording" in the early 1970s for his analysis of music making in the Central African Republic. He had the members of a group of instrumentalists perform their parts separately until the entirety of a musical fabric was built up, allowing for a subsequent analysis of the individual parts. Unlike Arom, however, we didn't ask the musicians to play "tutti" to create a version of the piece that they then used as a "base" upon which to (as mimetically as possible) perform their individual parts

Figure 3.4.   (Continued)

(Arom 1976: 485). Rather, we requested that they play along with the previously existing Tia Doca recording, itself a hybrid document, performed live but with some choral overdubs recorded later in a studio. Nor did we ask the instrumentalists to render their parts with minimal variation; one of the reasons we had the instrumentalists perform along with the Tia Doca recording was to approximate a "live" feel, and, as we show below, live *pagode* is premised upon continual variation, not the repetition of standardized patterns. Finally, the recordings we made at Estúdio Copacabana were video as well as audio. Given the various sonic layers present on each instrument, and the wide spectrum of sound-producing techniques, the mere isolation of one part from another would probably not have been sufficient to produce transcriptions with the grain of analytic resolution we hoped for.[28] Using video also enabled us not to ask the musicians to disarticulate their parts, performing one hand at a time for complex polyphonic passages on a single instrument, as Arom requested (1976: 488). We were concerned with tracking not just *what* sounds were produced but also *how* these sounds were produced. Ours was not a perfect technique; all kinds of misalignments happened, and the musicians were performing with a recording that they didn't themselves perform on (it was an earlier formation of the Tia Doca group that recorded the CD in 2000). And a recording studio—a rather sterile, "dead" environment—is almost antithetical to the kinds of live venues where *rodas de pagode* typically take place. But the results, we think, allowed us to peer into *pagode* performance from a highly specific and fruitful angle.

In particular, the video recordings not only aided us in our quest to transcribe the performances, but also facilitated the creation of another kind of representation for which we know no precedent. Synchronizing the videos with the audio, we were able to conjoin all the parts into a "virtual *roda*," an interface that allows readers to view and hear the studio performances individually or in any combination.[29] The placement of the videos in the interface approximates the way the musicians typically arrange themselves around the table at Tia Doca's *terreirão*. Combining the score and the interface allows readers to disambiguate the various sonic layers, both on the macro-level of ensemble playing and on the micro-level of the strands making up each instrumental part.

The virtual *roda* is intended to be used in conjunction with the "full score," figure 3.4, a highly detailed transcription of the first vocalise section,

---

28. Examples of transcriptions of *pagode* appear in very few sources. Galinsky's (1996) still is, as far as we are aware, the most detailed. His transcriptions, however, still adhere closely to generalized patterns—which he admittedly calls "prototypical" and "prescriptive" (1996: 128)—and not to specific performances. He also leaves out a fair amount of *pagode*'s micro-sound world. Lima (2001) transcribes vocal melodies but includes virtually no instrumental performance. Moura (2004: 203) includes a streamlined—almost Schenkerian—reduction of *pagode* and *partido-alto* rhythmic strata by Guilherme Gonçalves. For transcriptions of the samba of Rio's samba schools, see the figure "A rhythmic pattern played by a samba school's percussion ensemble" in Reily (1998: 315) and Gonçalves and Costa (2000).

29. The creation of the "virtual *roda*" would have been impossible without the expert Flash programming skills of Brian Lehrer.

Figure 3.5.   Keys to instrumental notation.

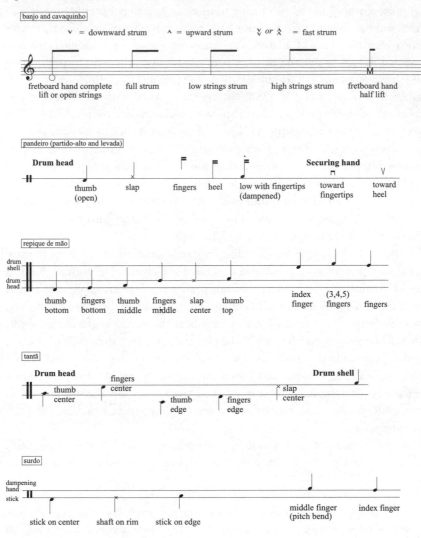

mm. 9–36. We notate both the prominent sounds each instrument makes and also the minor, barely perceivable residua of the players' hand motions. As seen in the notation keys (figure 3.5), each instrument is rendered idiosyncratically, with attentiveness to *how* sounds are produced.[30]

30. The notational scheme we created is an amalgam and modification of previously existing systems. With the exception of the *pandeiro*—for which we employed the notation devised by Carlos Stasi (explained in Gianesella 2009)—all the other percussion

Pagode sounds different from other forms of samba principally because of its distinctive instrumentation. To be sure, some of the instruments are utilized in other forms of samba and, indeed, across a wide spectrum of Brazilian musical genres: the conventionally tuned six- and seven-string guitars, *violão de 6 cordas* and *violão de 7 cordas* (nylon-stringed, the latter with an additional course in the low register typically tuned to C2); the diminutive, ukulele-like four-string *cavaquinho* (also called *cavaco* in Brazil and tuned D4–G4–B4–D5); the low-pitched *surdo* (alone among *pagode*'s main percussion instruments, played not with the bare hands but with a mallet in one hand); and the *pandeiro* (a small frame drum with metal jingles and—in the version typically used in *pagode*—a nylon head tuned tautly to produce a sharp, cutting slap tone). In contradistinction to these more widespread instruments, the *tantã*, the *repique de mão*, and the *banjo* are almost completely synonymous with *pagode*.[31] Developed by musicians who took part in the early *rodas* at Cacique de Ramos, these three instruments testify to the experimental ethos and sonic identity that typified the genre's emergence.[32] The *tantã* is a single-head, cylindrical drum that is the lowest pitched of all *pagode*'s hand percussion. The instrument played in the virtual *roda* has a wooden shell and a calfskin head, and produces an open tone with a fundamental pitched at Ab2 (approximately 104Hz, an octave above the *surdo*).[33] The *repique de mão* is a small cylindrical,

---

notations were expressly created for our transcriptions. There are a few examples of notation for *tantã*, *repique*, and *surdo* (Bolão 2003; Galinsky 1996) but none at this level of specificity. Although the guitars have long notational traditions, the *cavaquinho* and *banjo* do not, and we devised a few novel symbols to better represent how these instruments are played (see Habkost and Segura 2005 for some examples of *cavaquinho* transcriptions).

31. Three other instruments often heard at Tia Doca's *roda*s but not present in the virtual *roda* bear mentioning here: *cuíca, repique de anel,* and *chique-balde*.

32. The *tantã* was developed by Sereno (Jalcireno de Oliveira), and the *repique de mão* was invented by Ubirany (Ubirajara Félix do Nascimento), who, in an improvisatory flourish, used a drum set tom-tom and later a samba school *repinique*—both traditionally played with sticks—to play with his hands during *pagode* gatherings. Almir Guineto (Almir de Serra Souza), one of the primary and most popular architects of the *pagode* movement, is generally understood to be the creator of the *banjo*, a modified version of the "banjo americano" or "banjo norte-americano" that was common in Brazilian popular music in the 1930s but which, by the 1970s, had all but disappeared.

33. The terms *tantã* and *rebolo* are often used interchangeably in Brazil to designate the lowest pitched of the hand drums in the ensemble. In the most common usage, the *tantã* designates a larger and lower-pitched drum and the *rebolo* is slightly smaller, shorter, and higher-pitched. In some contexts, both a *tantã* and *rebolo* are used, the *tantã* performing the role taken by the *surdo* in the Tia Doca performance.

high-pitched, one-headed drum, its shell made of aluminum, and its head of plastic. The *repique de mão*'s timbre reflects a broader preoccupation of the Cacique de Ramos movement that initiated the *pagode* sound: its quest for tight and bright sound (a feature that separates *pagode* from much of the samba recorded in earlier decades).[34] In *rodas de pagode*, both the *repique* and the *tantã* are played on the lap, one hand striking the drumhead and the other the drum shell (some performers enhance the shell sound by using a ring on one of their fingers). Finally, *pagode*'s instrumentation includes the *banjo*, essentially a hybrid instrument that is a cross between the body of a small, North American banjo and the neck of a *cavaquinho*. Indeed, the *banjo* (also called *banjo-cavaco*) is, in some respects, virtually identical to the *cavaquinho*: it has four steel strings (the lower two wound), its neck has the same scale, and it is also tuned D_4–G_4–B_4–D_5. Yet its body—with a head made from cow or goat skin (or less frequently, plastic) pulled tight by a metal rim on a wooden resonator—produces a strident timbre different from the more mellow sound of the *cavaquinho*, sharply etched by the high overtones given off by its skin head and, in a sense, linked to the piercing timbre of the *repique de mão*. An idiomatic dimension of *banjo* playing—and one that indelibly connects it to the rhythmic figures of the *repique de mão*—is a kind of "*repicada*," a thirty-second-note flourish produced by a rapid left-hand motion.[35]

All of the instruments could be considered pan-timbral, producing a wide spectrum of tone colors and participating in a number of sonic strata simultaneously. The virtual *roda* and full score together reveal that instrumental figures in *pagode* alternate between different registers, often coalescing around high/low configurations. For example, hand-percussion parts are built around an open tone/slap nexus (*x*'s represent the slaps); the *cavaquinho* participates in the high/low alternation through a bifurcation of its four strings into two zones (alternating between these similarly to the *partido-alto pandeiro*); the *banjo* mixes a range of timbres—from penetrating full chords to duller muted and open-stringed ones—to achieve this high/low fluctuation; the six-string guitar, like the *cavaquinho*, also divides the instrument into two registers; finally, and perhaps most complexly, the seven-string guitar intersperses

34. This historical moment also coincides with the advancement of recording technology. Beyond the scope of this chapter, but important to mention nevertheless, is the fact that *pagode*'s ascendancy as a new *sound* for samba coincides with the full-fledged arrival of multitrack recording technology into Brazilian popular music. It's not far-fetched to posit that *pagode*'s integrated sound world has very much to do with recording techniques.

35. One of the meanings of "repicada" (past participle of "repicar") is to "cut or reduce to small portions." In this case, what is being cut is the beat.

upper-string chords with bass-register melodic figures that are produced with a metal pick worn on the thumb.

Citing the parts of the hand that generate these distinct timbral domains is not insignificant: as Grupo Fundo de Quintal's *repique de mão* player Ubirany has asserted, "The hand is our principal instrument" (Galinsky 1996:128). In contradistinction to carnival samba—which relies on sticks, mallets, and other beaters to achieve its almost brutal sonic onslaught—*pagode* is quintessentially a hand music. The *repique, pandeiro*, and *tantã*, for example, rely upon what might be called the "articulated hand" to produce their distinctive registrations and timbres: the thumb (or in the case of the *tantã*, the fingers) activating the open tone and the full hand generating the slap. Other parts of the hand help produce sounds that are like connective tissue between the open and slap tones (all notated in the full score). In this sense, the notation keys represent corporeal mappings as well as sonic ones.

Pagode's accompaniment is dense: all of the instruments play almost all of the time, saturating the sonic space.[36] Contained in these instrumental parts are distinct layers of sound, each with varying degrees of audibility, some almost audaciously present (open tones, slaps), some more submerged within the texture (clicks), and some virtually inaudible (residues of the dampening movements). Not immediately apparent in the score, however, is the music's dimensionality: concurrent, shifting, and contingent layers that emerge from combinations of sounds produced across the ensemble. For example, if we disarticulate the *pandeiro levada* part, we find that the open "thumb" tone correlates to other similar tones—the "thumb bottom" of the *repique de mão*, the "stick on center" of the *surdo*, the "finger's edge" of the *tantã*, the down-stemmed thumb tones of the *violão 6*. These correlations are not a function of general register. The open *pandeiro* tone is, for example, pitched more than two octaves above the open tone of the *surdo*. Yet, both tones—produced in the lowest registers of their respective instruments—might be considered as part of the same timbral and gestural grouping. Similarly, we might locate a "slap" complex across instruments—the relationship between the slap tones of the *repique de mão*, the two *pandeiros*, and the *tantã* is obvious (even though the *tantã's* thuddier slap is pitched lower than the others' taut slaps); and we could include the accented *banjo* chords in this grouping as well. Various "clicks" might also be heard in tandem, too. The *tantã* and the *repique de mão* both make heavy use

---

36. In *pagode* performance, textures are thinned out now and again but it's relatively uncommon for instruments to drop out.

of sounds coaxed from the shell of the drums (often amplified by a finger ring), and the *surdo*'s timbral universe includes the sound of the wooden part of the mallet against the instrument's metal rim. The *pandeiro*'s metal jingles could also be cited here. Much less apparent (and virtually undetectable without slowing down the recording), the *violão 6* has click sounds (denoted with an "x" in the full score) that, taken on their own, correlate with the click sounds in the other instruments. Finally, each instrument produces what might be called transitional sounds. The "thumb center" of the *tantã*, the muted chords of the *banjo*, the left-hand "index-finger" of the *surdo*—all barely audible—fall under this category. Of course, these timbral affinity groups (if we can call them that) are embedded within a highly particular temporal framework. Yet *pagode*'s rhythmic lineaments are deeply connected with its timbral contours.

Pagode *Rhythm*

For a first-time listener—especially one not able to engage with the Portuguese lyrics—*pagode*'s most immediately compelling feature might be its rhythmic language, from each instrument's idiosyncratic "swing" (what Brazilians call, variously, *balanço, suingue, cadência,* and *ginga*) to the cumulative groove that emerges out of the combination of the distinct nonhierarchical layers discussed above. Crucial here is that *pagode* (and samba in general) has no timeline or "topos";[37] there is no such thing as a "Brazilian *clave*," regardless of how tempting it might be to assign this status to one or another of *pagode*'s rhythmic parts. Rather, *pagode* is defined by the simultaneous presence of multiple and interpenetrate temporal reference points whose audible and structural availability to performers is based on a range of factors. These might include personal listening predilections, a player's proximity to certain instruments in the *roda,* the motions of dancers, the melodic line at a given moment, and so on. This orientation toward multiplicity also holds true for *pagode*'s periodic structure. As Julian Gerstin poignantly asks in his article on interaction between dancers and drummers in Martinican Belé, "What if performers relate varied, complex patterns to one another directly rather than through an imputed underlying layer of regularity?" (1999: 122). Gerstin goes on to ask whether the music's basic stratum of regularity might exist in "slower-moving 'main dance pulses'" or in "the quick-moving beats into which those

---

37. Agawu (2003: 73) defines *topos* as "a short, distinct, and often memorable rhythmic figure of modest duration . . . [that] serves as a point of temporal reference."

pulses are divided." "Or," he continues, "are all of these ways of relating patterns present, perhaps available to performers differentially as they focus their attention on various aspects of performance, perhaps utilized to different degrees in different genres?" (123). We would argue that "differential attention" to diverse temporal focal points aptly characterizes the kinds of listening that performers engage in as they enact *pagode*'s periodic framework. Such a claim places periodicity not within some ontological realm but within the epistemologies and capabilities of individual performers and instruments.

From a glance at the full score, it should be apparent that the sixteenth note functions as a minimal value, subdividing a quarter-note pulsation. However, keep in mind that the performers orient themselves to a range of audible and inaudible pulsations and figures. Moreover, the sixteenth note is a rather crude, isoperiodic representation of what is, in practice, an asymmetric flow of closely related yet nonidentical durations. For example, the *pandeiro levada* part in the full score consists of a virtually unbroken string of sixteenth notes. Listening to it by utilizing the isolating capacities of the virtual *roda,* however, reveals a slightly uneven pulsation, in which the second and third sixteenth notes are compressed within the center of each four-note figure, not perfectly represented by either sixteenths or sextuplets.[38] This "unevenness" is performed differently on each instrument and the music's rhythmic valences arise out of a combination of performative gesture and instrumental idiom.

Pagode rhythm combines two distinct yet codependent types of figures. The first emphasizes duple pulsations that string into what we might call "parity" groupings, and these align with *pagode*'s meter (one could say that they produce it). Following standard Brazilian convention, we have transcribed "Sorriso Aberto" in 2/4, but the music clearly contains various forms of parity—at the level of figure, meter, and phrase—that coalesce into cycles of two, four, and sometimes eight measures. The second type of figure moves in and out of alignment with the regular beats associated with the duple-oriented groupings. Mieczyslaw Kolinski (and later, Arom) labeled these two types of figures "commetric" and "contrametric," and, following Carlos

---

38. The topic of "Brazilian swing" has been taken up in Gerischer (2006). Assigning a generic sixteenth-note minimal value rests upon two basic assumptions, what we might call *horizontal equivalence* (that each sixteenth note in a single instrumental part is equidistant from the one that precedes it and the one that follows it) and *vertical alignment* (that each sixteenth note in one instrumental part or line occupies the identical temporal space as another being played "simultaneously." *Pandeiro* performance—like all instrumental samba performance—inheres in a staggered relationship to both the abstract, equidistant horizontal grid of the putative minimal value and the vertical alignments between instruments that produce *pagode*'s characteristic rhythmic textures.

Sandroni's convincing application of these to the analysis of samba, we incorporate them here.[39] While the tendency might be to assign commetricity a fundamental (or even generative) role (indeed, *contra*metricity seems to suggest some kind of deviance), Sandroni reminds us that neither com- nor contrametricity should be seen as "a priori more normal or regular" (2008: 22).

In Arom's view, a figure is commetric "when the majority of the accents—or in their absence, of the attacks—which identify it, coincide with the pulsation" (1984: 55). In the performance of "Sorriso Aberto" heard in the virtual *roda*, both the *tantã* and *surdo* are mainly commetric, typically alternating on each quarter-note beat between a high tone and a heavily accented low tone. Consistent with these instruments, the down-stemmed thumb tones of the *violão 6* and the open tone of the *pandeiro levada* (also produced with the thumb), almost always occur commetrically, with a quarter-note pulsation.

On the other hand, contrametric figures occur "when most of the accents or attacks are placed against the beat" (Arom 1984: 55). In the version of "Sorriso Aberto" analyzed here, the principal contrametric figures are performed by the *violão 6, repique de mão,* and *cavaquinho*. As we see below, these figures often vary, but each instrument can cycle back to its own particular *batida,* or "beat" (in the sense of a recurring pattern), that acts as a reference for improvisation. Here the *batida*s are characterized by what Arom calls "rhythmic imparity," having asymmetrical groupings that occur "within the interior of a periodically symmetrical framework, that is, one that is based on an even number of pulsations" (57). As Arom suggests, "any attempt of segmenting the figure, *nearest the point of central division,* will inevitably result in two uneven numbers" (57; emphasis in original).

In *pagode,* rhythmic imparity occurs in phrases lasting sixteen minimal values that is segmented into two unequal parts, seven on one side and nine on the other. Each side consists of two or three consecutive eighth notes (each two minimal values) and one dotted-eighth note (three minimal values). Due to this particular asymmetrical segmentation, the consecutive eighths on one side synchronize with the eighth-note pulsation of the meter, making that side commetric, while the consecutive eighths on the other side do not, making that side contrametric. Figure 3.6 presents a reductive transcription of the eighth and dotted-eighth groupings in the *violão 6* "stems-up" part, from mm. 25–28 of the full score. We can see that, in this case, the "7 side" is commetric and the "9 side" is contrametric.

39. Kolinski first used the terms "commetric" and "contrametric" in a critical review of A. M. Jones's *Studies in African Music* (1960). See also Kolinski (1973), Arom (1984), and Sandroni (2008).

Figure 3.6.   Imparity in *violão 6* "stems-up" part, mm. 25–28.

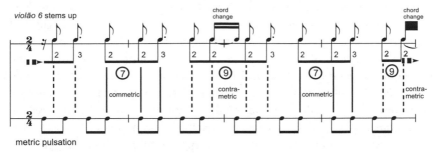

Figure 3.7.   Imparity in *repique de mão* and *cavaquinho*, mm. 13–16.

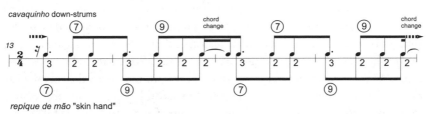

An imparity phrase is also found in the *cavaquinho* and the *repique de mão,* as seen in mm. 13–16 (figure 3.7). In these two instances, though, the phrase begins at different points within the period than it does in the *violão 6*. The *cavaquinho,* for example, starts its 7 side one eighth note before the 7 side in the *violão*. And although the *repique de mão* and the *cavaquinho* parts in mm. 13–16 align their attack points and durations, we suggest that they group those durations into 7s and 9s differently by timbre. The figure shows how we hear their respective 7–9 orientations.[40] In this reading, the *repique*'s imparity is 7 (3 2 2)–9 (3 2 2 2), and uniquely begins with the 3, rather than ending on it, as is the case with the *cavaquinho* and the *violão 6*.

These imparity phrases intersect in complex ways with timbral and harmonic formations. For example, on the full score we see that, with the crucial

---

40. The timbral distinctions that create the different grouping structures are evident in mm. 13–16 of the full score, figure 3.4. The beginning of each *cavaquinho* group is signaled by the beginning of a series of eighth-note down-strums on low chords following a single sixteenth-note up-strum on a high dyad. In the *repique de mão*, the onsets of the dotted-eighths that begin the segments are signaled, for the 7 side, by a fingered thirty-second-note flourish on the drumhead and, for the 9 side, by the first of a series of center slaps.

exception of the *banjo*, all of the harmonic instruments change chords (to Db7) on the last sixteenth note of m. 12. As suggested earlier, in *pagode's* harmonic world the same chord change often takes place *both* commetrically and contrametrically. Thus, to speak of "harmonic rhythm" in the singular is impossible. Rhythmically, the *banjo* is not alone; its commetricity aligns with the *surdo, tantã, pandeiro levada,* and the thumb of the *violão 6,* all resolutely accenting the downbeat of m. 13. To merely refer to these types of moments as harmonically or rhythmically dissonant or disjunct would be to miss the importance of *pagode's* diverse types of synchronization.

Pagode rhythm is articulated through specific timbral annunciations. For example, we find large numbers of recurring timbral-rhythmic correspondences between the *repique de mão* and the *surdo* and *tantã,* conforming, in many respects, to the contra-/commetric structures just discussed. If we track the *repique's* lowest tone ("thumb bottom") in relationship to the *surdo's* lowest tone ("stick on center"), one such correspondence becomes apparent. The *repique* begins its imparity phrase with its 7 side, which includes three low tones. As the last two of these come into phase with the meter, they align with the *surdo's* two open tones. This happens on second quarter-note beat of the four-beat cycle, in every odd-numbered measure from 9 to 33 of the full score. The *repique's* center slaps, which define the 9 side of its imparity phrase, might also be heard in reference to those of the *tantã.* The correspondence happens on the first and fourth sixteenth notes of the third beat of the four-beat cycle, as seen initiating in mm. 10, 12, 14, 18, 20, 22, 24, and 26. The first of these is commetric. Such pairings could be found between all instruments in the *pagode* ensemble. And, of course, timbral-rhythmic associations need not only take the form of unison vertical alignments. Consider, for example, the third quarter note of the four-quarter-note cycle, such as at the beginning of m. 10. The *partido-alto pandeiro's* slap on the third sixteenth does not coincide with the slaps in the *tantã* and *repique,* but it associates with them, thereby making that part of the cycle timbrally distinctive.

The anatomy of *pagode's* temporal world does not only reside in the periodic groupings of resonant open tones, incisive slaps, and, in the string instruments, fully fretted, ringing melodies and chords. There are sonic ligaments, even in the contra-/commetric structure we just presented, that, while almost undetectable in the context of a *roda de pagode,* are still essential to its periodicity. The subtle sounds buried in the folds of the instrumental accompaniment are much like the phoneme-level utterances analyzed earlier: they do not register as readily as full words and poetic lines, but they form the basis for the text's semantic presence. In the *banjo,* for example, we have notated a left-hand muting gesture, achieved by ever so slightly lifting the fingers (still in chorded position) off the fretboard. The *M* in the score does not simply

Figure 3.8. Regular contrametric patterning in *violão 6,* mm. 18–21.

denote an incidental sonic trace; it signifies an integral part of the *banjo*'s characteristic sound world, and, regardless of its "audibility," contributes greatly to the lineaments of its timbral and rhythmic profile. Similarly, the "thumb center" of the *tantã* often connects a downbeat slap tone and a second eighth-note shell click, and the "index finger" preparatory tone in the *surdo* almost invariably falls on the final sixteenth note of the first beat of a measure, leading to the instrument's primary emphasis of beat 2. Such almost inaudible "transitional" sounds play a crucial gestural role in linking more perceptible elements. *Pagode*'s rhythms therefore exist not only at the level of audible pattern but also in the micro-flows of articulated gesture.

The Gestural Economies of Rhythmic Variation

Alterations to *pagode*'s repetitive patterns—its *batidas*—generate variants that "poke out" of the texture. Any *pagode* performance is replete with such improvised figures and we offer only a few examples here (others can be gleaned from the full score). An extremely common variation can be heard in figures constructed out of a series of equal durations. They may occur within a single register, or in alternation of high and low registers, or in a succession that combines these single-register and alternate-register tendencies. The common thread is heightened attentiveness to registration. In figure 3.8 the *violão 6* persistently projects a "regular contrametric" pattern in the higher register (the up-stemmed fingers) against the stable commetric backdrop (the down-stemmed thumb).[41] The gestural sequence here—repeated seven times—is a straightforward thumb/fingers/fingers.

Figure 3.9 shows the *partido-alto pandeiro* and *cavaquinho* parts from mm. 78–86. Both instruments alternate high and low registers to create rhythmic displacement. A literal high/low alternation in the *partido-alto pandeiro* (mm. 81–82)—achieved through the gestural relationship of thumb (open tones)

41. According to Arom "contrametricity is *regular* when the position of the accents— or in their absence, of the attacks—in the figure is systematically invariable in relation to the pulsation" (1984: 55; emphasis in original).

Figure 3.9.   Contrametricity in *partido-alto pandeiro* and *cavaquinho*, mm. 78–86.

and palm (slaps) of the drum hand—is taken up by the *cavaquinho*, which has an uncharacteristic unbroken series of down-strums (mm. 82–84). As often happens, gestural alterations in one instrument trigger shifts in another.

Shifts in gesture often lead to the transient articulation of a new speed. In the following two examples this occurs through the repetition of a particular motion. In figure 3.10, consecutive downstrokes in the thumb produce straight triplets, uncharacteristic in *pagode*. Similarly, in figure 3.11 the *banjo*'s inexorable alternating up/down strumming is replaced by a variation figure in m. 203 with an almost unbroken succession of down-strums. (In measures after 106, the singers repeat the tune, but the instrumentalist play different variants of the lead sheet; see figures 3.2 and 3.3.)

One rhythmic strategy—employed at times by all instrumentalists—is the incorporation of successive dotted eighth notes into a prevailing commetric or contrametric process. This category of figures may be conceptualized as a 4 (dotted-eighth-note)-against-3 (quarter-note) polyrhythm or as a rephrasing of straight sixteenth notes in groups of three (in contradistinction to the predominating parity and imparity groupings described earlier). Regardless of the ambiguity of these figures, they project a "floating" character, one that introduces greater rhythmic variation into the texture.

Figure 3.12 shows the *partido-alto pandeiro* part regesturing the straight sixteenth notes into groups of three. As the usual rate of "thumb" attacks is one every quarter note, the temporary effect is one of speeding up, of temporal compression.

Similarly, Figure 3.13 shows a 4-against-3 pattern played on the *tantã*. But here each "strong-hand" tone (slaps and an open tone) is interspersed with two "weak-hand" clicks, grouping attacks into threes by the gestural alternation of strong/weak/weak. Given that the *tantã* typically has at least four

Figure 3.10.   Shift of speed in *violao 7*, mm. 168–171.

Figure 3.11.   Shift of speed in *banjo*, mm. 203–204.

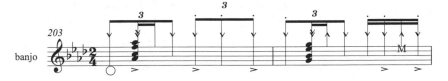

Figure 3.12.   Speeding up in *pandeiro levada*, mm. 15–16.

Figure 3.13.   Slowing down in *tantã*, mm. 20–21.

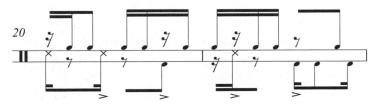

"strong-hand" tones per measure (see full score m. 19), the figure in this case could be perceived as a kind of slowing down.

The *surdo* example in figure 3.14 typifies the ambiguity of these figures. In general, the rate of activity for the stick-hand in the *surdo* part is an eighth note, and the "stick on center" sound happens every second stroke. The dotted-eighth figures beginning on m. 167 seem to slow down in relation to the eighth-note activity, even as the density of "stick on center" sounds increases.

These gestural shifts can help bring out connections that might otherwise be obscured. In figure 3.15, the relationship between the *tantã* and *surdo*, the two lowest pitched percussion instruments in the ensemble (tuned approximately an octave apart) is thrown into relief in m. 77, when the *surdo* omits its characteristic downbeat "stick on edge" sound (evident in mm. 73–76) and

Figure 3.14. Concurrent speeding up and slowing down in *surdo*, mm. 166–168.

Figure 3.15. Interaction of *tantã* and *surdo*, mm. 73–80.

enacts a strict alternation of "middle finger" and "stick center" gestures. This clears space for the open tone of the *tantã* to be heard in hocket-like interaction with the open tone of the *surdo*.

Such constellations are always shifting, always improvised. Unlike, say, with Cuban *batá* drumming, there is no "aggregate ostinato" or a "composite of tones . . . that together create recognizable melodies" (Moore and Sayre 2006: 126). *Pagode* does project what Moore and Sayre call a "composite texture," but it is extremely variable, based on moment-to-moment interaction and not intended to delineate a composite rhythm. In this sense, the more appropriate analogy might be the jazz rhythm section and not *batá* (or other West African drum traditions that subsist on interlocking patterns). Within the constraints of their idiom, *pagode* musicians perform roles similar to those of the members of small jazz ensembles who "take as their goal the achievement of a groove or feeling—something that unites the improvisational roles of the piano, bass, drums and soloist into a satisfying musical whole" (Monson 1996: 26). In *pagode* musicians do respond to one another, cajole certain rhythmic figures, and work collectively. But there is no "grammar" that provides a guiding logic. Rather the logic, as we show now, is a variation procedure that is attuned to a nuanced apprehension of song form.

Economies of Variation within Pagode's *Song Forms*

In much analytic literature on *pagode* and samba, one typically finds notated patterns that are presented as "standard" for each instrument, but we resist the temptation to code these into stock forms and argue that *pagode* subsists on continuous variation both within and among parts. Such variation might best be described as the result of a wide range of interactive practices, all bound together by attention to—and a concern for realizing—song form, from broad sectional divisions down to the nuances of individual words. The stories songs tell, their often ingenious use of the Portuguese language, the lilt and arc of their melodies, and their unique histories within the *roda* and the broader repertoires of Brazilian popular music are paramount to *pagode* practice.

The *roda*'s principal charge is to activate a corpus of songs and to increase audience participation until the line between performer and nonperformer is blurred. To someone unfamiliar with *pagode* (or more generally, with Brazilian Portuguese), the repertoire might seem rather repetitive; such a listener might claim that long sequences of songs do not change key or tempo, that most harmonies hover around a few basic progressions, that the accompanying role of each instrument remains fairly static. At a certain grain of resolution these observations are plausible.

But our sonic apertures do matter—both in terms of our desires and capacities—and within the *roda* we often witness an acute audition focused on the nuances of individual songs. This is not to discount other kinds of listening that might occur: distracted, rote, and combative are some, as well as a whole spectrum of states we might corral under the broad heading of "nonlistening." Yet, it is impossible to imagine a *roda de pagode* really working without a collective orientation to the songs. Each song's lyrical content and melodic structure conditions subtly different approaches and outcomes. And, crucially—lest we seem to imply that each song imposes its own rigid accompaniment codes—such attentiveness manifests along a spectrum of possibilities, all of which are fundamentally improvised. The passages we analyze below exemplify just a few of the many ways that an instrumentalist might demonstrate a commitment to *pagode* as extemporized song.

Mimetic Variation

Although one can, on occasion, hear improvised singing in the *roda*, a typical event is constructed around long sequences of well-known songs, often sung with heightened allegiance to performances found on commercial recordings. The familiarity of the repertoire allows *pagode* instrumentalists opportunities to render vocal lines mimetically. On the narrowest level, *pagodeiros* sometimes vary their characteristic patterns by matching their playing to local rhythms of the vocal melody over the course of a measure or two. Starting in the second measure of figure 3.16, the *partido-alto pandeiro* abandons its alternating high/low pattern, first to attack together with the voice on the strong syllables "fui," "vi-," and "lão," then to project a contra-metric series of regular attacks that prepares and synchronizes with the voice's next syllables, "Fiz al-." This form of mimesis requires an intimate prior knowledge; the through-composed nature of "Sorriso Aberto" makes it all but impossible that in-the-moment, predictive listening could reap this level of precision.

Similar matching appears in the relation between the *cavaquinho* and the vocal line in figure 3.17. Here, a floating, contrametric eighth-note pulsation characterizes both parts.

Heterophonic Variation

This tendency need not take the form of exact mimesis. At moments, instru-mentalists shift their playing by rendering an altered version of the vocal line's rhythm. This heterophonic form of variation highlights a specific portion of the song's melody by playing around it. In figure 3.18, for example, the *tantã* takes the rapid-fire delivery of "samba aqui, samba ali, samba lá"—a vocal *chamada* that is not part of the main lyrics—and creates a variation that highlights the vocal line's sixteenth notes.

Figure 3.16.   Mimesis, *partido-alto pandeiro* and vocals, mm. 43–46.

Figure 3.17. Mimesis, *cavaquinho* and vocals, mm. 94–96.

Subsectional Variation

A closely related tactic involves filling in brief pauses during vocal phrases. Instrumentalists often sing while playing, and they accompany themselves by taking account of a vocal line's breaths and filling up the spaces they generate. Here we are not alluding to the section-defining cadential variations addressed below; rather, these figures occur in the internal folds of individual verses and phrases (with the subsections labeled 1ª, etc., in figure 3.2). This type of variation can be found in the full score as well as in figure 3.19, where the *surdo* interjects a timbrally rich fill between "-gal" and "pra" (this corresponds to the break between 3ᵇ and 3ᶜ in figure 3.2).

Section Markers: Calls (In and Out)

Variation delineates song structures by audibly marking them with improvised musical figures that surface out of the general texture. Of course, this is a dual process: structure informs how instrumentalists shape their playing, even as performers manifest structure through the creation of a range of audible cues. These vary from very short, conductor-like phrases used to "call in" other musicians when singing is about to commence, to extended figures that evolve over many measures and connect sections.

Figure 3.18. Highlighting, *tantã* and vocals, mm. 105–106.

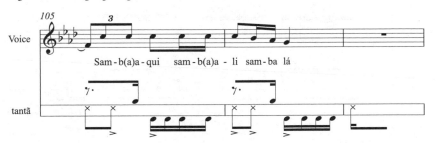

Figure 3.19. Fill-in at vocal breath, *surdo,* mm. 190–192.

"Sorriso Aberto" appears on the Tia Doca CD in the middle of what *pagodeiros* call a *pout-pourri* (with each song leading into the next without a break) and thus there was no need for the "call in" that is frequently used to begin songs. In such an instance, a single instrument (typically the *repique de mão* or *tantã*) plays an idiomatic figure to lead musicians into the song from silence. In this performance we do hear, however, a common type of call-in cueing the voices. In mm. 7–8 (immediately preceding the full score), the *violão 7, repique de mão,* and the *surdo* simultaneously play figures that lead the voices into the vocalise section (figure 3.20). These figures (such as the one for *repique*) can also be used unaccompanied, to cue in an ensemble at the beginning of a song (as mentioned above) or during a break when all instruments but one stop playing, leaving a space for a brief "solo."

A song's ending is also often audibly called, and sometimes emphasized visually through physical gestures. One such "call-out" interpolates a series of five dotted-eighths within four quarter-note beats, as is seen here in the *partido-alto pandeiro, repique de mão,* and *tantã* in figure 3.21. The forceful re-alignment of contrametrical rhythms and metrical pulsation on the downbeat

Figure 3.20.   Call-ins, *violão 7, repique de mão,* and *surdo,* mm. 7–8.

Figure 3.21.   Call-out, *partido-alto pandeiro, repique,* and *tantã,* mm. 231–233.

of the final measure is typical.[42] While other variations rely upon musicians using dynamic or articulatory emphasis to project their lines, call-outs often entail a marked increase in loudness.

Section Markers: Cadential Variations

Cadences—either at song endings or at significant internal arrivals—are typically marked with elaborate figures. These can take place over the course of the two measures leading into or coming out of a cadence, or they can extend over many measures, creating both an anticipation and a suspension of cadential arrival. In figure 3.22, the measures surrounding m. 205—the beginning of the final iteration of the vocalise section—illustrate the range of variations used at such moments. All of the instruments are transcribed except for the *pandeiro levada* and, taken together, reveal strategies for prefiguring a cadence and stabilizing the ensemble directly after. The measures surrounding a cadence present an opposition of densities: intense activity leading in, followed by relative calm.

Over the course of mm. 203–204 both the *partido-alto pandeiro* and the *tantã* resolutely repeat the same sixteenth-eighth-sixteenth figure, marking the quarter-note beat. Their inflection patterns are inverted, however: the *pandeiro* plays two open tones followed by an accented slap, while the *tantã* begins each three-note phrase with a slap followed by two open tones. The *repique* also plays a relatively unfluctuating pattern; its accents, however, emphasize the eighth notes off the beat, following each of them with a thirty-second-note "roll." The *banjo* pushes toward the cadence with eighth-note triplets, and the *surdo* plays one of its most complex patterns, sending a dotted eighth figure on a resonant closed tone in m. 203 into a flurry of sixteenths in m. 204.

A striking element of this passage is what we might refer to as postcadential "stabilization"; *violão 6* and *cavaquinho* fill up m. 205 with straight eighth notes, and the *repique de mão* emphatically plays three eighths to begin the measure. Although it is quite common to find such commetric partitioning of the 2/4 measure at cadential moments, it would be rare to hear this particular rhythmic subdivision at any other place in a song. The unadulterated eighth notes "re-collect" the energy and stabilize the ensemble after a frantic lead-up to the cadence. The *violão 7* performs a kind of cadential extension, delaying for a measure the arrival of the tonic in its bass line through the use of diatonic step-motion reminiscent of Brazilian *choro*. Two further examples of cadential

---

42. It is important to note here that the musicians stopped their performances in the studio even though "Sorriso Aberto" flows directly into the next song on the CD.

Figure 3.22.   Cadential activity in the ensemble, mm. 203–206.

extension can be found in figures 3.23 and 3.24. In both instances, the *tantã* ignores the cadence that occurs when the vocal line begins a new section ("Tristeza foi assim" at m. 61 and "É, foi ruim a beça" at m. 135). Instead, in the first example, the line is pushed through for an extra three measures using the sixteenth-eighth-sixteenth pattern we described above, finally returning to the basic groove in m. 65.

Figure 3.23. Cadential extension, *tantã,* mm. 61–65.

Figure 3.24. Cadential extension, *tantã,* mm. 134–141.

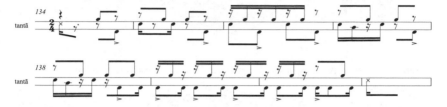

Figure 3.24 shows a slightly more elaborate extension. Beginning in m. 135 (the start of the first repeat of verse 1), the playing moves through a few different rhythms in quick succession. Measure 135 until the first beat of m. 138 replicates a pattern used commonly at key structural moments by the third *surdo* in *escolas de samba.* It suspends the flow strikingly, as the prominent low open tone is heard only five times in four measures. Starting at beat 2 of m. 138 the *tantã* takes the dotted-eighth subdivision mentioned above and renders it into a string of repeated eighths and sixteenths that comes in and out of phase with the meter, landing on the downbeat of m. 141, as if in quick response to the last syllable of "solução" (solution). This example is also characterized by another common cadential tactic: the break, or "drop-out." In m. 134 the *tantã* arrests the flow of the regular slap/open-tone alternation for a full dotted quarter. Flow, it seems, is suspendable only at such moments.

Similar to the *chamadas* (calls) discussed above, the placement and form of breaks are sometimes derived from famous recordings. More often, however, breaks are improvised and reflect attentiveness to the song form. In figure 3.25, the *banjo* and *violão 7* simultaneously stop playing as the repeat of the first vocalise section is brought to a close.

Reactions to Semantic Lyrical Content

Attunement to the vocal line need not revolve solely around rhythm or a broad marking of sectional divisions. Lyrics may condition reactions, prompting sonic codings of bits of text. Tia Doca's version of "Sorriso Aberto" has particularly good examples of this. As discussed, the lyrics refer to the instruments of the ensemble, and directly evoke *pagode* rhythm. At certain moments,

Figure 3.25.   Break in *violão 7* and *banjo,* mm. 133–134.

Figure 3.26.   Word painting of vocal "pandeiro" by the *pandeiros,* mm. 67–61.

"Sorriso Aberto" almost reads as a précis for samba practice. The line from verse 2 "se não fosse o pandeiro, e o ganzá, e o tamborim," for example, can provoke a vibrant response. The *pandeiro* is a prime candidate to participate in this kind of word painting, and in almost all performances of the song that we have heard or taken part in, the word "pandeiro" has been taken up by the *pandeiro* player in a self-referential move to emphasize the instrument's presence. This not only projects a kind of "*pandeiro*-ality," it also takes account of the mention of the "tamborim," referencing a phrase typical of *escola de samba tamborim*. In figure 3.26, the sixteenth-eighth-sixteenth open tone *levada* pattern anticipates the word "pandeiro" by a measure. The *partido-alto pandeiro* begins its illustration in sync with the mention of "pandeiro" in the text, and uses a pattern identical to the one used in the *levada,* although the final sixteenth is now a slap instead of an open tone.

Another word also serves as a catalyst for rhythmic responses. *Marcar*—the Portuguese verb for "mark"—is used in samba terminology to designate the maintenance of the music's basic pulsation. In the *escolas de samba* of Rio, for example, the "first *surdo*"—responsible for articulating the second beat of the 2/4 measure with the lowest pitched sound of the ensemble—is often referred to as "*surdo de marcação*." In figures 3.27 and 3.28, the *tantã* and *surdo,* two instruments in *pagode* that have the marcação as one of their primary functions, clearly respond to the sung *marcar.*

Figure 3.27. Word painting of vocal "marcar" by *tantã*, mm. 72–75.

Figure 3.28. Word painting of vocal "marcar" by *surdo*, mm. 170–173.

Figure 3.29. Word painting of vocal "malandro" by *cavaquinho*, mm. 184–187.

Finally, in figure 3.29 the *cavaquinho*, with a quick alternating up-down strum on the top three pitches of the chord in m. 187 (third and fourth six-teenths of beat one), gives a poignant evocation of the word *balança*. As mentioned above, Brazilian Portuguese is replete with words used to describe swing or groove—*suingue, cadência, ginga*—and *balança* fits into this category. Here it signifies the swagger of the *malandro*, the archetypal street-smart guy who uses his wily ways to take advantage of any situation, "balancing" but never falling.

Conclusion

"Sorriso Aberto" justifiably occupies an important place within the *pagode* repertoire. Its lyrics are poignant and elegantly constructed, its descending tetrachord progression distinctive, and its opening vocalise section one of the most convincing and catchy renderings of a ubiquitous singing practice. And any rendition of the song has the benefit of being in intertextual dialogue with Jovelina's original recording, one of the great performances in Brazilian popular music of the 1980s. Yet it is just one song in a repertoire of thousands. Each has its own sonic valences, and each has its own particular historical trajectories inside and outside the *roda de pagode*. It would be quite a stretch to suggest that "Sorriso Aberto" is an "ideal type" from which we could extrapolate an ontology for *pagode*. In many respects, the composition is rather idiosyncratic, with a chord progression that appears only infrequently in samba and with through-composed verses that have no structural analogue with any other *pagode* song. In other respects, however, it does provide a useful portal into *pagode's* sound world, sharing a number of features with other songs in the repertoire: lyrics that unwrap the poetry of the quotidian, rhythms that take a few elemental cells and spin these into a compelling groove, and melodies that are at once complex and singable.

We have both been at *rodas* when "Sorriso Aberto" has been performed (and, as instrumentalists, we have happily played it together on a few occasions). We can attest that the song is often sung with great zeal and joy and that it has a special ability to bring a vital energy to the *roda*, helping to, as its lyrics say, "even out life into good vibes." Its vocalise section can be especially affecting and powerful when taken up by large numbers of people who, formed into a fleshy circle, produce those afferent and efferent forces that we highlighted in the introduction. *Pagode's* lifeblood is, after all, the live event and what we have presented here is a nothing more than a prolegomena to future analyses that pay close attention to the micro-sonic world of *pagode*, spinning us, centripetally, back into the *roda*.

References

Agawu, Kofi. 2003. *Representing African Music: Postcolonial Notes, Queries, Positions.* New York: Routledge.

Arom, Simha. 1973. "Une méthode pour la transcription de polyphonies et polyrythmies de tradition orale." *Revue de Musicologie* 59(2): 165–190.

———. 1976. "The Use of Playback Techniques in the Study of Oral Polyphonies." *Ethnomusicology* 20(3): 483–519.

———. 1984 "The Constituting Features of Central African Rhythmic Systems: A Tentative Typology." *The World of Music* 26(1): 51–64.

Barata, Denise. 2002. "Permanências e deslocamentos das matrizes arcaicas africanas no samba carioca." XXV Congresso Anual em Ciência da Comunicação, Salvador/BA, http://www.academiadosamba.com.br/monografias/denisebarata.pdf (accessed July 18, 2010).

Bolão, Oskar. 2003. *Batuque Is a Privilege—Percussion in the Music of Rio de Janeiro.* Rio de Janeiro: Luminar Editora.

Cabral, Sérgio. 1996. *As escolas de samba do Rio de Janeiro.* Rio de Janeiro: Luminar Editora.

Carrilho, Maurício. "Violão de 7 cordas." http://ensaios.musicodobrasil.com.br/mauriciocarrilho-violao7cordas.pdf (accessed July 18, 2010).

Dicionário Cravo Albin dá Música Popular Brasileira [Online]. "Violão de 7 cordas." http://www.dicionariompb.com.br/violao-de-7-cordas/dados-artisticos (accessed July 18, 2010).

Diniz, André. 2008. *Almanaque do samba: a história do samba, o que ouvir, o que ler, onde curtir.* Rio de Janeiro: Jorge Zahar Editor.

Galinsky, Philip. 1996. "Co-option, Cultural Resistance, and Afro-Brazilian Identity: A History of the Pagode Samba Movement in Rio de Janeiro." *Latin American Music Review* 17(2): 120–149.

Gerischer, Christiane. 2006. "*O suingue baiano:* Rhythmic Feeling and Microrhythmic Phenomena in Brazilian Percussion." *Ethnomusicology* 50(1): 99–119.

Gerstin, Julian. 1998. "Interaction and Improvisation between Dancers and Drummers in Martinican Bele. *Black Music Research Journal* 18(2): 121–165.

Gianesella, Eduardo Flores. 2009. *Percussão orquestral brasileira: problemas editoriais e interpretativos.* Ph.D. thesis, Universidade de São Paulo.

Gonçalves, Guilherme, and Mestre Odilon Costa. 2000. *The Carioca Groove: The Rio de Janeiro's Samba Schools Drum Sections.* Rio de Janeiro: Groove.

Habkost, Nestor, and Wagner Segura. 2005. *The Beats of Samba.* Florianópolis, Brazil: NUP/CED/UFSC.

Kolinski, Mieczyslaw. 1960. "Review" [*Studies in African Music,* A. M. Jones]. *The Musical Quarterly* 46(1): 105–110.

———. 1973. "A Cross-Cultural Approach to Metro-Rhythmic Patterns." *Ethnomusicology* 17(3): 494–506.

Lima, Luiz Fernando Nascimento de. 2001. *Live Samba: Analysis and Interpretation of Brazilian Pagode.* Helsinki: International Semiotics Institute.

Lopes, Nei. 2003. *Sambeabá: o samba que não se aprende na escola.* Rio de Janeiro: Folha Seca.

———. 2005. *Partido alto: samba de bamba.* Rio de Janeiro: Pallas Editora.

Manuel, Peter. 2006. "Flamenco in Focus: An Analysis of a Performance of Soleares." In *Analytical Studies in World Music,* ed. Michael Tenzer, 92–119. New York: Oxford University Press.

McCann, Bryan. 2004. *Hello, Hello Brazil: Popular Music of Modern Brazil.* Durham, NC: Duke University Press.

Medeiros, Alexandre. 2004. *Batuque na cozinha: as receitas e as histórias das tias da Portela.* Rio de Janeiro: Senac.

Monson, Ingrid. 1996. *Saying Something: Jazz Improvisation and Interaction.* Chicago: University of Chicago Press.

Moore, Robin, and Elizabeth Sayre. 2006. "An Afro-Cuban Batá Piece for Obatalá, King of the White Cloth." In *Analytical Studies in World Music,* ed. Michael Tenzer, 120–160. New York: Oxford University Press.

Moura, Roberto. 2004. *No princípio, era a roda: um estudo sobre samba, partido-alto e outros pagodes.* Rio de Janeiro: Editora Rocco.

Pereira, Carlos Alberto M. 2003. *Cacique de Ramos: uma história que deu samba.* Rio de Janeiro: E-papers.

Reily, Suzel Ana. 1998. "Brazil: Central and Southern Areas." In *The Garland Encyclopedia of World Music,* vol. 2, *South America, Mexico, Central America, and the Caribbean,* ed. Dale A. Olsen and Daniel Edward Sheehy, 300–322. New York: Garland.

———. 2001. "Hybridity and Segregation in the Guitar Cultures of Brazil." In *Guitar Cultures,* ed. Andy Bennett and Kevin Dawe, 157–178. Oxford: Berg.

Salles, Marcos. 2000. CD Liner Notes, *Pagode da Tia Doca.* Paradoxx.

Sampaio, Luiz Roberto Cioce. 2007. *Pandeiro brasileiro.* Florianópolis, Brazil: Bernúncia Editora.

Sandroni, Carlos. 2008. *Feitiço decente: transformações do samba no Rio de Janeiro (1917–1933).* Rio de Janeiro: Jorge Zahar Editor.

Ulloa, Alejandro. 1998. *Pagode: A festa do samba no Rio de Janeiro e nas Américas.* Rio de Janeiro: Multimais Editorial.

Vargens, João Baptista M. 1987. *Candeia: luz da inspiração.* Rio de Janeiro: Funarte.

Veja. 1989. "Ritmo de festa: Uma boa safra de LPs para animar Carnaval" [Includes review of *Sorriso Aberto*]. June 20, 93.

Vianna, Hermanno. 1999. *The Mystery of Samba: Popular Music and National Identity in Brazil,* ed. and trans. John Charles Chasteen. Chapel Hill: University of North Carolina Press.

Vianna, Luiz Fernando. 2004. *Geografia carioca do samba.* Rio de Janeiro: Casa da Palavra.

CHAPTER 4

Thelonious Monk's Harmony, Rhythm, and Pianism

EVAN ZIPORYN AND MICHAEL TENZER

Photo: Thelonious Monk at the 1972 Monterey Jazz Festival. © Paul Slaughter. All rights reserved.

On February 28, 1964, jazz pianist, composer, and group leader Thelonious Monk (1917–1982) graced the cover of *Time* magazine, then America's major newsweekly. Coming at the height of the civil rights movement and amid dawning recognition for African Americans' achievements, it was a true breakthrough into mainstream media for him and for jazz. The moment was short-lived, with rock-and-roll's ascendancy to cultural dominance just around the corner, but it was also well-earned: Monk had been producing extraordinary music—often under difficult social and personal circumstances—for almost two decades, and would continue to perform for another nine years. Gnomic and inscrutable, he also magnified, for better or worse, popular clichés about the jazz artist as insouciant, hipster weirdo—aspects played up in *Time*'s account, and undoubtedly part of the reason its editors had singled him out, for the moment, as jazz personified.

Yet despite the typecasting, Monk was actually an unlikely icon, musically and personally. Jazz comprises a cluster of genres bound loosely by a symbiosis of individualism, commercial concerns, and high art leanings, but even given this, Monk's playing was in many ways too idiosyncratic to fit in to any niche. His music differed more from his contemporaries than theirs did from each others'. His small hands and distinctive piano technique often gave cause for his very skill and competence to be called into question, sometimes not without reason.[1] Such perplexities complicated Monk's reputation and that of jazz itself, which he was both part of and apart from. And as if to enhance this otherworldly aura, after touring and recording almost continually from the late 1940s until the mid-1960s, he simply faded away. He stopped playing piano soon after his last recordings in 1971 and retired into semi-seclusion for the last decade of his life.[2] Yet both his musical legacy and mythic status have continually strengthened ever since.

Our own lifelong obsessions with Monk's music started in the 1970s. It was a romance of recordings: the only performances we ever saw were on film, and that was much later. For us back then, "Thelonious Monk" was an *outré* persona conjured by liner notes and cover art. The cover of one LP—*Monk's Music,* from 1955—showed him writing music while perched in a child's red wagon, donned in hipster's garb and sunglasses; another—*Underground,* his last Columbia recording, from 1968—set Monk as WWII French resistance fighter, seated at an upright piano in a barn hideout, with several open bottles of wine, a live cow, weaponry, and a captured Nazi in tow. These manufactured

---

1. Celebrated jazz educator and author John Mehegan echoed a common jazz conservative's sentiment when he remarked that Monk's playing was "psychotic" (Mehegan, pers. comm. with Tenzer, ca. March 1975).

2. Spellman 1966 contains a memorable chapter-length portrait of Monk. Biographical sketches are easy to locate in jazz reference works or on the Internet, and Solis 2007 devotes a chapter to the task.

images suggested ways for the public to digest the music: Monk as idiot-savant, genius-child, rebel-recluse—a collection of quirky, individualistic, American countercultural personas. But, however these images may have hooked us as teenagers, we could not fail to hear his music as indispensable. His deadpan playing, stocked with "scribbled lightning" (Ross 2007: 519), and jabbing, stabbing, amazing chords, textures, rhythms, empty spaces, and clusters, was riveting, at once instantly recognizable, diverse and unpredictable, and full of the divine laughter that made it both deadly serious and hilariously funny. It invaded our musical selves-in-formation and led to insatiable fixation. Of course we were among many trying to internalize Monk and make him part of us. This chapter harvests fruits of our Monk incubation, and the friendship built partly from it.

Here we also position Monk to represent the multiplicity of jazz, something for which no one artist or performance is suited, and yet, for the same reasons *Time* chose him, no one is as well suited as he. Our aim is not so much to depict the dimensions of Monk's style as it is to show what he was able to achieve on one particular occasion. We consider a renowned April 1957 solo piano recording of "I Should Care" (hereafter *ISC*),◉ a song composed around 1944 as a number for the boilerplate Hollywood movie *Thrill of a Romance* and known to the public through recordings by Jimmy Dorsey, Frank Sinatra, and others.[3] It appeared repeatedly on the 1947 hit parade and was almost immediately adopted by Monk, (pianist) Bud Powell, and myriad other players. Our choice of a "standard," rather than one of Monk's numerous seminal original compositions, is deliberate, allowing us to focus on the deeply symbiotic relationship between Monk and the jazz mainstream, a microcosm of the relationship between jazz and American popular music as a whole.

Monk's decision to create a personalized, at least seemingly improvised (though in fact hardly at all) rendition of a popular song is itself "standard" practice for jazz. In general Monk's taste in standards leaned toward the

---

3. The song was composed by Axel Stordahl and Paul Weston, the lyrics by Sammy Cahn. These tunesmiths—like many in Tin Pan Alley during that era—were white. Many of the song's interpreters—Monk, Bud Powell, and Dizzy Gillespie, to name a few—were black. This dynamic of white (often Jewish-) American songwriter and African-American interpreter is a single point in a larger topic. Jazz was developed primarily by African Americans, though many of its luminaries, artistically and commercially, have been white. Any serious understanding of jazz must include issues of ethnicity and race. Historically jazz was made mainly by and for a minority community, many of whom were in the process of migration, both geographic and social. As such it has both been a symbol of and vehicle for the vital and ongoing socioeconomic issues that permeate race relations in America. These issues have been taken up insightfully; two good entry points are Monson 2007 and O'Meally et al. 2004.

popular music of his youth (DeVeaux 1999: 169–70), but he seems to have had a particular fascination with *ISC:* he recorded it at least four times for as many record labels, over a span of twenty years. Our chosen *ISC* is especially concentrated and allows us to frame Monk's idiolect against the background of some of the era's musical conventions and their milieu.[4]

Jazz, Monk, and Modern Jazz Technique

Jazz and Jazz Analysis

In the United States jazz was long ago pronounced "America's classical music," a phrase used so often as to now elude original attribution. Many Americans regard this African-American form as a birthright and know it when they hear it, even if hard pressed to say what it is that makes it "it." Born in late nineteenth-century New Orleans, it long ago permeated global culture, provoking cultural responses by the 1920s in places as distant as Japan and China (Atkins 2001; Jones 2001). To have even a passing acquaintance with Western culture is to have some awareness of jazz as an idea involving musical self-expression through improvisation. Beyond the "jazz buffs" that live in every country, this awareness can be expressed in indirect, idiosyncratic ways: a "jazzy" turn of phrase in a Bollywood production number, a rural Japanese man belting Sinatra-style while fronting his local high school's jazz band, or a lip-synching crooner in a Manila transvestite bar. These and thousands of other appropriations attest to jazz's potency.

Jazz history is often described in terms of a series of fast-morphing eras (until a pluralistic stasis set in after the mid '70s)—Dixieland, hot jazz, swing, bebop, cool, hard bop, free jazz, fusion, and so on—whose musics evolved but were also retained in coexistence. Throughout, it has been girded by poly-rhythmic, cyclical, repetitive principles tracing back to the West African music of slave ancestors, the dialects of song and rhythm in earlier African-American music (the blues, spirituals, etc.), the strophic ballad and popular song forms of Anglo-America, and the harmony and instruments of European art music. Jazz digested, synthesized, and transformed all of these.

The bebop style of Monk's era was typically played by combos of up to six players comprised of piano, stand-up bass, drum trap set, and possibly electric guitar (all comprising the *rhythm section*), fronted by saxophone(s), trumpet(s), or trombone(s). Most performances use the melody or "head'" of a popular song or a newly composed tune to launch solo improvisations stated over the tune's cyclically repeated harmonies, which are rendered by the rhythm section

4. For other commentary on this performance see Hodeir 2001: 126, Williams 2001: 221, and Blake 2009.

in constantly changing accompaniment patterns. Rhythm section members also take solos. Bebop players such as Charlie Parker (saxophone), Dizzy Gillespie (trumpet), and Bud Powell (piano) perfected a vocabulary of scales and patterns that brought out the color and quality of the "changes" (the chord sequence) while flying far from the original melody.

Jazz *is* improvisation, and the image of the spontaneously creative soloist, playing instinctually, is powerful. Some players can and do spin off very different solos from take to take and/or from night to night, but most draw from a personal lexicon of phrases, large and small, that constitute a player's style. The degree to which great improvisers plan their solos varies, and the line between improvisation and composition is fluid (Larson 2008). Aficionados have always known this, but today the ready availability of myriad "alternate takes" by Charlie Parker, Monk, and innumerable others proves that jazz improvisation can be a highly calculated act. The fixed, solo arrangement of *ISC* we selected is a case in point.

Jazz analysis, like all analysis, begins with listening, and is a multistage process proceeding from general stylistic features to consideration of players' own styles, and finally to the details of a performance. Knowledgeable listeners weigh a critical mass of musical markers including instrumentation, form, harmony, tempo, and rhythmic subdivision to identify and appreciate individual players. Even should such a listener first hear a recording of *ISC* "blindfolded"—that is, without being told who is playing—and fail to recognize Monk's musical signatures, he or she could still place the music at circa 1945–1965. This was an era encompassing related styles (bebop, cool, West Coast, and more) that we refer to for convenience as the era of modern jazz. The integrity of any durable genre rests on the tensile strength of its basic principles; Monk's relationship to modern jazz is a characteristic one of testing these strengths. Among the features relevant to this performance are certain types of harmonic and rhythmic complexity seen in relation to musical form, and a range of ways of laying these out on the piano keyboard. To analyze *ISC* in terms of these features, we will first survey their treatment in the genre. Then it can emerge how Monk mobilizes rhythm (especially fluctuations of tempo) and harmony on the one hand, while retaining form and melody on the other, to create a layered, asymmetrical reading of this standard song.

We later refer to a full transcription (figures 4.5 and 4.6) through which we can fix the performance in our minds at a glance. But even though we made every effort to make it accurate in pitch and harmony (though one can never be sure) and urge the reader to play it, not even a note-perfect performance will make it sound like Monk. This is because he plays with an embodied hand and finger pianism that even neurological and psychological description could hardly capture, let alone conventional music notation. Monk's touch at the keyboard vividly shapes surface rhythm and the envelope of the sound—its attack and decay contour. Playing it is worth doing, however, to encounter the sonic diversity of his style and wealth of unexpected piano sonorities.

Form and Fusion

ISC is composed in one of a small number of easily recognizable thirty-two-measure popular song types of the era (the top staff of figure 4.1 gives the melody). It consists of two sixteen-measure periods that are parallel, in the sense that the first eight measures of each are identical and the second eight differ.[5] This can be thought of formally as ABAC, in which each letter designates eight bars of melody and chords (actually the very first measures of B and C are also the same). Songs of this genre were written to be recorded by professionals and, if successful, were published as sheet music for amateurs. The sheet music arrangements, distributing the tones of the chords in various ways on the keyboard, were dispensable, but the harmonies were also represented by shorthand chord symbols (about which more below). A *lead sheet* consisting of these symbols over a single staff with the notated melody circulated among jazz players; a version of this can be seen by combining the top staff of figure 4.1 with the first row of symbols below the second staff. This version is from *The Real Book,* a latter-day "fake book" (originally a samizdat anthology of lead sheets for standard tunes and modern jazz compositions).

The "double period" form of *ISC* stems from European models. In non-jazz performances, such as for film or singers' nightclub acts, the songs last only as long as their words; that is, the music is read off the arranger or composer's notation and repeated (with preplanned small variants) as many times as necessary to sing the entire lyric. This is as it would be in many a Brahms *Lied* or an *aria da capo* in Mozart opera.

But jazz is a deep fusion of European and African music. This integration of independent, but in many ways compatible, musical systems was not only an ingenious cultural project directly contradicting the segregated social realities of America, but could be seen as providing that society with a compelling model of how to overcome those difficulties. Jazz harmony has roots in African melody based on flexible, unstandardized five- or seven-tone scales, but it acquired new depth of field (the range of colors and sensations of unique relation to a stabilizing "tonic" center that harmony evokes) by ingesting Europe's twelve-tone chromatic scale and its system of functional harmonic progressions. At a time when European composers largely eschewed it, jazz took up the mantle of enriching functional harmony.

5. See Forte 1995 for extensive analysis of these songs' form and features.

Figure 4.1. Melody and four harmonizations of *I Should Care*, with chord roots and harmonic functions.

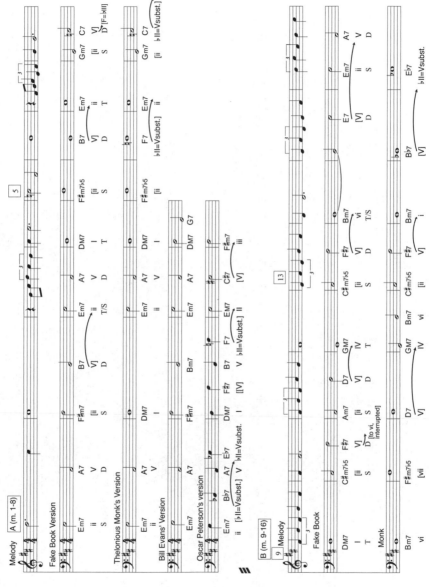

153

Figure 4.1. (Continued)

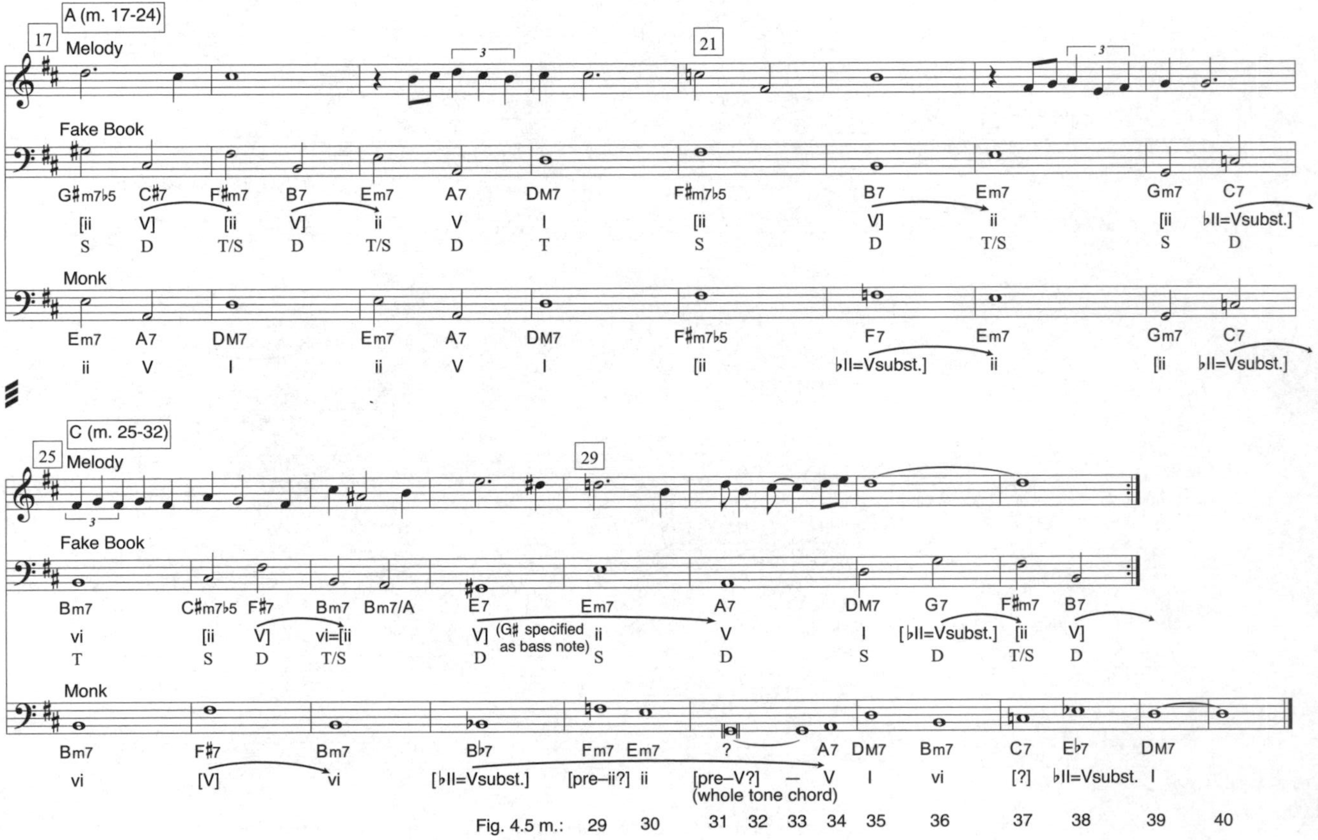

Jazz form evolved to become a cycle of harmonies reminiscent of analogous (though briefer) cycles in much African music, as well as in circular European forms based on a repeating bass line, such as the passacaglia. African cycles are configured with rhythmic and melodic patterns. These are given multiple, varied repetition, with the patterns locked in and aligned with the unchanging cyclic structure. Such *isoperiodicity* also defines most jazz, with regularly recurring chord progressions ("changes") instead of rhythms or melodies. Variation may last for as many cycles (isoperiods) as the soloist performs, organized by the harmonies linked to the cycle. Cycle and progression, seemingly as contradictory as circle and line, thus reconcile.

Jazz Harmony

So that Monk's style can soon be broached, let us pause to clarify our usage of three terms already in play:[6]

- *Harmony:* one of three essential functions of motion or rest perceived from pitch combinations at a given place in the form. These are the stable *tonic* (T) and the unstable *dominant* (D; leading to a tonic) or *subdominant* (S; leading to a dominant).
- *Chord:* specific root (fundamental tone) and quality (interval structure and sound) of a harmony specified by the lead sheet.
- *Voicing:* the specific, registrated pitches used to realize a chord.

Harmonic progression in European art music evolved from a conception of counterpoint that wove the simultaneous tones of concurrent melodies into a few stable chordal structures while retaining nuances like anticipation, suspension, and other kinds of melodic dissonances—tones that do not belong to a stable chord and that must resolve to those that do, else the tone combination parses as unstable. Stable chords contain only three tones in European practice.[7] Such triads come in and out of focus when the music's polyphonic

6. The condensed presentation in the ensuing sections is indebted to many published treatises on jazz harmony including Berliner 1994, Dobbins 1984, Levine 1995, Mehegan 1959, and Russell 1959. In an attempt to render jazz harmonic practice of the 1940s and '50s systematically we have deliberately not accounted for styles from before and after this time. Our summary is based on music of only a handful of the era's prominent pianists—Monk, Bill Evans, Oscar Peterson, Red Garland, Wynton Kelly, and a few others.

7. For the discussion to follow, basic knowledge of European triadic harmony and tonality is needed, although as a matter of pedagogical principle the analyses in this book and its predecessor (Tenzer 2006) strive to presume only an ability to read Western notation. To save space in this instance we refer the reader to Benjamin 2006: 368–369, where these fundamentals are reviewed.

strands either line up or diverge. Counterpoint oversees the management of dissonance, and this process, at various orders of magnitude, generates both harmony and form in great variety. Western music's *variation forms,* similar to jazz in some ways, act to restrain this tendency. But more culturally significant and musically distinctive is the fact that counterpoint, with its prolongation of dissonance and harmonic progression, historically urged Western music *in extremis* to long operas, symphonies, and other noncyclical structures.

In jazz, counterpoint and dissonance shape melodic lines and chord progressions, but cyclic structure prevails. The role of harmony is to identify, with particular colors (i.e., chords and voicings), the region of the cycle through which one is passing. Jazz harmonies are glued to their positions; nothing can dislodge them. It is not the chords themselves that are glued there, but their harmonic functions, and this allows (as we shall see) for many ways to substitute different chords of equivalent function, or to severely alter chords so long as their function is preserved. The functions have such a forceful progressive logic that the practiced ear can distinguish which of the many tones that may be sounding are operative in establishing the harmony, and which are more or less ornamental. Even if crucial tones are absent, expert listeners can infer harmonic function from the context. What identifies harmonies and how they are realized in sound must thus not be thought of as the same thing; indeed, the two can vary seemingly to the point of severing their relationship—but not quite.

Harmonic Principles and Chords

Songs like *ISC* are composed in the tonality of one of the twelve equal-tempered chromatic notes, and end with tonic harmony, though some, like *ISC,* do not begin with it. The tonality, which may be major or minor in quality, shifts fluidly and temporarily at many points in the cycle. We restrict discussion to *ISC*'s home key of D major for illustration; figure 4.2a shows the root-position triads (major, minor, or diminished[8]) in open note heads with roman numerals, indicating the scale tone that is the root of the chord, on the first line below the staff.

The second line below the staff labels each with tonic (T), dominant (D), or subdominant (S) function.[9] With rare exceptions, a jazz chord has a harmonic meaning only if it can be confidently heard as having one of these three functions. Thus iii and vii chords are rare in jazz major keys because the former is functionally ambiguous and the role of the latter is understood as a weak version of V. In

---

8. Augmented triads, the fourth type, have no role in *ISC.*

9. In European practice the term *subdominant* applies to the harmony built on scale degree 4; harmonies on steps 2 and 6 are called *supertonic* and *submediant,* respectively.

Figure 4.2a.   Harmonic functions and chords in D major (with ii–V–i progression in B).

Roman numeral/ scale degree in D major:	I	ii	iii	IV	V	vi	vii
Function (in D major):	T	S	(–)	S	D	S	(D, weak)
Triad quality:	major	minor	minor	major	major	minor	diminished
Root name and 7th chord quality:	DM7	Em7	F♯m7	GM7	A7	Bm7	C♯m7♭5

fact, each of the S, T, and D functions is normally linked to a single chord, which progresses to one of the others strongly because their roots are a fifth apart: ii for S, V for D, and I for T. IV and vi chords are very often heard as equivalent to ii (note that the roots of ii, IV, and vi together form a ii triad). The constituent tones of iii, IV, vi, and vii chords may appear as voicings of *other* chords, or the chords may function in other *keys* where they play the roles of ii, V, or I.

Jazz chords and voicings were influenced both by the tonal language of other African-American forms such as the blues, and by the sonorities of early twentieth-century French composers like Debussy and Ravel.[10] Evolving style came to allow sevenths (tones that are the interval of a seventh above the root; shown with black note heads) not to be considered dissonant, and to inhere to virtually all chords. This is also true of many other nontriad tones (figures 4.2b and 4.3), but sevenths are essential and assumed. Adding them to triads produces *seventh chords* of various distinctive qualities depending on the type of the triad and the size of the seventh. The major seventh chord (labeled M7) has a major triad plus major seventh. The dominant seventh chord (labeled 7) is the same but with a minor seventh. The minor seventh chord (m7) has a minor triad plus minor seventh, and in the half-diminished seventh chord (m7♭5) the minor seventh is joined to a diminished triad.[11] These are labeled in the fourth line below the main staff of figure 4.2a.

10. "Blue notes" fall outside the scale or even between the cracks of the piano keyboard, most often around the third, fifth, and seventh steps of the scale. Originating in African music's flexible approach to tuning and tonality, they were developed into expressive tools by singers, guitarists, and almost all nonpiano instrumentalists, who could bend and alter pitches. The piano cannot do this, but adding extra tones to harmonies was one way of evoking blues expression.

11. A fifth type, the (fully) diminished harmony (minor third, diminished fifth, diminished seventh), is omitted because it plays no role in *ISC,* nor indeed in jazz. It and other seventh chord qualities combining different types of thirds, fifths, and sevenths are possible and do occur, but they are considered as voicings of one of the four basic types.

Mention of the half-diminished seventh chord occasions a brief diversion into the role of major and minor tonalities in jazz. The exact nature of this relationship is multifarious, varying from era to era and player to player, and intertwined with devices absorbed from other practices such as the blues. As with much European tonality, the distinction between major and minor modes is retained as an overall affect—in other words, tunes are one or the other—but in actual practice the two freely commingle. In essence, this comes down to the unique case of the half-diminished seventh chord, built on the second degree of the minor scale.

Consider that in D major in jazz, one may often encounter an E-rooted seventh chord that uses B♭, from D minor, instead of B, making the chord a half-diminished seventh rather than a minor seventh. Also, as shown above the staff in figure 4.2a, the vii7 chord in D major has the same root and half-diminished-seventh quality of the ii7 chord in B minor, so it can be used to temporarily change to that key, or even to B major. And by playing a half-diminished seventh when a tonic function is expected, jazz musicians can create a chain of ii–V progressions. This is our first example of "chord substitution," a principle of harmonic modularity at the core of jazz practice (see "Chords and Voicings" below).

In jazz, motion from S to D to T functions usually reflects root motion by fifth, as in the iconic ii–V–I progression. Mastery of jazz harmony involves the ability to manipulate ii–V–I in all keys and combinations. In D major, ii–V–I is most simply expressed as Em7–A7–DM7, which occurs twice right at the beginning of *ISC,* but the same *functional* progression, transposed and with substitutions, occurs in many places throughout the song. In the *fake book* (the lead sheet) version shown in the second staff of figure 4.1, the vocabulary is varied, close to what an accomplished player might actually play, and the progression is sometimes interrupted. For example, the ii–V in mm. 8 and 24 suggest that a richly chromatic F major is coming, but the progression is not allowed to complete. Measures 17–20 bring a dovetailed chain of ii–V motions, each one leading to the next, as the arrows show. All staves of figure 4.1 and all harmony in *ISC* can be explained in ii–V–I terms.

Dominant function chords contain the crucial interval of the diminished fifth (also known as the tritone) between the third and seventh. In the A7 chord, this means C♯ and G. The tritone's distinctive sound is absent from major and minor seventh chords, but their occasional substitutes, the borrowed half-diminished seventh and the dominant seventh sonority itself—which does double duty as tonic in blues forms—include it. The interval impels forward motion in ii–V–I progressions, which sometimes concatenate and elide into strings of descending tritones in inner voices, creating, if artfully done, a spinning vortex of dominant resolutions. The approach to and departure from the tritone is more expansive in the music of Monk's era—and certainly to an even greater degree in Monk's own music—than it is in classical music; it is without question the most important source of the feeling of harmonic progression in the music. The tritone is the structural hub orienting and ordering the tremendous vocabulary of idiomatic chord voicings.

Chords and Voicings: From Lead Sheet to Performance

In modern jazz, seventh chords specified by lead sheets may appear simply as shown in figure 4.2a, but musicians rarely follow what the lead sheet specifies to the letter. Well before Monk came on the scene, jazz pianists vied to distinguish themselves with ingenious voicings. A kind of common practice prevailed in bebop, though we emphasize that musicians can and did step outside this practice in search of particular expressions and logics. In the main, though, four complementary techniques developed (see also Berliner 1994: 63–88 and 531–539), two concerning voicing as such and two concerning chord choice—what chord to play where:

Voicing
- *Extension and omission:* addition of tones foreign to the chord proper, and/or dropping tones that are part of it
- *Spacing and doubling:* distribution of a voicing on the piano or among instruments in an ensemble.

Harmonic Choice
- *Substitution:* replacement of one chord by another with equivalent function
- *Insertion and deletion:* increase or decrease in the rate of harmonic motion by adding to or subtracting from changes specified on the lead sheet

Extension, Omission, Spacing, and Doubling

Figures 4.2b and 4.3 illustrate possibilities for extending minor seventh, dominant seventh, and major seventh harmonies, and apply them to the initial ii–V–I of *ISC*. In the first staff each chord is extended upward by thirds beyond the seventh to include the ninth, eleventh, and thirteenth above the root. Each of the resulting seven-note stacks of thirds includes all notes of the D major scale. The fact that all three chords extend through the exact same pitch collections, in the same intervallic arrangement (i.e., a stack of thirds), demonstrates the fundamental role that harmonic function—and *not* chord or voicing—plays in determining tonal meaning in jazz. The chords could in some cases even be voiced in identical ways, but their functional context would make them heard and understood differently. Here is a significant way in which, it seems to us, jazz harmony differs in emphasis from European practice.

To the extent that the distinction between ii, V, and I voicings blurs, what is it precisely that distinguishes their functions? The second staff shows which of the seven diatonic tones are directly involved in the progression toward and away from the V chord's tritone. Typically these tones are necessary and sufficient to convey harmonic function. Surprisingly for anyone familiar with European harmony, neither the fifth nor the root of the chord are necessary; indeed these may be dropped (and possibly supplied by a bass player, but not necessarily). But in order to convey function and quality most effectively, the essential tones are typically arranged in the lower register of the voicing, with extension tones higher up.

The third staff of figure 4.2b distills the optional diatonic tones, which may be used without diluting function or quality, and the fourth staff shows how the tonic note (D) and the fourth scale step (G) are carefully avoided in the dominant and tonic chords, respectively, so as not to carry them over from the chords that precede them, which would impede the ii–V–I motion (see dashed arrows).

Outside the diatonic pitch collection remain five tones completing the chromatic aggregate, which can provide rich "upper structures" to voicings. In some cases these work against important diatonic intervals; for example, using a G♯ with the Em7 chord could obscure the minor third between E and G; using it with the A7 chord would weaken the C♯/G tritone. But with the DM7 it sounds all right because its diatonic "shadow," G, is already avoided. Figure 4.3 sketches the effect of chromaticism in each chordal context.

All optional diatonic and chromatic tones may be withheld or used, and they may be spaced from low to high in limitless ways. Attention is paid to the choice of lowest pitch, the registers of all others, thickness (number of notes played at once), and the use of some pitches in more than one octave doubling. This topic is discussed later in reference to specific instances in short excerpts by pianists Bill Evans and Oscar Peterson (figures 4.4a and b), and also at length in relation to Monk.

Chord Substitution, Insertion, and Deletion

Because every dominant-quality seventh chord shares its tritone with the dominant-quality seventh chord whose root is a tritone away, the chords in each such pair may be *substituted* for one another (figure 4.2c, first staff).

Figure 4.2b.   Chord extensions: ii–V–I in D major (see also figure 4.3).

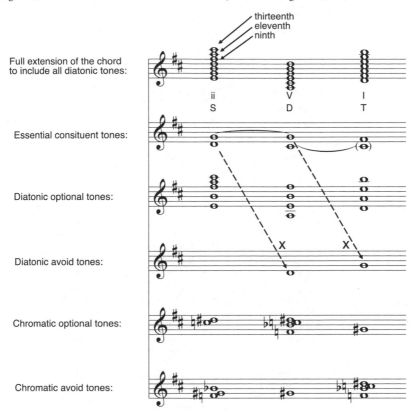

Figure 4.2c.   Substitution.

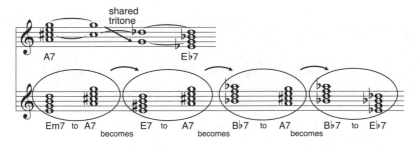

Substitutions for V are idiomatic in ii–V–I motion. In D major, this turns
Em7–A7–DM7 into Em7–Eb7–DM7 and causes the roots to descend chro-
matically by half step rather than by fifth, an especially characteristic marker
of modern jazz sound. The second staff of figure 4.2c illustrates another kind
of substitution, involving change of chord quality. In the first stage, the ii of

Chords:		
E minor 7th (ii: subdominant)	A dominant 7th (V: dominant)	D major 7th (I: tonic)
Diatonic tones:		
D	7th: **essential**	11th(=root of I): **avoid**	root: optional
E	root: optional	5th: optional	9th: optional
F#	9th: optional	13th: optional	3rd: **essential**
G	3rd: **essential**	7th: **essential**	11th(=7th of V): **avoid**
A	11th: optional	root: optional	5th: optional
B	5th: optional	9th: optional	13th: optional
C#	3th: optional	3rd: **essential**	7th: optional
Chromatic tones:		
D#/E♭	OK as D#(#7) if 7 is absent; **avoid** as flatted root (E♭)	Optional as #11th (D#) or ♭5 (E♭); esp. since 11th (D) is absent	**avoid** as sharp root (D#) or ♭9 (E♭)
E#/F	**avoid** as #root (E#) or ♭9 (F♭)	Optional as #5th (E#) or ♭13th (F): do not clash with 5th/13th	**avoid** due to clash with essential diatonic 3rd
G#/A♭	Strong tendency to be heard as major 3rd (G#): **avoid**	Strong tendency to be heard as major 7th (G#): **avoid**	Optional as #11th, esp. since 11th (G) is absent
A#/B♭	♭5th: **avoid**	Strong tendency to be heard as ♭9th (B♭); use only if 9th is absent	**avoid** due to clash
B#/C	#5th/♭13th: do not clash with 5th/13th	Strong tendency to be heard as #9th (B#); use only if 9th is absent	Strong tendency to be heard as minor 7th (C): **avoid**

Figure 4.3. Essential, optional, and avoid tones in chord extensions.

the ii–V–I progression is intensified by raising its third from G to G#. This makes it E7, a dominant seventh chord, that is, V7 in relation to the A7 chord, and thus "tonicizes" the root of A7 as if A were momentarily the home key. From here it is a matter of applying the tritone substitution principle just discussed to convert the pair of chords into progression from B♭7 to E♭7. Monk does just this in *ISC* (figures 4.1 and 4.5, mm. 15–16).

Harmonic rhythm is the rate at which harmonies change. A scan of the various versions of *ISC* in figure 4.1 shows chords changing usually every two or four beats, though Oscar Peterson achieves special intensity in mm. 1–2 by changing on each beat, and there are scattered instances of chords held longer. Since harmony's depth of field is rich, even with these severe constraints on harmonic rhythm there can be infinite ways to realize the harmonies in a song and suggest unexpected aural routes through it.

Sometimes root progressions by fifth are concatenated, as in figure 4.1, staff 2, mm. 2–3. Here, rather than have mm. 3–4 be a repetition of mm. 1–2, as it is in Monk's version (staff 3), the ii chord of m. 3 is treated as a local tonic and preceded by its own ii–V. The two new bass tones F# and B are part of the D major scale, so the motion feels activated but the connections do not jar. The major third (D#) of the B7 chord is the only chromatic alteration implied. In Bill Evans's version, the bass player faithfully provides the root tones (figure 4.4b), but Evans does not reflect the change on the piano. Without the D#, the feeling of tonicization is absent and we have labeled the chord as Bm7.

Earlier we mentioned a more deeply hued insertion, at mm. 8 and 24, which introduces a ii–V (Gm7 to C7) progression borrowed from F major, a key built on a tonic foreign to the D major scale. This motion is so distinctive that it might be heard as one of the strongest markers of the song as a whole. In the *fake book* version, after slipping momentarily toward F in this way the music slips right back to DM7 in m. 9. Monk, however, reinterprets the C7 as a tritone substitution for an F#7, and resolves in m. 9 to Bm7 (the *fake book* does this too, but later, at the parallel moment in mm. 25). Another insertion in the *fake book* version, reflecting a mix of diatonic and chromatic moves, comes at the final measures (31–2). This characteristic "turnaround" revs up the motion, propelling the music toward the next repetition of the form. Monk's seeming extension of this passage and the two prior measures reflect a musical action we shall describe later; in figure 4.1 we condense his chords into the thirty-two-measure form (the actual measure numbers corresponding to mm. 29–38 of the transcription in figure 4.5 are shown below the lowest staff).

Deletions put the brakes on chord progression. In this idiom they are somewhat rarer than insertions but noteworthy for that reason. When Monk slows down the *fake book* chords at m. 2 he wants to focus on the very repetition of the chord progression in the initial two pairs of measures, and when he does it again at mm. 15–16 it is as if we are asked to savor the tritone substitutions selected for those moments. Modern jazz harmonic practice often seems to be founded on the intensification and complexifying of its diatonic basis in the several ways we have just described all at once—so the instances in which this process is slowed or impeded provide a special repose.[12]

12. Harmonic complexity increased in jazz through the 1950s until John Coltrane, Miles Davis, and other notable players introduced forms of relatively immobile (harmonically speaking) so-called modal jazz, in which chord changes were drastically curtailed and sometimes abandoned.

Rhythm and Pianism

Rhythm

The rhythmic traits for which jazz is known and at which it excels—groove, swing, speed, heat, cool, polyrhythm, conversational interaction among players, dense and irregular improvised motives and phrases, antiphonal call and response, and more—are all but absent in *ISC*. Most modern jazz group performance emphasizes strict periodicity with terrific forward momentum created by players' rhythmically propulsive contributions. Formidable mastery, poise, and virtuosity are needed to play. Tempi are characteristically either fast enough to scare off would-be pretenders, or, just as daringly, cooled off to an unruffled "ballad" speed, and steady in either case. The metric backbone is the succession of harmonies with the beat usually actualized and propelled by the walking quarter notes of the bass and the drums' "ride" cymbal. Though harmonies change on measure downbeats and sometimes middles, the beats in between—beats 2 and 4 in a four-beat measure—are stressed to create a driving backbeat.

Solo performances and recordings are almost exclusively the provenance of pianists, who could use the left hand to simulate the roles of the rhythm section, with either walking bass lines or the evocation of earlier styles such as stride or boogie-woogie. Monk himself made extensive use of these latter techniques on his own solo records, as well as on the unaccompanied numbers that were generally included in his live sets. Solo performers such as Art Tatum would also "extemporize," straying from steady time in introductions, quasi-cadenzas, and so on. For Monk, though, a solo ballad like *ISC* was an opportunity to stretch time in a far more radical manner, eschewing steady time almost completely.

Swing, an idiomatic variation of the timing of the subdivided beat, depends on underlying regularity. It involves a dynamic relationship between measured periodicity and the realm of unmeasured music, a rhythmic freedom that can be implied through soloists' styles. This dynamism in turn references a melodic vernacular—the sense that a soloist is "speaking through their horn." Some would argue that this has to do with the lyricism of the human voice, others that it represents some kind of middle ground between a discursive, rhetorical European way of making music and a more interactive, polyrhythmic African approach. Others might say that both are true or that it simply feels good, and that, having been discovered and developed at the turn of the twentieth century, it proved irresistible.

Monk's *ISC* can be said to swing only in the colloquial sense of being compellingly musical, that is, simply because he is saying something in a distinctive way. But strictly understood, swing can exist only against a conception of steady time, and in this recording nothing keeps time. Except fleetingly in a few spots, it is impossible to move the body in any regular pulsation to Monk's playing. He is clearly not keeping steady time internally—or else he has a very different clock. If we listen intently for the regularity most bodies crave—and which we expect from familiarity with more standard versions of the song—we must jolt in and out of time with him. The slow regular beat of the tune's harmonic progression remains impassively present, a law both obeyed and mocked. Monk often played solo ballads in this manner, a meditation with outbursts, with an affect both reverent and ironic. In live performance with a group, this number would be surrounded by tunes that swung hard. In other words *ISC*'s rubato is heard—and is meant to be heard—in terms of the *absence* of jazz's most authentic rhythmic traits, and of Monk's abandonment of them in the service of other qualities.

Pianism

One of the most ergonomic inventions in human history (Gelernter 1999: 132), the piano and its eighty-eight-key action are among jazz's essential European legacies. Its technology has empowered musical cultures as distant as Burmese and African American to adapt it to their own idioms, extending out from the panoply of European approaches to the instrument on completely unforeseen trajectories. Jazz piano's trajectories crisscross and meld into a great tradition of their own.

No one gains entrance into the pantheon of jazz pianism without a strongly identifiable voice on the instrument. The differences among pianists are bread and butter to jazz lovers, from earlier era virtuosi like Jelly Roll Morton, James P. Johnson, Fats Waller, Earl Hines, and Art Tatum through beboppers like Bud Powell and Mary Lou Williams and on to a diversity of post-bop players far too numerous to cite or describe. But, as we have said, even among these names Monk comes in at a different angle due to a tightly bound combination of pianistic idiosyncrasies, harmony, and rhythm. Yet we cannot properly appreciate these elements outside the context of what his peers developed for the instrument.

Keyboard concept, technique, and historical currents conspire to shape pianists' approaches. All pianists have to consider multiple aesthetic issues determining what kinds of textures to favor in developing a style. Individual tunes suggest their own approaches, but players develop idioms that carry over from tune to tune. Voicings can be played with from one to ten fingers—or sometimes, in Monk's case, with flattened palms. Overall motion can be dense or sparse. The hands can be independent or interdependent. One can move freely around the entire keyboard or stay closer to its more conventional, "vocal" center. Nuances of touch, phrasing, and dynamic are essential.

Piano styles also group historically. The "orchestral" ways of playing that developed in jazz's first few decades were strongly influenced by brass band marches and ragtime, and by the fact that before World War II jazz was primarily dance music. Pianists of those years tended to provide a clear beat and full harmonic support. Some, like bandleader Count Basie, favored economy of notes and texture. In contrast, there was nothing in piano technique or harmony that Art Tatum could not execute astonishingly, nor did he hesitate to infuse most everything he played with the encyclopedia of approaches at his disposal, in all kinds of combinations and throughout the entire range of the keyboard.

Bebop was for listening, not dancing, and its speed an excuse for cutting— that is, outplaying and stumping cohorts. The competition nudged piano technique to become lighter, fleeter, and sparser. The walking bass and drums safeguarded the time so pianists needed to do less in that regard, and the bass register was to some degree forsaken. Bud Powell's style often rested on a chassis of insistent, rhythmically irregular, somewhat grating left-hand "shells" (the root of the chord played in the bass register, plus the seventh directly above it). Jutting from below, they cut in under single-line right-hand melodies that looped around the upper two-thirds of the keyboard, equaling Charlie Parker's saxophone lines in their density and irregular phrasing.

In the '50s, jazz cooled off, tributaries of eclectic styles blossomed, and it became necessary to know how to play in many ways. Red Garland could imitate the fast-moving close harmonies of big band saxophone sections in passages featuring thick, parallel, two-handed chords moving with melodic gestures. Wynton Kelly emphasized idiomatic blues riffs. Influences of Cuban and Brazilian styles, and of modern European composition, gradually took root. But in the main, Powell's saxophone-like approach to the right hand prevailed, while in the left hand many developed harmonically richer voicings, deployed somewhat like Powell's shells.

Analysis of Two Peers

Compare figure 4.4's transcriptions of the opening of *I Should Care* as played by Oscar Peterson and Bill Evans, two strikingly different but equally iconic pianists of the time. Peterson, stylistic and technical heir to Tatum, plays solo here with mid-range voicings of up to eight notes, some with left-hand shells, most containing all triad tones and the seventh. As mentioned earlier, he doubles the harmonic rhythm to quarter-note speed, which allows interpolation of tritone substitution dominants preparing the V and the I chords of mm. 1–2. The Eb7 at m. 1, beat 4 is voiced with a pungent #9 in addition to the seventh chord itself. Peterson exploits the hidden presence of an F# major triad within this sonority, playing it with the right hand to separate it from the Eb major triad

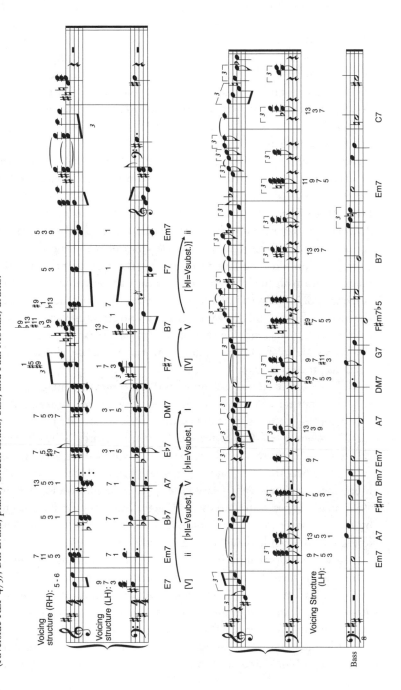

Figure 4.4a. Opening measures of Oscar Peterson's version of *I Should Care* (transposed to D from the original key of B♭). From *Soul-O!* (Prestige PR 7595); Oscar Peterson, solo piano.

Figure 4.4b. Opening measures of Bill Evans's version of *I Should Care* (transposed to D from the original key of C). From *How My Heart Sings!* (Riverside RLP 473); Bill Evans, piano, Chuck Israels, bass, and Paul Motian, drums.

167

he places in the left. The left-hand triad then slides down in parallel motion to the downbeat of m. 2, but in the right the A♯ moves to A while the other tones remain in place. This reveals an F♯ minor triad comprising the third, fifth, and seventh of the DM7. The superpositions of triads and impeccable voice leading of this chord change are of a special richness in this region of the keyboard.

Shooting up in register, the F♯7 chord on the second triplet eighth of m. 2, beat 2 is V of the B7 chord on beat 3, itself an applied V to the Em7 of m. 3. The F♯7 is notable for its ♯9 (A) and the ♯5 (D), which is perhaps there only because Peterson has omitted the fifth of the chord (C♯; see also figure 4.3, middle column and second row under "Chromatic Tones"). On the next beat, where he brings the melody to a local peak, the fifth (F♯) is again omitted, but both thirteenth (G♯) and ♭ thirteenth (G) are included. This B7, voiced with the root as an afterbeat, contains additional extension tones C and F that, combined with the others, conceal G♯ major, F major, C minor, and A diminished triads all at once. This sequence of lavish chords, texturally full and smooth, steady and propelled in rhythm and with a legato touch, give *ISC* sumptuous treatment.

Evans's bass player Chuck Israels provides all of the chord roots in metrically secure positions, so rather than double them or their rhythm, the pianist parries them with the left hand, playing deft off-beat rhythmic punches that converse polyrhythmically with the right hand's intricate embellishment of the melody. Beyond this, however, Evan's chord structures are similar to, albeit thinner than, Peterson's. He remains in the piano's central register, and he is equally fastidious about voice leading: the majority of the chord-to-chord connections proceed by step.

The elegantly contoured right-hand line begins by hugging the original tune, but transforms it completely after m. 4 (while still brushing the original C♮, B, and A in mm. 5–7). Evans sometimes uses melody to enrich the voicings, as when A–F♯–D (thirteenth, ♯eleventh, ninth) is heard over the C7 chord in m. 8. He also gingerly clashes with them by using avoid tones, as with the F♮ (♯7) over the F♯7♭5 in m. 4, or the E♭ similarly related to its Em7 harmony two measures later (see figure 4.3, left column and top row under "Chromatic Tones"). In both cases, though, Evans is careful to promptly lead by step to a more consonant resolution: the former moves up to F♯ at the end of the measure, while the latter goes directly down to D.

As we take up analysis of Monk's *ISC,* we will find that features creating continuity in these two short excerpts—stepwise motion, propulsive rhythm, mid-range voicing, and a consistent level of density and dissonance—are missing. Monk did not by any means invent the notion of favoring discontinuities in these parameters. He did not come from nowhere, and it is well established that his style is part of a lineage extending from before Duke Ellington, through Monk, and on to later figures like avant-gardist Cecil Taylor, not to mention the many who deliberately emulated Monk in recent decades. To hear those connections is a project for another time that would enable a crucial historical and stylistic narrative. But to frame Monk against the prevailing, more conventionally tasteful modern jazz aesthetics illustrated by figure 4.4 is to hear him at his most inimitable and strange.

Monk's ISC: *Analysis*

The dialog between Monk's *ISC,* the tune itself, and other versions like Evans's and Peterson's, is shaped by harmony, touch, texture, register, and time in the form of rubato rhythm. By stressing discontinuity in all of these dimensions, Monk creates an irregular sonic crystal. The sensation of rupture comes from the way the melody is studded with a limited number of irregularly timed events arranged in layers of mobile-like combinations. Bounding and rebounding from event to event, we acutely feel the durations changing between them and can perceive them as if they were suspended in the ether.

The analysis starts with a catalog of the techniques followed by a depiction of the temporality, but first, as suggested earlier, an adjustment must be made to our understanding of the form. There is a large rubato "hidden" in figure 4.5's transcription: mm. 29–38 of figure 4.5, lasting 47 seconds, from 2:13 to 3:00. The rhythms and measures in the transcription suggest the sound, but in this region sound and function are diverging. Part of the passage (mm. 31–34) has three events that occur only here: an improvised-sounding single line in swing rhythm, a swooping five-octave plummet through a whole-tone scale (a trademark gesture), and then a slow rising approach from a bass A (V's root) to the tonic voiced in m. 35. Because of the tritone G–C# at m. 31 (these essential V7 tones are quite low here; more on this below), the plunge to the bass A, and the overall cadenza-like, last-hurrah rhetoric, we understand these four measures as a single stretched-out "measure" of dominant harmony that would (should) fall in the song's thirtieth measure. This assertion derives from the axiom that the thirty-two-measure form is immutable, its harmonies locked in.

Analogously, the Fm7–Em7 progression of mm. 29–30 is a lengthening of Em7's subdominant function, with the Fm7 as an insert.[13] The D# at the end

---

13. One could argue for including m. 29 as the second half of an extended "measure 28," since the melody's D#/Eb properly belongs there. The moment is certainly ambiguous; however, because the inserted Fm7 harmony is syntactically unidiomatic both after the preceding Bb7 and before the following Em7. We elect to speak of an extended "29" because of the textural break after m. 28 (and continuity with m. 30), and the slow arpeggio in m. 28, which has the character of an anacrusis and makes m. 29 feel like an arrival.

of the original melody's m. 28 (see figure 4.1, staff 1) is respelled E♭ and delayed to m. 29, where it is the seventh of the Fm7. Measures 35–38 are equivalent to a two-measure turnaround progression that leads, via tritone substitution of E♭7 for A7, to the DM7 chord at m. 39. The ten notated measures 29–38 thus

Figure 4.5.   *I Should Care*, as performed by Thelonius Monk on April 12 or 16, 1957. Transcribed by Evan Ziporyn.

Figure 4.5.   (Continued)

segment into 2 + 4 + 2 + 2 and can be understood as four-measure group map-
ping to mm. 29–32. The full performance therefore comprises exactly one
thirty-two-bar statement plus an ending tonic harmony. We refer to the four
extended "measures" henceforth as "29," "30," and so on. With durations of 12,
18, 8, and 8 seconds, respectively, they have a glacial average quarter-note tempo
near MM 20. One view of the durational scheme of the whole, with its irregular distribution of events, is given by the proportional transcription shown in
figure 4.6.

Figure 4.6.   Monk's *I Should Care,* transcribed in proportional notation. Each system
lasts about 15 seconds. Accidentals apply only to notes they directly precede. Solid
barlines shown every 8 measures.

Figure 4.6. (Continued)

Techniques and Events in Texture and Harmony.

Some layers of events do promote continuity in *ISC*. The original melody is always present in the uppermost note of Monk's right hand, albeit with occasional octave displacement and with limited embellishments such as minor changes in rhythm or inserted arpeggios. With the sole exception of m. 3, we can identify downbeats in Monk's performance by the attacks of new harmonies that mark the corresponding downbeats in the lead sheet. Save for mm. 1, 11, 15, 16, 17, and the extended "measures" "29," "30," and "31," these are built from shell voicings in which the root plus the seventh immediately above it are the lowest notes heard. These first-beat events track the series of harmonies, and, remembering the tune, we understand the varying times between them to represent equal durations. They ought to help us entrain a meter but do not, due to slow tempo and rubato. Some measures (such as 2 and 4) contain little or nothing more than one of these events, sustained until the next one.

Seen differently, it is because of the rubato that these first-beat moments interact with others to become reference points on the discontinuous soundscape. Monk paints them with many refined techniques that the ear can distinguish and type. They can be understood in terms of how they are shaped by pianism and texture from one perspective, and as voicings from another.

These techniques of pianism and texture are presented below in ascending order of how much discontinuity and contrast they create:

- *Register changes.* Monk plays the melody in parallel octaves emphasizing the tune's sixteen-measure parallel structure at mm. 1–2 and 17–18 (foreshadowed at 15–16) and again nearing the conclusion at mm. 28–"30." (Mm. 17, 28, and "30" are doubly marked with added tremolo.) The registral acme and nadir of the whole song are linked via the whole-tone run later in m. "30."
- *Arpeggios (fast and slow).* Monk inserts this insouciant cocktail piano flourish at mm. 5, 17, 20, 21, and "29." He uses triad and seventh-chord collections except at m. 20, where he pointedly avoids the root and fifth in keeping with the voicing on the first beat of the measure. A slow arpeggio on the single tone B♭ sets the stage for m. "29."
- *Surfacing an inner voice.* Beginning with m. 6 and reemerging in mm. 10, 12, 14, 18, and 22, chromatic lines are brought out during moments of repose in the main melody. Presented first as parallel voicings, the tenor line within them is the most independent, venturing forth alone at mm. 12, 14, and 18.
- *Attack-sustain.* A signature Monkism is to sharply attack a voicing containing a second, tritone, or seventh, and immediately release one or

more tones to leave the rest sustaining. The technique stands out vividly and is closely linked to the voicing of clusters (below). It is first heard at m. 6, where the A–B major ninth stands out, and then at m. 8, where, in the first chord, the sustained G is part of the melody, but in the second chord the sustained Db is an inner voice. In mm. 9 and 11 both tones involved (G and F♯) are part of the melody, whereas in m. 13 both melody and an inner voice tone remain. The sustained A♯ over Bm7 (a ♯7 in a minor seventh chord) at m. 27 spotlights this pivotal dissonant note from the original tune. A series of five attack-sustain chords concludes the performance, beginning at m. "31."

Figure 4.7a illustrates how this technique and the previous one conspire to highlight a special contrapuntal, inner-voice activity. Monk carefully leads the sustained G–Db tritone, introduced one note at a time in m. 8, stepwise down the linear distance of a tritone to the same two tones, inverted and played as a vertical interval in m. 16. We hear the lower of the two voices against *ISC*'s melody in the upper until m. 16's exposed Db, which completes the descent alone just before the melody itself vaults upward. Figure 4.7b is an example of an opposite technique: disjunct, tonally disorienting voice leading. A peculiar "nontonal" descending line, D–A♯–F♯–Eb–B, is brought out from m. "31" to the end; its bass support, D–B–C–Eb–D, is equally odd. Together they endure a series of pouncing attack-sustain chords. Monk is here singling out important prior moments for our reconsideration, frozen in reverse order and decontextualized. The bass is silenced just as the A♯ in the line, and the voicing that introduces it, reconfirm the significance Monk imputes to m. 27; the next event recalls the third beat of m. 8. The last two chords bring back sustained bass for the bII–I cadence, but with crunching voicings new to the performance, and reserved for its austere conclusion.

The following voicing techniques are ordered by increasing density and dissonance:

- *Single tones and silence.* Rare moments are reserved for withholding voicings on downbeats. An unadorned root tone played low on the keyboard is the very first sound we hear, creating a powerful solo bass stratum that returns only at m. 28, on the last beat of m. "30," the "third beat of m. 32," and at the very end. The sequence of these unaccompanied roots, E–Bb–A–Eb–D, supports a ii–V–I progression with two inserted tritone substitutions: an essence of jazz harmony. Measure 3, meanwhile, begins silently. Since mm. 3–4 repeat the chords of mm. 1–2, the silence retrospectively calls attention to the bass tone of m. 1, while throwing us off the scent of rhythmic regularity.
- *Seventh-chord voicings, some with doublings and omissions.* On beats 1 and 3, Monk often uses voicings consisting only of an unadorned

Figure 4.7a.　Linear motion by tritone, mm. 8–16.

Figure 4.7b.　"Nontonal" descending line, mm. "31" to end.

Figure 4.7c.　Derivation of Monk's "whole-tone dominant," and its neutralization of tritone substitution.

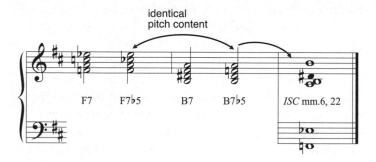

complete seventh chord (mm. 7, 9, 11, 19, 23, 24, "29, beats 1 and 3"). Peterson or Evans might have played these, and their ordinariness gives them a quality of repose. Sometimes Monk omits one or more tones for a stringent sound (mm. 5, 13, 14), and sometimes he omits the third or fifth but doubles the seventh, a biting Monk sonority (mm. 2, 4, 12, 18, 20, 21). The fifth chord in the concluding attack-sustain series omits the seventh of DM7 and adds only the sixth (B).

- *Voicings with avoid tones and other dissonance.* Monk creates special dissonance by including avoid tones, sometimes omitting essential ones simultaneously. The voicing of A7 at the end m. 3 contains the avoid tone D. The motion over the bar line to DM7 is additionally grating because the seventh of the first voicing, G, moves by a tritone to C♯ instead of resolving downward, forming a bare octave C♯ with the melody. The abrasive voicing at m. 8 contains both the seventh (F) and ♯ seventh (F♯) of its minor seventh chord; the latter note rubs up against the root (G). A similar situation obtains at mm. 27, "31, beat 3," and "32, beat 3."

- *Whole-tone voicings.* Monk loved the two whole-tone scales (CDEF♯G♯B♭ and C♯D♯FGAB), and a whole-tone voicing consisting of a dominant seventh chord with a flat fifth. This chord is made up of two tritones a major third apart, and as figure 4.7c shows, when transposed by a tritone the pitch content does not change.[14] With this chord it is not a matter of choosing whether to use V7 or its tritone substitution, for the two are now (enharmonically) equivalent. Measures 6, 10 (beat 3), 15, 16, 22 (minus the A♯), 26, and 28 include voicings like this. But even with this preparation, we are not quite ready for the thick whole-tone voicing at m. "30," with its triple C♯. Though we have identified this region as functionally dominant harmony, when we first hear the voicing it is ambiguous: the G–C♯ tritone is down uncharacteristically low, and there is no root or shell as there is in most other places in *ISC.* Then, when Monk starts swinging the right hand, a lonely solo line suggesting a C♯7 harmony, we feel blindsided. This is a more conceptual kind of dissonance. Suspended in rubato, the irony of this nod to conventional jazz at the most tonally and temporally remote moment makes it the climax of the performance. The ensuing whole-tone run jolts us back to reality— Monk's reality, that is.

14. This is a French augmented sixth chord, whose invariant properties were well exploited by late nineteenth- and early twentieth-century European composers.

• *Tone clusters.* The very first right-hand sound we hear contains a tart cluster of the root, third, seventh, and ninth of the Em7 chord. On the third beat of m. 8, Monk lassoes the root, third, seventh, ♭ ninth, and ♯ ninth of C7, omitting some tones in the parallel return at m. 24.

In all, Monk's voicings range from pure triads (unique to the final two sounds we hear) to plain seventh chords, attack-sustain events, and thornier constellations, all the way to clusters (m. 1). That these extremes are manifest at the opening and closing of the piece makes the point a bit too neatly: this is a constructed, conscious effort, a dissonance continuum that is a dimensional extension of the idea of the chord change itself. He bobs and weaves across this terrain, tracing an unpredictable path. Few composers in *any* idiom roam so widely in so short a span of time between understood areas of consonance and dissonance, developing timbre as a compositional parameter. That Monk manages this movingly in a standard tune is miraculous.

Monk works some of his signature gestures, such as whole-tone runs, into almost every performance of almost every tune. Then there are certain chords or gestures that he clearly associates with specific songs—accessories, if you will—but that he uses in different locations within the performance. The distinctive chords in mm. "31–32," for example, are the *introduction* to his first recording of *ISC,* on his 1947 Blue Note debut.[15] In both cases they are used once and only once, either as coda or introduction; in other words, for Monk these particular chords and voicings are associated exclusively with *ISC,* even though they have little to do with the tune's chord changes. This practice is not necessarily exclusive to Monk, but in combination with the distinctive nature of the gestures themselves, it is a considerable factor in distinguishing his style.

Figure 4.8 illustrates all the aforementioned techniques in two ways: evenly distributed in relation to the thirty-two-measure form, and in a quite different distribution in proportional clock time. Vertical alignments of events are linked to notated beats in the upper matrices and seconds in the lower. In the first pair of matrices, the two representations of mm. 1–16 (0:00 to 1:17) are juxtaposed; the next pair shows mm. 17–32 and the ending. The latter pair of matrices is widened in deference to the extended duration of the passage, though this causes measure width to be different than in the upper pair.

15. *Genius of Modern Music,* Blue Note, 1947.

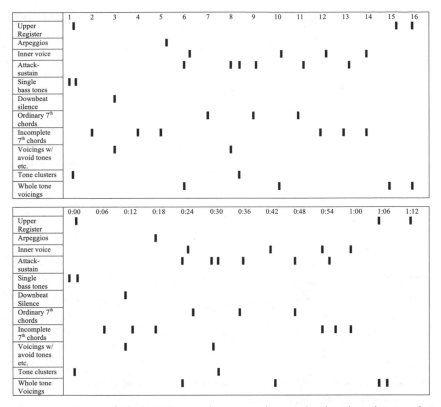

Figure 4.8.　Onsets of Monk's voicings and pianism techniques distributed in relation to the two halves of the form. The top matrix distributes events in measures evenly by measure, the bottom one by clock time. The "climactic" whole-tone voicing in m. "30" is shown as a dot.

Quantified Monk Time

The constantly changing flow in *ISC* is created almost entirely without apparent reference to a coordinating pulsation.[16] The only exceptions appear to be the "swung" moment, and perhaps also the tiny capsule bursts of fast notes released for the arpeggios (but do these begin or end on a beat or elsewhere?). Otherwise, each event exudes its own impulse, enticing us to monitor the length of the intervening silences as much as we follow the sounds. With his

16. In this light, the rhythms shown in figure 4.5 are subjective and rest on educated guesses as to what Monk may have intended to evoke, based on style characteristics—if indeed he had in mind a metric representation or a meter at all. It is not our concern here to rationalize the transcription, but rather to describe some of what it conceals.

	17	18	19	20	21	22	23	24	25	26	27	28	"29"	"30"	"31"	"32"	End
Upper Register	I											I	I	I			
Arpeggios		I		I	I							I		I I			
Inner voice			I			I											
Attack-sustain							I		I	I					I I	I	I
Single bass tones												I		I		I	I
Downbeat silence																	
Ordinary 7th chords			I				I	I						I I			
Incomplete 7th chords		I		I	I												I
Voicings w/avoid tones etc.											I				I	I	
Tone clusters								I									
Whole tone voicings				I		I				I	I			I	•		

	1:18	1:24	1:30	1:36	1:42	1:48	1:54	2:00	2:06	2:12	2:18	2:24	2:30	2:36	2:42	2:48	2:54	3:00	3:05
Upper Register	I									I I									
Arpeggios	I		I	I					I	I	I								
Inner voice		I																	
Attack-sustain				I		I	I								I	I I	I	I	
Single bass tones									I					I			I		I
Downbeat silence																			
Ordinary 7th chords		I		I I					I I										
Incomplete 7th chords	I	I	I																I
Voicings w/avoid tones etc.						I									I	I			
Tone clusters				I															
Whole tone voicings		I I		I		I		•											

Figure 4.8.   (Continued)

unfashionable and disinterested antivirtuosity, Monk's performance is "letting the silence speak" (Solis 2007: 22).

Verification of rubato's pervasiveness can be had from figure 4.9, which charts to the extent possible the arrival time and duration of every beat and measure to the nearest tenth of a second. Where there is no activity near a notated beat, it can in a way be said not to exist. Nevertheless, in such spots we calculate durations by averaging the total duration between the nearest on-beat events. These numbers are preceded with tildes (~), but the beat arrivals themselves are left blank. Where closer-by rhythms make an approximation possible (such as beat 3, before the group of eighth notes in mm. 6 and 22) onsets are notated with tildes as well. The only exception of this type for measure beginnings is the silent onset of m. 3.

The diversity of Monk's durations is impressive, and the warping of steady time is in play from the outset. There is a nearly fourfold difference in the durations of the first two measures (9.1 and 2.4 seconds). Although m. 1's "beats" are of vastly different lengths, they have an average tempo of about MM 26.4. This means the average beat lasts 2273 microseconds, longer than the 1500–2000 ms. extreme of what one can perceive as a regular periodicity (London 2004). As explained, mm. "29–32" bring the end of the song to the downbeat of m. 39, at 3:00. From this we calculate that the average tempo of

Measure #	Beat 1 onset	(beat 1 length)	Beat 2 onset	(beat 2 length)	Beat 3 onset	(beat 3 length)	Beat 4 onset	(beat 4 length)	(Measure Length)
1.	:00	2"	:02	3.6"	:05.6	~2.7"	-		~.8"	9.1"
2.	:09.1	~.6"	-		~.6"	-		~.6"		~.6"	~2.4"
3.	~:11.5	~1"	~:12.5	~1.1"	:13.6	1.4"	:15	.5"	4.0"
4.	:15.5	1"	:16.5	~.93"	-	~.93"	-	~.93"	3.8"
5.	:19.3	~.75"	-	~.75"	:21.8	1.9"	:23.7	.6"	5.0"
6.	:24.3	~1.55"	-	~1.55"	:27.4	~.7"	~:28.1	~.7"	4.5"
7.	:28.8	.9"	:29.7	.8"	:30.5	.8"	:31.3	1.1"	3.6"
8.	:32.4	1"	:33.4	2"	:35.4	~1.6"	-	~1.6"	6.2"
9.	:38.6	.4"	:39.0	1.8"	:40.8	1.5"	:42.3	.6"	4.3"
10.	:42.9	.6"	:43.5	2"	:45.5	~.85"	-	~.85"	4.3"
11.	:47.2	1.8"	:49.0	1.8"	:50.8	~1.25"	-	~1.25"	6.1"
12.	:53.3	~.95"	-	~.95"	:55.2	~.9"	-	~.9"	3.7"
13.	:57.0	1"	:58.0	1.3"	:59.3	~.8"	-	~.8"	4.9"
14.	1:01.9	~.9"	~1:02.8	~1"	1:03.8	.5"	1:04.3	1"	3.4"
15.	1:05.3	.7"	1:06.0	1.7"	1:07.7	1.6"	1:09.3	1.3"	5.3"
16.	1:10.6	1"	1:11.6	2"	1:13.6	2"	1:15.6	1.8"	6.8"
17.	1:17.4	~1.5"	-	~1.5"	1:20.4	2.4"	1:22.8	.5"	5.9"
18.	1:23:3	~1.4"	-	~1.4"	1:26.1	.9"	1:27.0	.6"	4.3"
19.	1:27.6	~.7"	-	~.7"	1:29.0	~.8"	~1:29.8	~.9"	3.1"
20.	1:30.7	.9"	1:31.6	1.6"	1:33.2	~.85"	-	~.85"	4.2"
21.	1:34.9	~1.05"	-	~1.05"	1:37.0	1.5"	1:38.5	.5"	4.1"
22.	1:39.0	~1.45"	-	~1.45"	1:41.9	~.6"	~1:42.5	~.6"	4.1"
23.	1:43.1	.7"	1:43.8	.8"	1:44.6	.8"	1:45.4	.8"	3.1"
24.	1:46.2	1.1"	1:47.3	2.1"	1:49.4	~.65"	-	~.65"	4.5"
25.	1:50.7	3.1"	1:53.8	1.1"	1:54.9	1.1"	1:56.0	1.5"	6.8"
26.	1:57.5	.8"	1:58.3	~1.03"	-	~1.03"	-	~1.03"	3.9"
27.	2:01.4	~.9"	-	~.9"	-	~.9"	2:04.1	1.6"	4.3"
28.	2:05.7	2"	2:07.7	2.4"	2:10.1	.9"	2:11.0	2.6"	7.9"
29. ("29")	2:13.6	~.85"	-	~.85"	2:15.3	~.8"	-	~.8"	3.3"(12")
30.	2:16.9	~1.8"	-	~1.8"	2:20.5	~2.1"	2:22.6	3"	8.7"
31. ("30")	2:25.6	~2.6"	-	~2.6"	2:27.8	.7"	2:28.5	.6"	3.5"(18.4")
32.	2:29.1	.7"	2:29.8	.7"	2:30.5	.7"	2:31.2	1.5"	3.6"
33.	2:32.7	~.7"	-	~.7"	-	~.7"	-	~.7"	2.8"
34.	2:35.5	2.6"	2:38.1	2.8"	2:40.9	.6"	2:41.5	2.5"	8.5"
35. ("31")	2:44.0	~1.27"	-	~1.28"	-	~1.27"	-	~1.28"	5.1"(8.0")
36.	2:49.1	~.72"	-	~.73"	-	~.72"	-	~.73"	2.9"
37. ("32")	2:52.0	~.62"	-	~.63"	-	~.62"	-	~.63"	2.5"(8.0")
38.	2:54.5	~1.37"	-	~1.38"	2:27.2	~1.37"	-	~1.38"	5.5"
39.	3:00.0	~1.8"	-	~1.8"	3:03.6	~.9"	-	~.9"	5.4"
40.	3:05.4		-		-		-		(fade)

Figure 4.9. Durations of individual measures and beats.

the whole is about MM 42.67 (1406 ms.), but, even were this consistent, it too is near the low threshold of our ability to entrain.[17]

Even in the variously distributed measures sharing equal durations (such as mm. 9, 10 18, and 27) beat lengths within them vary widely. This is equally true when the measures are contiguous (mm. 10–11; 21–22) and one might expect some momentum to accrue. Overt long-range contrasts are of course also of great interest, such as the nearly tenfold difference in duration between

17. Note that 32 measures contain 128 beats, and over three minutes this averages to 42.67 beats per minute, or 1.4 seconds (1400 microseconds) per beat. London gives 1500 microseconds as the slowest entrainable pulsation.

mm. 2 and "30," or the more than sevenfold difference between m. 1, beat 2 and m. 17, beat 4. The 6.5-second "beat 1" of m. "30" (i.e., the full duration of the original m. 31) is such a whopper that it doesn't even seem fair to compare it with anything else.

In figure 4.10 we illustrate the relationship between the thirty-two-bar structure and its realization in two ways. The inner circle is subtended thirty-two times to create identical arcs of 11.25 degrees, one for each measure of the song. The outer circle's arcs are generated from the actual durations of Monk's measures, and one can see by comparison how far afield he goes.

Figure 4.10 depicts *ISC* as a cycle. Earlier we defined jazz as typically cyclic but avoided treating it as such in the analysis because Monk plays through the tune only once. Is cyclicity indeed neutralized in this nonrepetitive context? The concluding tonic harmony is different from the subdominant with which

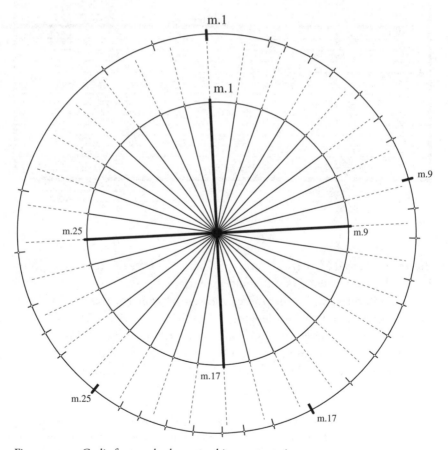

Figure 4.10.   Cyclic form and rubato: graphic representation.

the song begins, which may further weaken any sense of cycle. But in jazz it is normal to play a set of chord changes many times and then conclude with a contrived progression or other figure that may not be there in the original tune, as a way of arresting momentum. We would still stress the cultural understanding that *ISC* is jazz, and therefore it is *supposed to* repeat. The fact that it doesn't is another dimension of Monk's wise irony: it is jazz, yet it isn't; it repeats, yet it doesn't; Monk will play for us, but he knows better than we when to stop (perhaps our chapter should end right here). We maintain that acculturation to jazz is more than sufficient to encourage listeners to step out of time, as it were, and experience a beautiful tension between jazz's norms of steady pulsation and cyclic repetition—which were Monk's cultural referent too—and the through-composed, extreme rubato of this performance. This leads us to assert that *ISC* can be experienced as cyclic, metered, and in free rhythm all at once.

A Note on Monk's Style.

Tracing Monk's approach over his complete career and repertoire, one will hear the same melodies and chord voicings in the same contexts, over and over again. In almost every case, he's "figured out" what to do and simply applies it to each version. Yet his playing *sounds* spontaneous, and this tossed off, vernacular feel contributes to the music's deep empathy and all-too-human charm.[18] Pinning this feeling down to a quantifiable list of attributes or abstracting it to an underlying aesthetic is a large task. It may have something to do with "cool," and perhaps with some notion—to borrow a phrase from a different genre—of "keeping it real." Making it seem loose, even by calculation, is a way of connecting with the listener, reminding us that behind the sound there is a human deciding what notes to strike (hence the hesitations in *ISC*, even when multiple takes reveal that Monk knew exactly what chord he would play next), and risking a wrong note every time he strikes them. We empathize with the feeling of risk and hence take pleasure when he plays the "right wrong notes," which range from deliberate attack-sustain tones to *actual wrong notes*—for without the spontaneous risk of these, a "right wrong note" is just a composed-in dissonance. No better demonstration of this can be imagined than the recently released first take of the Riverside *ISC*, which begins with twelve—twelve!—attempts at an opening arpeggio, all slightly different, all equally "spontaneous" yet calculated, and all unsatisfactory to Monk.

18. One contemporary, of equal stature to Monk, and speaking very much off the record, has gone so far as to say, in private conversation, "Monk and Mingus always wanted their bands to sound under-rehearsed."

There is a doggedness to Monk's *sui generis* formulations—the dissonance continuum and signature gestures—that is hard to wrap one's mind around. How is it possible that Monk could fix on a particular, individuated way of playing a three-minute tune in 1947—distinctive, crystal clear, and packed with formal logic and creativity—and then stick to it for twenty-five years? How did Monk arrive on the scene with such individuality—one can hear the whole-tone scales even on recently unearthed live recordings from the early 1940s—and then maintain it, intact and unchanging, for his entire career? Why do none of his versions change over time? Where did it all come from?

Jazz and World Music, Monk and Personal Musicianship

These unanswerable questions are compounded and enriched by reflecting on jazz as twentieth-century America's underdog in the realms of musical legitimacy and hybridity. For decades its creative development was hidden in plain sight. It occupied a position with respect to Western music's institutions and structures of power analogous to the one that many of the contributions to this book (plus its predecessor and other similar writings) occupy with respect to the practice of music analysis generally. Then things changed. Following decades of exclusion, jazz's ultimate inclusion in the academic canons of musical value let the cat out of the bag in that world, implicitly affirming openness to all music. As jazz led the way, it gradually penetrated the awareness even of musicians who do not practice it, as other world traditions do today. It is a vehicle for the individual's quest for self-realization.[19] Its irreducibly hybrid origins offered a paradigm for viewing any music, if not people and social relations. We now have decades' worth of neo-hybrids involving jazz and other world music, and generations at home in both jazz and other traditions. If jazz and other African-American musics had not long ago made the case for this evolution, would other traditions have been in a position to do so since? Jazz has made us more musical than we thought we could be.

The problems raised by Monk, however, transcend these issues in a way that we can suggest by recounting a transformational moment we shared. In the late '70s, European art music was just beginning to emerge from its postwar hyper-modernist isolation. At that time, Robert Moore, our composition teacher, taught a course called "American Experimentalists," in which he cited Monk and composer Steve Reich in the same breath as in a special category among the most important musicians of the century (to date). Coming from

---

19. Monson (2007: 283–311) explores this theme in depth.

a professor back then, this link struck us as brazenly counter-hegemonic, and also a cosmic truth. He said it was their indifference to traditional virtuosity, combined with intense desire to perform, that *forced* them to be visionaries and use their minds to invent ways to bend the tradition in their directions. There are examples of similar outsider-inspired change in other cultures.[20] It is certainly the case that musicianship with the power to transform is more in the mind and spirit than it is in the hands or throat. And this is both unsettling and inspiring because it deflects back to each listener that necessity of finding a concept, both a general sensibility and a specific idea to be developed, that can define the self and contribute to the world. But Monk had already made that clear to the two of us in sheer sound, from the instant we first heard him.

References

Atkins, E. Taylor. 2001. *Blue Nippon: Authenticating Jazz in Japan.* Durham: Duke University Press.

Benjamin, William. 2006. "Mozart: Piano Concerto No. 17 in G Major, K. 453, Movement 1." In *Analytical Studies in World Music,* ed. Michael Tenzer, 332–376. New York: Oxford University Press.

Berliner, Paul. 1994. *Thinking in Jazz: The Infinite Art of Improvisation.* Chicago: University of Chicago Press.

Blake, Ran. "Monk, Thelonious." In *Grove Music Online. Oxford Music Online,* http://www.oxfordmusiconline.com/subscriber/article/grove/music/18962 (accessed December 2, 2009).

De Veaux, Scott. 1999. "Nice Work If You Can Get It: Thelonious Monk and Popular Song." *Black Music Research Journal* 19(2): 169–186.

Dobbins, Bill. 1984. *The Contemporary Jazz Pianist.* 4 vols. New York: Charles Colin.

Forte, Allen. 1995. *The American Popular Ballad of the Golden Era, 1924–1950.* Princeton, NJ: Princeton University Press.

Gelernter, David. 1999. "Bound To Succeed: Big Hands, Little Hands, and Keyboards." *New York Times Magazine,* April 16.

Hodeir, Andre. [1959, 1962] 2001. "Monk or the Misunderstanding." In *The Thelonious Monk Reader,* ed. Rob van der Bliek, 119–134. New York: Oxford University Press.

20. French composer Hector Berlioz (1803–1869) revolutionized the use of the orchestra but played the guitar, at that time not yet a concert instrument, and was poorly schooled in traditional harmony. "The belief in the clumsiness of his harmony, the naïveté of his counterpoint, and the negligence of his forms has not been dissipated. Few contest his greatness: what is in question is his competence" (Rosen 1984). Gdé Yudane is a Balinese composer who completely and influentially overthrew the norms of contemporary Balinese composition in the 1990s. Unlike his composer peers, he was not primarily a performer and composed through abstract conceptualization rather than intuition derived from fluency with the tradition.

Jones, Andrew. 2001. *Yellow Music*. Durham, NC: Duke University Press.

Larson, Steve. 2008. "Composition versus Improvisation?" *Journal of Music Theory* 49(2): 241–275.

Levine, Mark. 1995. *The Jazz Theory Book*. Petaluma, CA: Sher Music.

London, Justin. 2004. *Hearing in Time: Psychological Aspects of Musical Meter*. New York: Oxford University Press.

Mehegan, John. 1959. *Jazz Improvisation: Tonal and Rhythmic Principles*. Vol. 1. New York: Watson-Guptill.

Monson, Ingrid. 2007. *Freedom Sounds: Civil Rights Call Out to Jazz and Africa*. New York: Oxford University Press.

O'Meally, Robert G., Brent Hayes Edwards, and Farah Jasmine Griffin, eds. 2004. *Uptown Conversation: The New Jazz Studies*. New York: Columbia University Press.

Rosen, Charles. 1984. "Battle Over Berlioz." *New York Review of Books,* April 26.

Ross, Alex. 2007. *And the Rest Is Noise: Listening to the Twentieth Century.* New York: Farrar, Straus and Giroux.

Russell, George. 1959. *The Lydian Chromatic Concept of Tonal Organization for Improvisation*. New York: Concept.

Solis, Gabriel. 2007. *Monk's Music: Thelonious Monk and Jazz History in the Making*. Berkeley: University of California Press.

Spellman, A. B. 1966. *Black Music: Four Lives in the Bebop Business*. New York: Pantheon.

Tenzer, Michael, ed. 2006. *Analytical Studies in World Music*. New York: Oxford University Press.

Williams, Martin. [1970] 2001. "Thelonious Monk: Modern Jazz in Search of Maturity." In *The Thelonious Monk Reader,* ed. Rob van der Bliek, 210–223. New York: Oxford University Press.

Original Recordings

Evans, Bill. May 17, 1962. "I Should Care" on *How My Heart Sings!* (Riverside RLP 473). Bill Evans, piano, Chuck Israels, bass, and Paul Motian, drums.

Monk, Thelonious. April 5, 1957. "I Should Care" on *Thelonious Himself.* (Riverside RLP 12–235). Thelonious Monk, solo piano.

Peterson, Oscar. 1968. "I Should Care" on *Soul-O!* (Prestige PR 7595). Oscar Peterson, solo piano.

CHAPTER 5

Dynamics of Melodic Discourse
in Indian Music

Budhaditya Mukherjee's Ālāp in Rāg Pūriyā-Kalyān

RICHARD WIDDESS

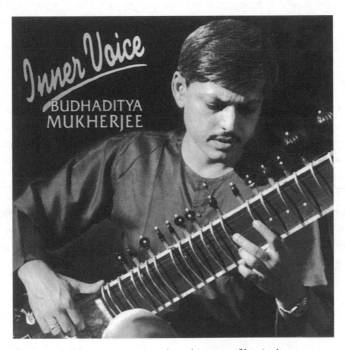

Photo: Budhaditya Mukherjee, as portrayed on the cover of his Audiorec compact disc *Inner Voice*. Reproduced by permission of Audiorec Ltd., London.

1. Introduction

This chapter presents an analysis of a performance of *ālāp,* with reference to the compositional principles that it demonstrates. Following a long succession of ethnomusicological and musicological studies, including Nettl (1974), Lortat-Jacob (1987), Nettl and Russell (1998), Treitler (1974, 2003), Nooshin (2003) and many other contributions, it is clear that compositional principles are no less important in music that is unwritten and "improvised" than in music that is written and "composed"; and that, indeed, one can no longer speak of "improvisation" and "composition" in any oppositional sense. It also seems clear that the importance of compositional principles in unwritten music, such as *ālāp,* is related both to the performer's need to recall memorized material and invent new material that is grammatical, and at the same time to the listener's need to engage with, comprehend, and be stimulated by an auditory experience that happens in real time, whether a written score exists or not, and whether the experience is of a live performance or a recording. In this essay I will consider primarily the listener's perspective; how far the cognitive processes involved in performing and listening to *ālāp* are equivalent remains an open question, but that they are closely related seems likely.

1.1 Ālāp *and* Rāga

The Sanskrit word *ālāpa* signifies speaking to, addressing, hence speech, conversation, or communication (Monier-Williams 1899: 153); it overlaps in meaning with the English word *discourse. Ālāp* in Indian classical music is a process rather than a genre, but it typically occurs in the form of a nonmetrical "improvised" prelude, often quite extended, preceding a composed metrical piece. "Improvised" in this context means that *ālāp* is not normally a fixed, memorized item of repertoire, but rather a technique or style of performance that can be applied to any *rāga. Ālāp* is intimately related to the concept of *rāga,* and in canonical theoretical sources it is explained as a "manifestation" or "making clear" (*prakaṭīkaraṇa*) of the *rāga* (Widdess 1981). Without *rāga,* therefore, there would be no *ālāp.*

Rāga, an elusive but fundamental concept, denotes "passion" or "delight,"[1] and as a musical term refers to the unique aesthetic qualities of a particular

---

1. Not, as so often asserted, "color" in a general sense. The root *rañj,* from which *rāga* derives, connotes *red* color, hence passion (Monier-Williams 1899: 861, 872; Widdess 2006).

melodic configuration. Each such configuration, each *rāga,* has a number of melodic features besides scale structure, which may include strong and weak pitches, transilient and recursive features, melodic motives and formulae, special ornamentations, and distinctive aesthetic qualities (for examples, see Bor 1999, passim). It is the combination of all its features that makes a *rāga* unique, and it is this combination that must be brought out in *ālāp.* [2]

Van der Meer states that *ālāp* "is considered the most complete and sublime method for exposing a *rāga*" (1980: 32). [3] He suggests that *ālāp* is concerned with two "issues": (1) the "melodic and tonal coherence" of the *rāga,* and (2) the unique identity of the *rāga,* that is, its distinctiveness from all other *rāga*s. We may note here that it would require different skills on the part of the listener to appreciate these issues. The "melodic and tonal coherence" of the *rāga* presumably emerges from the current performance, whereas the distinctive identity of the *rāga* implies the listener's awareness of this and other *rāga*s as entities existing outside the current performance. Clearly listeners will vary as to their familiarity with Indian classical music, and therefore in the extent to which they can appreciate the second of these issues.

It is in any case doubtful whether these two issues alone are sufficient criteria for an effective *ālāp* performance. In addition, the materials of the *rāga* must be organized successively, over what is often an extended period of time, in such a way as to engage the listener's attention. Van der Meer states that *ālāp* is "divided into a number of parts, each of which highlights an aspect of the *rāga,* progressing from low to high [register]" (1980: 32). This essentially means that different scale degrees are emphasized in turn, in ascending order. This is the fundamental organizational principle of *ālāp,* known as *vistār* ("expansion").

But Van der Meer makes clear that there can be more differentiation than this between "aspects" of a *rāga.* The example of *ālāp* that he analyzes is a performance of *rāga* Hindol, which he regards as a relatively "straightforward" *rāga,* but he nevertheless observes that, for example, "a slow [glissando] from ma to ga [scale degree 4 to 3] is avoided in the foregoing parts . . . as this [glissando] will become predominant in the next parts." And he continues, "In many other *rāga*s the beauty and aesthetic pleasure derive precisely from a process of hiding and unveiling, of avoiding certain tones only to introduce

2. Studies of ālāp with reference to North Indian classical music include Jairazbhoy 1961; Sorrell and Narayan 1980: 105–109 and 149–152; Van der Meer 1980: 32–42; Widdess 1981; Widdess 1994; Widdess 1995a: 312–367; Powers and Widdess 2001a: 193–194; Sanyal and Widdess 2004: 141–208; Khan and Widdess, forthcoming, and so on.

3. Van der Meer is writing specifically about ālāp in the *dhrupad* vocal style, but the comments quoted apply equally to instrumental performances of the kind to be analyzed here.

them later, or of choosing such patterns that a suggestion of another *rāga* emerges" (1980: 35).

Such statements indicate a dynamic view of *rāga,* according to which different sections of a performance may be characterized by different melodic material. This view runs somewhat counter to, or deeper than, the typical assumption that a *rāga*—often represented as a scale or a simple ascent–descent pattern—remains unchanged throughout any performance as a matter of principle in Indian music. It is true that a change to a different *rāga* would not normally be contemplated in mid-performance, but within a single *rāga* it may be possible to exploit different melodic components or configurations.

Similar ideas have been also expressed by other writers. Jairazbhoy (1971: 73) associates alternative melodic configurations of a *rāga* with the accompanying drone, which always includes at least one other pitch besides 1 (normally 5 or 4), thereby offering the possibility of different tonal orientations. He further notes the use of more than two drone pitches by modern sitārists, an innovation that he attributes to Vilayat Khan (Jairazbhoy 1971: 187–189). Powers (Powers and Widdess 2001b: 840–842) associates different "modal nuclei" of a *rāga* with different stages of *ālāp,* but without linking these to tonal centers. In particular, Powers points to "mixed" *rāga*s, formed by combining particular motives or pitch areas from two or more different *rāga*s, as offering scope for this dynamic structure.

On the other hand, Indian musicians typically assert that every *rāga,* even a composite one, must form an integrated whole, with a distinctive aesthetic identity, and that the display of its separate elements should not compromise its "melodic and tonal coherence." There is thus a potential tension between dynamic and integrated approaches to *rāga* performance.

Van der Meer notes that "an artist in his long hours of practice [may have] done research into a special [particular] *rāga* which allows him to display new aspects of the *rāga*" (1980: 39). I will argue that in the present example, the artist demonstrates a considerable degree of "research" into the rich melodic possibilities afforded by a composite *rāga,* and displays, if not new aspects as such, at least an analytical approach to its performance that exploits the different aspects of the *rāga* in a dynamic way within the *ālāp* framework.

1.2 Analyzing Performance on CD

The CD *Inner Voice* (Budhaditya Mukherjee) was released by Audiorec in 1991 (ACCD 1014).⁴● It features the sitārist Budhaditya Mukherjee, one of the finest exponents of North Indian classical instrumental music, affiliated to the

4. The CD is available from http://www.audiorec.co.uk/.

leading stylistic school (*gharānā*) of sitār playing founded by Imdad Khan (1848–1920).[5] The first 14'23" of track 2, comprising an *ālāp* in *rāga* Pūriyā-Kalyān, forms the subject of this analysis. I became closely acquainted with this CD because I was asked to write the liner notes. Listening with perhaps unusually close attention, I was struck by the formal craftsmanship displayed in this *ālāp*, and by the artist's exploitation of the contrasting melodic materials that combine to make up this "mixed" *rāga*.

But one is immediately faced with a methodological issue in analyzing material of this kind. Ethnomusicologists are accustomed to analyzing musical performances in context. The immediate circumstances of performance and the wider cultural background are seen as inseparable from the sounds of the music: the latter cannot be understood, it is believed, in isolation from their context. But a commercial recording captures only the sounds (apart, perhaps, from a small amount of contextual information provided in the liner notes): the material to be analyzed in this case is thus an almost completely decontextualized artifact. The context of the performance is, in any case, totally separated from the context of listening: the music will be heard in a different context each time the CD is played. There is no possibility of vocal or visual interaction between listeners and performers, as there would be in a live event. On the other hand, the recording is infinitely repeatable, unlike a live performance; it may take on new meanings, for the same or different listeners, at each playing.

Here therefore I pose this twofold question: from the point of view of the listener to the recording,[6] how is the *ālāp* discourse audibly structured, and what part in this process is played by the manipulation of contrasting aspects of the *rāga*? Admittedly we cannot predict the experience of any given listener on any given occasion, but we can at least ask, what kind of musical experience does the performance afford, through the medium of sound alone?

Huron (2006: 231, 235) has drawn some basic distinctions among the kinds of musical expectations that listeners to any music might have, as follows (I have changed the order of presentation for convenience):

---

5. Dates from Parikh 2007. According to information given on his website, Budhaditya Mukherjee learned sitār from his father, Bimalendu Mukherjee (1925–?), who studied with Imdad Khan's son Inayat Hussein Khan (1894–1938), father of the world-famous sitārists Vilayat and Imrat Khan, and with three of Inayat's senior disciples. Bimalendu also studied with a number of instrumental and vocal teachers from other traditions. See http://www.budhaditya.com/.

6. I am perhaps rather artificially imagining a listener who has not read the CD liner notes, written by myself, which briefly prefigure some of the content of this study.

1. *Unconscious expectations*
   a. *Veridical* expectations: expectations based on long-term memories of musical patterns, arising from "repeated exposure to a single episode, token or work." For example, hearing the start of a well-known melody may arouse veridical expectations that it will continue in the familiar way.
   b. *Schematic* expectations: expectations based on the conventional patterns and structures of the musical style, absorbed into long-term memory through repeated exposure to that style. In Indian music, for example, one might expect the overall pitch of the melody in *ālāp* to rise, tempo in metrical contexts to increase, the scale to remain constant throughout the performance of one *rāga,* the *sthāyī* to be repeated after the *antarā* section of a composition, and so on.
   c. *Dynamic* expectations: expectations based on the perception of patterns emerging as the music unfolds, inferences that are "updated in real time, especially during exposure to a novel auditory experience such as hearing a work for the first time." For example, the repetition of a pitch or phrase may induce expectation of further recurrences of the same pitch or phrase.
2. *Conscious expectations*
   Expectations based on explicit, consciously accessible knowledge acquired through training or experience. They might be triggered by, for example, the performer's announcement (or the CD track listing) specifying the *rāga* to be played, arousing the expectation of a particular aesthetic mood or melodic features; or by the performer's identity as a member of a particular stylistic lineage, implying to the knowledgeable listener that he/she will display particular techniques of sound production or other stylistic preferences.

Helpful as this categorization undoubtedly is, there is inevitably overlap among its categories. Expectations that are fully conscious for some, based on explicit knowledge of music theory, may be unconscious for others, on the basis of prior direct experience. The unacculturated listener may be able to infer dynamically, even consciously, patterns that are engrained but unconscious schemas for an acculturated listener. Patterns that are unique to the performance, and therefore only inferable dynamically, may be schematic in structure.

Empirical research in this area with reference to Indian music has hardly begun. Nevertheless we may speculate that in an oral musical tradition that does not emphasize fixed compositions so much as partly improvised performances that are different each time, veridical expectations—knowing exactly what comes next—will be less important than schematic expectations—knowing what is likely to come next. Similarly, given that the experience of a live performance of Indian music effectively amounts to "hearing a work for the first time" (since different performances of a *rāga* even by the same artist are likely to be different to some extent), we may assume that dynamic expectations—inferring what is about to follow from what has just been heard—play an important role in the auditory experience. Listening to *ālāp* would seem to require a combination of schematic and dynamic expectations, the former drawing on long-term memories of other *ālāp* performances, the latter based on short-term memories of the performance itself. Only in the case of listening to a recording would veridical expectations be likely to form, if one listened to the recording so frequently as to memorize parts of the performance.

With these distinctions in mind, empirically untested for Indian music though they are, I propose to analyze three aspects of the chosen performance. First, a "close reading" of the opening two and a half minutes, to see how the performer engages the unknown, unseen future listener in the process of discourse; secondly, a "top-down" overview of the whole *ālāp*, tracing broad processes of change; and finally, a closer examination of selected passages that illustrate the interaction of small- and large-scale patterns.

My division of the *ālāp* into segments—phrases, phrase groups, and sections—in this analysis is heuristic. It seems intuitively clear that the melody proceeds in phrases, and that phrases cluster into phrase groups separated by distinctly perceptible changes—for example, the introduction of a previously unheard pitch. My division and numbering of phrases and phrase groups reflects my perception of such changes; some phrase groups are clustered into larger units, introducing a further layer of hierarchical organization.

The first two notation examples show a detailed pitched and rhythmic transcription in which pitch events are mapped against a time scale. In subsequent examples I show only a melodic outline, without precise rhythmic indications and with reduced melodic detail, in order to show synoptically the relationship of successive phrases to each other and to an underlying contour schema. In all cases, timings are included to enable the reader to refer to the original recording, either on the CD or on the website associated with this book.

I will refer frequently to the widely used concept of cognitive schemas. These are a type of memory structure, a template in which cognitive categories are arrayed in a specific sequential order or other spatial relationship (Snyder 2000: 95–103): a "mental preconception of the habitual course of events" (Huron 2006: 419; see also 203ff., and passim). Cognitive schemas are believed to play an important part in our perception of the world and our ability to interact with it or communicate about it (D'Andrade 1995; Lakoff 1987; Slingerland 2008: 162–166). Similar cognitive structures have frequently been posited in music analysis, especially of orally generated melody (e.g., Treitler 1974; Widdess 1995b: 320ff.), and in studies of oral poetry (Rubin 1995: 21–37). I will refer to two types of schema: a pitch schema, which encapsulates the static, quasi-spatial, hierarchical relationships among a group of defined pitches (such as a scale); and a contour schema, which is a temporal sequence of pitches, stated repeatedly with embellishment and variation.

2. The Ālāp Begins

2.1 The Introduction

The recording begins with a short introduction, the function of which is partly to establish a basic pitch schema (figure 5.1). We hear first (00:00) the drone lute *tambūrā*, the open strings of which are gently plucked in rotation to provide an almost continuous background drone throughout the performance. Two of the strings are tuned to the tonic (approximately C♯, transposed to C in the examples below), one to the octave below, and one to a semitone below the tonic. In the relative-pitch cipher notation for scale degrees that I will use in the text of this essay, with a subscript dot denoting the lowest and a prime the highest of three octaves respectively, we hear: 7 1 1 1, repeated continuously.

The sitārist then enters above the *tambūrā* drone. Before introducing any melodic content, he sounds the various drone strings (*cikārī*) of the sitār, tuned to the tonic (1) at three different octave levels, and to 3 and 5 in the lower octave. In addition, he sounds in descending succession the sympathetic strings (*tarab*), which are tuned to the scale of the chosen *rāga;* these are not normally plucked during the performance, but sound by sympathetic resonance in response to notes played on the melody strings. Adding these to the *tambūrā* drone, and collapsing the various octaves into one, we can represent the pitch schema articulated here (following a method adapted from Lerdahl 2001: 47) as shown in figure 5.2.

Figure 5.1.   Introduction to the *ālāp*.

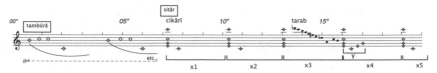

Level a:	1									1		*cikārī, tambūrā*
Level b:	1			3			5				7	1	*cikārī, tambūrā*
Level c:	1	♭2			3		♯4	5		6		7	1	*tarab*
Level d:	1	♭2	[2	♭3]	3	[4]	♯4	5	[♭6]	6	[♭7]	7	1	[theory]

Figure 5.2.   Pitch schema I.

Figure 5.2 means that in this performance, the octave is divided into seven unequal steps (level c). These can be mapped onto a general scale (level d) of twelve, notionally equally spaced loci (*svarasthān*), represented in Indian notation systems as the theoretical basis of all *rāga*s. Microtonal differences that may arise between the same locus as rendered in different phrases, performances or *rāga*s need not concern us here. The intertonal pitch space between the steps of level c is heard in oscillations and glides produced by deflecting the vibrating string at the fret, but it cannot be measured in terms of fixed microtonal increments. In cognitive terms, there are seven pitch-class categories in this pitch schema, and the intervening pitch continuum is heard as nuance (Snyder 2000: 85). As a matter of principle in Indian classical music, no pitch-class category foreign to the *rāga,* that is, none of the bracketed scale degrees on level d, may be explicitly articulated.

Level b shows that four of the seven scalar degrees are highlighted by the drone strings of the sitār and *tambūrā*; and of these, the tonic (1) is reinforced still further by additional strings at different octaves (level a). Levels a–c constitute the hierarchically structured pitch schema within which the entire *ālāp* performance will be heard. We will refer to it as pitch schema I.

However, figure 5.2 is not a complete representation of the pitch domain of this performance. Levels a and b will be almost continuously audible; their constant sounding by the sitārist and *tambūrā*-player make them a permanent frame of reference for the listener. But those pitch classes of level c that do not appear on levels a and b will be heard only intermittently, in the melody itself. The melody can promote shifts of emphasis among level c pitches, and even among those at the higher levels, thereby suggesting alternative pitch relationships without introducing any additional pitches. Such alternatives will become extremely important as the *ālāp* unfolds: in effect, a kind of bimodality emerges.

An acculturated listener might consciously recognize the configuration at level c as the scale known as Mārvā ṭhāṭ. Several important *rāga*s are associated with this scale, but most of them omit pitch 5. The inclusion of this degree in the sitār's sympathetic strings, which are tuned to the actual pitches required by the selected *rāga*,[7] strongly implies that the *rāga* will be Pūriyā-Kalyān, the only well-known *rāga* that employs all seven degrees of the Mārvā ṭhāṭ scale. The sounding of the sympathetic strings at the beginning of the performance, evoking a pitch schema corresponding to a known scale type and *rāga,* might therefore arouse very specific, conscious expectations in the expert listener.[8]

The introduction (figure 5.1) may also establish, or at least suggest, a structuring of time. The sitārist's five plucks of the drone strings (marked x1–x5 in figure 5.1) are sufficiently equidistant to suggest the possibility of a metrical unit, approximately 3 seconds in duration; but 3 seconds is at the upper limit of short-term memory's ability to judge duration (Snyder 2000: 162), so the degree of regularity is hard to estimate.[9] Intermediate plucks on the strings tuned to 1, 3 and 5 (at y) suggest a subdivision of the x4 unit into eight roughly equal durational values, but only the first three subdivisions are expressed, and this subdivision is not subsequently confirmed. The other plucks in x1, x2, and x3 are highly ambiguous as to regularity. In the following, melodic sections, there are again suggestions of a quasi-metrical unit of around 3 sec or its binary subdivisions, but these are again ambiguous. Although the performer may have perceived a regular pulse while playing, and some listeners may intuitively be able to reconstruct it, it is not explicit in the data. Probably most listeners will compare each duration only with preceding durations, not with any perceived constant unit of duration (Snyder 2000: 189ff.). For this reason, and because our interest here is in melodic rather than rhythmic procedures, we will not attempt to define the rhythm in terms of an inherent pulse.[10]

2.2 Opening the Rāga: *Phrase Groups A1–A6*

Figure 5.3 shows the beginning of the sitārist's improvised melody (00:21–2:29), comprising phrase groups A1 and A2. The notation maps musical events against a time scale: each tick bar line marks one second, and each line of

7. Pitch 5 can be included in drone tunings even when missing from the rāga, although normal practice today would favor replacing it by a different pitch that is present in the rāga.

8. The artist plucks the *tarab* strings in descending scale order, except for the last four, which he plays in the order b2'–6–1'–7 (followed by 1 in the *cikārī*). This melodic fragment may also be intended to indicate the rāga: it foreshadows the first phrase played on the melody strings, beginning 6–1–7–b2.

9. The durations x1–x5 are in fact not quite equal, but respectively: 3.0, 2.9, 2.9, 3.0, and 2.7 seconds.

10. The issue of rhythmic perception in ālāp has been addressed in Widdess 1994, 1995a, Sanyal and Widdess 2004, and Widdess 2005.

Figure 5.3.   Phrase groups A1 and A2.

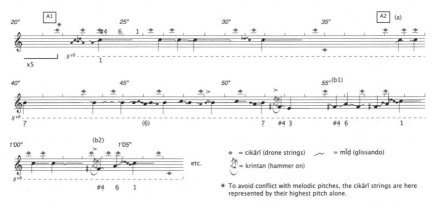

notation represents 20 seconds. The notation distinguishes prominent melodic pitches from more transitory ones with larger and smaller note heads, respectively. The most prominent pitches are represented as quarter notes, but this symbol has no durational implications. Where several pitches are played in *mīḍ* (glissando, produced by pulling the string) after a single pluck, the inflections of pitch are shown as glide lines between pitch symbols.[11]

The artist's opening melodic gesture (phrase group A1, 00:22–00:35) is to reiterate the tonic (1), established in the introduction. It is normally considered important that the *rāga* should be identifiable within the first few phrases of an *ālāp,* so A1 begins to explore intervallic relations surrounding the tonic, embellishing the tonic with *mīḍs* tracing the circuitous path 6–1–7–♭2–6 6–1. Reiteration of 1 is again embellished by ♭2 before the end of the phrase group (followed by a pause for plucking of high and low drone strings).

Phrase group A2 (00:38–01:07, figure 5.3) is longer and more complex than A1, comprising two distinct phrases, moving away from and returning to the tonic, respectively (the second phrase is repeated). Phrase (a) begins with a step down from 1 to the adjacent 7, which is then reiterated five times at irregular time intervals. Between these reiterations, *mīḍs* explore the surrounding pitches, 6 and 1, always returning to 7. Eventually the melody leaps from 7 to ♯4, coming to rest on a prolonged 3. In this descent 5 is heard, if one notices it at all, only as a momentary passing note (*kaṇ*) immediately preceding and following ♯4.[12]

11. For a comparison of this method of notation with a spectrogram, see Sanyal and Widdess 2004: 330–345.

12. The notes 6 and 5 are not plucked with the right hand here, but played by "hammering on/pulling off" with the left hand fingers (*krintan*); they are consequently quieter than the plucked notes.

Pitch Schema I:	1		3		5		7	1
Phrase-group A2:			3	♯4		6	7	1

Figure 5.4. Configuration of pitch space in phrase group A2.

Phrase (b1) returns us to the tonic by a different route. Two convoluted *mīḍs* embellish a sequence of main pitches: ♯4–6–1. Here 5 is again heard only fleetingly in embellishment of ♯4, 7 is relegated to an embellishment of 6, and ♭2 is again a momentary upper leading note to 1. The underlying ♯4–6–1 is even clearer in the repeat of this phrase (b2).

The two phrases of phrase group A2 together trace in outline a descent from 1, via 7 and ♯4 to 3, and a return via ♯4 and 6 to 1. This suggests a configuration of pitch space conflicting with pitch schema I (figure 5.4); we shall have more to say about this alternative configuration shortly.

An acculturated listener hearing only these phrases might conclude that the artist is playing the *rāga* Pūriyā. This is a major *rāga,* suitable for extended *ālāp* treatment because of its serious character. It uses the intervallic structure of the Mārvā scale, but 5 must be omitted.[13] Scale degrees 3 and 7 are strongly emphasized, and ♯4 is also important. In order to avoid confusion with the equally well known *rāga* Mārvā (after which the scale is named), in which 6 and ♭2 are strongly emphasized, these two pitches are treated as weak notes in Pūriyā. To avoid emphasizing 6 in descent, 7 characteristically falls to ♯4, and thence to 3, as we hear in A2(a). The ascending line ♯4–6–1 heard in A2(b) is a typical, though not distinctive, way of approaching 1 from below in Pūriyā; although it briefly foregrounds 6, it moves quickly through this pitch to 1, whereas to include the strong pitch 7 might necessitate some prolongation or elaboration of that pitch before 1 could be reached.

Phrase group A3 (outlined in figure 5.5) repeats and expands the falling–rising contour of A2. But in the course of A3, a new aspect of the *rāga* is revealed. Phrase A3(a) begins in the same way as A2(a), with a step down from 1 to 7, again reiterated five times with *mīḍs* elaborating the small complex of tightly adjacent pitches around 1. This time the phrase resolves through stepwise descending movement 7–6–5—, coming to rest on the pitch that was avoided in A2, 5. The artist underlines the novelty of this gesture by repeating the prolonged 5 and by arpeggiating 1–3–5 in the drone strings of the sitār, as if to remind us that 5 has all along been present in the background pitch schema I. In phrase (b), he further reinforces the 5 by repeating the motive 5–6–7–6–5—: this contextualizes 5 in relation to its upper neighbors and links

---

13. Some allow 5 as a *kaṇ* between 6 and ♯4 in this rāga (N. Magriel, pers. comm.).

Figure 5.5. Phrase group A3.

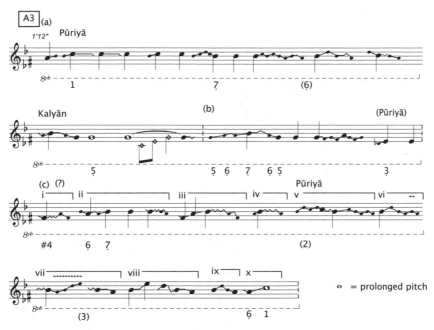

with the emphasis of 7 in the preceding phrase, but it contradicts the impression or "image" (*svarūp*) of Pūriyā presented in A2 and confirms the hint of Pūriyā-Kalyān in the *tarab* scale. The phrase ends with a fall to 3. This completes the downward movement from 1 to 3 in parallel with phrase A2(a), and a touch of ♭2̤ reminds us of the Pūriyā "image" established in A2, which the 5̤ has strikingly disrupted.

Continuing the elaborated parallel with A2, phrase A3(c) returns to 1 by the route ♯4–6̤–1. This time, however, 7 is included between 6̤ and 1, and this is developed into an elaborate excursus; a resolution on 1 may be foreseeable, as a dynamic expectation raised by A2(b1) and (b2), but the resolution is delayed by the excursus. The development here illustrates a process which in an earlier publication I termed "internal scalar expansion," in which a phrase is expanded by inserting material into it that reaches one or more higher pitches before regaining the original conclusion of the phrase (Widdess 1981; see further below). The process is outlined in figure 5.6.

The arrows here indicate how the single pitch 6̤, in the underlying melodic progression ♯4–6̤–1, is elaborated by the cumulative insertion of 7, 1, ♭2, and 3, followed by a corresponding contraction to 6̤. The resulting succession of motives also shows a process of end repetition that Budhaditya Mukherjee often uses in *ālāp*, whereby a succession of motives or phrases all

199

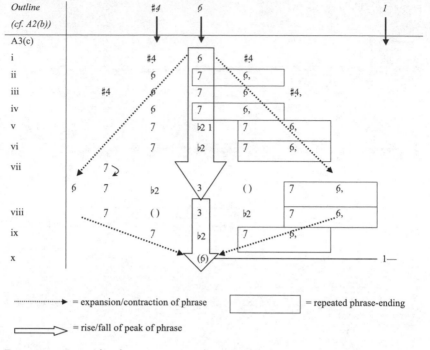

Figure 5.6.   Internal scalar expansion in phrase A3(c).

end with the same sequence of two or more pitches, here: 7 –6 (shown by the boxes in figure 5.6). The effect here is to defer the goal of the phrase (1) repeatedly and with increasing intensity.

A knowledgeable listener would have no difficulty in identifying the *rāga* in phrase group A3 as Pūriyā-Kalyān. As its name suggests, this is a composite *rāga;* it has been described as "a beautiful combination of Pūriyā in the lower tetrachord and Kalyān (or Yaman) in the upper tetrachord" (Bor 1999: 134). Kalyān is the name given to a large group of *rāga*s, and to the basic scale that most of them share:

$$1 \quad 2 \quad 3 \quad \sharp 4 \quad 5 \quad 6 \quad 7 \quad 1'$$

Rāga Pūriyā-Kalyān substitutes Pūriyā's ♭2 for the 2 of the Kalyān scale, and adds the 5 of Kalyān that is missing from Pūriyā (figure 5.7).

As Bor observes, the lower tetrachord of the resulting scale resembles Pūriyā, the upper tetrachord Kalyān. But this tetrachordal division is not watertight: *all* the pitches apart from ♭2 and 5 are common to *both* Pūriyā and Kalyān scales. Furthermore, the combination of *rāga*s involves more than simply scalar material. The best-known representative of the Kalyān group of

Pūriyā:	1	♭2	3	♯4	( )	6	7	1'
Kalyān:	1	2	3	♯4	5	6	7	1'
Pūriyā- Kalyān:	1	♭2	3	♯4	5	6	7	1'

	Pūriyā		Kalyān	

Figure 5.7. *Rāga* Pūriyā-Kalyān as a combination of Pūriyā and Kalyān scales.

*rāga*s is the *rāga* Yaman (sometimes known as Yaman-Kalyān[14]). Pūriyā-Kalyān is usually interpreted as a combination of Pūriyā and Yaman, and Budhaditya Mukherjee clearly follows this view.[15] Pūriyā and Yaman have two features in common besides elements of scale structure:

- In both, 3 and 7 are considered the most emphasized pitches (theoretically termed *vādī* and *samvādī*, respectively). Scale degree 5 in Yaman, and 1 in both, are also important. Adding these together, we arrive at level b of pitch schema I:

$$1 \quad 3 \quad 5 \quad 7 \quad 1'$$

- In both Pūriyā and Yaman, there is a tendency to omit 1 and 5, especially in ascending contexts. Scale degree 5 is permanently omitted in Pūriyā; it is also omitted in many phrases of Yaman, though it invariably returns.[16] The tonic may similarly be omitted in both *rāga*s, and in both it invariably returns. This tendency carries over into the combined *rāga* Pūriyā-Kalyān, and suggests a temporary alternative pitch-hierarchy (figure 5.8). This alternative configuration, which we may call pitch

14. According to some musicians and theorists, Yaman and Yaman-Kalyān are distinct, though closely related, rāgas.

15. Most musicians would probably agree with this interpretation, but not all. A recording of Pūriyā-Kalyān by Kesarbai Kerkar appears to combine Pūriyā with Śuddh Kalyān, and the result is effectively a different rāga from the one played by Budhaditya Mukherjee. The history of Pūriyā-Kalyān is somewhat unclear. Jairazbhoy suggests (1971: 99) that it represents a historical stage in the evolution of Pūriyā from Yaman. Earlier authors Ṭhākur (1962: 91ff) and Bhātkhaṇḍe (1956: 239ff) describe a similar rāga called "Pūrva-Kalyān"; it is not clear how far this equates with modern Pūriyā-Kalyān.

16. See Jairazbhoy 1971: 82ff. for discussion of this phenomenon.

Level a			3				7	
Level b		♭2	3	♯4		6	7	
Level c	1	♭2	3	♯4	5	6	7	1

Figure 5.8.   Pitch schema II.

> schema II, perhaps owes its apparent stability, despite
> its polytonal or dissonant relationship with the drone, to the fact
> that level (b) can be enharmonically understood as an anhemitonic
> pentatonic series.[17]

There is thus scope for a closer integration of the *rāga*s Pūriyā and Yaman than a simple juxtaposition of tetrachords. The two common features— emphasis of 3 and 7, and tendency to omit 1 and 5—link Pūriyā and Yaman into a closer bond than would be the case with entirely unrelated *rāga*s: other things being equal, the group of pitches {3, ♯4, 6, 7, 1} could indicate either *rāga*.[18] Thus phrases A3(c) i–iv, taken out of context, could be interpreted as either Pūriyā or Yaman.

Having introduced the basic elements of the *rāga* Pūriyā-Kalyān in phrase groups A1–3, the artist reverts to the pitch and temporal schemas of the intro- duction, in a formulaic phrase known as *mohrā* ("seal") (A4, figure 5.9). This is by convention distinguished from the remainder of the *ālāp* by rhythmic plucking of the drone strings of the sitār,[19] after which the tonic and sur- rounding pitches are stated on the melody strings. The *mohrā* ends with a *mīḍ* that alludes to the ascent ♯4–6–1, which in combination with ♭2 (taken twice in *mīḍ*) reaffirms Pūriyā.

Further development of the material of A2 and A3 in phrase group A5—a series of six phrases that exploit further the contrasts and ambiguities inherent

17. That is, a scale of five degrees containing three whole-tone intervals, two minor thirds, and no semitones between successive degrees. In Indian terms, 6 here corresponds to the 1 of Bhūpālī. A similar pentatonic schema is characteristic of a number of other rāgas, including Mārvā (where ♭2 and 6 would be projected at level (a) in place of 3 and 7). In Yaman, 2 is substituted for ♭2, but the result is again an anhemitonic pentatonic series (2 = 1 of Bhūpālī).

18. The ascending motive ♯4–6–1' is sometimes used in Yaman as well as in Pūriyā. Cf. Jairazbhoy 1971: 204–205, especially 11. 5–6 of the ālāp notation on p. 205.

19. The isochronous pulsation of the *mohrā* (or *mukhṛā*) may be a temporary mani- festation of an underlying metrical unit that is present throughout the ālāp. See discus- sion of this issue in Sanyal and Widdess 2004: 177–180.

Figure 5.9. *Mohrā.*

in the combined *rāga*—and a second *mohrā* in A6 (03:38) complete the first major section of the *ālāp*, in which the *rāga* is unfolded in the low register of the instrument. Although the conventional requirement to establish the identity of the *rāga* in the opening phrases of the *ālāp* has been fulfilled, the artist has also shown that the *rāga* has two aspects, and has highlighted the contrasts and ambiguities between them, thus creating a dynamic tension that continues throughout the *ālāp*.

3. Vistār *and* Rāga

3.1 Expansion (Vistār)

Figure 5.10 presents an overview of the whole *ālāp*, expressed as a pitch-time graph. The vertical axis represents the pitch dimension of the performance, comprising a total range of two octaves and a sixth, divided into low, middle, and high registers (*saptak*). The internal division of each octave according to pitch schema I is represented with horizontal lines, which are thicker for 1 and 5 (dashed) to aid visual orientation. The horizontal axis represents time, divided into one-minute increments.

Within this spatial and temporal grid is plotted a "pitch-focus line." This shows the most emphasized, or "focal" pitch at each stage of the melody, and the points at which this focal pitch changes. In section A, the focal pitch fluctuates within the low register, but in section B, it rises gradually through the middle octave. In section C, it continues to rise as far as 5 in the upper octave, before falling rapidly to the starting point, 1 in the middle register.

The pitch-focus line was established by making an outline transcription in which prolonged pitches were distinguished; the most prolonged pitch in each phrase group was identified as the focal pitch. The validity of this analysis can be demonstrated either by playing (or singing) the pitch-focus line while listening to the recording at normal speed, or alternatively by playing the recording at fast speed, whereupon the pitch-focus line becomes clearly audible, at least in sections B and C.

In sections B and C, the artist himself draws our attention to most of the focal pitches in turn, by echoing the focal pitch an octave lower (figure 5.11). I

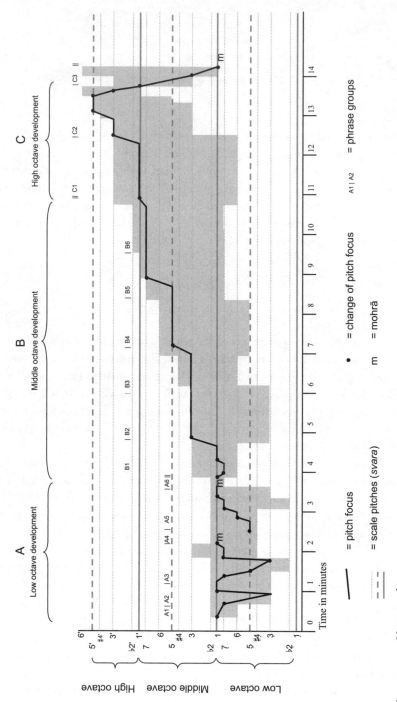

Figure 5.10. *Vistār* in *ālāp*.

Figure 5.11.   Consonant reinforcement in sections B and C.

will call this phenomenon "consonant reinforcement."[20] The lower pitch may be connected with the upper by a glissando, or by consonant leap (perfect fourth or fifth) to a pitch midway (e.g., 3–7–3). The latter may be embellished by a rapid scalar flourish, often involving the *krintan* technique (pitches sounded by hammering on/pulling off with the left-hand fingers). Pitches 3, 5, 7, and in the upper register 3' and 5' are all treated in this way. Pitch ♯4 is evidently not sufficiently stable to be treated with this degree of emphasis. The reasons for avoiding this gesture in connection with 1' will emerge later (p. 218). Meanwhile we may note how this consonant reinforcement evokes pitch schema I when 5 is the focal pitch, or pitch schema II when 3 or 7 is the focal pitch.

In sections B and C, the artist does not develop every degree of the scale of the *rāga* equally: the notes ♭2, ♯4, and 6 do not appear in the pitch-focus line, although they are of course present in the melody. The pitch-focus line thus passes through the following:

20. Although this device of consonant reinforcement seems to be very commonly employed in ālāp, I have never seen or heard it discussed. In vocal dhrupad, it often takes the form of a sweeping glissando, falling an octave and immediately returning.

I 3 5 7 I' 3' 5'

This sequence replicates pitch schema I. It reflects the structure of the *rāga,* in which 3 and 7 are inherently strong pitches, whereas ♭2 and 6 must be de-emphasized in order not to imply the *rāga* Mārvā. Pitch #4 is relatively strong in both Pūriyā and Yaman, and so receives some emphasis in the middle octave, but no consonant reinforcement. 5 is a strong pitch in one of the components of Pūriyā-Kalyān, namely Yaman; just as this pitch appears in the sitār drone strings, it also appears at the midpoint of the *vistār* of the middle octave, and at the highest point of the *vistār* in the high octave, even though at other times it is virtually absent from the melody for long periods.

The shaded area in figure 5.10 indicates the approximate range of the melody. A more precise indication of the pitches used in each phrase group will be found in figure 5.13.

The structure shown by figure 5.10 illustrates a standard procedure for performance of *ālāp* in any North Indian *rāga,* termed *vistār,* "expansion." The melody "expands" through the three octave registers, first the low octave (section A), then the middle (section B), and finally the high octave (section C). The middle octave development is the longest and most gradual. This is the heart of the *ālāp,* invariably present even in the shortest performances,[21] whereas the lower and higher octave developments may be abbreviated or dispensed with in a short performance. The note-by-note *vistār* of the middle octave is the essential part of the *ālāp* and has been a part of performance practice and theory at least since the thirteenth century (Widdess 1981, 1995: 361–367; Sanyal and Widdess 2004: 144–147).

In an earlier publication (Widdess 1981), I suggested that in *ālāp,* "the principle of range expansion operates at the level of individual phrases, as well as in the organisation of the whole." I suggested that a small-scale generative process that I termed "internal scalar expansion" drives the large-scale development of *vistār.* In this process, "a rising and falling phrase is expanded at successive repetitions, by adding higher and higher notes at the apex." We have already seen an example of this process in section A of Budhaditya Mukherjee's *ālāp* (figure 5.6). Figure 5.12 illustrates an abstract model of this process.

---

21. In *khyāl* performances, singers normally only perform a short ālāp, perhaps only a few phrases, before introducing the composition; this short ālāp may not present the complete middle octave. However, after the composition, the ālāp is normally resumed from the point at which it was interrupted, and completed with tablā accompaniment.

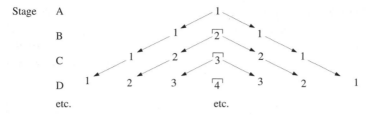

Figure 5.12.   Abstract model of internal scalar expansion.

Here small horizontal brackets mark the introduction of higher pitches in successive stages. In actual melody, the model is modified to take account of the characteristics of the *rāga,* including omitted pitches, differences between ascent and descent, "crooked" (*vakra*) pitch order, and so on. Parts or the whole of each stage may be repeated, with or without variation, or omitted, or divided across successive melodic phrases, in ways that show the artist's inventiveness and sensitivity to the *rāga.* Each stage may be repeated many times, in whole or part, with as much variation in articulation and emphasis as the performer's imagination can produce, before introducing the next stage. Typically, the ascent and peak area of each stage tend to be repeated more frequently and varied more extensively than the descent.

Analysis of Budhaditya Mukherjee's *ālāp* in Pūriyā-Kalyān suggests that the internal scalar expansion process underlies the gradual expansion of range and rise in pitch focus in sections B and C, and can be connected with the relationship of the pitch focus and the phrase group final, the artist's tendency to end successive phrases in the same way, and his separation of contrasting *aṅgs* of the *rāga.* We will discuss these connections with specific examples in section 4.

We might expect the process of *vistār* in *ālāp* to elicit schematic and even conscious expectations, since the process of *vistār* on both the small and the large scale is almost universal in *ālāp.* For the listener unfamiliar with Indian music, the insertion of new material within the phrase might initially come as a surprise, but after some occurrences might also become dynamically expected, as successive insertions tend in the same (rising) direction.

A related expectation, dynamic or schematic, might be that the ascending beginning of a phrase or phrase group will be balanced by a descending conclusion. Ascent in *ālāp* is incomplete, and implies the completion of descent. This idea is supported by the tendency for the descending line of successive phrases to be similar each time, and relatively infrequent, whereas the ascent and peak phases tend to be highly varied, and are often repeated recursively before leading to the descent (see later, figure 5.14). The arrival of the descent is thus another expectation that the artist frequently defers, but when it comes it tends to follow a predictable pattern.

Part of the art of *ālāp* performance consists in both arousing such expectations, and delaying their fulfillment through elaboration of each stage of the process. As Huron notes (2006: 328),

> When a future event is highly probable, listeners experience a strong sense of the inevitability of that outcome—an experience we can call the "feeling of anticipation." Anticipating events leads to changes of attention and arousal whose physiological concomitants are akin to stress . . . A common way to increase the feeling of anticipation (and the accompanying tension) is through *delay*. By delaying the advent of the expected event, the state of anticipation can be sustained and so made more salient for a listener.

In the context of *ālāp*, "highly probable" events include both the ascent to new, higher pitches, normally in mid-phrase, and the corresponding descent to lower ones, normally at the ends of phrases. Delaying the advent of such events may be particularly effective when the absence of a clear metrical framework makes it difficult to predict precisely when an expected event might occur.

3.2 *Phrase Group and* Rāga

Figure 5.10 shows one aspect of the process of this *ālāp* performance, namely, the relationship between pitch focus, pitch space, and time. Figure 5.13 adds further information on this relationship, and enables us to see how the artist articulates the two sides of the *rāga*, in sections B and C of the *ālāp*. The pitch content of each phrase group is shown in successive lines. Focal pitches are shown as whole notes, and the final pitch of each phrase group is marked. The solid arrows indicate changes of pitch focus, whether between phrase groups or within a phrase group, and the dotted ones, changes of phrase group final.

Note that the focal pitch and phrase group final are not always the same pitch. In phrase groups B1–3, pitch 1 remains the final, while the focal pitch rises to 3; this is because the artist returns repeatedly to the tonic at the ends of phrase groups and of many individual phrases. In B4, however, both the focal pitch and the final shift upward to 5. This represents a major structural and aesthetic change: the artist no longer feels the need to return to the tonic, and instead is content to rest on 5. Pitch 5 remains the final in B5, while the pitch focus rises to 7; but in B6, both the pitch focus and the final rise to 1'. In C1 and C2, the pitch focus rises to 3' and 5', but 1' remains the phrase group final

Figure 5.13. Pitch material, pitch focus, phrase-group finals, and *rāga aṅgs*, in phrase–groups B1–C3.

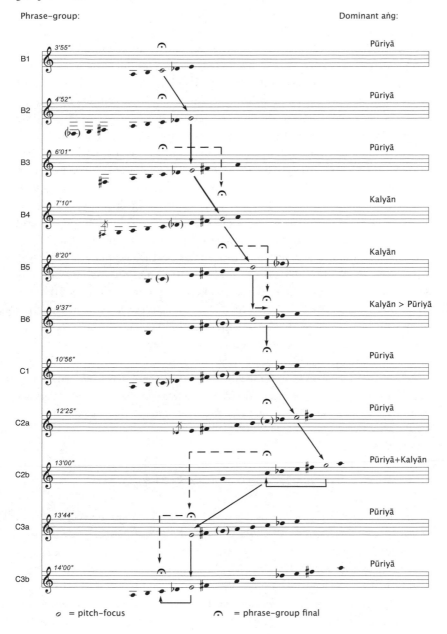

until C3, where it falls to 1. What is striking here is that 1 and 5 are the only pitches that are used as phrase group finals. Pitch 5 thus fulfills an important structural role, equivalent to 1, despite its omission from parts of the melody and from one component of the *rāga*.

We can also read from figure 5.13 the artist's separation and ultimate integration of the two *aṅgs* of the *rāga*. In B1–B3, 5 does not appear, and ♭2 is prominent, because in these phrase groups he plays almost exclusively Pūriyā material. In B4, however, 5 becomes both pitch focus and phrase group final. At the same time, ♭2 almost disappears, because here the artist plays mainly Yaman material. This continues in B5, where the pitch focus rises to 7; but a hint of ♭2' betokens not only the ascent to 1' but also a shift back to Pūriyā. Both occur in B6, where 5 gradually disappears and ♭2' becomes prominent in its place. Pūriyā remains dominant as the high octave development begins in C1–2a; in C2a the omission of 1', a typical feature of Pūriyā, is very striking, although it remains final for this phrase group. In C2b, 5' reappears and becomes the focal pitch; but ♭2' remains in play. Here, for the first time in the *ālāp* since section A, the artist combines Yaman and Pūriyā materials, playing phrases that explicitly include both 5 and ♭2. This is the culmination, not only of the *vistār* process, but also of the analysis and resynthesis of the *rāga* that has taken place in this performance. But the synthesis is short-lived: as the artist returns to the starting point of the *ālāp*—the middle octave 1—in C3, he also returns to Pūriyā. Pitch 5 is reduced once more to the status of a lingering *kaṇ* in C3a, and disappears altogether in C3b.

This overview of *vistār* and *rāga* indicates the overall narrative structure of the performance, but close attention to each phrase group would be necessary to understand in more detail how the artist weaves together the elements of his musical story.

4. The Dynamics of Melodic Discourse

In the light of the preceding overview of the whole *ālāp,* we will consider three extracts that represent key passages in the performance. They demonstrate, respectively: the approach to and arrival at pitch 5, involving a transition from Pūriyā *aṅg* to Kalyān *aṅg;* the approach to pitch 1', involving a transition from Kalyān *aṅg* to Pūriyā *aṅg;* and the development of 5', involving a synthesis of the two *aṅgs*, and concluding descent, in which the synthesis is dissolved again. My analysis here will show in particular how the artist structures each passage by using contour schemas (underlying pitch sequences), thus facilitating comprehension and expectation on the part of the listener.

4.1 Ascent Phase 1: Approaching 5 (Phrase-Groups B3–4)

The first passage to be analyzed begins at 6:01, and constitutes phrase groups B3–4. Immediately before this, the artist has developed the lower part of the middle octave, introducing the pitch 3 and combining it with the lower pitches already introduced in section A. In phrase groups B1–2, he plays almost exclusively Pūriyā material, emphasizing 7 and 3, though not yet ♯4, and avoiding 5 or 5̱.

In phrase group B3, shown in outline in figure 5.14, the pitch focus remains 3, and the final of each phrase remains 1, but higher pitches are also introduced, leading toward the next stage of the *vistār*. Figure 5.14 highlights four features of this passage:

- Each phrase from (a) ii onward follows a contour schema structured as a pair of balancing statements; that is to say, an antecedent–consequent structure. The antecedent ends on the focal pitch (3), the consequent on the phrase group final (1). Each antecedent ascends from the tonic or below to end on 3; after a momentary pause, the consequent descends to the final. In phrases (a) and (c), the antecedent is elaborated by recursion and repetition, whereas in the other phrases, the antecedent leads to the consequent directly. This passage illustrates the technique of improvising a sequence of phrases all ending in the same way.
- In the antecedents, the artist employs internal scalar expansion to introduce the new, higher pitches ♯4 and 6. Pitch ♯4 appears, for the first time in the middle register, in phrase (a) ii. It is important in both Pūriyā and Yaman, but a change to Kalyān *aṅg* is deferred until later. Indeed, the next higher pitch in Pūriyā, 6, is introduced by internal scalar expansion in phrase (c) iv, even though the next higher pitch in the scale of the *rāga*, 5, has not yet arrived. Clearly the artist wishes to maintain the Pūriyā *aṅg*, thereby deferring the rise of the focal pitch to 5, for as long as possible.
- The introduction of ♯4, in phrase (a) ii, allows an important motive of *rāga* Pūriyā to emerge, namely the descending interval ♯4–3; this motive reinforces the pitch focus on 3 and the image of Pūriyā, and is frequently repeated in this phrase group, with particular emphasis in phrase (c). In the consequent of each phrase, this motive is extended downward to the phrase group final: ♯4–3 ♭2–1, again making Pūriyā very apparent.
- From phrase (b) onward, every phrase articulates pitch schema II, resolving onto 1 only at the final pitch of the phrase.

Figure 5.14. Analysis of phrase group B3.

B3 is the last phrase group devoted to the pitch focus on 3, and the introduction of #4 and 6 already suggests impending change. The logic of *vistār*
dictates that the pitch focus must move to the next higher strong pitch
of the *rāga*, 5. But by the beginning of phrase group B4, pitch 5 has been

scrupulously avoided for the past three and a quarter minutes, apart from an occasional fleeting hint in ornamentation of ♯4—hardly enough to disturb the dominance of the Pūriyā *aṅg* from the beginning of section B to this point, except perhaps for a very expert listener. Indeed, the expansion to 6 and the resulting interval ♯4–6–♯4 seems to emphasize the absence of 5. However, 5 has been quietly but persistently present throughout among the *cikārī* drone strings of the sitār. Its arrival in the melody, early in B4, could therefore occasion feelings both of surprise, and of resolution of the extended conflict, over several minutes, between the pitch schema of the melody (pitch schema II) and that of the accompanying drone (pitch schema I).

The artist devotes phrase group B4 to introducing and confirming pitch 5 (figure 5.15). This involves several changes to the melodic discourse:

- The pitch schema changes to that of the Kalyān *aṅg*, stressing 1, 3, and 5 (see figure 5.15, phrase (b)). Pitch ♭2 is either skipped over (7–1–3) or played so lightly as to be almost inaudible (7–[♭2]–3 or [♭2]–1–7–1) in this phrase group.
- The antecedent–consequent structure, so consistent in the previous phrase group, disappears. Despite an initial tendency for 5 to drop back to 1 (phrases (a), (b)), 5 is quickly established as the final pitch of each phrase, approached by ascending lines from 1, 7, 6, or 5. There are no balancing descending phrases returning to 1. Both the pitch focus and the phrase group final have shifted to 5, as we noted earlier (p. 208 and figure 5.13). Pitch 5 has taken over the function of 1 as the pitch on which phrases end.
- Pitch 6, introduced in the previous phrase group, is here reintroduced in phrase (c), and from then on each phrase ends 6–5. This pitch belongs to, and thus connects, both aspects of the *rāga*, but its meaning changes. In B3 it is defined as part of Pūriyā *aṅg*, preceded and followed by ♯4; but in B4 the same pitch becomes part of Kalyān *aṅg*, and instead of ♯4–6–♯4 (leading to 3), we now hear ♯4–6–5. 6–5 is further highlighted in different registers in B4(h), connected by a dramatic rising glissando.

The underlying contour schema in this phrase group, as we have seen, is not articulated as an antecedent–consequent alternation, but as an ascent of variable length and configuration leading to a repeated 6–5 cadence. This change in melodic sentence structure (so to speak) further emphasizes the special significance of phrase group B3, in which the midpoint of the middle octave development has been reached, and the Kalyān *aṅg* has emerged in contrast to the earlier dominant Pūriyā.

Figure 5.15.   Phrase group B4.

4.2 Ascent Phase 2: Approaching 1' (Phrase-Groups B5–6)

Having securely established 5 as both melodic focus and phrase group final in phrase group B4, in B5 (figure 5.16) the artist begins the lengthy ascent of the upper tetrachord of the middle octave; he will not reach the goal of 1' until the very end of B6. This prolonged transition from 7 to 1' is not only due to the tension between a "leading note" and a "tonic," to borrow the Western terms for a superficially similar phenomenon; in this performance it is also because 7 is a pivot between the two *aṅgs*. In effect, the artist creates an ambiguity between two different 7s: one falls through 6 to 5, and evokes Yaman; the other rises by way of b2' to 1', and evokes Pūriyā. At the start of B5, we are in the Kalyān *aṅg*, and the former 7 prevails. By the end of B6, we have returned to Pūriyā *aṅg*, and it is the Pūriyā 7 that finally rises to 1'.[22]

Figure 5.16 analyzes the beginning of this transition in phrase group B5. The whole phrase group is a development of its first phrase, (a), where the sequence 5–6–7–6–5 is the Yaman phrase that was prefigured an octave lower in A3(b) (figure 1.5). This phrase introduces 7 for the first time, at the apex of the rise–fall contour, and this pitch continues to play a pivotal role as the focal pitch in what follows. Pitch sequence 7–6–5 is an unambiguously Yaman cadence on the current phrase group final, 5. So far, the *rāga* "image" has not changed significantly, though the somewhat whimsical ending of the phrase,

---

22. I do not intend to imply that the two 7s are of consistently different pitch. But there may be a significant rise in pitch of 7 from the beginning of B5 to the beginning of C1. (7 at 8:22.8 is approximately C-48 cents; 7 at 11.16 is approximately C-5 cents. Intervening samples are in the range C-22 to C-14. Rise = 53 cents, about half a semitone.)

Figure 5.16. Analysis of phrase group B5.

* = pitch is repeated several times

with a 6–3 glissando, seems to hint at some new departure. This follows in phrases (b) and (c), which develop (a) as a contour schema, summarized at the foot of figure 5.16.

The contour schema consists of an ascent (X) and two alternative descents (Y, Z). Z is the Yaman descent 7–6–5, and it can be heard as a balancing consequent to the ascent in X, coming to rest on the current phrase group final (5) and reaffirming Yaman. Y is an inconclusive answer to X, ending on ♯4 or 3; by leading into another X ascent, Y repeatedly defers the conclusion in Z. In X, the omission of 5 in ascent (typical in either Yaman or Pūriyā) prepares for its reappearance in Z; but at the apex, 7 (expanded to 7–1'–7 from (b) iii onward) can lead to either Y or Z. Most often it leads to Y, where both 6 and 5 are heard only fleeting in rapid descending runs to ♯4. These bring to the fore the sequence 7–♯4 (–3), which hints at Pūriyā (compare 7–♯4–3 in phrase group A2, figure 1.2). In phrase (b), there are seven repetitions of X + Y, in which the omission of 5 and foregrounding of 7–♯4 prepare the ground for Pūriyā to emerge, before X + Z reconfirms Yaman.

In phrase (c), the artist rebuilds the schema in reverse order, starting with Z, before a full statement of X + Y leads to a conclusion with Z. In (c) v, the omission of 5 in both X and Y again prepares for Pūriyā without leaving the domain of Yaman. But in (c) vi, just as 7 begins to fall to 6 and 5 (Z), the artist introduces a momentary ♭2' (twice) that unequivocally hints at Pūriyā (boxed in figure 5.16). If the reader experiences this ♭2, as I do even after repeated hearings, as a shock, almost as if the artist had played a pitch outside the *rāga*, that is a measure of the success with which he has created the impression of Yaman in the preceding phrases (from B4 onward): an impression that the Pūriyā-like tendencies of Y have not sufficiently challenged, in my perception, to induce me to expect the ♭2.[23] The appearance of this ♭2 in the context of the Yaman-affirming 7–6–5 makes it doubly unexpected. This is perhaps the first phrase in the whole of section B in which both 5 and ♭2 are explicitly stated. But the result is not so much a synthesis as an ambivalence, a division of ways, as if the artist is saying: from here we can go *either* 7–♭2–1' *or* 7–6–5, either upward into Pūriyā or down into Yaman. As we move on into phrase group B6, the down-into-Yaman option is abandoned in favor of up-into-Pūriyā, as the *vistār* process demands.

The second stage of the ascent from 5 to 1', accomplished in phrase group B6, features the most impassioned improvisation in this performance. After the confident assertion of 5 in B4, and the poignant fall of 7 to 5 at the end of

---

23. It also suggests that dynamic expectations induced by the preceding phrases are stronger than the veridical expectations that I have acquired as a result of listening repeatedly to the recording.

B5, a sense of greater urgency and instability, presaged by the unexpected ♭2’ at the end of B5, becomes pervasive. The pitch focus on 7 must now rise to 1’; at the same time, Kalyān gives way to Pūriyā. The artist embellishes this double transition with the most varied stylistic palette, using quivering ornamentation, rapid flourishes, insistent repetition of small phrases, consonant leaps, long glissandos, quiet *krintans,* and other devices. His fingers ascend and descend the area of most intense development—between 3 and 7—so rapidly, so many times, and in so many varied ways as to severely challenge analysis. Nevertheless, what allows us to make sense of the artist's turbulent musical thought process here is its underlying logic, broadly outlined in figure 5.17.

As shown on the first two lines of figure 5.17, the phrase group follows a contour schema, of which the first half is repeated before proceeding to the conclusion; the third and fourth lines show how this schema is implemented in the phrase group, with approximate timings of the main junctures. From 7 at the outset, the contour rises to 1’ at the conclusion of the schema. Pitch 7 is emphasized throughout, but a tendency for it to fall to 6 (implying the possibility of returning to 5?) is eventually replaced by its rise to 3’, which falls to 1’. At the same time, emphasis on 3 at the beginning of the schema, articulated very clearly at the outset through consonant leaps 7–3–7, shifts early in the schema to ♯4: the interval ♯4–7 is articulated at several points, as a leap, or filled with ♯4–6–7 or rapid 7–6–5–♯4 in *mīḍ* or *krintan.* This interval becomes increasingly hearable as Pūriyā, as ♭2’ and 3’ are gradually introduced, and 5 is reduced to a passing *kaṇ.*

Figure 5.17. Analysis of phrase group B6.

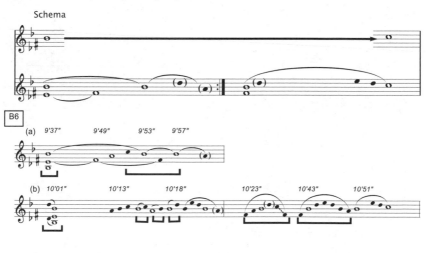

L___J = repeated (with variation)

At the end of this phrase group we have arrived not only at the upper tonic, the final goal of the middle octave *vistār*, but also back in the Pūriyā *aṅg*. As if to drive the point home, the first phrase group of section C (10:56) sweeps down and up the whole of the middle octave stressing pitch schema II, and ends with the characteristic Pūriyā ascent to 1: ♯4–6–1', which we heard an octave lower at the opening of the *ālāp* (see A2, figure 5.3). It is now clear why the artist does not emphasize 1' here, as he does the other strong pitches reached in the *vistār*, by "consonant reinforcement" (figure 5.11). The sequence 1'–5–1–5–1' would negate the transition back to Pūriyā that has been so strenuously achieved.

4.3 Synthesis and Closure (Phrase-Groups C2–3)

Our final examples (figures 5.18–19) represent the denouement of the melodic discourse and its return to the beginning. In phrase group C2, as we have already noted, some of the characteristics of Pūriyā and Kalyān coalesce for the

Figure 5.18.   Analysis of phrase group C2.

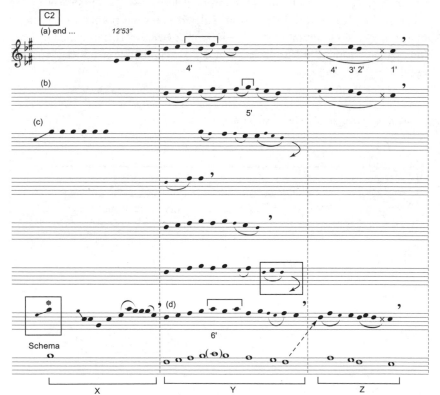

first time. The artist has reserved this synthesis for the climax of the *vistār* process, where the highest pitches of the entire *ālāp*—5' and 6'—are reached.

Before C2 begins, the artist has established the upper tonic and begun the development of the high octave by advancing the *vistār* to 3'. The Pūriyā *aṅg*, established during B6, remains dominant as we enter phrase group C2. After repeated consonant reinforcement of 3, the development continues as shown in figure 5.18. The underlying contour schema comprises a rising–falling antecedent contour Y, repeated recursively, followed by a descending consequent Z, comprising the sequence #4'–3'–b2'–1', which was used in the same way an octave lower in B3 (figure 5.14). The difference here is that Y peaks around and emphasizes 5', while at the same time ascending from and returning to b2'.

At two points, the artist interrupts the alternation of Y and Z, in order to emphasize the arrival of 5' by prolonging and repeating it (X), supporting it on the second occasion with the fifth and octave below: 5'–1'–5–1'–5'. Despite this emphasis on 5', neither Pūriyā nor Kalyān is dominant in the phrase group: elements of both are combined, in pitch sequences that include both b2' and 5', such as b2'–3'–#4'–5' and b2'–3'–5' (in the recursion from Y to X, boxed in figure 5.18). This last sequence, remarkably, echoes a fifth higher the typical Pūriyā ascent to 1, namely #4–6–1', which has been heard several times (e.g., in phrase A2b, figure 5.3): this implied parallelism would not be possible in either of the component *aṅgs* of the *rāga* alone.[24]

	b2'	3'	5'
=	#4	6	1'

Immediately when this synthesis of Pūriyā and Kalyān has been established, the final descent phase of the *ālāp* begins (figure 5.19); and immediately the dominance of Pūriyā is reasserted. The whole descent of the middle octave is accomplished in two phrases (C3a and C3b)—North Indian musicians rarely linger over this portion of an *ālāp*.[25] But the artist avoids a simple scalar descent, by reordering the pitches of pitch schema II, taking them in *vakra* ("crooked") order; and also by recursion, repeatedly returning to a higher pitch and repeating parts of the descent before continuing downward. Thus in C3a, he repeats the descent as far as #4, and reiterates this pitch, before descending from there to 3, evoking the Pūriyā motive #4–3. Similarly, an emphasis on 7 and #4 evokes Pūriyā; the fleeting appearance of 5 in ornamentation of #4

---

24. On consonant parallelism as a structural principle in modern and early rāgas respectively, see Jairazbhoy 1971: 77–89 and Widdess 1995: 210–223.

25. South Indian musicians often treat the concluding descent phase more elaborately than the ascent phase.

Figure 5.19.   Analysis of phrase group C3.

indicates the last vestige of Kalyān *aṅg*. In C3b, the artist takes a final sweep of the middle and high registers, touching again the highest point reached earlier (6'), before descending in consonant leaps that lay bare the structure of Pūriyā: 3'−7−♯4−3 (and at the end 7). This phrase explicitly articulates pitch schema II, completely omitting 1, and thereby deferring its highly foreseeable return to the very end. The *ālāp* ends with the tight constellation of pitches around 1 with which it started, and the third and final *mohrā* (14:15), prefaced by a final strum of the *tarab* scale.

5. Conclusions

This analysis illustrates with reference to Indian classical music the contention with which we began: that compositional principles are as characteristic of unscripted musical performances as of written compositions, and that they reflect the needs of performers, composers, and listeners. Indian classical musicians take pride in their independence from notational models, and in the oral transmission of musical knowledge and skills through distinguished lineages rather than through texts. Like "oral" performers in many cultures, they are highly successful at engaging the attention, comprehension, and appreciation of audiences over long time spans, in performances that involve preparation, memory, variation, and spontaneous invention in varying proportions. While it is intriguing to ask "How do they do that?" it is equally illuminating to inquire what their performance might mean to a listener.

I have argued that Budhaditya Mukherjee's dynamic approach to *rāga* in this performance is only one aspect of a highly structured melodic discourse, in which many devices are employed that allow, and encourage, the formation of dynamic, schematic, and conscious expectations on the part of the listener: a melodic discourse that affords the listener an experience of engagement, anticipation, surprise, and fulfillment. As is well known, Indian audiences certainly experience live performance in an engaged manner. Martin Clayton writes (2007) that "North Indian *rāg* performance, especially as practised in intimate and informal settings, is often distinguished by a lively interaction involving both musicians and listeners, mediated by both gestures and vocal interjections." Clayton has observed that listeners' physical reactions often anticipate events in the music, showing that they form precise dynamic expectations; and performers, of course, interact with the audience by arousing, delaying, and (perhaps unexpectedly) fulfilling such expectations.

Does this discourse displace the objectives of *ālāp* adduced by Van der Meer, namely, to demonstrate both the internal coherence of the *rāga* and its distinctness from other *rāga*s? It could be argued that what Budhaditya Mukherjee demonstrates is the composite character of Pūriyā-Kalyān rather than its internal coherence; only in the lower and the higher octaves do we briefly hear what an integrated Pūriyā-Kalyān might sound like. Similarly we might argue that this performance does not demonstrate the distinctness of Pūriyā-Kalyān from all other *rāga*s, but rather its close relationship to the two *rāga*s of origin, Pūriyā and Yaman, and how it can be made to sound at times closer to one or to the other. In an informal experiment, I played two extracts from the *ālāp,* with no explanatory information, to a highly expert listener, and invited him to say what *rāga* he heard in each. He easily identified the pervasive features of Yaman in one and Pūriyā in the other, but nevertheless percipiently speculated that both extracts could come from a performance of Pūriyā-Kalyān, if "the artist is going out of his way to show incomplete or partial *aṅg*s of the *rāga.*"[26] That is precisely the approach that I am suggesting that this performance demonstrates: an approach that is perhaps more concerned with articulating a dynamic, engaging melodic narrative than with delineating an integrated *rāga* image. As Van der Meer and other writers observe, "hiding and unveiling" different aspects of a *rāga* is an accepted technique: it is only the extensive, structural use of the technique that is exceptional here.

What, then, does the artist achieve by treating the *rāga* in this somewhat unconventional way? Is it an approach especially suitable for a CD recording marketed originally to an audience outside India? The listener who has never heard Pūriyā or Yaman can make sense of the recording only in terms of the sounds themselves; but the artist has used those sounds in such a way as to create an internal dialogue, a narrative flow that perhaps helps to stimulate or maintain the listener's attention. Structural complexity and variety are

---

26. The listener was Dr. Nicolas Magriel, a highly experienced performer and analyst of Indian music. The extracts were, first, B4 (b) to B5 (b); and second, B2 to B3. I did not tell him that the extracts were from the same performance.

perhaps also appropriate for a recording, if they reward repeated listening with new insights.

One could extend this argument to say that equally the other compositional principles and structural features of this *ālāp*, which are broadly typical of *ālāp* in general, lend themselves to comprehension by unacculturated as well as by more experienced listeners. Thus the compositional principle of *vistār* seems designed to permit the development of schematic or dynamic expectations on the part of the listener. Many parts of this *ālāp* are based on contour schemas, such as those shown in figures 5.16–18, which, being based on repetition, afford the possibility of immediate recognition and anticipation. The alternation of ascent and descent, operating on both the large and the small scales, the tendency for successive ascents to reach successively higher pitches, and the less frequent but more abrupt and formulaic descents, appear to exemplify the "stimulus ramp archetype" described by Huron (1992): a pattern found in many musics, whereby "regular [small] increments of stimulus level [are] followed by occasional large decrements of stimulus level." Huron attributes this archetype to the operation of an automatic neurological orienting response mechanism, by which the listener's attention can be sustained over extended periods.[27]

Of course, *vistār* is a process of which performers, at least, are fully conscious; but if Indian classical musicians take advantage of their listeners' neurological responses and unconscious dynamic expectations, as well as employing culture-specific schemas (such as *rāga*s), this may help account for their success, since the mid-twentieth century, in communicating with unacculturated audiences both within and outside India, and for the development of a significant national and international niche market for commercial recordings. This success was, in turn, necessitated by the change in classical music patronage in India itself, in the first half of the twentieth century, from aristocratic connoisseurs to a broader public audience, reached by radio and sound recordings as well as live concerts. Many changes in Indian musical performance and culture have been attributed to this change in social and economic environment; the use of abstract structural procedures and neurological response mechanisms in music does not guarantee its autonomy from such social and historical motivations. These cultural factors are comparatively well documented, but to help us understand further the dynamics of musical discourse, both analysis of performance, and empirical research into the perception of structures and processes in Indian music, will be required.

27. Unusually, perhaps, the process operates at several hierarchical levels of formal organization in *ālāp,* from individual motives to the whole *ālāp,* whereas the examples of ramp archetype analyzed by Huron appear to operate at only one level.

References

Bhātkhaṇḍe, Viṣṇunārāyaṇ. 1956. *Bhātkhaṇḍe Saṅgīt-Śāstra (Hindusthānī Saṅgīt Pad-dhati)*. Hāthras: Saṅgīt Kāryālaya.

Bor, Joep, ed. 1999. *The Raga Guide.* Wyastone Leys, UK: Nimbus Records.

Clayton, Martin. 2007. "Time, Gesture, and Attention in a Khyāl Performance." *Asian Music* 38(2): 71–96.

D'Andrade, Roy. 1995. *The Development of Cognitive Anthropology.* Cambridge: Cambridge University Press.

Huron, David. 1992. "The Ramp Archetype and the Maintenance of Passive Auditory Attention." *Music Perception* 10(1): 83–92.

———. 2006. *Sweet Anticipation: Music and the Psychology of Expectation.* Cambridge, MA: MIT Press.

Jairazbhoy, N. A. 1961. "Svaraprastāra in North Indian Music." *Bulletin of the School of Oriental and African Studies* 24(2): 307–325.

———. 1971. *The Rāgs of North Indian Music: Their Structure and Evolution.* London: Faber.

Khan, Wajahat, and Widdess, Richard. Forthcoming. *Wajahat Khan Plays Rageshri.* London: Navras Records. Audio CD and CD-ROM.

Lakoff, George. 1987. *Women, Fire, and Dangerous Things.* Chicago: University of Chicago Press.

Lerdahl, Fred. 2001. *Tonal Pitch Space.* New York: Oxford University Press.

Lortat-Jacob, Bernard, ed. 1987. *L'improvisation dans les musiques de tradition orale.* Paris: Selaf.

Monier-Williams, Monier. 1899. *A Sanskrit–English Dictionary: Etymologically and Philologically Arranged with Special Reference to Cognate Indo-European Languages.* Oxford: Clarendon Press.

Nettl, Bruno. 1974. "Thoughts on Improvisation: A Comparative Approach." *Musical Quarterly* 60(1): 1–19.

Nettl, Bruno, and Melinda Russell, eds. 1998. *In the Course of Performance: Studies in the World of Musical Improvisation.* Chicago: Chicago University Press.

Nooshin, L. 2003. "Improvisation as 'Other': Creativity, Knowledge and Power—The Case of Iranian Classical Music." *Journal of the Royal Musical Association* 128(2): 242–296.

Parikh, Arvind. 2007. *The Glorious Tradition of Etawah-Imdadkhani Gharana: The Greats of Seven Generations.* Mumbai: International Foundation for Fine Arts.

Powers, Harold S., and Richard Widdess. 2001a. "India, Sub-continent of. §III.2 *Rāga.*" In *The New Grove Dictionary of Music,* 2nd ed., ed. Stanley Sadie, vol. 12, 178–188. London: Macmillan.

———. 2001b. "Mode. §V.3 South Asia: '*Rāga.*'" In *The New Grove Dictionary of Music,* 2nd ed., ed. Stanley Sadie, vol. 16, 837–844. London: Macmillan.

Rubin, David C. 1995. *Memory in Oral Traditions: The Cognitive Psychology of Epic, Ballads, and Counting-Out Rhymes.* New York: Oxford University Press.

Sanyal, Ritwik, and Richard Widdess. 2004. *Dhrupad: Tradition and Performance in Indian Music.* London: Ashgate.

Slingerland, Edward. 2008. *What Science Offers the Humanities: Integrating Body and Culture.* Cambridge: Cambridge University Press.

Snyder, Bob. 2000. *Music and Memory.* Cambridge, MA: MIT Press.

Sorrell, Neil, and Ram Narayan. 1980. *Indian Music in Performance: A Practical Introduction.* Manchester: Manchester University Press.

Ṭhākur, Omkārnāth. 1962. *Saṅgītāñjali.* Vol. 6. Hāthras: Saṅgīt Kārālaya.

Treitler, Leo. 1974. "Homer and Gregory: The Transmission of Epic Poetry and Plainchant." *Musical Quarterly* 60(3): 333–72.

———. 2003. *With Voice and Pen: Coming to Know Medieval Song and How It Was Made.* Oxford: Oxford University Press.

Van der Meer, Wim. 1980. *Hindustani Music in the 20th Century.* The Hague: Martinus Nijhoff.

Widdess, Richard. 1981. "Aspects of Form in North Indian *Ālāp* and Dhrupad." In *Music and Tradition: Essays Presented to Laurence Picken,* ed. D. R. Widdess and R. F. Wolpert, 143–181. Cambridge: Cambridge University Press.

———. 1994. "Involving the Performer in Transcription and Analysis: A Collaborative Approach to Dhrupad." *Ethnomusicology* 38(1): 59–80.

———. 1995a. "*Free Rhythm* in Indian Music." *EM: Annuario degli Archivi di Etnomusicologia dell'Accademia Nazionale di Santa Cecilia,* III: 77–95.

———. 1995b. *The Rāgas of Early Indian Music: Modes, Melodies and Musical Notations from the Gupta Period to c. 1250.* Oxford: The Clarendon Press.

———. 2005. "'Free Rhythm' in *Ālāp:* Performers' Perspectives." Paper presented at the 50th annual conference of the Society for Ethnomusicology.

———. 2006. "*Rāga.*" In *Keywords in South Asian Studies,* ed. Rachel Dwyer. http://www.soas.ac.uk/southasianstudies/keywords/ (accessed March 22, 2011).

→→ CHAPTER 6 →→

Timbre-and-Form

The BSC and the Boston Improvising Community

Lou Bunk

Photo: The BSC performing on October 15, 2008 at The Outpost Gallery in Cambridge Massachusetts as part of a weekly concert series, called "The Series," produced by Dave Gross. From left, front: James Coleman, Bhob Rainey, Greg Kelley, and Liz Tonne. From left, back: Howie Stelzer, Chris Cooper, and Vic Rawlings. Photo by Seth Tissue; reproduced by his permission.

1. Introduction

Once a month, the sound of electronic crackles, noisy multiphonics, gurgling, hissing, quiet vocalized gibberish, bowed metal, blowing sounds, and a thousand shades of hullabaloo can be heard coming from the Third Life Studio. This unassuming yoga studio and performance space in the gritty Union Square neighborhood of Somerville, Massachusetts, is the venue for Opensound, a concert series I have coproduced since 2006 with Tim Feeney its founder, and Lou Cohen, a local performer.

Opensound features musicians who perform a recently invented genre of music that explores timbre and form through free improvisation. There is no currently accepted name for the genre, so for this chapter I will adopt *timbre-and-form* as a makeshift moniker. Timbre-and-form musicians perform with a broad assortment of sound making objects, synthesizers, effects pedals, laptops, DIY (do-it-yourself) electronics, and uniquely modified instruments. When traditional instruments are played intact, it is often with an assortment of extended techniques, enhancing the sonic palette. In these concerts, conventional melody and harmonic progression are overshadowed by transforming spectra and the beautifying of noise.

Opensound concerts, and others like them in the Boston area, are often casual events akin to an art opening in a private loft. Attendance ranges anywhere from a handful of friends to a small crowd of fifty or so. Fifty is rare. There is a community atmosphere among the concertgoers and musicians, as many people know each other and have been making music together for years. When the music starts, the room becomes absolutely silent, and the intensity of listening is profound. For sets that may last an hour or longer, the audience will sit in close quarters, perfectly quiet and still, sometimes with eyes closed, transfixed by every nuance of sound. For me, the allure in these events, and indeed the music, is how, without self-conscious assertion, the solemnity of a classical performance seems reconciled with the visceral liveliness of a local rock show.

Especially in North America, many trained contemporary composers seek to square the dynamic energies of the popular music that surrounded them all their lives with the refined European-derived techniques they acquired formally. As a composer attempting to digest these worlds, I am cautious of an oversimplified outlook when observing the many trajectories toward fusion that comprise this part of today's new-music landscape.[1] Some

---

1. Once-underground organizations like the Bang on a Can marathon concerts, first held in the 1980s, have morphed into major establishment events, while newer generations

of these streams, many now decades old, stand well on their own integrity; others are glib and short-lived. But however long they may ultimately endure in their current shape, the fusions taking place in Boston at concerts like Opensound eschew the driving rhythms of rock and the virtuoso complexity of much art music. They draw instead on the avant-garde sensibilities of composers such as John Cage, Morton Feldman, Helmut Lachenmann, and Giacinto Scelsi, and merge them with an arguably compatible and updated "hitting a baseball bat on a street-sign punk-rock" (Rawlings) energy and DIY ethos.[2] Rawlings adds that "there is something about the music that is very academic and schooled, and something else that is as easy to do as appreciate a found object." In these sources, traditional instrumental technique is valued less than an openness to sound in the moment, and a conviction that any sound is potentially very beautiful. Indeed, formal training is not a prerequisite for participation: one needs only a willingness to play and patiently listen. This community draws me in not only because of this unforced amalgamation of styles, but also because its lovely and peculiar music echoes the sonically spare, inventive work of some of my own favorite composers (listed just above), while the process (free improvisation) gives the music a dirty perfection, a rock 'n' roll emancipation. These handmade mediations on timbre embody an attractive aesthetic paradox: "letting go" while maintaining purpose.

Tim Feeney, the founder of Opensound, describes first hearing timbre-and-form in a 2002 concert called Autumn Uprising:[3]

> James Coleman, Liz Tonne, and Tatsuya Nakatani[4] spun my head around. Here's this guy with half a drum set just contorting himself like this [contorts his arms], and is still just making these really small sounds. And these two other people just not moving! It was still. Things were changing enough to bump the vibe along. There was this

---

of composers such as Trey Spruance, Matthew Welch, and others (see Zorn 2000, 2007) create unprecedented and eclectic merging of popular musics with self-conscious "art-music" thought and techniques.

2. Unless otherwise noted, all direct quotes are from unpublished interviews I conducted in person and over email between August 2008 and January 2009. This quote is from Vic Rawlings, the cellist/circuit-ist of the BSC.

3. *Autumn Uprising* was a yearly festival in Boston started in 1997 by Dave Gross, a local saxophonist. It ran until 2002 and featured a wide array of improvised music.

4. Coleman (theremin), Tonne (voice), and Nakatani (percussion) played an improvised trio.

hush around the thing that was really really powerful, and I said *oh,*
I'm hooked!

Like Feeney, I too was struck, and wondered how this music could be so
captivating without planning. Although timbre-and-form has been the subject of many magazine articles and critical reviews,[5] scholars are only beginning to analyze it.[6] Through ethnographic portrayal of the performers, and an
analytical study of a representative recording, I will investigate the shared
musical and social values of this nascent genre, focusing on a 2007 performance by the BSC,[7] led by saxophonist Bhob Rainey. The entire transcription, along with a recording of the performance, can be accessed at www.oup.
com/us/accswm◑.[8]

Interestingly, many familiar ways of describing and listening still apply
to this new music. The BSC's innovation is its idiosyncratic improvisational
process in which each performer plays an equal part. Despite starting without score, chart, or illustrative instruction, and with the use of minimal pitch
and harmonic progression (also unplanned), the BSC realizes a perceivable
formal structure mainly though the real-time shaping of timbres, rhythms,
and textures.

The first half of this chapter examines the timbre-and-form subculture,
investigating how its history and shared values have contributed to the distinctive music and process of the BSC. In the second half I analyze how the BSC
creates a music primarily of timbral events, and I specifically show how the
collaborative intentions of individual improvised decisions lead to an instantly
discovered form. I attempt to deduce in these decisions how an implied yet
unknown formal strategy informs the moment-to-moment artistic tactics of
each performer, thereby highlighting the immediate yet thoughtful process of
structuring inherent in the BSC's music.

5. *Signal to Noise* and *The Wire* are two English language magazines that cover this
music.

6. One can find copious scholarship on pitch-based improvisation (see Nettl 1998;
Fischlin and Heble 2004), and on timbre-based composed music, particularly electroacoustic (see Simoni 2006 and the journal *Organised Sound*), but there is still little
analysis of timbre-based improvisation.

7. BSC is not an acronym. When asked if the name had meaning, several members
said it might have in the beginning, but not anymore.

8. Though I include parts of this transcription in figures whenever necessary, there
are times when I assume the reader has at hand the entire transcription. A discussion of
the issues surrounding the making of this transcription will come in a segment just
before the analysis begins.

2. Music and Methodology

2.1 Musical Precedents, Local History, and the Founding of the BSC

Throughout the twentieth and now twenty-first centuries, musicians have extensively explored ways to compose music out of transforming timbre, and what some might call "noise." The BSC extends this vibrant tradition. Before the advent of electronic music, composers investigated timbre acoustically through percussion and orchestration. Futurist composer and painter Luigi Russolo rejected the classical orchestra, and invented his own "intonarumori" (noise instruments) while proclaiming that "noise is triumphant" in his futurist manifesto "The Art of Noises" (Russolo [1913] 2004: 10). Though more traditional, Edgard Varèse invigorated the orchestra's percussion section, subjugated the strings and winds to supporting static sound structures, and composed "the movement of sound masses" as described in "The Liberation of Sound" (Varèse [1936] 2004: 17). The BSC echoes these cacaphonics, though without Russolo's political bombast. In the founding of electronic music, the BSC is indebted particularly to the microvariations of intricate electronic sounds, like the elaborate massing of sine tones one hears in the early *Elektronische Studien* of Karlheinz Stockhausen. Indeed, *musique concrète* is also a precedent, not only in terms of the recontextualizing of found sounds, but also in the "instrumental *musique concrète*" of Helmut Lachenmann (see Feller 2002: 254), where Pierre Schaeffer's "acousmatics"[9] is applied to live performing instruments. The BSC shares these influences with, and also reflects, the various subgenres of "punk"-inspired "noise" music[10] exemplified by "no wave" guru Thurston Moore,[11] and the "Japanoise" of Merzbow (Hegarty 2007: 153), though without the sheer loudness.

The BSC's approach to improvising is informed by the aleatoric music of John Cage, as well as the spontaneity of some European free improvisers[12] and

9. "Acousmatic, adjective: is said of a noise that one hears without seeing what causes it" (Schaeffer [1966] 2004).

10. Both Hegarty 2007 and Toop 2004 provide an updated and thorough history of "noise" in music. While Hegarty focuses more on the many subgenres of "noise," Toop paints a broader cultural portrait.

11. Thurston Moore fronts the highly influential group Sonic Youth, formed in 1981 in the wake of the New York City punk scene.

12. MEV (Musica Elettronica Viva) and AMM (not an acronym) are two influential improvising groups that emerged in Europe in the late 1960s. AMM's many members (Cornelius Cardew, Keith Rowe, Lou Gare, and Eddie Prévost) have roots in free jazz, but over the years have shed most of these, particularly harmony and melody. MEV, populated by Alvin Curran, Richard Teitelbaum, Frederic Rzewski, and Allan Bryant,

free jazz, though the BSC strips away the "jazz" approach to harmony, melody, and rhythm, leaving just the "free." The more current "Onkyo" of Japan (Sachiko M, Otomo Yoshihide; see Hegarty 2007: 146–148) share these values of improvisation, and have similarly evolved them to a more reduced and quite timbre-based music. The influences of the BSC extend further yet; its members have cited Hindustani music, Shakuhachi, the microtonal improvisations of Joe Maneri,[13] Chinese poetry, and the paintings of Cy Twombly, to name just a few. The gamut of these influences enables us to contextualize timbre-and-form music as a characteristic art form of our era, with influences conflating space, time, genre, context, and multiple meanings.

In particular, the music and ideas of John Cage strongly resonate with James Coleman, the thereminist of the BSC. He contends that through "youthful brashness," the BSC made the claim that "John Cage is an idiom that you can improvise," much like one can improvise in a bluegrass or bebop style. Perhaps Cage's wide-ranging oeuvre cannot be characterized as being in a single idiom, and indeed some in the improvising community thought this was "incredibly outrageous." However, Coleman's intention is not to pigeonhole Cage, but to identify certain aspects as models for free improvisation. Coleman believes that it was "probably our greatest achievement."

The BSC formed in the summer of 2000 during a period when Bhob Rainey was touring and performing often. Rainey criticizes the larger free-improvising groups of that time as being "pretty uniformly bad" and as having "little focus throughout." He complains that the "balance was just horrid" and that it often sounded "like a bunch of people with different ideologies demonstrating their ideologies together. There is a received wisdom that above a certain amount of people improvising you lose any chance of doing something good unless you start structuring it." Rainey found this structure in playing "game" pieces like John Zorn's *Cobra* and in Fred Lonberg-Holm's Lightbox Orchestra.[14] He was moderately satisfied with the results, but confided that "it

---

among others, emerged as a counterpoint to the studio-based electronic music of their day. They made electronic music a live event by improvising on DIY sound making objects (olive oil cans, contact microphones, etc.) and a Moog synthesizer.

13. Many of the players in the BSC took classes with Maneri at the New England Conservatory of Music and cite his influence on their compositional approach to improvisation. "Joe was hugely important in those days. Many people, myself included, studied with him and admired his playing" (Rawlings).

14. *Cobra* consists of a set of cues notated on cards, and rules about the cues that direct the players what to play. The Chicago-based Lightbox Orchestra uses cue lights and projected images to control the improvisation.

really wasn't a pleasure to play." A key component of improvisation, "that incredible struggle to try to make it good," was not present, and for Rainey "it was a poor compromise."

The impetus for forming the BSC came to Rainey in San Francisco after a particularly successful performance of a larger ad hoc free improvising ensemble in February 2000, assembled by Jack Wright.[15] Rainey remembers that Wright "gave some simple speech at the beginning about trying to leave space for other people, and not turning it into a solo-fest." The success inspired Rainey to found a larger ensemble in Boston, where he had been performing among a community of musicians that espoused an aesthetic "that really allows for space." Unbeknownst to Rainey at the time, Greg Kelley, the trumpeter for the BSC, had similar ideas. Several months later, the BSC took shape.

For the Boston improvisation community this time was exciting and pivotal, but also politically fraught. Various approaches to timbre-and-form improvisation were emerging as innovations within, and on the fringe of, a well-established and vibrant free jazz scene. At first, improvisers of many styles would split shows at the same venues, notably the Playground music series at the Zeitgeist Gallery. Rawlings regarded this mingling as "awesome, idealistic and quasi-utopian" saying that "the music we play now was developed there," but a certain tension became evident. Free jazz musicians were playing "kickin'-ass" (Rawlings) fast and virtuoso pitch-based music that spotlighted the "heroic" (Coleman) soloist, while some timbre-and-form improvisers cultivated the opposite—a sparser, timbre-based music that valued "group sound" (Stelzer).[16] "We were talking a lot about minimalist aesthetic, the beauty in things that were slow and small and quiet. There was especially a lot of talk about [Morton] Feldman" (Coleman). Indeed, Coleman saw the timbre-and-form perspective as a "loving critique" of jazz, and not "anti-jazz" or a "dismissal." Rawlings concurs:

> Jazz became a thing to get away from aesthetically. It was a pre-existing form, and that was enough of a constriction right there. Speaking for myself, leaving those inflections out made my playing much more my own thing. I had no animosity for the people. I had gratitude to them for being a part of a community that was awesome.

15. Jack Wright is a Philadelphia-based saxophonist and free improviser who has been performing since the early 1970s.

16. Although my account focuses on the tension between free jazz and timbre-and-form music, the Playground featured many hybrid approaches that explored the intersection of free jazz, timbre-and-form, punk rock, noise, and drone, to name just a few.

Howard Stelzer, who became acquainted with many of the BSC musicians during his regular attendance at the Zeitgeist, recalls the growing tension:

> While many established jazz and improv players were open to collaboration, there were elements of scene politics left over from earlier days. Some jazz guys seemed hung up on history, respect and hierarchy. I think they saw us as coming in and doing things that were [way] out there, but doing it in their space.

This "us and them attitude" (Stelzer) boiled over into a "sandbox fight" (Rawlings) in 2000, in the wake of Autumn Uprising 4 (AU4), which hosted AMM. Coproducers Dave Gross and James Coleman broke with precedent by booking "a lot of non-jazz" (Stelzer), reflecting AMM's timbre-and-form style; initially, Gross and Coleman planned to headline the festival with Bill Dixon, a well-known free jazz trumpeter, but negotiations fell through. The Jazz community felt "left out" (Stelzer). "Spectacular"[17] attendance at AU4 inspired and validated the timbre-and-form community, but a handful of free jazz players complained of a "lack of diversity" in the programming.[18] This suggestion of racism—a "pious" charge that Rawlings also regarded as thinly veiled "petty scene politics"[19] raised hackles and exacerbated aesthetic

17. Katt Hernandez, a violinist and improviser who attended AU4, said that "the festival was a really, really wonderful thing."

18. On October 10, 2000, Taylor Ho Bynum, a local improviser, wrote an open letter to Gross and Coleman on a listserv popular with the Boston improvisation community. While genuinely constructive and at times complimentary in tone, it did contain one harsh criticism: "I find the lack of diversity in this year's Autumn Uprising really disturbing. The overwhelming whiteness and maleness is fairly staggering." The responses to this letter continued for several months, some defending AU4, others echoing Ho Bynum. Similarly inflammatory was Stu Vandermark's remark in *Cadence*: "It is impossible for me to come up with a justifiable explanation for the lack of black improvisers in the festival." A broader social context for this controversy, considering how the history of jazz relates to the civil rights movement, is theorized in Monson 2007.

19. Hernandez suggests that the lack of diversity in AU4, and in the timbre-and-form community generally, is a consequence not of overt racism, but of its secondary manifestation in Boston's socioeconomic balkanization. Noting that "it wasn't African Americans who made the complaint," she observes of the Playground series, "It was just one or two dudes running it out of their own shallow pockets, and if you asked them for a show, or ran into them on the street, you could play. But since Boston is hyper-segregated, the chances of an African-American musician [from] Roxbury or Dedham or Quincy just running into Dave or James on the street was a lot more remote than all of us who were living and working near them in Somerville, Allston, or Cambridge."

differences.[20] The musicians involved felt hurt and misunderstood. "At that moment," Stelzer reflects, "things sort of changed." Gross elaborates:

> It really shut things down. Before, I was booking two sets a night [at the Zeitgeist] and would try to have disparate groups, so you have people who don't know each other get exposed—a cross-pollenization [sic]. After Autumn Uprising 4, that was not possible because it became very divisive, and you have these camps.

This split gave the developing "new style" (Rawlings) space it needed to grow.[21] Although free improvisation was the common ground that initially brought all these musicians to the same performing venues, ironically it was different conceptions of freedom that drove some of them apart.

The timbre-and-form community that emerged was a "great mash-up of people who weren't interested in any kind of Dogmatic Improv 101 absolutism."[22] Kelley contends that there is "no scene," or if there is, then "ours is a scene of scene-hoppers," saying that "you'd be as likely to run into people at a noise show by RRRon Lessard,[23] [or] at a Scelsi piece played by [new music piano virtuoso] Stephen Drury over at the New England Conservatory."

The BSC's story is about the emergence of a new musical style made by people with shared influences, philosophy, vernacular, and vocation. Most of them work at jobs unrelated to the music, and few if any make a living from playing. A critic of timbre-and-form or the BSC might see their fetishizing of noise and indifference to mainstream appeal as self-indulgent. The music may come across as remote, reactionary, or even rude because of its purposeful disregard for meter, melody, harmony, and other standard musical markers. Its aesthetic even rejects the assaulting volume of other urban noise youth cultures, taking some of their ugly and proudly aggressive sounds and insisting that we listen to them reverentially, at the amplitude of a whisper. One could be forgiven for thinking that the musicians are lost in a self-involved rapture that drugs them into believing their expression is art despite lacking recognition from beyond its immediate subcultural

---

20. Gross admits that the programming may have been "too in-crowd" but stands by their curatorial decisions. He recalls trying to sincerely discuss the issue of diversity at a community meeting but laments that "nobody wanted to talk about anything [racism], and were more concerned with splitting up the pie."

21. In retrospect, says Rawlings, "none of this shit is important," and "it would be good to forgive and forget."

22. Greg Kelly in Panzner 2004.

23. Ron Lessard runs a record store and record label called RRRecords in Lowell, Massachusetts, which stocks hard to find "noise"-based music groups.

context.[24] The group might be viewed askance for adopting a self-conscious elitism and inflated sense of their own worth, since rejection by the mainstream is occasionally worn as a badge of honor. One need not resolve these questions, however, to take this music and its creators' statements at face value, acknowledge its freshness, and try to hear it as its modest but devoted audience does.

2.2 Background and Instruments

The BSC formed out of a common artistic interest in timbre-and-form music. Though geography played a part, they all lived in the Boston area, their particular instruments are less important to the musical potential then the sensibilities of each player; I imagine that if they all played kazoo for one show, they would somehow find a way to make music that still sounded like the BSC. When recruiting members, Rainey did imagine roles; in particular, he invited Chris Cooper (guitar) and Howie Stelzer (tapes), hoping they would "throw a few wrenches," "keeping people from being too polite and sinking into nice sounds for 20 minutes."

The BSC's eight members come from disparate backgrounds. This was unplanned but can be seen as a reflection of the music's inclusiveness. Greg Kelley sums this up: "I come from a classical background, Bhob comes from a jazz background, Vic and Liz came more out of rock and indie rock, Chris Cooper, Noise and weirdo stuff, James, who knows . . . art rock, Brian Eno, Cage kind of thing." Vic Rawlings remarks that while some have "full-on master's degrees," others "couldn't play a major scale on a damn piano," adding, "that is pretty awesome as a band."

The instruments are evenly divided between acoustic and electronic.[25] The performers on acoustic instruments are Bhob Rainey (soprano saxophone), Greg Kelley (trumpet), Liz Tonne (voice), and Mike Bullock (bass). They often play using extended techniques that maximize the creation of noisy yet intentional and clearly defined timbres. For instance, Bhob Rainey and Greg Kelley sometimes remove their mouthpieces and blow into them at various angles to produce shades of white noise. Liz Tonne will often speak and sing

---

24. Simon Reynolds sees extreme examples of noise music as a "drug or intoxicant" calling the "noise buff" a "hip vegetable." He continues: "Noise hipsters have uprooted themselves so successfully from their parent culture, they can cope with absurd levels of outrage/dissonance, and therefore require extreme after extreme in order to feel stimulated/mindblown" (Reynolds [1990] 2004: 57).

25. Of the eight members of the BSC, Coleman is the only one not present on the recording that is the subject of this chapter.

in gibberish, produce multiphonic overtones, screech in an extreme high register, as if mimicking animals and machines. Of the four, Mike Bullock (bass) plays the most traditionally, but incorporating scratch and microtones.

Of the four electronic instruments, James Coleman (theremin) plays on the most familiar, though his approach avoids theremin clichés. Instead of sci-fi glissandos and precise Clara Rockmore-style melodies, Coleman uses the theremin to explore delicate and tiny microtonal gestures that at times sound like vocal murmuring.

Vic Rawlings plays a cello that he modified himself. He installed a set of resonating strings behind the standard four, to which (while performing) he attaches pieces of metal to attain different sonic effects. He has also permanently installed a thin metal bar for bowing, scratching, and tapping, which extends out from the cello's bridge. The cello is amplified, magnifying quiet sounds that would otherwise remain unheard.

Rawlings rounds out his setup with a surface of exposed guitar pedal circuits. He turns the workbench activity of "circuit bending"[26] into perfomance, by placing small pieces of metal into these live circuits, producing sounds that crackle, whirl, hiss, and beep. He projects these sounds through a mishmash of cheap and blown-out speakers arranged on the floor before him. Because each speaker is individualized (through its destruction), the sound is filtered differently depending on which speaker it is sent through.

Howie Stelzer's setup for the BSC is made up of "cassette tapes, cassette players, a microphone, a couple of electronic effects" (a delay, loop, and distortion pedal), which he uses sparingly. The microphone is not used to sing or vocalize, but to generate feedback and to amplify the tape decks "through the air." Only one speaker is used; "I only play in mono for the BSC." The cassette tapes tend to be of the band. "It kind of blurs things, so that we sound less like a bunch of people playing instruments, and more like a unified sound" (Stelzer).

Chris Cooper plays "a very broken guitar, various metals and plastics, and a handful of effects." The "guitarishness of the guitar" is downplayed by treating it like "a big wooden pickup"; resonant pieces of metal are placed in the strings, and remote controls are activated near the guitar pickup to amplify "otherwise inaudible beepings." Cooper continues: "When the strings *are* more in use, they're tuned either to keep the metal accoutrements well-balanced and sproingy, or to be a useful level of floppy or taut." "A broken pencil sharpener" is used to spin different implements that, along with "various serrated knives and threaded rods," are rubbed against the strings. Electric

---

26. Both Ghazala 2005 and Collins 2006 are exemplary technical manuals in the art of circuit bending, which also provide some interesting personal philosophy.

guitar pedals, such as delay, distortion, and an envelope follower,[27] are applied to feedback loops, the result sounding like "some cranky synthesizer oscillator: every little change to a pedal can make a huge change to the sound" (Cooper).

2.3 Values, Aesthetics, and Rehearsal

The BSC values an approach to improvisation that results in a perceptible form made of structured parts, though without predetermination. The musicians simply start from nothing, listen intently to one another and to the perceived wants and needs of the music, and act accordingly. Discernable "parts" emerge from an often seamless timbral surface that, when finally breaking, can create an environment ready for structural articulation. The players have trained themselves to listen and respond to these opportunities for movement to the next part. They seek a strong sense of cause-and-effect by placing a high value on taking "decisive" (Stelzer) musical actions. Despite this, the players never take solos. "Even when playing alone, it is not soloing; it is performing with the silence" (Rainey).

Rainey developed a critique-based rehearsal method that has helped the BSC refine its ways of discovering form. Early on, there would be more rehearsal, but now they do so only before an important gig:

> [We] leave it open and play a short piece. [Then] there will be an analysis of what went down in that five-minute piece. Someone might say "I think so-and-so might have been hearing this and trying to introduce something, but other people were sort of stuck." We couldn't move to the next thing. Sometimes I come up with a little exercise, made up on the spot, based on the problems that arise, just to force people to do things that they wouldn't ordinarily do. (Rainey)

Rainey explains that in the early days, people were "too nice" and there was "too much agreement." The result was music with "no bounce . . . no soul [and] no grit." These early faults have led the BSC from just making a music that "works" with elements "that fit" (Rainey) to an improvisational system that generates a dynamic form rife with surprise and discovery. Rainey adds, "Part of the thing about working with other people is trying to break open new ground you alone would not have thought of."

Stelzer comments on a "compositional style of thinking" that has evolved out of this approach to rehearsal. He points out that they "always have a strong

---

27. An *envelope follower* is a device that tracks the amplitude changes of an audio signal. This information can then be used as a control signal to change parameters of other devices, most often equalizers and other timbre filters.

beginning," and particularly highlights the purposefulness and communal aspect of every musical decision: "We are all responsible for every sound that we make. Everything that we do has to have a purpose within the piece. It has to be part of a *group mind.*"

Paradoxically, the BSC balance this purposefulness with a hybrid of humanly influenced natural processes and the inhuman by-products of technology. This leads them to place aesthetic value on a variety of electronic sounds such as feedback (as in a Hendrix guitar solo) and the hums of appliances (e.g., refrigerators). While the players do value active and decisive participation in creating the music, they also acknowledge some passivity to a larger BSC group-*machine*-mind with its own natural, seemingly mysterious, mechanisms and rules. Rainey hints at this algorithmic side of the BSC, a Xenakian[28] thread, when he says, with a touch of hyperbole and facetiousness, that "improvisation is one big justification for one stupid mistake at the beginning." Certainly, the BSC is not a machine that spits out a composition from the input of a short musical gesture. Cooper explains that while he explores expression that "can't accidentally sound like a human" he also makes "slight adjustments" that blend "this inhuman process with the rest of the band." Rawlings says "there is a line between being active and passive, and if it is too active it always fails." If it is too passive, it is not "decisive" (Stelzer). In a way, the BSC "pull back the pinball and let it go" (Rainey), where the compositional silver ball is guided by both *passive* machine bumper and *active* humanly controlled flipper. In the following sections, I will show specific examples of some of these ideas and aesthetic principles put into action.

2.4 Overview of Timbre and Pitch in Phoneme (3)

The BSC's values and process are evident in its September 15, 2007, performance for the third night of Phoneme,[29] or *Phoneme (3)*. This relatively compact improvisation (twelve minutes) exhibits a litany of timbres reflecting the BSC's sound palette: metal scrapes, static, crackles; tape-player mechanisms warbling, whooshing, and spinning; wordless vocalizing, cooing, and ululating; blowing, gurgling, multiphonics on saxophone; distorted

---

28. About Iannis Xenakis's stochastic music from the 1950s and '60s, Rainey comments, "The absolute ambivalence of that stuff is horrific, and is not like a Cage ambivalence. It seems to have a cause and effect that is not human. It is like weather, like being in a tornado. It is like this thing has a motive and I will never figure it out. I think I am a bit attracted to that."

29. Phoneme is a three-day series of concerts organized during the Philadelphia Live Arts Festival and Philly Fringe.

trumpet (using sheets of metal); test tones, quavering string sounds, and microtonal beating.

My reading of how these timbres function in the music is, like all analyses, subjective, that is, I offer my own perceptions as one of many possible readings. Yet this music's idiosyncrasy poses special problems. Though it has its cultural context, we have few inherited ideas about its structural norms or underlying theory. What is common in the listening experience is negotiable; what I hear may be both "correct" and contrary to other "correct" hearings. Denis Smalley describes the "intrinsic-extrinsic threads" of electroacoustic music:

> The wide-open sonic world of electroacoustic music encourages imaginative and imagined extrinsic connections because of the variety and ambiguity of its materials, because of its reliance on the motion of colourful spectral energies . . . (Smalley 1997: 110)

The "transcontextuality" of electroacoustic music that Smalley describes primarily entails the recognition of sound sources. To analyze the BSC, I identify not only sound sources (the players and means of sound production), but also what each player might be thinking as an improviser, and I seek metaphors to comprehend the musical moment that results from that perceived intention. Such metaphors could be descriptive phrases or images, imagined actions, or full-blown allegories. Therefore my analysis will weave this type of subjectivity with detailed accounts of how the players use timbre to project form, to demonstrate how this fundamental value of the BSC manifests in the music.

For example, careful listening and responding by the performers are evident in *Phoneme (3)* at 1:00–1:30, transcribed in figure 6.1. As the sustained tones (sax and trumpet: 1:04–1:08) are fading, the entrance of the bass snap pizzicato and tape spins (at 1:04.5 and 1:05.5) make the moment a vivid ending and also initiate the next beginning. The crackling of Vic's circuitry (at 1:09) enters soon after, seeming to respond to Howie's tape spins, and forming a second layer to the continuing bass snap pizzicatos. This composite event (pizzicatos, spins, crackles) ends as the trumpet introduces a new sustained tone D♯4 (1:11); the three players act with one voice as they seem to recognize the freshness of this pitch and stop playing to give its entrance breathing space.

Transforming timbres like these overshadow stable pitch throughout, hence pitch's purpose and organization in *Phoneme (3)* is mainly timbral. Whether the harmonies are microtonal or tempered, I mostly hear the pitches as components of some larger spectral event. Progression from one pitch to the next is present, but is perceptually subsumed by the emphasis on spectral movement. The most salient type of pitch event is the sustained tone, perhaps because its own stability directs the focus to its timbre, allowing more

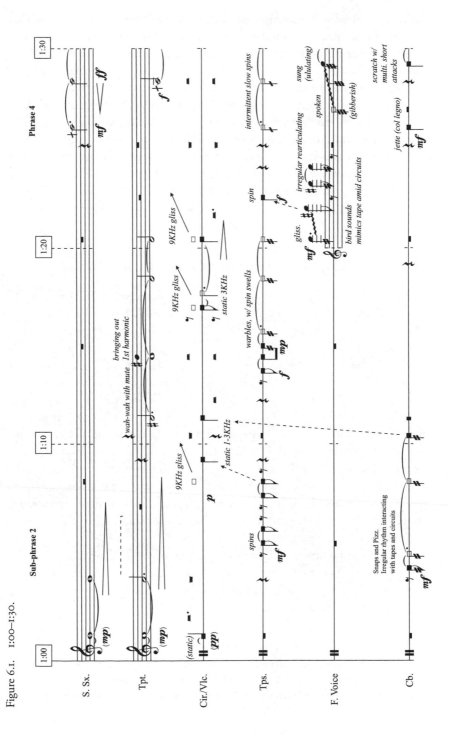

Figure 6.1. 1:00–1:30.

239

unfettered blend with other timbres and masking the linear connections that can result from pitch change. For example, the trumpet begins the piece with a sustained A4 and is joined by the saxophone (at 0:28.5) with a detuned A4, causing a microtonal beating effect that fuses pitch and timbre. Soon the saxophone sinks to G↓4[30] against the trumpet's A4 (0:46.5), increasing the timbral beating to create a thicker pitch mass. Only with the trumpet's D♯4 at 1:11 do the trumpet and saxophone begin to shorten the length of the sustained tones and explore new pitches in new registers (A↓5, A↓3, and F♯4).[31]

Besides sustained notes, there are few other pitched events, the pizzicato bass and the occasional bird-call-like figures of the voice, as well as the fragile melodic quality of the trumpet between 6:00 and 7:00, all projecting relatively stable pitch. Occasionally these pitches add up to what one might hear as harmony, though using no structured system.

2.5 Discovered Form and the Fantasy of Analysis

I hear the form of *Phoneme (3)* as a series of time spans organized hierarchically into sections, each containing two or more phrases. Phrase beginnings are often marked by the onset of timbral contrast, or sometimes by material previously heard as a beginning. Cadences bring phrases to an end, and are often a distinctive, sometime contextually formulaic, process of timbral, textural, rhythmic, and dynamic relaxation that creates repose and a sense of goal; occasionally phrase endings are elided with the next beginning and therefore involved with the introduction of new material. Consecutive phrases that feature similar textures, rhythms, and timbres cohere into sections, and sectional beginnings are thus articulated not only by the previous phrase cadence, but also by substantial changes of timbre, rhythm, and texture. In some phrases, the essential textural, rhythmic, and timbral continuity is altered or interrupted briefly but clearly enough to articulate them into shorter subphrases. Figure 6.2 shows the hierarchal relationship of sections, phrases, and subphrases in *Phoneme (3)*.

By way of preliminary illustration, we can observe in figure 6.3 that the first phrase of *Phoneme (3)* ends in a cadence at 0:27 after the trumpet's held tone A4 ends (0:24.5), and the intensifying bass scratch figure transforms into a decrescendo rising glissando.

---

30. Quarter tones are notated as follows: one-quarter sharp = ↑, one-quarter flat = ↓, and three quarters sharp = ♯. Three-quarters flat is not used.

31. The structural significance of these pitch movements will be discussed later in the analysis.

Figure 6.2. Hierarchic levels of sections, phrases, and subphrases.

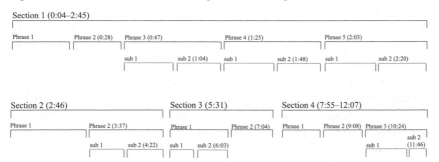

Figure 6.3. Phrase 1.

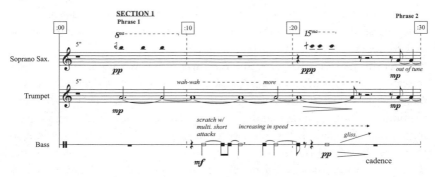

In this phrase, as in much of *Phoneme (3)*, progression toward cadence results from timbral transformation and rhythmic determination, or rhythmic will. The bass intensification in this phrase exemplifies this kind of progression through its four accelerating scratch-tone events, each made up of multiple articulations that grow faster from one to the next. Its first three events (0:11, 0:13.5, and 0:17) are all relatively loud and supply much of the rhythmic momentum that urges the music forward. The fourth (0:22) breaks from this pattern by being quieter and changing timbre; it functions like a goal of the first three, as it captures and ingests their rhythmic energy, transforming it into a rising glissando fading to silence.

The transforming timbre in the trumpet A4 sustained tone also adds momentum to this progression toward cadence. Greg (trumpet) begins the note stably, but after only a few seconds he evolves the timbre into a slowly oscillating "wah-wah" sound (most likely created by covering and uncovering the bell with a mute), creating a subtle rhythmic energy and timbral shift that supports Mike's (bass) forward motion.

The music comes to a local closure (0:27) when Greg and Mike spontaneously and collectively recognize the potential to create it. As Mike continues to augment the scratch tones in the third scratch event (0:17–0:20), Greg responds by slightly increasing the "wah" effect on his A4. With this, Mike begins the rising glissando-diminuendo. Greg hears this and instantly decides to join the lessening dynamic. Through synchronizing with Mike at this moment he helps shape the glissando into an event of concurrence and purpose, a cadential gesture. The music comes to full repose when Greg and Mike, and the rest of the band, arrive in silence together.

As this shows, the BSC's *process* is an approach to "free" improvisation that encourages the *discovery* of such structures through careful listening and responding to the music's potential at any given moment (recall Stelzer's comments on "group mind"). Thus, *discovered form* emerges from a process in which these improvisers establish and support musical structures. The success of this relies on their shared artistic goals, and a long history of playing together.

But this leads to a paradox. The BSC seems to exemplify Edwin Prévost's statement that "sensing, evaluating and acting, in a creative dialogue, are the medium of the meta-musicians," his term for improvisers. The "work" in this medium is "finding a new sound, mastering its production, and then projecting it" (Prévost 1995: 3). Yet "once you slap that [work] on some medium so that it can be heard over and over again," it becomes more like a composition than an improvisation experienced live (Rainey). Indeed, the BSC values sounding "composed," whether on recording or live. Analysis should take into account the music's immediate nature, but can equally proceed as if the music had been composed beforehand.

This leads to my writing about *Phoneme (3)* both in terms of the architectonics I hear, shedding light on how musical events gird these underlying structures (phrases, cadences, and sections), and also in terms that highlight the real-time process of discovery. Through *analytical fantasy,* I will surmise the intentions behind the player's musical decisions as a way to dramatize the real-time dimension of discovering the formal structures I describe in the first way of writing.[32] Obviously, the intentions of each individual performer of the BSC, at each moment in *Phoneme (3),* cannot be ascertained; I can infer only the *possible* and *likely* motivations for members' decisions.[33]

---

32. Heinrich Schenker evoked the idea of "fantasy" in music analysis by enigmatically titling his theoretical trilogy "New Musical Theories and Fantasies," which includes the volumes "Harmony," "Counterpoint," and "Free Composition."

33. For more on subjectivity in music analysis, see Guck 1994 and 1997.

When the perspective shifts to analytical fantasy I will invoke the players' first names, as for example, when I wrote above, "Greg hears this and instantly decides to join the lessening dynamic." The verbs *hear* and *decide* suggest that I presume to know what Greg is thinking, as if he is a character in a novel I am writing. I do not know *for sure* what Greg is "hearing" or what (if anything) he is "deciding," but by posing this fantasy as a likely reality, I can illustrate my and the group's conviction that their process leads to a structured form, a discovered form that is comprised of sections, phrases, and cadences. Through this dialectical strategy, the analysis preserves a compositional outlook and attempts to stay true to the live medium.

2.6 Transcription

A detailed transcription of this performance is an essential tool for building the in-depth analysis that follows. In making the transcription, I primarily use Western notation. Though the timbral nature of this music stretches this system, the transcription is still an invaluable reference for both the reader and analyst by indicating approximately what (and when) each instrumentalist plays, each on its own staff. In my interview with Stelzer, he disagreed with this principle of separating the music into individual instrumental lines:

> I am not sure if that is the most useful way to listen to the BSC. It doesn't make any difference to us who does what. We don't make this clear within the music. It is all part of the group sound. It is more like composed electroacoustic and tape music where you can point to a sonic event, but not a person making it or what technique is being used.

To understand Stelzer's idea of "group sound," I nevertheless believe it is essential to consider the individual lines. First, when I listen to the music, I *am* cognizant of individual performers, particularly when the texture is simpler. I switch back and forth between listening to the whole and to what each instrumentalist is playing.[34] Second, a key component of listening to this music is observing how the performers respond to each other, and to the overall ensemble. In order to represent this process in the analysis, I need to be able to make specific observations about who is doing what, for example,

---

34. Later in the analysis, I will describe in more detail this "whole" versus "part" listening experience.

Figure 6.4.   0:40–0:50.

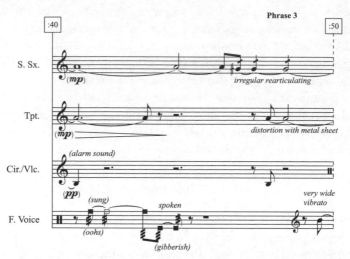

that at 0:40.5 (see figure 6.4) Liz (voice) enters with "oohs" and a quieting "gibberish" to help articulate the ending created by Greg's (trumpet) decrescendo. Through such analytical fantasy I can show how Liz and Greg work together to form a unified event. By separating out who plays what, when, and why, I am able to better understand the whole, its motion, and its purpose.

3. Analysis

In *Phoneme (3)* I hear the improvisers discover a form, but I am also intrigued by the transforming spectra of sounds. By highlighting the critical moments that help articulate the musical structure, the analysis evokes both this spontaneously invented narrative and its timbral processes. My metaphors are intended to lift this intimate musical experience out of the abstract, to personalize and demystify *Phoneme (3),* and timbre-based music like it, for a listener who might feel like an outsider.

3.1 The Discovery of a Section

As figure 6.2 shows, I segment *Phoneme (3)* into four sections of rough coherence, each having nearly the same duration, except for the final, longer section:

Section 1   0:00–2:45
Section 2   2:45–5:31
Section 3   5:31–7:54
Section 4   7:54–12:06

The music operates differently in each section. In section 1, a textural coherence develops through the use of hushed sustained tones on and around A4, shaping a clear phrase structure and forming a center of gravity for orbiting events of timbre. The texture of section 2 is denser; the sustained tones dissipate, rhythmic activity increases in the first half, and phrases are longer and fewer. With the start of section 3, the rhythmic energy dissolves, the pacing of events is slower, and a haunting "blowing" sound dominates; it is toward the middle of this section that a fragile trumpet melody emerges and recedes. Section 4 marks a faint return to the sounds and events of the first two sections; section 1's sustained tones commingle with the rhythmic activity of section 2. In section 4 three arch-like phrases, of which the second reaches the loudest dynamic peak, deliberately retreat to a final cadence.

Cadences at section endings are moments of repose that carry more structural weight than cadences that bring shorter, more hierarchically surface spans of music to rest without disrupting a section's inner coherence. From a standpoint of analytical fantasy, a sectional cadence is an event at which the players "agree" to jettison an established coherence in search of something new. For example, the first sectional cadence (figure 6.5) is triggered by a sudden loud multiphonic in the saxophone (2:35–2:45); section 2 is established in its wake.

Though sustained, as were other tones before it, the saxophone's sheer amplitude and intensity seem to wipe away everything that preceded it, perhaps acting as a king of sustained tones, banishing further ones in its wake, and mandating new developments. The players comply, but not unanimously, as evidenced by the bass's sustained C3 tremolo (2:42.5) that enters about halfway through the multiphonic. This provides support to the multiphonic, while its new timbre (tremolo) and register reframe perception. The multiphonic becomes a point of elision, morphing during the course of its very duration from the cadence function into a clarion call for fresh material. The players soon respond.

The new section is fully exposed when the multiphonic ceases (2:46). At this moment, the bass adds a sustained C♯4 to the C3, and the tape's intermittent sounds (henceforth onomatopoetically designated "FT") are more prominently heard, as they are no longer masked by Bhob's sax. Soon after (2:49), Chris (guitar) enters with "intermittent distortion rumbles" to which Mike

Figure 6.5. Sectional cadence, 2:30–3:00.

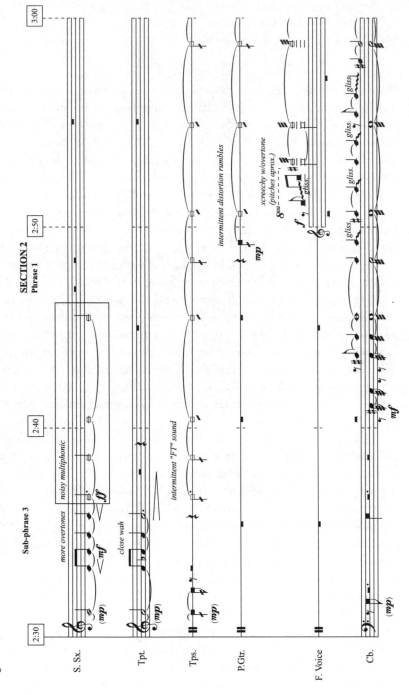

246

(bass) responds by turning the sustained C#4 into short falling glissandos. Liz (voice) adds to this increased activity with skyscraping "screechy" sounds. The result is a dense texture of highly rhythmicized actions that carry forward the increased loudness of the multiphonic through a decidedly new character.

Amid this louder and denser music (figure 6.6), the trumpet's sustained G#4 (3:18) appears as a beckoning of the past. The players seem to gravitate toward its quieter energy; soon after it fades, they begin to tamp down the overall activity and loudness, though not in a meaningful way until the A2 pizzicato in the bass (3:29). It is as if they recognize, but are reluctant to join in, a reprise of the tranquil landscape of section 1. It takes a fresh event (the A2 pizzicato) to motivate the group to change. Soon after (3:36.5), a second pizzicato event on Bb2 and G2 creates the critical mass to convince the players that the first cadence in the new section has arrived; in response, they pull back further. Chris (guitar) stops playing, and the others slightly decrease their rhythmic activity, as the first phrase (of the second section) ends and the second begins.

3.2 The Discovery of a Subphrase

A subphrase is created when a moment of articulation is achieved without disrupting the ongoing making of a phrase, that is, without full repose. Phrase 3 in section 1 is the first I hear dividing into subphrases (0:46.5–1:04.5 and 1:04.5–1:24.5; see figure 6.1) due in part to the sudden and fleeting rhythmic volatility of the bass and tapes (1:04.5). This is a particularly beautiful moment that highlights the subtle way in which the BSC discovers form, and therefore demands a thorough description of its context.

Phrase 3 begins when the saxophone moves from its sustained A4 to G#4 (figure 6.4). The trumpet is silent, having recently dropped out (0:40–0:43.5) as part of the cadential formula at the end of phrase 2. But soon after the saxophone entrance, the trumpet quickly returns to the sustained A4, which is now familiar as a phrase initiator as each phrase so far has begun in this way.

The close association of this phrase beginning with the previous two is made "rough" by the saxophone, which becomes more rhythmically active and expands its interval from the trumpet to a quarter tone. The vocal "oohs" also cultivate a rough coherence by bridging the end of phrase 2 to the start of phrase 3, thus binding all the music so far into a single section. After about eight seconds the vocal "oohs" end (0:56) and the music becomes particularly still. Vic (cello/circuits) enters at Liz's (voice) exit with a murmuring static sound. Soon after, Bhob (sax) ceases the irregular rearticulations and cleanly sustains the G(4. Greg (trumpet) timbrally supports this diminishment by gradually fading the distortion effect on his A4.

Figure 6.6. 3:10–3:40.

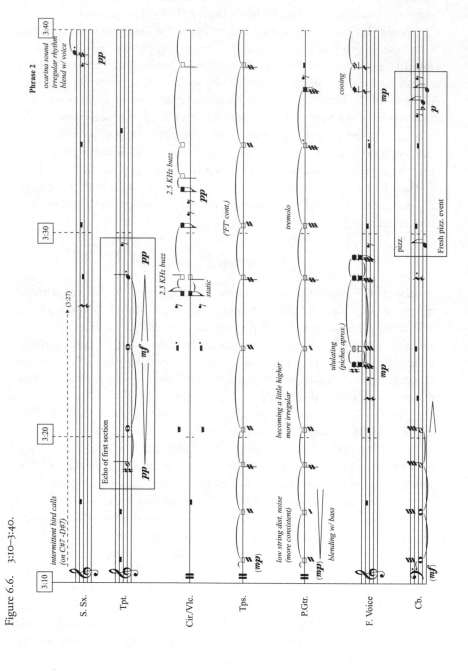

248

At this moment, just before Mike (bass) enters (1:03; see figure 6.1), the players seem to be bringing the music to cadence. Mike interrupts this imminent repose with a new and startling snap pizzicato gesture. Howie (tapes) supports Mike's entrance similarly with a new sound (tape spins); the two engage in rhythmic dialogue. It is as if Howie agrees that a cadence should not come here, again in the same way, with the saxophone and trumpet playing a diminuendo on a sustained tone; it is here perhaps that Howie exemplifies his role as a "wrench," described by Rainey.

Through these new gestures, and their increased rhythmic and dynamic fervor, the second subphrase of phrase 3 is initiated; the saxophone and trumpet still do die away, though this time submitting to an interruption, as opposed to progressing to cadence. The music shifts. Perhaps at this *very* moment, without knowing what comes next, as a listener I could perceive a strong enough transformation that a new phrase, or even new section, might be beginning. But because of the instability caused by the interruption, there lingers doubt of a more substantive change. Greg's entrance on a sustained D♯4 (1:11) signals that this is not the next section, or even the next phrase, because it forms a strong link back to, and is a clear development of, the earlier sustained A4s. My perception of a more substantive change dissolves.

As the D♯4 persists, Howie continues the "spins," perhaps resisting the erstwhile eminence of the sustained tone, but Mike (bass) does not join, giving another signal that the interruption was fleeting, and that the flow of the first subphrase, and thus the sectional coherence of all the preceding music, is still operative. At 1:16.5, Vic deepens his static, but Howie's spins are now evaporating. With Liz's (voice) entrance (1:20) she seems to try to reinvigorate Howie's seditious tape spins by mimicking their rhythmic excitement through birdlike sounds. Howie responds with a single loud tape spin (1:22) in clear rhythmic dialogue with Liz; however, the mutiny in this gesture fails as the now formulaic sound of a slowly fading trumpet pitch announces, "the phrase is now cadencing." The players consent by coming to a brief silence (1:24), paralleling the cadential formula from the ends of phrases 1 and 2; disappearing trumpet tone leads to silence.

3.3 Whole versus Part Listening

There are moments at which I am not concerned with, nor equally able to distinguish, what each member of the BSC is playing. I conceive of their group sound as if it is created by an individual, as Stelzer described in his account of the BSC group mind. This type of *whole* listening does not imply undervaluation of polyphony in a complex texture; I just imagine this multi-instrumental polyphony as if it were coming from a single source. A good moment to hear this is at the beginning of section 2, as described above in the discussion of the first sectional cadence, in which the tape, guitar, voice, and bass meld together as a single complex sound, following the saxophone multi-phonic.

At other times, particularly when the texture is less dense, I track each individual instrument, paying attention to entrances and exits, and especially observing how players respond to and complement one another. These two types of listening experiences, whole and part, are not mutually exclusive. There are moments when the texture is less dense, and one set of instruments seems to form a composite sound, while others act independently at the same time. An example of this is at the opening between the saxophone and the trumpet (0:05–0:24.5; see figure 6.3); while the trumpet holds an A4, the saxophone squeaks out short B♭5s, which sound as if they could originate from the sustained tone, as if some kind of rogue partial. These two instruments meld even more in the second and third phrases (0:28.5–1:07), where, as described, the saxophone joins the trumpet's sustained tone in a close interval.

While the saxophone and trumpet are fashioning this composite, the other players form an independent counterpoint. In phrase 1, the bass scratch tones develop an autonomous line. In phrase 2, at 0:30.5, the voice enters in the "winds" register, but with a contrasting timbre (spoken-like) and rhythmic momentum that yields its own distinct part. As a listener, I hear these added distinct parts help create a perception of only two voices, of which the composite is one.

3.4 How Timbre Alone Can Be Music: Section 2, Phrase 2

An important assumption for the BSC is that timbre without a stable fundamental pitch or harmonic grounding can be a primary component of music, that it can *be* the music. It is axiomatic that music unfolds beginnings, middles, and ends. This paradigm is operative on every hierarchic level from the smallest subphrases to wholes. In pitch-based music, harmony, melody, and voice leading, supported by rhythmic determination, generate *potential* in a "beginning," *momentum* and *anticipation* through a "middle," and *repose* and *arrival* at an "end." This unfolds in accordance with culturally validated structural formulas.

As I have shown, timbre aided by rhythm can also lead to perception of beginnings, middles, and ends on multiple hierarchic levels. Though the BSC does not employ metric patterning to project form (common in African drumming and electronica), they do create a more fluid free massing and lessening of rhythmic density common to some modern Western classical composers such as Varese, Xenakis, and others mentioned earlier.

For example, we have seen how, in phrase 1 of *Phoneme (3)*, the shifting spectra and rhythm of a scratch tone helps to move the music through a "middle" toward a cadential goal. At the end of section 1, a piercing saxophone multiphonic first "ends" section 1 and then "begins" section 2. Though these examples both involve pitch, it is timbre that creates the motion forward; the scratch tones craft momentum for the sustained A4 (trumpet), and the multiphonic is pitched, though with a complex timbre that is at the center of the sound experience. The first span of music in which pitch is put aside almost completely is the second phrase of section 2, transcribed in figure 6.7, where timbre alone becomes the music.

A quiet, monolithic texture emerges after the first phrase of the section 2 cadences on the two bass pizzicatos mentioned earlier; the players meld into a whole. The pacing decelerates as they settle into this slowly evolving sound texture, which forms a new phrase. Its shape and direction are evident in its two subphrases (3:37–4:22 and 4:22–5:30), which together form an arch of activity that peaks twice: once at the beginning of the second subphrase (4:22) and again fifteen seconds later. This shape is composed through the careful control of rhythmic momentum and the timing of sounds' entrances and exits.

As the tape FTs and the 2.5-kHz buzz of Vic's circuits persist, the end of phrase 1 is not crisply defined, although the slowing rearticulation of the FTs does ease the momentum. Two entrances signal the start of the next phrase: subtle and rhythmically irregular ocarina-like sounds from the saxophone blend with high-pitched vocal cooing. By 3:54 both players (sax and voice) stop, allowing the music to settle further into the static environment created by Howie's tape and Vic's buzz. Forward momentum essentially halts, and for the next thirteen seconds (3:54–4:07) the other players remain silent, allowing the music to just *be* this lovely crackling and spitting sound. The prolonged stasis, gradually approached and departed, suggests a calm "middle" distinct from a cadential kind of repose.

The music nudges forward when Vic adds a 500 Hz "purr" (4:07). Liz enters soon after with sporadic and playful notes (B5 and C♯6) that add to a building momentum. Vic joins this increased activity by allowing more and more articulative attacks, which very quickly excite the overtones of the buzz and build the drive of this "middle" toward *something*. He thrusts the phrase to its first peak with the sudden entrance of a loud "crackle-rumble" (4:22). Its novelty is nearly substantive enough to articulate a new phrase, but considering the continuation of Howie's tape and Vic's buzz, and the lack of any repose before it, it only initiates a new subphrase.

This first peak, at the beginning of the second subphrase, begins to die away as the crackle-rumble weakens and becomes more focused, sounding like a Geiger counter (4:36). With this, Liz sings a "quiet scream" in slowly swelling,

Figure 6.7.   Phrase 2, section 2.

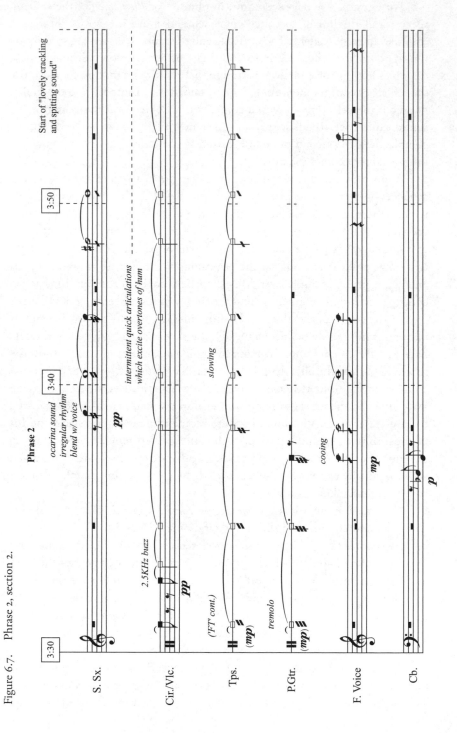

252

Figure 6.7. (Continued)

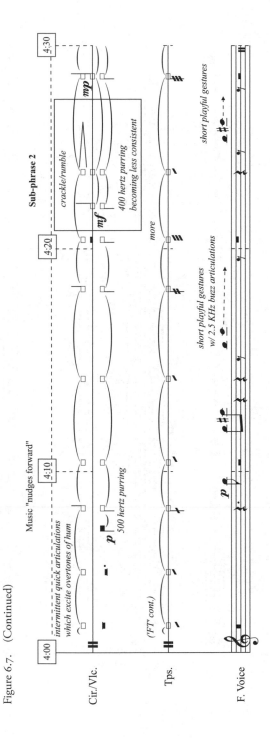

253

Figure 6.7. (Continued)

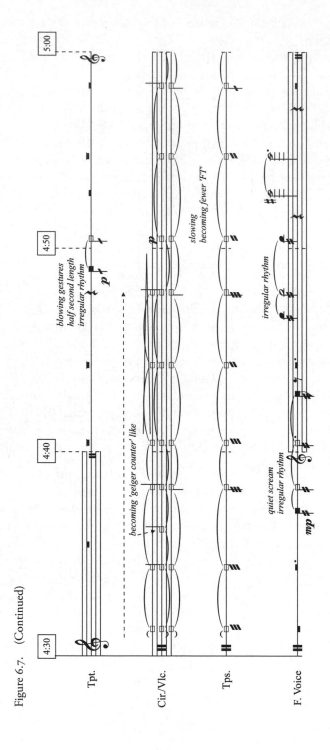

Figure 6.7. (Continued)

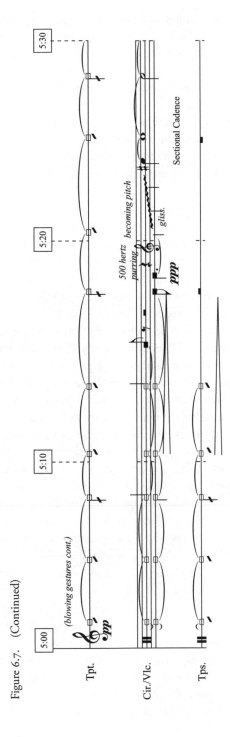

irregular rhythms. Vic and Howie reply by similarly intensifying their respective continuing sounds, leading to the second peak, a musical moment that is an arrival within a "middle" (of the second subphrase). This intensity sustains until 4:57, when Liz concludes her quiet scream. Vic and Howie immediately sense this ending and curtail the intensity of their sounds; there are fewer FTs, and the complexity of Vic's buzz and purr diminishes. Though the entrance of trumpet "blowing" adds a new layer of timbre, the gesture still recedes and progresses toward stasis, as the entire phrase arch comes to completion. With this, a cadence ending section 2 is achieved as Howie withers to silence and Vic reduces his contribution to a single tone at 5:18.5.

3.5 Melody and Timbre in Section 3

Description of the first subphrase of section 3, notated in figure 6.8, will reveal how and why a melody emerges in the second subphrase. Transforming timbre alone continues to be the music in this first subphrase, the piece's quietest span, where Bhob (sax) and Vic (circuits) come to the fore.

The beginning of this section is hard to pinpoint. The first indication is at 5:20 where Vic morphs the "purr" from the last phrase into a *very* quiet sustaining tone around C#5. During and after this transformation, Greg (trumpet) continues the subtle irregular blowing gestures from the previous section. By 5:30, seven seconds after the C#5 has fully emerged, the players have still not completely shifted out of the internal coherence of section 2; they are slowly segueing into section 3 with a fusion of old (blowing) and new (C#5). As a listener at this moment, I sense a change, but I am still unsure of its formal significance.

At 5:31 the music begins to operate in a new way, with a new kind of coherence. Greg accents his irregular trumpet blowing with a new "lip" sound. Bhob answers by commencing his own blowing sound on the sax, which will come to dominate the entire third section. The other players seem to recognize a suggestion in this blowing and leave space for him to explore this delicate trademark sound. Their next articulations, encouraging Bhob, are decisive and collective, and so at last clarify that a new section is dawning: Mike (bass) places a low C2 toward the end of Bhob's first blowing; then Chris (guitar) scuffs a low "scrape and rumble"; Greg seems to answer both of them by increasing the articulations in his irregular blowing, which merge with the timbre of the guitar (this is the last of Greg's "blowing" prolonged from the previous section); Vic joins Greg and Chris by initiating a "3.5-kHz buzz" and moving his C#4 to D#4 a rare example of voice leading.

Soon after the end of this combined sound (Chris, Greg, and Vic) (5:38.5), Bhob recognizes the opening created for him and walks through with a second

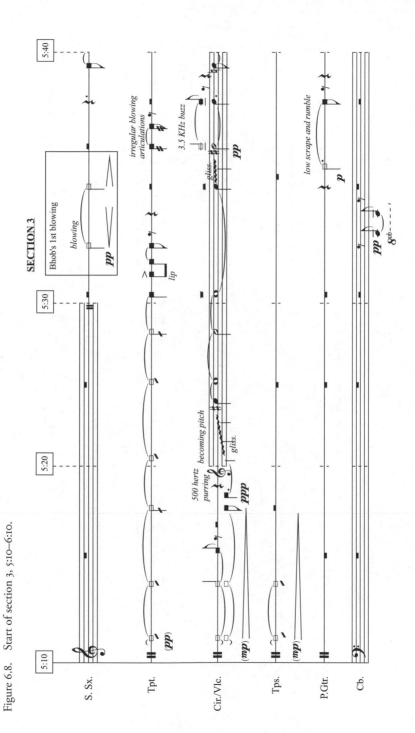

Figure 6.8. Start of section 3, 5:10–6:10.

257

Figure 6.8. (Continued)

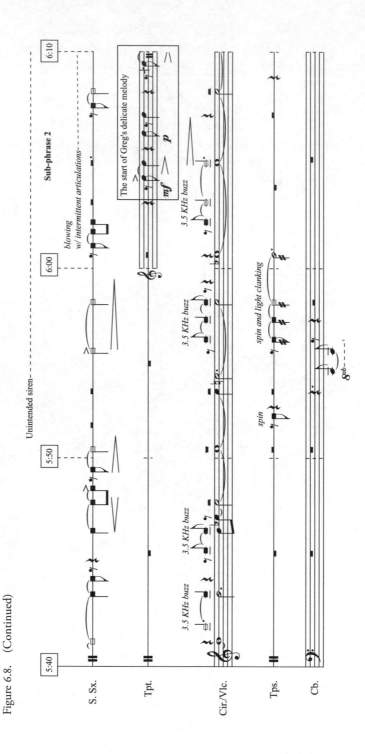

blowing sound. From here, the music settles into an otherworldly stasis; I imagine the blowing as the irregular breathing of an astronaut and Vic's circuits as the ambient sound of a spacecraft. The music is still and *"concrète"* like a field recording of some mysterious extraterrestrial place coming to the fore in a tape collage.

Unexpectedly, a siren (5:51) from outside the concert hall breaks the stillness. The musicians respond to the chance event by moving away from atmosphere and back toward progression.[35] Howie's tapes produce a transient and hushed "spin" (5:52.5), while Mike adds C2 (5:55.5), familiar from the phrase's beginning. Soon after, Bhob enunciates a stronger blowing sound, after six seconds of not playing. With this, Vic for the first time synchronizes his 3.5-kHz buzz with the blowing, while Howie joins this harmonization with "clanking and spins."

This increased momentum, as well as the crescendo of the approaching siren, seems to spur Greg to act with an even more intentional (and more intense) gesture. His loud and short D5 (6:03.5) instantly suggests a new beginning, but it is only of a subphrase, not a phrase, as both Vic and Bhob unaffectedly maintain their respective sounds. Building upon his decisive D5, Greg begins to unfold a very delicate melody, the only unambiguous melodic moment in the piece. He thereby imputes an accompanimental role to Bhob's blowing and Vic's buzz, though he does not completely allow this melody to be the focus. This handmade tune, with its complex and unstable spectra, seems to balance the interests of pitch and timbre. Here, my focus remains on the heightened timbre, and less on the actual pitch movement. As a result, I hear Bhob's blowing as both accompaniment and counterpoint to Greg's melody. In this rare moment, timbre and melody unite.

4. The Immediacy of a Timbre

I have written about timbre in *Phoneme (3)* as an agent of change: its contextual novelty can establish a new phrase, its rhythmic acceleration can drive toward a cadence, and its gradual spectral transformation can make sections cohere, all while steering to and from cadential repose.

---

35. It is common (but not obligatory) for the musicians to respond to unintended concert hall noise, whether it be coughing, someone taking off a noisy jacket, or a cell phone. The musicians very much play off the energy of the audience, and responding to their sound (or that of a passing fire truck) is an effective method of engagement.

Timbre also has immediacy. As a listener, I am drawn in by the beauty and originality of a sound's spectrum. Often an engaging timbre is enough to create an extraordinary musical moment, even without context. The microstructures of overtones and tiny irregular rhythms grant timbre the potential to evoke a universe of complexity and mystery in every moment. From this vantage point, it could seem unnecessary to know what comes before, or surmise what comes next.

The BSC embraces this outlook, but through their music also posit that a sound without context can say only so much, for so long. They put forward two, often simultaneous, listening experiences: timbre for timbre's sake, and timbre in a context, as part of a narrative. For example, in the "middle" of the second phrase of section 2, as a listener, I am absolutely engaged by the intricate flux of sound created by a "lovely crackling and spitting," and for a moment may forget the formal context. I engage the musical now in the midst of a larger narrative. The potential to listen this way exists throughout.

The BSC thus create what could be called a *now-focused* linear narrative, evoking "vertical time" through beautiful timbres, and evoking "linearity" when these timbres shape a clear form (Kramer 1988). I hear this kind of narrative in the music of many cultures using timbre to balance "now" and "forward," from the intricate detail of breath sounds in Japanese shakuhachi flute playing to the dancing spectra of Tuvan throat singers.

What is perhaps unique to the BSC, and other groups like it, is how the live process of improvisation creates an anxiety of anticipation. On improvisation, Rainey says, "it is always in danger of completely falling apart, and there is nothing there to save it." It is performance "without a net" (Rainey), and as a listener, I am on the edge of my seat, and as a result, the *moment* of music making is more lucid. The BSC, and the timbre-and-form subculture from which it was born, values this intimate and immediate engagement with its audience and extend that to the room itself. Rainey continues:

> You are taking into account the space in a way that composed music never does, unless it is composed for that space. The tempos that you choose, the sonorities are so specific to that place and that time. And that is really conveyed [to the audience]. (Rainey)

It seems fitting to end by asking if and how the now-ness of timbre stems from its inseparable bond with form, and, for the BSC, a form that is discovered through improvisation. Were the BSC and the timbre-and-form community originally attracted to timbre because of its now-focused nature? Or did an interest in timbre come first, leading to encounter and eventual valuation of its immediacy? The circularity of the questions underscores how timbre and form are intermingled. One might say the same of pitch and form, although pitch events are cognitively speaking more perceptually discrete than timbral ones, and offer our listening faculties more ways to group and parse. Most BSC musicians first played music based in pitch and harmony and then adopted a timbre-based approach. This influence could account for why the BSC, at least in the case of *Phoneme (3)*, discovers a hierarchal form whose sections, phrases and cadences, as I have described them, could be seen as modeled on the structures of more definitely pitched music.

The BSC puts forth a system of values based in time-honored principles of composition, balance, form, and texture, while downplaying pitch and harmonic progression, perhaps because pitch's forward trajectory undermines timbre's now-ness. In pitch-based music I may linger for a moment "in the now," and perhaps focus on the beautiful tone of a violin or guitar, but the main interest is in how pitch, melody, and harmony progress. In timbral narrative it is possible to follow a line forward, but the line is elusive. The BSC can guide listeners onward through and to the next beautiful sound, inviting them to linger, perhaps outside of the form for a moment. In the tale of *Phoneme (3)*, it is not clear, nor does it matter, whether this now-focused linearity results from form serving timbre, or the timbre serving form. As listeners, we can decide this at every moment.

References

Bailey, Derek. 1992. *Improvisation: Its Nature and Practice in Music*. New York: Da Capo Press.

Collins, Nicolas. 2006. *Handmade Electronic Music: The Art of Hardware Hacking*. New York: Routledge.

Feller, Ross. 2002. "Resistant Strains of Postmodernism: The Music of Helmut Lachenmann and Brian Ferneyhough." In *Postmodern Music/Postmodern Thought*, ed. Judy Lochhead and Joseph Auner, 249–262. London: Routledge.

Fischlin, Daniel, and Ajay Heble, eds. 2004. *The Other Side of Nowhere*. Middletown, CT: Wesleyan University Press.

Ghazala, Reed. 2005. *Circuit-Bending: Build Your Own Alien Instruments*. Indianapolis, IN: Wiley.

Guck, Marion A. 1994. "Analytical Fictions." *Music Theory Spectrum* 16(2): 217–230.

———. 1997. "Rigors of Subjectivity." *Perspectives of New Music* 31(1): 306–314.

Hegarty, Paul. 2007. *Noise/Music: A History*. New York: Continuum.

Kramer, Jonathan. 1988. *The Time of Music*. New York: Schirmer.

Monson, Ingrid. 2007. *Freedom Sounds: Civil Rights Call Out to Jazz and Africa*. Oxford: Oxford University Press.

Nattiez, Jean-Jacques. 1990. *Music and Discourse: Toward a Semiology of Music*. Trans. Carolyn Abbate. Princeton: Princeton University Press.

Nettl, Bruno, ed. 1998. *In the Course of Performance*. Chicago: University of Chicago Press.

Panzner, Joe. 2004. "The Stylus Interview Series." Rev. May 10, 2004. http://www.stylusmagazine.com/articles/weekly_article/nmperign-the-stylus-interview-series.htm (accessed December 8, 2009).

Prévost, Edwin. 1995. *No Sound Is Innocent.* Harlow, Essex, UK: Copula.

Reynolds, Simon. [1990] 2004. "Noise." In *Audio Culture: Readings in Modern Music,* ed. Christopher Cox and Daniel Warner, 54–58. New York: Continuum.

Russolo, Luigi. [1913] 2004. "The Art of Noises: Futurist Manifesto." In *Audio Culture: Readings in Modern Music,* ed. Christopher Cox and Daniel Warner, 10–14. New York: Continuum.

Schaeffer, Pierre. [1966] 2004. "Acousmatics." Trans. Daniel W. Smith. In *Audio Culture: Readings in Modern Music,* ed. Christopher Cox and Daniel Warner, 76–81. New York: Continuum.

Simoni, Mary ed. 2006. *Analytical Methods of Electroacoustic Music.* New York: Routledge.

Smalley, Denis. 1997. "Spectromorphology: Explaining Sound-Shapes." *Organised Sound* 2(2): 107–126.

Toop, David. 2004. *Haunted Weather.* London: Serpent's Tail.

Varèse, Edgard. [1936] 2004. "The Liberation of Sound." In *Audio Culture: Readings in Modern Music,* ed. Christopher Cox and Daniel Warner, 17–21. New York: Continuum.

Zorn, John, ed. 2000. *Arcana: Musicians on Music.* New York: Granary Books.

———. 2007. *Arcana II: Musicians on Music.* New York: Hips Road/Tzadik.

CHAPTER 7

Rhythm and Folk Drumming (P'ungmul) as the Musical Embodiment of Communal Consciousness in South Korean Village Society

Nathan Hesselink

Photo: Folklorized version of communal labor team percussion music (*ture kut*), Kyŏnggi province.

Introduction

Rhythm has always been central to the Korean cultural experience. According to some of the earliest documentation of the fledgling nation—namely, Chen Suo's third-century *Sanguo zhi* (*History of the Three Kingdoms*)—music, dance, ritual, and the agricultural cycle have enjoyed an intimate relationship on the peninsula since Korea's inception, and at the heart of such interactions lies percussion music and dance. While drumming became an integral component of Korean life on every level of society and in nearly every social context, including formal court ceremonies and more public large-scale religious celebrations, in this chapter I will focus on such expressions borne of the everyday experiences of the commoner classes in the villages. Because of its longevity and ubiquity, musicologists and historians have forwarded the argument that rhythm as an object and activity has been witness to and participated in the development of a foundational Korean identity (Yi Sangjin 2002: 27–34; Kim and Vermeersch 2004).

Over the centuries village musical life began to coalesce around a percussive tradition that came to be known alternatively as *p'ungmul* (literally "wind objects"[1]) or *nongak* (farmers' music), an art form representing a repository of indigenous and imported musical, religious, philosophical, and material cultural elements (Hesselink 2006: 48–89). What this means on the purely rhythmic level is that *p'ungmul* has acquired Korea's rich variety of patterns and cycles, a sampling that includes simple, compound, and composite meters, as well as rhythmically unmeasured passages. In the world of generalities, however, South Korea is often placed in contradistinction to other East Asian drumming traditions, emphasizing a ternary division of the beat versus the binary divisions common to neighboring Japan and China (Hwang 2004: 10–11; Komoda and Nogawa 2002: 571–573; Jones 1998: 124). While this is certainly a reductive reckoning of the East Asian rhythmic scene,[2] a predominance of compound meters highlighting the creative potentials and possibilities between what in the West we would identify as 12/8 and 6/4 does immediately distinguish Korea's "groove" from others in the region.

---

1. The preferred generic term for rural drumming and dance throughout much of the twentieth century, *p'ungmul* is a composite of the two Sino-Korean characters *p'ung* (wind) and *mul* (object). Most likely this is a cultural borrowing from China, where legend has it that wind stirs humans to dance and sing, hence the use of "wind objects" (see further Hesselink 2006: 15–16).

2. Unmeasured rhythm is not uncommon in Japan and China, and the idea of *ma*—"space" or elasticity—is central to Japanese rhythm and musical aesthetics.

In this chapter I will use musical-theoretical concepts to describe the means by which the rhythms and performance practices of one village *p'ungmul* tradition embody a sense of communal consciousness, a core theme in South Korean folklore and anthropology. My analysis will focus on the group known as Imshil P'ilbong Nongak (P'ungmul), one of the last vestiges of rural, village-style drumming and dance from North Chŏlla province directly connected to activity associated with the agricultural cycle. P'ilbong's repertoire includes a set of work rhythms (but with strong religious overtones) drawn from the age-old custom known as *ture kut* (communal labor *p'ungmul*), commonly acknowledged as the oldest form of *p'ungmul* and one exhibiting the strongest reliance on group participation (Yang Chinsŏng 1989: 14, 39; Chu Kanghyŏn 1997; see also Yi Pohyŏng 1984). Today this group of rhythms is subsumed as a movement titled *Ch'aegut* within a more general, entertainment-oriented "piece," a historical survivor unmoored to its original context due to the discontinuation of communal labor *p'ungmul* in the past three decades.

An examination of these rhythms' structure and organization at the micro and macro levels reveals two key principles that contribute to such a communal awareness, principles I will refer to as *recurrence* and *reinforcement*. My approach will draw on two methodologies now well established within Korean folk music studies: (1) look at the internal construction and logic of individual cycles/patterns, then identify underlying units found across other rhythms (Kim Hyŏnsuk 1991; Pak Chongsŏl 1991); and (2) interpret the larger ordering and placement of these rhythms and what this might mean or suggest for the performers' and/or onlookers' appreciation and enjoyment (Kim Inu 1993). The more specific task of this analysis will be an accounting of various surface-level structures and processes and their connection to the deeper, foundational motivation of communal consciousness. The broader goal will be to remind us of music's meanings and efficacy beyond the purely aesthetic realm, and more specifically within the Korean context, that rhythm and folk drumming can act as a vehicle by which the past is presented in a tangible way to modern experience.

History, Ideology, and Personal Motivation

As political and geographical boundaries settled during the Chosŏn dynasty (1392–1910), diverse regional varieties of dialect, personal character attributes, and melodic-rhythmic styles formed and became associated with their respective local drumming traditions. In the first half of the twentieth century, however, folk music and musicians suffered tremendous neglect and injustice as a consequence of war, modernization, and societal indifference, and so in the early 1960s the South Korean government established a means by which to discover, support, and promote such traditional arts and artists—in English often referred to as the "Cultural Asset Preservation Law" (*munhwajae pohobŏp;* see Hesselink 1998 and Howard 2006). The end result was the recognition of five *p'ungmul* organizations considered the representative models (cultural assets) of each one's particular regional practice. And so while the metropolis came to define and dictate the locus and nature of most musical activity in late twentieth-century South Korea, village folk drumming (and dance) remained alive in rural and semirural locales out in the provinces, reflecting a combination of local dedication and perseverance encouraged by governmental policy and financial support. It also has become a bastion of nostalgia and national pride.

Segments within the broader *p'ungmul* community became overtly politicized beginning in the 1970s. With the rise of the so-called people's (*minjung*) movement—a political, religious, and aesthetic collective that strove to establish a national identity and ethos in the world of ordinary citizens—activist college students and labor union members embraced *p'ungmul* as a powerful visual and sonic indicator of what was deemed to be a "pure" expression of Korean-ness. Support came from higher levels of academia as well: *minjung*-inspired folklorists and anthropologists often spoke of the remnants of a "communal consciousness" (*kongdongch'e ŭishik*) in village society, a contemporary marker of what was believed to be an older and broader egalitarian worldview that was manifest socially through the political and familial ties of the village inhabitants and identifiable in events featuring performances of *p'ungmul* (O Chongsŏp 1989; Kim Inu 1993). In these academics' writings and related theorizing, however, proof of *p'ungmul* as instigator and maintainer of communal consciousness was offered through association alone, not by a structural analysis of its constituent elements.

My own initial encounter with *p'ungmul* came in 1994. I was fortunate to have been invited to see a famous cultural asset troupe from the southwest present a full ninety-minute performance at an outdoor venue in Seoul. Like many newcomers to the tradition, I was completely bowled over by the boisterous mixture of sound, color, and movement, all accompanied at a deafening level by gongs and drums. The complexity and diversity of the rhythms being performed by musicians who were simultaneously dancing, alongside the fantastic array of geometric shapes being created in the air by spinning-tasseled hats, all competed for my rapt attention. It seemed wonderfully coordinated and chaotic at the same time.

This encounter also prompted a much deeper connection and meaning for me that became apparent as I began to attend more performances, formally study, and eventually teach *p'ungmul* to others. I had always been attracted to percussion music, especially drumming. It engaged a part of me beyond the immediate pleasure of physically moving along with what I was hearing to include a special consciousness of multidimensional space in and around me, a kind of synesthesia that linked motion and choreography with percussive timbres and rhythmic structures. With *p'ungmul* I finally felt that I was fully embracing all of these modalities, because I was now required to move in time (the rhythms) and in space (individual choreography, group ground formations). Drumming and dancing in this Korean context thus brought together the external and internal aspects of my past experiences with rhythm to form a single, unified entity.

Embedded within this highly personal sense of awareness was the equal acknowledgment that others were contributing to the sounds and motions of the music. Under the right conditions—which often meant a large, enthusiastic, and socially close group of performers (i.e., friends, neighbors, and relatives) performing for a longer period of time (at least thirty minutes)—there came a moment or moments when I suddenly felt the loss of individual self, so that it seemed that the group was now moving and breathing in perfect synchrony. I was struck by how intense my feelings of group cohesion and communal awareness had become, sentiments I similarly discovered in the above-mentioned literature. In one specific circumstance I even lost my sense of time, so that afterward while sharing drinks with fellow performers, I reckoned that I couldn't account for nearly twenty minutes of the performance. I now realize that these experiences were not unique to me, and that the Korean literature even has terms for both a heightened sense of togetherness and a kind of focused attention frequently experienced as a suspension of time (to be discussed below). These phenomena, however, are generally only described on the surface level or theorized sociologically without any real explanation as to how the music's structure might contribute to their existence. And so I was drawn to the assignment of this volume to analyze a world music tradition with an eye to both explaining the particularities while simultaneously suggesting parallels with the wider world. This chapter can be seen as a way of analyzing and intellectualizing these experiences and processes through a musicological lens.

Repertoire and Instrumentation

Imshil P'ilbong Nongak is based in the mountainous area encompassing the village of P'ilbong, located in Kangjin district, Imshil county, North Chŏlla province, in the southwest part of the peninsula. Historically considered one of the poorest areas in the entire region, P'ilbong's inhabitants were nonetheless able to maintain a satisfactory farming existence and thriving *p'ungmul* tradition until the 1980s. The exodus of many younger village members to the cities during this decade posed the first real threat to the livelihood of the local *p'ungmul* group. As a result, beginning in 1980 a number of large-scale and high-profile communal *p'ungmul* performances were staged in the village with accommodations made for the media and academics (Chŏng Pyŏngho et al. 1980; Kim Sunam et al. 1986), efforts repeated as recently as 2002 (Kwon 2005: 142–148). Alongside the initial push to preserve these inherited practices was the desire to acquire cultural asset status, a move that if successful would guarantee an adequate amount of security from governmental support and increased student fees. After nearly a decade of hard work, luck, and considerable financial depletion, P'ilbong's troupe was designated the fifth and last such cultural asset for *p'ungmul* in 1988 (Hesselink 1998: 319–322). In spite of this success—including the building of a new training institute to accommodate the flow of students that began to pour in—as late as 1996 many homes in the village were still without electricity and running water.

Of the five designated organizations, P'ilbong (along with the cultural asset troupe Kangnŭng Nongak on the east coast) maintains the closest roots to an older agrarian and communal village lifestyle. *P'ungmul* continues to be found and enjoyed in most of its original contexts, including ritual fund-raising (*kŏlgung* or *kŏllippae p'ungmul*), village cleansing (*mae kut*), and the more secular entertainment-oriented performance (the *p'an kut*), though cultural asset status has forced the ensemble to focus more on its entertainment-based repertoire, to the slight detriment of its religious and work activities. Within the *p'an kut* we find the movement *Ch'aegut,* the collection of rhythms based on communal labor of yesteryear that is analyzed in this chapter. In the past *p'ungmul* was typically performed by an ensemble of adult male villagers playing on gongs and drums, with little or no distinctions made between performers and onlookers in terms of active involvement. Today women and youth have joined the ranks (a combination of expediency and the effects of democratization). Out of necessity, P'ilbong now also recruits new members from neighboring villages and provincial centers.

Ties to a more "traditional" Korea have helped bolster P'ilbong's star status as an institution. For reasons not always entirely clear, P'ilbong's troupe has been singled out almost exclusively by musicologists and political theorists as encapsulating the one true, "authentic" expression of Korean folk performative culture (Kim Wŏnho 1999; Yi Yŏngbae 2000; see also Pak Sangguk et al. 1999). Its location in the heart of the Chŏlla provinces—an area commonly viewed as the cradle of Korea's most influential folk music genres (Song Pangsong 2007: 426–458)—provides a partial explanation, although it is not hard to identify similar small-scale communities with active *p'ungmul* in other provinces. P'ilbong's training institute was the most frequently visited and emulated by urban South Korean youth in the past two decades, with Korean college students sharing belief in the village's older, authentic essence (Hesselink 2006: 143–147). P'ilbong members also frequently come to the United States to conduct master classes and workshops for college and university Korean drum circles (Kwŏn Hyeryŏn 2001: 52).

All *p'ungmul* ensembles share the same core set of two gongs and two drums that are either strapped to the body or are held in the hand. The performers simultaneously dance while playing, a practice that further distinguishes Korea from the rest of East Asia (at least pre-touring folkloric troupes of China in the latter twentieth century), as well as most other world drumming traditions. Although there are many variations in instrument design depending on the troupe and province, here I will concentrate on the standard models of the core instruments used in entertainment-oriented performances (the *p'an kut*). Those who have attended a *p'ungmul* event will also recall the sound of the double-reed shawm known as the *hojŏk* (*t'aep'yŏngso*), the gritty melodic element in what is otherwise a predominantly percussive showcase. Despite the widespread use of this instrument, however, its music and musicians occupy a separate domain in terms of group interaction (most are independent of any troupe affiliation) and provincial loyalties, because it is possible for nearly any shawm player of any regional repertoire to play with any group in any manner they see fit. And so its inclusion in the analysis is beyond the scope of this chapter.

Gongs

The *sangsoe* (lead *soe* player) traditionally leads the ensemble. The *soe* (literally "iron" or "metal"), also known as the *kkwaenggwari* (an onomatopoeic designation), is a small, handheld gong made of brass. *Soe* are produced by either pouring liquid metal into a mold or by forging, the latter process considered superior in quality. The instrument is struck on its front surface by a mallet held with the free hand, while the hand holding the *soe* manipulates the sound through a number of available damping techniques. *Soe* are commonly divided into male and female, the former generally associated with a higher and sharper toned pitch and the latter with a lower and more subdued one. It is customary for the lead player to play on a male *soe,* accompanied by the second player (*pusoe*) on a female *soe,* and for the rest of players in the section to be likewise paired. Most likely an import from the Chinese imperial court, the *soe* is listed as an accompanying instrument to Confucian dance and ritual in the 1493 *Akhak kwebŏm* (Guide to the Study of Music).

The companion to the *soe* is the *ching,* a large, handheld gong also made of brass (by casting or forging). The *ching* is struck with a padded beater; a good instrument produces an after-tone characterized by three undulations of sound that in Korean is referred to as *samp'aŭm* (three-wave sound). *Ching* strokes tend to coincide with the first beat (downbeat) of each rhythmic pattern and are thought of as the "sonic glue" that binds together the rest of the ensemble. The sound of the *ching* has also been employed as a signal for retreat in the military, and as a means of sounding an alarm in village society; there is also the noteworthy but minority viewpoint that the gong's sound is capable of changing the bone structure of an unborn child in the womb of a shaman (Kim Myŏnghwan 1992: 71). The *ching* is listed under similar contexts with the *soe* in the *Akhak kwebŏm;* it is unclear when and how these two gongs made their way from the court and aristocracy to the commoner classes.

Drums

The best known and most easily recognized instrument in a *p'ungmul* troupe is the *changgo* (stick drum), a double-headed, hourglass-shaped drum. Its body is hollow and is usually carved from a single piece of paulownia wood (*odong namu*), then spun on a lathe. *Changgo* are customarily finished with a clear varnish or are lacquered a deep red or maroon color. Two circular drumheads made of cow, sheep, horse, or dog leather are then stretched over the bowls and secured with rope or cotton cords. The larger, lower pitched side of the drum is struck with a mallet fashioned from the root of a bamboo tree and associated with the earth and female energy. The smaller, higher pitched side, in contrast, is struck with a stick carved from the stalk of the bamboo tree and associated with the heavens and male energy. *Changgo* are strapped to the body securely with white cotton cloth so that both hands are free to play while dancing.

The first literary reference to the *changgo* dates to the year 1076 in chapter 80 of the *Koryŏsa* (History of Koryŏ). Chapter 70 of the same document records the gift of twenty *changgo* from Sung China in 1114, though it should be noted that the *Koryŏsa* was written in 1451, some time after the events it chronicled. A pottery body of an hourglass-shaped drum was excavated from this same period, and tenth-century reliefs depict a smaller hourglass drum laid on the knees, accompanied by a pair of cymbals. Line drawings of an instrument more closely resembling a modern-day *changgo* appear in the 1454 *Sejong shillok* (Annals of Sejong) and the aforementioned *Akhak kwebŏm,* all suggesting elite roots. The use of two earthenware jars strapped to a wooden frame, called a *chil* (jar) *changgu,* as used in Miryang, South Kyŏngsang province, however, hints at the possibility of indigenous origins.

The sound of the *changgo* is supported by the *puk*, a double-headed, barrel-shaped drum. Considered the only indigenous percussion instrument in a *p'ungmul* group, the body of the *puk* is constructed with interlocking slats of wood. Leather (usually cow) skins are then stretched over both openings and laced together with rope. Tension is maintained by optional wooden chucks wedged between the rope and the body of the instrument. The *puk* is generally suspended from the performer's shoulder by a long cord of cotton cloth and is struck with a stick made of hardwood. Mythological tales imbue the *puk* with magical powers, and in the military this drum was used to signal advances (in contrast with the *ching* sound, indicating retreats).

Many *p'ungmul* troupes also feature a number of performers on the *sogo* (small drum), a small, double-headed frame drum with a handle. The *sogo* is primarily used as a dance prop; its method of construction and manner of playing produces very little sound, so that one seldom hears it being struck.

The Recording

My knowledge of P'ilbong's repertoire came primarily through my association with the community *p'ungmul* troupe known as Puan P'ungmulp'ae, led by one of P'ilbong's leading disciples, Mr. Yi Sangbaek. During my fieldwork period with him in the later 1990s, Yi was in direct contact with the P'ilbong village cultural asset instructors, engaged in his own often overlapping research agenda. Puan P'ungmulp'ae was Yi's brainchild, a working laboratory in his hometown of Puan (also located in North Chŏlla province) in which he would teach and re-create P'ilbong's "true village flavor" in as direct and untainted a manner as possible. After nearly a year of weekly rehearsals, a "model" performance—one that contained all possible movements and most of the existing rhythms within the "official" version of the entertainment-oriented piece the *p'an kut,* as established by the appropriate cultural asset documentation—was staged on June 17, 1996, in the troupe's rehearsal hall in downtown Puan◗. This structure and its compositional makeup are provided and discussed later as figure 7.2.

Puan P'ungmulp'ae was then composed of fifteen founding performers with a total extended membership numbering forty-nine (all are heard on this recording). Yi directed the performance as lead *soe* player, with the remaining group representing a mixture of men and women ranging in age from twenty to nearly sixty years old. The event was organized primarily "for the tape recorder," and so no arrangements were made for the visually alluring aspects of *p'ungmul,* such as the special costumes and spinning–tasseled hats. Puan P'ungmulp'ae was also still in the process of locating a regular shawm player, so the instrument was omitted on this occasion.

As pointed out above, the *Ch'aegut* movement found within the larger *p'an kut* piece is a historical survivor of earlier agricultural practices and life-styles. Today it occupies only a very small space in the total performance; in the June taping session, only one *ch'ae* rhythmic cycle (*ch'ilch'ae*, or "seven strokes") was played as part of this movement (more discussion on this process follows shortly). For illustrative and later analytical purposes, therefore, I have prepended the closing section of the first movement (*Mŏrigut*)—a *samch'ae* (three stroke) cycle sequence that would be realized in this manner if played in *Ch'aegut*—to the complete *Ch'aegut* movement. This provides an example of how two *ch'ae* rhythmic cycles might be joined together in a longer performance (see figure 7.1).

Analysis

Most writings on the topic of communal—and, by extension, folk—consciousness focus on its sociological construction in village life, both past and present (Eikemeier 1980: 128; Eckert 1993: 114–115; Samuel Kim 2003: 41). Folk arts are the most studied and represented examples of such social action in the public sphere, and *p'ungmul* is no exception. Regardless of its performance context, whether as accompaniment to communal labor, ritual fund-raising, or entertainment, *p'ungmul* as rhythm, dance, and even theater is a collective, public activity, inviting participant and onlooker alike to join together in a truly participatory event. Such happenings are characterized by an informal, largely amateur performance aesthetic, with the often stated

Movement I (*Mŏrigut* excerpt)

0:00	*samch'ae* (three strokes)	2.5 times
0:07	*iŭmsae* [joining rhythm]	1 time
0:10	*nŭrin kaenjigen* (slow *kaenjigen*)	5 times
0:17	*iŭmsae* [joining rhythm]	1 time
0:18	*hwimori* [closing cycle]	26 times (fade out)

Movement III (*Ch'aegut* complete)

0:52	*ch'ilch'ae* (seven strokes)	10 times
2:03	*tumach'i* (two strokes)	7 times
2:27	*iŭmsae* [joining rhythm]	1 time
2:29	*nŭrin kaenjigen* (slow *kaenjigen*)	13 times
2:49	*iŭmsae* [joining rhythm]	1 time
2:51	*hwimori* [closing cycle]	17 times (fade out)

Parenthesized terms are direct English translations of the corresponding Korean terms, and square-bracketed terms are English descriptions of Korean terms for which there are no good translations.

Figure 7.1. Audio track contents and timings (with number of repetitions).

rhythm	meter	duration in beats	# times stated

I. Mŏrigut (1 min. 53 sec.)

rhythm	meter	duration in beats	# times stated
ŏrumgut I	free	n/a	2
hwimori	12/8	4	10
iŭmsae I	12/8	8	1
samch'ae	12/8	8	2.5
iŭmsae II	9/8	3	1
nŭrin kaenjigen	6/8	2	5
iŭmsae III	12/8	4	1
hwimori	12/8	4	26
ŏrumgut I	free	n/a	1
insagut I	12/4	12	1

II. Oemach'i chilgut (kilgut) (4 min. 3 sec.)

rhythm	meter	duration in beats	# times stated
kilgut	12/8	16	5
nŭrin kaenjigen	6/8	2	15
iŭmsae III	12/8	4	1
hwimori	12/8	4	19

III. Ch'aegut (2 min. 26 sec.)

rhythm	meter	duration in beats	# times stated
ch'ilch'ae	12/8	16	10
tumach'i	12/8	8	7
iŭmsae II	9/8	3	1
nŭrin kaenjigen	6/8	2	13
iŭmsae III	12/8	4	1
hwimori	12/8	4	17

IV. Hohŏgut (8 min.)

rhythm	meter	duration in beats	# times stated
chindadŭraegi	4/4; 12/8	8; 4	14; 15
ŏrumgut I	free	n/a	1
hohŏgut	12/8+8/8 +10/8+ 12/8	24	3
tol hohŏgut	12/8+8/8 +10/8+ 12/8+9/8 +12/8	23	2
chajin hohŏgut	12/8	8	24
chung samch'ae	12/8	8	7
iŭmsae III	12/8	4	1
hwimori	12/8	4	12
tchaksoe	12/8	8	11
hwimori	12/8	4	21
tchaksoe	12/8	8	21
hwimori	12/8	4	15

V. P'ungnyugut (7 min. 26 sec.)

rhythm	meter	duration in beats	# times stated
insagut II	12/8	8	1
p'ungnyu	12/8	8	38
pan p'ungnyu	12/8	8	9
pparŭn kaenjigen	12/8	4	5
iŭmsae IV	12/8	4	1
hwimori	12/8	4	48

VI. Pangulchin'gut (14 min. 18 sec.)

rhythm	meter	duration in beats	# times stated
ŏrumgut II	12/8	4	9
hwimori	12/8	4	18
ŏrumgut II	12/8	4	12
hwimori	12/8	4	13
iŭmsae I	12/8	8	1
samch'ae	12/8	8	4.5
iŭmsae II	9/8	3	1
nŭrin kaenjigen	6/8	2	7
iŭmsae III	12/8	4	1
hwimori	12/8	4	6
tchaksoe	12/8	8	7
hwimori	12/8	4	14
iŭmsae V	12/8	16	1
pan p'ungnyu	12/8	8	117
pparŭn kaenjigen	12/8	4	24
iŭmsae IV	12/8	4	1
hwimori	12/8	4	65

VII. Mijigi (5 min. 7 sec.)

rhythm	meter	duration in beats	# times stated
ŏrumgut I	free	n/a	2
tchaksoe	12/8	8	4
hwimori	12/8	4	7
tchaksoe	12/8	8	7
hwimori	12/8	4	25
iŭmsae V	12/8	16	1
pan p'ungnyu	12/8	8	33
pparŭn kaenjigen	12/8	4	12
iŭmsae IV	12/8	4	1
hwimori	12/8	4	16

VIII. Yŏngsan (13 min. 21 sec.)

rhythm	meter	duration in beats	# times stated
ŏrumgut I	free	n/a	1
kajin yŏngsan	12/8	80	10
tadŭraegi yŏngsan	12/8	12	14
hwimori	12/8	4	72
tchaksoe	12/8	8	31
hwimori	12/8	4	31
ŏrumgut I	free	n/a	2
insagut I	12/4	12	2

Figure 7.2.   *P'ungmul* performance based on model of P'ilbong's *p'an kut*. Rhythms identified by meter, number of beats, number of repetitions, and whether a pattern [P] or cycle [C]; patterns/cycles occurring more than once set apart by different fonts.

goal of achieving a feeling of oneness or unity (*shinmyŏng* in Korean). Rhythm and movement are recognized as central contributing factors to such phenomena, though the nature of such constructions is seldom discussed or analyzed. Close readings of the musical details, however, may be the only way to show how communal experience is sustained at the moment-to-moment level.

Recurrence

I refer to the two key organizing principles of *p'ungmul*'s rhythmic and performance structure as recurrence and reinforcement. They are complementary and interactive realms, feeding into one another on many levels. Recurrence as a practice in various forms—procedurally, musically, choreographically—is a significant part of communally based musics around the world. Music that recurs ensures that everyone participating has many chances to acquire the specific knowledge required; and when it is acquired, recurrence then reinforces it. I chose the word *recurrence* in place of *repetition*, as the latter can suggest mechanical or identical reproduction (though recurrence, repetition, and iteration can all be subsumed under the rubric of *periodicity;* see Tenzer 2006: 22).

In performance, recurrence constitutes a space of tremendous potential, created through anticipation both of what will/might happen and of what will/might change in comparison to previous events. Over time— both of an individual performance and the life of a performer—shared experiences of recurrence become deeper in musically and socially transformative ways. Here *p'ungmul* joins other amateur and/or improvisatory group musical activities grounded in oral tradition that allow for, or even feature, "discrepancies" within this framework of recurrence that creates a dynamic and open structure for all participants (Chernoff 1979: 112; see also Keil 1995). Whether they are intentional (variations, improvisation) or not (mistakes by beginners, lapses in memory), such deviations, far from breaking down a sense of community, actually serve to enhance it. The American ethnomusicologists Charles Keil and Steven Feld (1994: 23) have referred to this as "participatory consciousness," and described the way slight variations within repetition achieve a "changing same" (L. Jones 1970), grounding the performance in the here and now, between the physical you and me (see further Hesselink 2007). Recurrence occurs at both the macro and micro levels in a symbiotic universe of performance, musical structure, and aesthetics.

Figure 7.2 provides the model of the basic musical structure of P'ilbong's *p'an kut,* the entertainment-oriented event traditionally held in the village communal meeting space (*p'an*) as a celebration at the end of a long day of hard manual labor or ritual fund-raising. The largest structural unit is the movement, or *madang* in Korean, identified by uppercase Roman numerals. Each movement can be considered a discrete and self-contained piece composed of a predetermined series of rhythms and danced ground formations performed in order without fail. It is customary for the lead small-gong player (*sangsoe*) to signal the beginnings and endings of these movements, provide cues for moving from one rhythm to another (in the case of cycles), and regulate the overall tempo. Actual speed and number of internal repeats are gauged by the *sangsoe* according to audience response and related energy level of the musicians (cycled rhythms are shaded, to more clearly show the alternation between cycles and patterns). Names of rhythms are drawn from structural designations (*tumach'i*, or "two strokes," refers to two strokes on the large gong), performance contexts (*kilgut*, literally "road ritual," was used for processions), and onomatopoeia (*kaenjigen*, representing strokes on the small gong). Figure 7.3 provides a graphic representation of the performance temporally, so that a better sense of proportion can be gleaned from figure 7.2. Figure 7.3 will also visually support the following analysis of repeated structures.

Names of movements are drawn from three types of classification: (1) the structural placement of the movement; (2) the name of the movement's characteristic rhythm; and (3) the type of ground formation employed. Movement I is an example of type 1 (*Mŏrigut* means, literally, "beginning ritual"), while movements II, III, IV, V, and VIII are examples of type 2. In type 2 movements the characteristic or featured rhythm is introduced within the first two or three rhythms encountered. Movements VI and VII are both type 3, named after the distinctive ground formation enacted (*Pangulchin[gut]* means "to form a drop" [i.e., wind and unwind in a series of "drops"], and *Mijigi* is a reference to the "thrust and fall back" military formation). Regardless of type, each movement closes with a cadential formula comprised of a fixed series of rhythms and transitions.

Beginning at the macro level, it is in the use and ordering of each movement's closing rhythms in which recurrence is first recognizable (refer again to figures 7.2 and 7.3). Regardless of opening rhythmic material or ground formation employed, all movements essentially end with the four-beat cycle *hwimori* played by the group within a circular dance formation; movements I and VIII add on the *ŏrumgut*—*insagut* dyad, an opening/closing flourish (*ŏrumgut*) coupled with the "greeting ritual" (*insagut*) rhythm (*insa* can mean both hello and goodbye). In most cases, *hwimori* is preceded by a form of the *kaenjigen* cycle (named after the small gong line's oral mnemonics) and the transition or "joining" rhythm *iŭmsae* (meaning "joint" or "juncture"; see figure 7.2). Instances of *hwimori* with its preceding *iŭmsae* can be heard on the track from 0:17 to 0:51 and from 2:49 to the end.

On a purely rhythmic level this recurrence brings about a feeling of closure, a kind of cadence in which the group comes back to familiar material. Physically and symbolically, however, this return signals a celebratory *communitas* as the group regularly "comes back together," reestablishing a circle ground formation in closer bodily proximity. In movements IV and VIII— respectively the midpoint and conclusion of the performance—the final

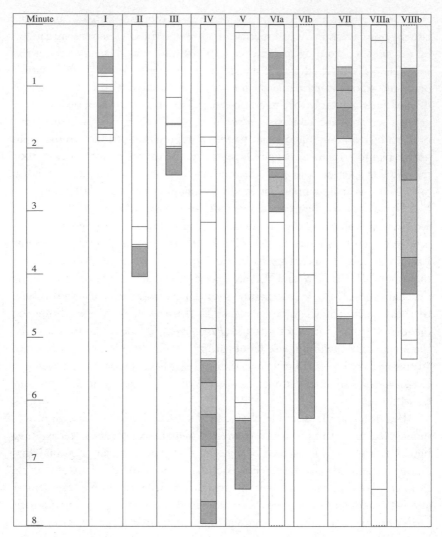

Figure 7.3. Graphic representation of *p'ungmul* performance by movement in minutes. Shaded boxes represent *hwimori* segments (darker = *hwimori,* lighter = *tchaksoe*).

hwimori rhythmic cycle is elongated through a variant known as *tchaksoe* (pair of *soe*), a call-and-response section in which the small gong (*soe*) players play densely interlocking patterns.

The number of occurrences of *hwimori* and the number of times it is repeated at each occurrence in fact intensifies as the performance progresses. Elongations of *hwimori*—the call-and-response *tchaksoe* sections—begin in movement IV, then reappear in movements VI, VII, and VIII; "stand-alone" *hwimori* cycles are also added at the beginning of movement VI (refer again to figure 7.2). Moreover, no new material is introduced in movements VI and VII. Figure 7.4, which catalogs the number of successive statements of *hwimori*, including the *tchaksoe* sections, demonstrates a dramatic expansion from movement IV onward: 26, 19, and 17 times in the first three movements, then 112, 48, 65, 16 (a brief lull), and 165 in movements IV through VIII.

At the level of the individual rhythm, such as those indicated by each line on figure 7.2, *p'ungmul* performances are mainly cyclic. This means that most rhythms—called *karak* (strand or phrase) or *changdan* (literally "long and short") in Korean—repeat a distinctive series of durational proportions lasting a fixed number of beats. Roughly two-thirds of the rhythms are immediately repeated to form cycles (seventeen of twenty-six), the significance of which is magnified when we consider that rhythms that do not normally repeat, and hence do not create cycles, occur infrequently and only last for a few seconds at a time. Within these seventeen cycles, fourteen last twelve beats or fewer, meaning that their relatively short length translates into easily digestible units for the beginning and/or amateur participant when first encountering and learning the tradition. Confidence in one's skills to contribute to the greater whole (the ensemble) is cultivated with a pedagogy initially stressing the use of a primary form of the cycle, called the *wŏnhyŏng* ("standard/primary form"). The *wŏnhyŏng* outlines the basic stroke order and series of accented or unaccented beats (or divisions of the beat), and is learned at an early stage. Once this form is internalized, the student then learns a set of more difficult stock variations, with the final goal of being able to improvise

I: $\|: \textit{nŭrin (slow) kaenjigen}^{\text{5 times}} :\| \textit{iŭmsae} \|: \textit{hwimori}^{\text{26 times}} :\| [\textit{ŏrumgut, insagut}]$

II: $\|: \textit{nŭrin kaenjigen}^{\text{15 times}} :\| \textit{iŭmsae} \|: \textit{hwimori}^{\text{19 times}} :\|$

III: $\|: \textit{nŭrin kaenjigen}^{\text{13 times}} :\| \textit{iŭmsae} \|: \textit{hwimori}^{\text{17 times}} :\|$

IV: $\| \textit{iŭmsae} \|: \textit{hwimori}^{\text{112 times}} :\|$

V: $\|: \textit{pparŭn (fast) kaenjigen}^{\text{5 times}} :\| \textit{iŭmsae} \|: \textit{hwimori}^{\text{48 times}} :\|$

VI: $\|: \textit{pparŭn kaenjigen}^{\text{24 times}} :\| \textit{iŭmsae} \|: \textit{hwimori}^{\text{65 times}} :\|$

VII: $\|: \textit{pparŭn kaenjigen}^{\text{12 times}} :\| \textit{iŭmsae} \|: \textit{hwimori}^{\text{16 times}} :\|$

VIII: $\|: \textit{hwimori}^{\text{165 times}} :\| [\textit{ŏrumgut, insagut}]$

Figure 7.4. Closing rhythms of each movement (*madang*), with number of repeats.

in performance.[3] This activity is encouraged and supported by the sheer number of times many rhythms are repeated (especially *hwimori*).

We are now ready to get at the heart of the analysis, a discussion of the third movement *Ch'aegut* (stroke ritual/performance). The term *ch'ae* commonly refers to the number of strokes played on the large gong (*ching*) per cycle, so that in a rhythm called *ilch'ae* (one stroke) the *ching* would be struck once, in *ich'ae* (two strokes) twice, and so on. In the context of P'ilbong's village tradition, rhythms so named are considered a direct remnant of *ture kut,* music played as accompaniment to the work of communal labor teams (*ture;* a picture of a folklorized version of this performance is provided on the chapter opening page). I mentioned above that this repertoire of rhythms is considered to exhibit the greatest antiquity with the deepest roots in communal, traditional society. *Ch'aegut* theoretically contains the full complement of such rhythms, progressing from *ilch'ae* (one stroke) on through to *ch'ilch'ae* (seven strokes) omitting only *och'ae* (five strokes), a rhythm with strong shamanistic associations no longer played today.[4] Standard procedure, however, dictates that only one or two of these rhythms be cycled during *Ch'aegut.* A further twist on this practice is that the selection of the *ch'ae* rhythmic cycle(s) is generally decided by the lead small-gong player, often with considerable variation from performance to performance. Other members of the group, therefore, must first listen to the rhythm played by the lead gong once through before they can contribute to the cycle. This movement in its entirety featuring the seven-stroke cycle *ch'ilch'ae* (the rhythm chosen in the model performance) is heard beginning at 0:52.

What on the surface appears to be a substantial amount of musical material to learn and internalize readily breaks down into only a few and significantly related gestures. This is because the *ch'ae* rhythms have an additive structure in which a limited number of short basic rhythmic cells are added or manipulated to create a large repertoire, representing a kind of generative recurrence in that earlier building blocks are used to construct later larger entities. In figure 7.5 I have listed the six commonly used *ch'ae* rhythmic cycles

---

3. While some may feel that *improvisation* is an imprecise term in a *p'ungmul* context, implying a concerted and mature compositional effort "in the course of performance" (after Nettl 1998), I use the word here and throughout this chapter to refer to an individual's decision to alternate between standard and variant forms of the rhythms, as well as add, delete, or even alter strokes and footsteps as the particular moment or spirit dictates.

4. According to Yi Sangbaek, *och'ae*'s unusual structure (when compared to the other 12/8-based *ch'ae* rhythmic cycles) made it difficult to dance to, hence its omission. *Och'ae* is made up of five phrases: 8/8 (2 + 3 + 3), 9/8 (3 + 3 + 3), 10/8 (2 + 3 + 3 + 2), 10/8 (2 + 3 + 3 + 2), 9/8 (3 + 3 + 3).

"One stroke" cycle (*ilch'ae*): A̲ B
"Two stroke" cycle (*ich'ae*): A̲ A̲ B
"Three stroke" cycle (*samch'ae*): **B̲¹** **B̲²**
"Four stroke" cycle (*sach'ae*): A̲ A̲ **B̲¹** C
"Six stroke" cycle (*yukch'ae*): A̲ A̲ **B̲³** **B̲**
"Seven stroke" cycle (*ch'ilch'ae*): A̲ A̲ **B̲³** **B̲¹** C

Figure 7.5.   Additive structure in the compositional makeup of all possible *ch'aegut* (movement III) rhythmic cycles (underlined letters = phrases with single *ching* strokes, bold underlined letters = cells with two strokes).

of the *Ch'aegut* movement (III) in ascending numerical order. Each basic rhythmic cell is assigned an uppercase letter, with derivative forms marked by a number in superscript. The total number of distinct cells used in this collection of rhythms, therefore, is six: A, B, B¹, B², B³, and C (this number is reduced to five if one further breaks down B¹ into its two constituent parts: first half of B + A). Some cells include one *ching* stroke, while others (indicated by underlines in figure 7.5 and by bold boxes below) include two. Regardless of length of the rhythmic cycle, however, the *ching* is struck every two beats until the proper number of strokes has been reached (once for *ilch'ae*, twice for *ich'ae*, and so on). The only exception to this rule is *samch'ae* (three strokes), which features only two strokes on the *ching* symmetrically placed at every four beats (*samch'ae* is eight beats long), thus making "*samch'ae*" a misnomer. Perhaps this occurs because of *samch'ae*'s life outside of the *Ch'aegut* movement in the rest of the *p'an kut*, in which *ching* strokes every four beats is the norm.

For the musical examples that follow, I have chosen to use a modified form of *chŏngganbo*, or Korean traditional mensural notation. Each box represents an equal unit of time, with boxes strung together in a row that is read from left to right. Beats—established by the placement of the foot when dancing—are marked by bold vertical lines. In all instances within the *Ch'aegut* movement, each beat is divided into three time units, hence all rhythms are in some kind of compound meter. The symbols within the boxes indicate small gong (*soe*) strokes: O = loud stroke, o = weaker stroke, and ⊃ = damping (cutting off) the sound with the hand holding the gong. Modification has occurred in my choice of small gong stroke symbols (*soe* dynamics and damping techniques were not notated in older scores), the horizontal arrangement of the boxes (*chŏngganbo* is conventionally written and read from top to bottom), and the identification of *ching* strokes by boxes in bold (for a full rationale of my choice of modifications, see Hesselink 2001).

The initial rhythm *ilch'ae* (one stroke) contains two distinct cells with ternary subdivision, A and B. Cell A is two beats long, and cell B is four beats:

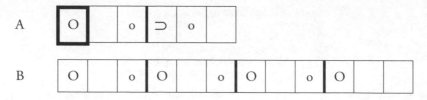

By repeating cell A, we then get the complete rhythm *ich'ae* (two strokes):

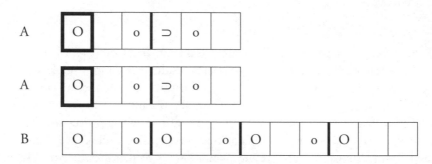

To generate the next rhythm *samch'ae* (three strokes), two derivative forms of the four-beat B cell, B¹ and B², are combined:

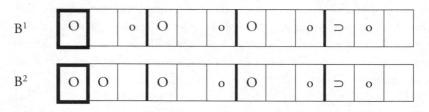

As mentioned, B¹ can be thought of as composed of the first two beats of B followed by cell A. B² differs from B¹ only in the first beat: a strong stroke is added to the second division of the beat, and the weaker stroke from the third division is removed. Otherwise parallel cells with a change only in one beat are a common construction of *ŭm-yang changdan,* or *ŭm* [*yin*] and *yang* rhythms; a leading scholar and performer has specifically identified the long-plus-short figure (first beat of B¹) as reflecting the female (*ŭm*) gesture of a mother's open embrace, its reverse gesture of short-plus-long (first beat of B²), the male (*yang*) strong arm (i.e., firmness) of the father (Kim Tongwŏn 1998: 111; personal communication). *Samch'ae* is heard at the beginning of the track.

Sach'ae (four strokes) marks a return to the A cell, played at the beginning twice like *ich'ae* (two strokes), followed by B¹. New material is then introduced with cell C, a syncopated four-beat pattern:

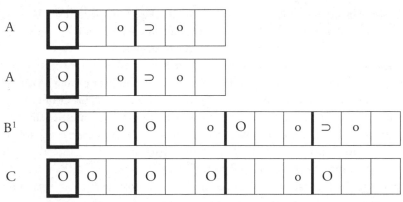

The *yukch'ae* (six-stroke) rhythm combines two A cells with a B³ cell (a new derivative form of B) and cell B itself (with two added ching strokes):

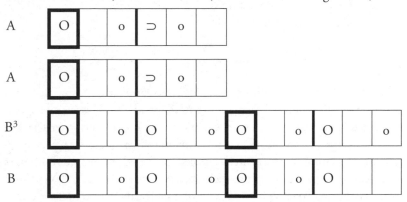

And the final *ch'ilch'ae* (seven-stroke) rhythm is composed of the cells A, A, B³, B¹ (with an added ching stroke), and C:

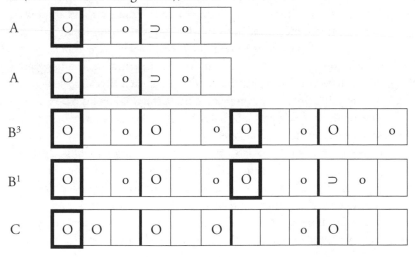

Ch'ilch'ae is heard at 0:52 (the first time through played by the lead small-gong player alone). For the performance analyzed in figures 7.2 and 7.3, only one *ch'ae* rhythmic cycle was chosen (*ch'ilch'ae/*seven strokes).

The organizational and performative logic here involves a cycle of rhythms composed of short rhythmic cells, the existence of a simple or primary form of the cycle's rhythm (*wŏnhyŏng*), and the return to a cadential cluster of closing rhythms at the end of each movement repeated numerous times. Even after learning just a small amount of material, then, novices can create and partici-pate in recurrence at two levels of structure. This draws them into the per-forming community without confrontation or competition, a hallmark of premodern, communal labor practices and related musical activity. This same logic then serves to reinforce the internalization and appreciation of the rhythms for mid-level and more senior performers, and creates opportunities for advanced players to both acknowledge their "juniors" while increasing their technical and improvisatory skills.

Reinforcement

Reinforcement is an outgrowth of recurrence and familiarity; I now also wish to discuss the notion of reinforcement as interdependence. During a *p'ungmul* performance, a mutual reliance among the participants is constructed by the interrelationships among the various instrumental lines. Figure 7.6 provides a representative example of these interrelationships found throughout P'ilbong's repertoire, a score of the rhythmic cycle *samch'ae* (three strokes) drawn from *Ch'aegut*. As noted, *samch'ae* is composed of eight beats with ternary subdivi-sions (two measures of 12/8). This example is also read from left to right, with the first phrase of four beats placed above the second phrase. Three of the four core *p'ungmul* instruments that provide the cycle's defining strokes are shown: the barrel drum (*puk*) line on the bottom, the hourglass drum (*changgo*) occu-pying the two middle positions (one hand holds a mallet, the other a stick), and the small gong (*soe*) on the top. The fourth instrument, the large gong (*ching*), is a timekeeper that marks the beginning of each rhythmic cell (struck twice in an iteration of *samch'ae* on beats 1 and 5, marked by bold boxes).

The barrel drum (*puk*) part alternates loud strokes (beats 1, 2, 3, 5, 6, and 7) with softer ones (beats 4 and 8). The same dynamics and rhythms are played by the mallet hand on the hourglass drum (*changgo*). Large circles in the lower row of the *changgo* part represent strong strokes by the mallet on the mallet side of the drum (beats 1, 2, 3, 5, 6, and 7); large circles in the upper row indi-cate movement by the mallet hand over to the opposite (stick) side of the drum, which produces a softer stroke (beats 4 and 8). This movement from head to head with the mallet hand thus matches and reinforces what the barrel

Soe	O		o	O		o	O		o	⊃	o	
Changgo (stick side)	I		'	I		'	I		I	O	I	'
Changgo (mallet side)	O			O			O					
Puk	O			O			O			o		

Soe	O	O		O		o	O		o	⊃	o	
Changgo (stick side)	I	I	'	I		'	I		I	O	I	'
Changgo (mallet side)	O	O		O			O					
Puk	O	O		O			O			o		

Key

Soe (small gong) strokes	Changgo (hourglass drum) strokes	Puk (barrel drum)
O = loud stroke	O = mallet stroke	O = loud stroke
o = weaker stroke	I = stick stroke	o = weaker stroke
⊃ = damp sound with hand holding gong	' = stroke by tip of stick	

Figure 7.6. *Samch'ae* (three strokes) rhythmic cycle.

drum plays, a vital identity relationship that performers may acknowledge through playful glances, or exploit if memory fails. The small gong (*soe*) line is similarly a near carbon copy of the stick hand of the *changgo* player, matching the rhythm—and even at times dynamic contour (beats 1, 2, 5, and 6)—of the stick strokes (listen to the beginning of the track for *samch'ae*).

The same principle dictates the construction of the closing rhythm *hwimori* (see figure 7.7). *Hwimori* is a four-beat, ternary subdivision cycle (12/8) played quickly. Signaling the closing of each movement, as we have seen, *hwimori* provides an arena for performers of all skill levels to improvise, either rhythmically and/or choreographically with their feet and upper bodies. Referring again first to the *puk* line, we observe that the first two beats are played loudly, followed by two weaker strokes. This is mirrored in the movement of the mallet hand from the mallet side of the drum (strong strokes on beats 1 and 2) to the stick side (weaker strokes on beats 3 and 4). The *soe* line matches the stick strokes and dynamic contour almost stroke for stroke (heard from 0:18–0:51 and from 2:51–end).

The interrelationship between instrumental lines can be characterized as a timbral elaboration of a core rhythm, given by the hourglass drum (*changgo*). As a metaphor for the performers themselves, this idea suggests different sounds or voices—a collective of individuals—contributing to a sense of unity

Soe	O		o	O		o	O		o	O		o
Changgo (stick side)	I		,	I			I	O	,	I	O	,
Changgo (mallet side)	O			O								
Puk	O			O			o			o		

Figure 7.7. *Hwimori* rhythmic cycle.

and the creation of an interconnected musical family. Such reinforcement is experienced in multifaceted ways by the performers, including feelings of support, camaraderie, joy, and community.

Conclusion

From its genesis in rural, premodern society through its transformation into a self-conscious vehicle and musical emblem of pan-Korean identity, *p'ungmul* has remained rooted in collective group activity. Far from historical revisionism or romantic abstraction, communal consciousness is a reality, tangibly experienced and embodied through the playing of rhythms in village-style folk drumming and dance. Through the complementary and interdependent principles of recurrence and reinforcement, an acute sense of community is reenacted every time a *p'ungmul* group convenes to share in the common endeavor. By engaging the tools of musical analysis in this chapter, grounded in a local cultural context, I have hoped to demystify, while at the same time quantify, how this music achieves its emotional and communicative powers.

There are, of course, many senses of musical "community" found worldwide in which both smaller group and larger societal cohesion is the aim. One can certainly acknowledge parallels between South Korean practices and those of many West African drumming ensembles, in which a similar feeling of togetherness is generated through rhythm, dance, improvisation, and even a preference for compound meters (but with a focus on creative tension—rather than reinforcement as I have defined it—between different rhythmic lines in the African context). What fascinates me as an observer of East Asian culture, however, is how the much more closely related Korean and Japanese societies mimic each other on the general social level in their adherence to group conformity, yet differ so radically in conception in their folk drumming traditions. My earlier description of *p'ungmul* as "coordinated and [yet] chaotic" quite neatly sums up the aesthetic distance one feels when experiencing Japanese folk drumming and its emphasis on perfect gestural and choreographic coordination, generally without improvisation (Malm 1986: 22–35). The earliest forms of *p'ungmul* took root in an agricultural, primarily egalitarian society, one that predated waves of later Chinese influence and the crucial introduction of Neo-Confucian thought with its tightly defined hierarchies. Japanese rural society followed a similar historical trajectory, as did apparently social attitudes surrounding the production of its folk percussion and dance (a move toward the loss of the sense of the individual), yet for complex reasons meriting further study, *p'ungmul* seems to have withstood this trend in its greater allowance of personal freedom and expression.

As I have described elsewhere (Hesselink 2007), *p'ungmul* for me holds tremendous potential as a model of democratic behavior. In its transmission and performance, one is challenged to navigate the complementary currents of responsibility (to set rhythmic patterns, individual dance steps, and group choreography) and independence (improvisation as personal voice within these constraints). Furthermore, by allowing all manner of participants within the same performance to contribute at their own specific skill level, the promise of universal participation—in this case, a rhythmic call to unity—is made that much more strongly.

References

Chernoff, John Miller. 1979. *African Rhythm and African Sensibility: Aesthetics and Social Action in African Musical Idioms.* Chicago: University of Chicago Press.

Chŏng Pyŏngho, Yi Pohyŏng, Yi Chuyŏng, and Chŏng Chun'gi. 1980. *P'ilbong nongak [Nongak of the Village of P'ilbong].* Seoul: Munhwajae kwalliguk, Munhwajae yŏn'guso.

Chu Kanghyŏn. 1997. *Han'guk ŭi ture* [Communal Labor of Korea]. 2 vols. Seoul: Chimmundang.

Eckert, Carter J. 1993. "The South Korean Bourgeoisie: A Class in Search of Hegemony." In *State and Society in Contemporary Korea,* ed. Hagen Koo, 95–130. Ithaca, NY: Cornell University Press.

Eikemeier, Dieter. 1980. *Documents from Changjwa-ri: A Further Approach to the Analysis of Korean Villages.* Wiesbaden, Germany: Otto Harrassowitz.

Hesselink, Nathan. 1998. "Of Drums and Men in Chŏllabuk-do Province: Glimpses into the Making of a Human Cultural Asset." *Korea Journal* 38(3): 292–326.

———. 2001. "'*P'ungmul* Is Played with Your Heel!' Dance as a Determinant of Rhythmic Construct in Korean Percussion Band Music/Dance." *Ŭmak-kwa munhwa* 4: 99–110.

———. 2006. *P'ungmul: South Korean Drumming and Dance.* Chicago: University of Chicago Press.

———. 2007. "Taking Culture Seriously: Democratic Music and Its Transformative Potential in South Korea." *World of Music* 49(3): 75–106.

Howard, Keith. 2006. *Preserving Korean Music: Intangible Cultural Properties as Icons of Identity.* Aldershot, Hampshire, UK: Ashgate.

Hwang, Byung-Ki [Hwang Pyŏnggi]. 2004. "Beat: In Search of the Original Form of Korean Culture." In *The Korean Beat: In Search of the Origins of Korean Culture,* comp. Kim Tschung-Sun Kim [Kim Chungsun] and Sem Vermeersch, 7–13. Daegu, Korea: Academia Koreana of Keimyung University.

Jones, Leroi [Amiri Baraka]. 1970. *Black Music.* New York: William Morrow.

Jones, Stephen. 1998. *Folk Music of China: Living Instrumental Traditions.* New York: Oxford University Press.

Keil, Charles. 1995. "The Theory of Participatory Discrepancies: A Progress Report." *Ethnomusicology* 39(1): 1–19.

Keil, Charles, and Steven Feld. 1994. "Dialogue 1: Getting into the Dialogic Groove." In *Music Grooves: Essays and Dialogues,* ed. Charles Keil and Steven Feld, 1–30. Chicago: University of Chicago Press.

Kim Hyŏnsuk. 1991. "Nongak-esŏ ch'aebo-wa punsŏk ŭi munje" [Problems of Transcription and Analysis with *Nongak*]. *Han'guk ŭmak yŏn'gu* 19: 73–89.

Kim Inu. 1993. "P'ungmulgut-kwa kongdongch'ejŏk shinmyŏng" [*P'ungmulgut* and Communal Spirit]. In *Minjok-kwa kut: Minjok kut ŭi saeroun yŏllim-ŭl wihayŏ* [Folk and Ritual: Toward a New Understanding of Folk Ritual], 102–144. Seoul: Hangminsa.

Kim Myŏnghwan. 1992. *Nae puk-e aenggil sori-ka ŏpsŏyo* [There Is No Voice That Can Match My Drum(ing)], ed. Kim Haesuk, Pak Chonggwŏn, Paek Taeung, and Yi Ŭnja. *Ppuri kip'ŭn namu minjung chasŏjŏn 11: Kosu Kim Myŏnghwan ŭi hanp'yŏngsaeng* [The Deep-Rooted Tree Oral Histories (11): The Life of the *P'ansori* Drummer Kim Myŏnghwan]. Seoul: Ppuri kip'ŭn namu.

Kim, Samuel S., ed. 2003. *Korea's Democratization.* Cambridge: Cambridge University Press.

Kim Sunam, Im Sŏkchae, and Yi Pohyŏng. 1986. *P'ungmulgut: Han'gugin ŭi nori-wa cheŭi* [*P'ungmulgut:* Play and Ritual of the Korean People]. Seoul: P'yŏngminsa.

Kim Tongwŏn. 1998. "Han'guk chŏnt'ong changdan ŭi kusŏng wŏlli" [Organizational Principles of Traditional Korean Rhythmic Patterns]. In *Han'guk chŏnt'ong yŏnhŭi ŭi ihae-wa shilche I* [The Practice and Appreciation of Korean Traditional Performing Arts I], ed. Kim Tŏksu, 95–149. Seoul: Han'guk yesul chonghap hakkyo.

Kim, Tschung-Sun [Kim Chungsun], and Sem Vermeersch, comps. 2004. *The Korean Beat: In Search of the Origins of Korean Culture.* Proceedings of the Keimyung International Conference on Korean Studies in Celebration of the 50th Anniversary of Keimyung University. Daegu, Korea: Academia Koreana of Keimyung University.

Kim Wŏnho. 1999. *P'ungmulgut yŏn'gu* [A Study of *P'ungmulgut*]. Seoul: Hangminsa.

Komoda Haruko and Nogawa Mihoko. 2002. "Theory and Notation in Japan." In *East Asia: China, Japan, and Korea,* ed. Robert C. Provine, Yosihiko Tokumara, and J. Lawrence Witzleben, 565–584. New York: Routledge.

Kwon, Donna. 2005. "Music, Movement and Space: A Study of the *Madang* and *P'an* in Korean Expressive Folk Culture." Ph.D. dissertation, University of California, Berkeley.

Kwŏn Hyeryŏn [Donna Kwon]. 2001. "Miguk-esŏ ŭi p'ungmul: Kŭ ppuri-wa yŏjŏng" [The Roots and Routes of *P'ungmul* in the United States]. *Ŭmak-kwa munhwa* 5: 39–65.

Malm, William P. 1986. *Six Hidden Views of Japanese Music.* Berkeley: University of California Press.

Nettl, Bruno, with Melinda Russell. 1998. *In the Course of Performance: Studies in the World of Musical Improvisation.* Chicago: University of Chicago Press.

O Chongsŏp. 1989. "P'ungmulgut-esŏ ŭi kongdongch'e ŭishik-e kwanhan yŏn'gu" [A Study of Communal Consciousness in *P'ungmulgut*]. Master's thesis, Seoul National University.

Pak Chongsŏl. 1991. "Minsogak changdan kujo-e kwanhan punsŏk yŏn'gu" [An Analytical Study on the Structure of Folk Music Rhythmic Patterns]. *Han'guk ŭmak yŏn'gu* 19: 41–65.

Pak Sangguk, Yi Chongjin, Yi Chunsŏk, and Kim Chongok. 1999. *Imshil P'ilbong Nongak.* Seoul: Kungnip munhwajae yŏn'guso.

Song Pangsong. 2007. *Chŭngbo Han'guk ŭmak t'ongsa* [An Expanded Broad History of Korean Music]. Seoul: Minsogwŏn.

Tenzer, Michael. 2006. "Introduction: Analysis, Categorization, and Theory of Musics of the World." In *Analytical Studies in World Music,* ed. Michael Tenzer, 3–38. New York: Oxford University Press.

Yang Chinsŏng. 1989. *Honam chwado: P'ilbong maŭl p'ungmulgut* [Chŏlla-Province "Left Side" Style: *P'ungmulgut* of P'ilbong Village]. Namwŏn, Korea: Honam chwado p'ungmul p'an kut palp'yohoe shilmut'im.

Yi Pohyŏng. 1984. "Nongak-esŏ kilgut (kil kunak)-kwa ch'aegut" [*Ch'aegut* and *Kilgut* [*Kil kunak*] Rhythmic Patterns in *Nongak*]. *Minjok ŭmakhak* 6: 31–47.

Yi Sangjin. 2002. *Han'guk nongak kaeron* [An Introduction to Korean *Nongak*]. Seoul: Minsogwŏn.

Yi Yŏngbae. 2000. "P'ilbong P'ungmulgut ŭi kongyŏn kujo: Wŏlli-wa sahoejŏk ŭimi" [The Performance Structure of P'ilbong P'ungmulgut: Its Principles and Societal Meaning]. Master's thesis, Chŏnbuk University.

CHAPTER 8

Strophic Form and Asymmetrical Repetition in Four American Indian Songs

VICTORIA LINDSAY LEVINE AND BRUNO NETTL

Photo: The Chickasaw Nation Dance Troupe. Courtesy of the Chickasaw Nation Department of Libraries, Archives, and Collections.

The songs of Native North Americans have been the subject of intensive musical analysis since the late nineteenth century[*]. Preponderantly they are in strophic form, meaning that they repeat the same music during each successive stanza or verse of the text. But oddly enough, the nature and the variety of these strophic designs have not been addressed. Many of these songs incorporate what we call *asymmetrical repetition,* that is, the alteration of a musical phrase when it is repeated. There are several sorts of alteration. Upon the repetition of a strophe, one phrase, usually the first phrase, may be omitted, or a phrase can be lengthened or shortened. Within the strophe itself, one phrase may be followed by one or more altered versions; and these alterations may be subtle changes in pitch, rhythm, or vocal production.[1] All of these alterations introduce some nuance into a musical form that otherwise would be highly redundant. Asymmetrical repetition thus energizes songs meant to be performed communally in various social or ceremonial contexts.

Previous scholars have described this approach to design as "incomplete repetition" in reference to War Dance songs, which constitute a specific genre that originated among Plains Indians and is now associated with intertribal powwow music. However, the term *incomplete repetition* has been criticized because of its negative connotation.[2] Furthermore, the principle of asymmetrical repetition is of central importance in Native American music; it is not exclusive to the Plains region or powwow songs alone. On the contrary, asymmetrical

* The authors wish to express their gratitude to the members of the Chickasaw Nation for their generous assistance in obtaining the audio recording and photograph that illustrate this chapter, especially Dr. Amanda Cobb-Greetham (Administrator, Division of History and Culture), Michelle Cooke (Director, Department of Libraries, Archives, and Collections), Robyn Elliott (Administrator, Division of Communications, Media and Community Development), and Meredith Johnson (Division of History and Culture). We also wish to thank Jason Baird Jackson for his insights and helpful suggestions.

1. *Asymmetry* usually refers to a difference in the lengths of phrases or sections, and so applies naturally to the first three types of alteration we identify. Strictly speaking, the fourth sort of alteration affects only the *parallelism* of the phrases, because changes of content do not necessarily change phrase lengths, but for convenience we will regard it as a sort of asymmetry as well.

2. The term *incomplete repetition* has been used by music scholars since the mid-twentieth century to describe the kind of strophic form that may be diagrammed as A A1 BCD / BCD, where A A1 BCD represents the first half of the strophe, and the second BCD stands for the second, shorter half. The strophe in its entirety is normally repeated several times. Browner suggests that the terms *traditional form* or *war dance form,* as used by Native American singers, are preferable to the term *incomplete repetition* (Browner 2002: 68–69). By contrast, Judith Vander uses the terms *dynamic symmetry* or *inexact repetition* to describe the form of Shoshone *Naraya* (Ghost Dance) songs, which combine paired phrase structure with asymmetrical repetition (Vander 1986: 17).

repetition is manifested in a variety of musical genres throughout Native America, and it may be what tends to distinguish American Indian strophic forms from those performed elsewhere in the world.

In this chapter, we present four case studies of American Indian strophic songs that employ different kinds of asymmetrical repetition: an Arapaho Wolf Dance song, a Kiowa Peyote song, a Yahi Yana Flint Song, and a Chickasaw Friendship Dance song. The four songs are of diverse origins and provenance. Each song represents a different genre from a different community and has its own history and performance context. The songs were recorded at various times and places for various purposes. Our goal in bringing these four case studies together is to explore the role of asymmetrical repetition in American Indian musical design. We argue that the use of strophic forms and asymmetrical repetition in Native American songs is connected to larger social systems and reflects aspects of the deep history of Native North America. Following the introduction, the chapter is organized in six sections. We begin with a note on the musical style, transcription, and analysis of American Indian music. Then each of the four songs is analyzed as an individual case study. Finally, we offer some general observations about how strophic songs featuring asymmetrical repetition express shared concepts of time and place, facilitate participation in intertribal performance, and contribute to a broader perspective on American Indian music history.

A Note on the Musical Style, Transcription, and Analysis of American Indian Music

Since some readers may not be familiar with the general stylistic characteristics of American Indian music, we offer a brief introduction here. Most Native songs are monophonic and are performed in either blended or unblended unison, although songs in some genres are performed as solos, and certain genres from the Eastern Woodlands region employ call-and-response with occasional moments of parallel harmony. Native singers accompany most songs with unpitched drums and rattles, and occasionally other idiophones. Although a variety of scales exist in Native North America, many songs feature anhemitonic pentatonic scales with an average range of about an octave. Form in Native American songs is generally fixed, clear, and precise. Most Native songs feature strophic, sectional, or iterative forms; they are rarely through-composed, except in the case of flute melodies. Songs in some genres, such as lullabies, may be quite short, lasting one or two minutes. A ceremonial dance song, by contrast, may last ten minutes or longer, depending upon the performance context, the choreography, and the number of dancers participating. Ceremonial events as a whole tend to last many hours or may extend over several days, involving scores and sometimes hundreds of songs. There is little improvisation, but most songs have a flexible structure that encourages a degree of spontaneity and individual artistry in the course of performance, or between one performance and the next. Timbre and methods of vocal production vary greatly, and are a significant expression of personal, tribal, and regional identity.

Native North American music has been transcribed using European music notation since the early seventeenth century,[3] and despite claims to the contrary, this repertory can be notated reasonably effectively. Most Native singers use musical materials that can be notated with a few modifications to indicate microtones, vocal ornaments, slight prolongations or abbreviations of durational values, and similar stylistic elements (figure 8.1). American Indian songs tend to emphasize syllabic or neumatic melodies with little melisma. Melodies are not usually heavily ornamented, although singers use special vocal techniques, such as pulsation on sustained tones or glottal shakes, to create special rhythmic effects as well as variety in timbre. Melodic phrases are clearly defined, often by aspirated attacks and releases. The underlying pulse is generally regular and even, although Native musicians achieve rhythmic complexity through several techniques, some of which are described in the following case studies. Metric structures in Native American songs often appear to be irregular, and therefore contemporary scholars sometimes omit time signatures from transcriptions of American Indian songs.

One of the greatest challenges for transcribers of American Indian music is vocal timbre. Because this is difficult to adequately represent in music notion, transcriptions are usually supplemented by verbal commentary that describes vocal production as relaxed and resonant, tense and nasal, or similar adjectives. Another challenge is the precise representation of pitch, in that we do not always know whether a group of tones that are very close in pitch would be conceived by the singers as different pitches or as variants of a single pitch category. The composer Bob Snyder explains that musicians within a given culture develop pitch categories as a means of recognizing individual pitches, "despite local variations in their values" (Snyder 2000: 86). Snyder further states that "In some musical systems, . . . especially those having scales with few pitches, certain controlled types of small-scale variation are allowed precisely to blur categorical pitch boundaries" (Snyder 2000: 143). Other than George List, music scholars have not yet addressed North American Indian pitch concepts in depth (List 1985).

3. For information on the history of transcribing American Indian music, see Levine 2002.

+   Placed above a notehead indicates microtonally raised pitch

−   Placed above a notehead indicates microtonally lowered pitch

X   Used as a notehead to indicate note of indefinite pitch; the stem indicates the note's durational value

⌐   Placed leading up to a notehead indicates an upward portamento as an attack at the beginning of a phrase

⌐   Placed descending from a notehead indicates a downward portamento as a release at the end of a phrase

/   Indicates an upward portamento between two notes

\   Indicates a downward portamento between two notes

>   Placed above a notehead indicates a strongly accented note

⌢   Placed above a notehead indicates a slightly longer durational value

⌣   Placed above a notehead indicates a slightly shorter durational value

NOTE: Dots above or below notes indicate vocal pulsations. The use of key signatures in the Chickasaw Friendship Dance, Figure 8.6, does not imply the use of functional harmony in this song.

Figure 8.1.　Key to transcription modifications.

　　　Michael Tenzer points out that musical transcription and analysis are closely intertwined, "since the act of notating music requires deciding how to represent virtually all music elements" (Tenzer 2006: 8), and this statement certainly applies to scholarship on Native American music. Most American Indian songs have been transcribed from audio recordings since the early twentieth century, and therefore we would add that recording technology also contributes to the way scholars have come to understand form and design in American Indian songs. From 1890 until the mid-1930s, researchers used cylinder phonographs to record Native music. While cylinder recordings and the transcriptions and analyses based on them are important historical documents, the technological limitations of the recordings skewed early representations of Native music. Sound distortion in cylinder recordings limited the perception of vocal timbre, which is a central component of American Indian musical style. Cylinders came in two sizes: a four-inch cylinder, which could record about three minutes of music, and a six-inch cylinder, which could record up to nine minutes (Brady 1999: 22). These time limitations distorted representations of form when the singer could perform only one part of a multisectional song, one song within a song set, or one verse of a strophic song. Transcriptions and analyses based on early recordings created the mistaken impression that all Native songs are short and simple in form, an idea that persists to some extent. We hope to offer a richer interpretation of American Indian musical form through the following case studies.

Arapaho Wolf Dance Song

The Arapaho, who speak an Algonquian language, are from the Northern Plains region. During the early nineteenth century they lived in Wyoming and eastern Colorado, but in the 1850s they split into two bands: members of the northern band now live on the Wind River Reservation in Wyoming, while members of the southern band settled in Oklahoma (Fowler 2001). Prior to the twentieth century, Wolf Dance songs were a significant part of the Arapaho repertory. The literature on Arapaho culture mentions a Wolf Dance only occasionally, and identifies it as a ceremony of one of the men's societies, which had certain duties in social life and warfare. Frances Densmore describes Arapaho Wolf Dance songs as focused on preparations for warfare, and explains that these songs were performed at communal dances prior to the departure of a war party (Densmore 1936: 102). Further insight into the genre may be gleaned from the musical culture of the Arapaho's near neighbors, the Cheyenne. Virginia Giglio states that the Cheyenne called their warrior scouts "wolves" in the nineteenth century, and they sang wolf songs to honor and encourage warriors preparing for battle. Giglio explains that "wolf songs were sung between sweethearts before war parted them from each other; these are sometimes known as 'war journey songs,' serving to sustain memories of important relationships during the stress of war" (Giglio 1994: 12). Wolf Dance songs were eventually absorbed into the repertory of Forty-Nine dances (Giglio 1994: 15), a social event that became associated with intertribal powwows during the twentieth century.

In 1949, the Czech-American linguist Zdenek Salzmann recorded a group of Northern Arapaho singers, two men and two women, on the Wind River Reservation in Wyoming. The Wolf Dance song analyzed here is from Salzmann's collection, in which this genre figures prominently (figure 8.2, track 1).[4] In a number of ways, this performance is typical of many songs as they are sung by groups in the Northern Plains. Men's and women's singing styles differ. The men's style is loud and tense, with heavy pulsations on long tones and strong accentuation. The women's style is more nasal and less strongly accented; instead of pulsations, the women use a slow vibrato with pitch variation of about a half step to ornament the long tones. The singers use a tetratonic scale, consisting of slightly large whole tones with octave duplication of

---

4. Salzmann recorded about forty songs on wire; these recordings were deposited in the Archives of Traditional Music, Indiana University.

Figure 8.2.   Arapaho Wolf Dance song.

two tones.[5] They sing homorhythmically in virtually perfect unison and octave. They also drum in rhythmic unison, maintaining a steady pulse throughout the song. But the relationship of the drumming to the melody line is not so simple. One round of the strophic-form song contains 93 drum beats, while the melody line has 133 beats (transcribed in figure 8.2 as eighth notes). Thus there are approximately, but not precisely, two drum beats for every three beats in the melody. It should be clear that the dotted eighths representing the drum beats in figure 8.2 would not provide a reliable guide for someone wishing to reproduce the song from this notation. The drum beats do not regularly coincide with the beginnings of melody notes, nor is there a regular syncopated shift. However, in the repertories of which this song is representative, it is not proper performance practice for drum beats and melody beats to coincide. We conclude, therefore, that the two structures of melody and drum exhibit a degree of independence. Ethnographic accounts do not shed light on this phenomenon.

This slight discrepancy between the two rhythmic structures, vocal and percussive, which are performed simultaneously by all of the musicians, raises questions. Is there a fundamental metric unit, or pulse, or other musical structure that unites the drumming and the melody? What do the drum beats and sung notes have to do with each other? Are there alternate ways of transcribing this song that would illuminate the complexities of the rhythmic structure? One possibility is that the two lines are independent, have little to do with each other, and the singer-drummers therefore maintain the two in mind simultaneously. In fact, some Plains Indian drummers and singers insist on the independence of the drum from the melody. Another possibility is that the

5.   The assumption of the relevance of octave equivalence is supported by the use, an octave apart, of a distinct motif, and also by the fact that men and women sing together in octaves.

musicians intend to provide a regular relationship—two drum beats per three-eighth units, but with little attention to precision of the relationship between the two lines. This interpretation, however, is contradicted by the care with which the singers sing—and drum—in unison. Another possibility was suggested by Hewitt Pantaleoni, who proposed that a very rapid gait—units of perhaps 1/20 of a second—could unite the two independent parts, and that perhaps Plains singers and dancers were accustomed to feel this kind of micro-unit (Pantaleoni 1987). Finally, it should be noted that offbeat drumming does not appear to be as widespread now as it was in the mid-twentieth century.

In considering the rhythmic structure of the melody alone, earlier transcribers were inclined to represent American Indian songs according to European metric schemes, but with shifting meters. For example, the first phrase of the Arapaho Wolf Dance song could be represented as 3/8, 5/8, 4/8, 4/8, 5/8. Indeed, the total number of eighth-note equivalents in the transcription is twenty-one, but the beginnings of the measures do not share a characteristic such as dynamic stress. To Euramerican listeners there is no metric "feel," and the irregularity of metric units, and of note lengths, suggests that European meters are not helpful here.

Ethnographic descriptions of Plains singing style typically refer to pulsations on sustained tones as a characteristic of performance practice. The Arapaho Wolf Dance song, however, suggests that the pulsations may actually be the basic unit of rhythmic organization. The pulsations are equidistant, and some of them are so pronounced as to constitute the articulations of notes. The grouping of pulses derived from the pitches they accompany is:

3–4–1–12 (+ 1 silent) [:3–4–3–3–3–3–1–12 (+ 1 silent)
3–4 (a bit long) 1–2–12 (+1 silent):]

The characteristics to be noted are that there is a germinal motif of 3 + 4 heading each phrase, and each phrase ends in a long series of pulses on one tone, plus a short rest. Thus each of the three phrases of the strophe, two of which are repeated, consists of the head motif, the closing long pulsed tone, and material, different in each phrase, that connects the head to the closing.

It is a short leap from these descriptions of rhythmic structure to a consideration of the overall form of the song. The Arapaho Wolf Dance song conforms in important ways, but not completely, to the type of strophic form used widely in the Plains. The first three notes are sung by the leader, who is then joined by the other man; the women enter in the course of the second phrase, and the singers repeat the second and third phrases before repeating the strophe as a whole. In typical performances, the entire strophe is repeated a number of times; singers told Nettl that four times is the ideal norm. In the recording at hand, only the final two renditions of the strophe are given.

The strophe is normally repeated with precision, but in the case of the Wolf Dance songs and some other Arapaho songs, it was customary, in the last rendition of the strophe, for the singers to pause before the final phrase. In the recording at hand, singing and drumming stop briefly at the end of phrase 2, after which the singers—the drumming following after two or three notes—complete the song, slowing a bit for the final note.

The form of this song conforms significantly to the typical form of Plains songs used in public ceremonies and at social dances. Very commonly, the first phrase is repeated, and it is conceivable that in other renditions, the first phrase of the song at hand is repeated; that was the case in other Wolf Dance songs recorded by Salzmann. The form might then be something like A1 A1 B A2 B A2 (ignoring for the moment thematic relationships between A and B).

Due to a lack of documentation, we are not able to comment on how the singers of this Wolf Dance song conceptualized its form. However, an Arapaho singer interviewed by Nettl in 1951 suggested that the way the song is constructed is to sing it, and then to sing it again, leaving off the beginning. This would conform to the form of the song at hand. Basically it is ABA(8), followed by a partial repetition, BA(8), where A(8) indicates the A-section melody stated an octave lower. Songs with a larger number of distinct phrases (and the Peyote song discussed below) conform to the same principle, as in A A B C A(8)—the basic song—followed by B C A(8)—the partial repetition.

In Nettl's interviews with Blackfoot singers, three approaches emerged. One singer suggested, again, the dominance of the incomplete repetition principle. A second singer stated that a proper song had four parts, such as (1) A; (2) A; (3) BCA(8); (4) BCA(8). A third singer spoke of the need to have a good beginning, middle, and end. Although this may apply to virtually anything, here the singer seemed to have in mind that the beginning and end were often identical except for octave displacement, whereas the middle contrasted.

In summary, the Arapaho Wolf Dance strophe could be described thus: a short head motif states a germinal motif (C–D) twice. Its last note is sustained, and it is followed by a cadential pause. A second phrase begins with the same germinal motif, moves quickly to the lower octave and ends as did the first phrase with another statement of the germinal motif, but an octave lower. A third phrase is a variation of the first, an octave lower. The second and third phrases are then repeated. The strophe can thus be considered as consisting entirely of the head motif (C–D–C–D) and its variations and octave displacements, with the exception of the passage in phrase 2 that moves the melody to the lower octave. By the same token, one can describe the song as based entirely on the rhythmic motif 3–4–1-long and its slight variations, which appears throughout except during the part of the second section that moves the the melody to the lower octave. The three phrases that comprise the strophe are all variants of the same musical idea, the second essentially an expansion of the first, and the third, an inexact transposition of the first; thus this three-phrase structure is an example of asymmetry within a strophe. A major characteristic of this song, even when compared to other songs in the Plains repertory, is the economy of its construction, since it is built of a four-tone scale, it is rhythmically supported by equidistant pulses, and it is dominated by a single motif.

Kiowa Peyote Song

A rather typical Kiowa Peyote song exhibits similarities to, as well as significant differences from, the Arapaho Wolf Dance song (figure 8.3, track 2)◐. This song, performed by Edward Humming Bird, comes from an undated commercial recording, *Songs of the Redman,* released by American Indian Soundchiefs. The Kiowa, who speak a Kiowa-Tanoan language, probably originated in Montana but gradually migrated east and south; at the time of European contact they were separated from the Arapaho by about a thousand miles (Levy 2001: 907). The Kiowa tribal headquarters are now located near Carnegie, Oklahoma. Peyote songs constitute only one genre within the broader Kiowa repertory, and the style of Peyote songs is very different from

Figure 8.3. Kiowa Peyote Song

Drum and rattle in unison eighth notes.
At end of the last rendition, the last four quarters and the accompanying percussion speed up slightly.
Quarter notes are very slightly shortened.

other Kiowa genres, particularly in terms of rhythm and vocal production. Peyote songs are performed throughout North America by members of the Native American Church, a spiritual tradition that became prominent in the late nineteenth century. Members of the Native American Church sing Peyote songs during an intertribal ceremony, and therefore the songs share a musical and textual style that transcends the boundaries of culture and musical areas. The songs are usually performed by a solo singer accompanying himself with a rattle, while the person seated to his right plays a special water drum. Described thoroughly by David McAllester (1949) and more briefly by Nettl (1953), the style of Peyote songs exhibits a great deal of internal diversity along with significant unifying features. A few Peyote songs have been diffused intertribally; more important, the style of composing and singing this genre has moved from culture to culture. For reasons unknown to us, the Peyote songs of the Kiowa people appear to be formally and rhythmically the most intricate.

Our purpose here is not to discuss the Peyote ceremony and its cultural background.[6] But a word about the way Peyote songs are said to be composed may help in the appreciation of the song selected for analysis. Some composers of Peyote music assert that new songs come to them during or after a ceremony when under the influence of peyote. Others report that new songs come to them in dreams when sleeping after a ceremony, which reflects the widespread Native American belief in dreams as a source of knowledge and creativity. One composer explained that as he sang songs to himself while at leisure, or even while working, he gradually mixed themes from different songs and eventually constructed a new song from these previously extant materials. Finally, Nettl learned that some composers simply improvise Peyote songs in the appropriate style during the course of a ceremony. The repertory of Peyote songs is vast, and new songs are continually being composed. In general, the repertory consists of songs known to all or many of the participants and they can be sung at any time during the ceremony. However, four songs—the beginning, midnight, sunrise, and ending songs—are prescribed. If new songs are indeed improvised, they may be simply variations of known songs.

Compared to the mainstream of Plains songs, Peyote songs are sung in a more relaxed, less heavily pulsating or accented style, without the use of falsetto, and that is true of the song at hand. Its most notable features are the sharply descending melodic contour (shared by the Wolf Dance song), the asymmetrical form, the use of a rhythmic ostinato, the restriction of the rhythmic vocabulary to two note values (eighths and slightly shortened quarter

6. An introduction to some of the extensive literature on this topic is provided by White (2000).

notes), and the rattle beats equivalent to and coinciding with the eighth notes of the melody. It is worth noting the wide range—a major thirteenth—of the tune. All of the pitches can be subsumed within the European chromatic scale. The two main pitches, G and C, and their lower octave duplicates dominate the melody and serve as its tonal anchors. In addition to these pitches, a high A and a mid-level B and B-flat appear, but their infrequent use and the complementary distribution suggest that they might be three variants of the same pitch category, or, in any event, units that play a role different from C and G. Whether there is an unarticulated Plains Indian music theory that interprets the pitches of a song as a hierarchy is certainly not clear. Since the great majority of pitches in Plains and Peyote songs are separated—in songs and in the abstract scales derived from songs—of intervals larger than a major second, it might be reasonable to suggest the following: in the collection of tones that comprise the "scale" of a song, tones separated by an interval approximating a half-step that never appear successively in the song itself might be functioning as variants of a single pitch category, in a way perhaps analogous to the raised and lowered seventh in the ascending and descending harmonic minor. While the overall structure of the strophe is similar to that of most Plains songs, and to the Wolf Dance song, it is somewhat different in its details. The strophe of a Peyote song usually consists of eight to twelve phrases, some repeated, some presented successively in melodic sequence, some that are variations of earlier ones, and some reappearing in the lower octave.

The verbal texts of Peyote songs have been discussed in the ethnomusicological and anthropological literature because of their unusual character, but questions remain about their meaning. The song is constructed almost entirely of presentations and variants of a rhythmic pattern accompanied by an identical series of syllables; variations in the rhythmic pattern produce variations in the vocables. They are similar to the syllable patterns that serve as texts of Peyote songs wherever these are sung, but these patterns do not have lexical meaning in any Native American language, as far as has been determined. Everywhere, syllable patterns coincide with rhythmic patterns in the manner of this Kiowa Peyote song. We should point out, however, that there are a few Peyote songs in which lexical texts appear during the second of the two main sections. These texts are occasionally in English. The principal lyrics of this song are *yana howi nayo*, with variants *yana howi no* and *yana howi na he ne yo we*. These are similar to *heyo wici, wici nai, yo wici ni, heyo wa ne ne kaya tini, kaya tina yo, he ne ne hato wici na yo*, and others heard in Kiowa and other Peyote repertories. Lexical meaning may be absent, but these syllable patterns are unique to Peyote songs and each song always maintains its vocable text. Sometimes songs are referred to by the initial syllable patterns. Finally, virtually all Peyote songs share the use of a musical and textual closing formula, sung on four long (quarter-note) pitches on the tonic with the vocables *he ne yo we*. This almost always appears at the end of the song, but it may also appear at the end of the first section. Some members of the Native American Church, while unable to give a specific meaning to this vocable pattern, compare it to the use of "Amen" as a closing formula in Christian hymns.

During a ceremony, each Peyote song is normally repeated four times, and it is important to note that all repetitions are virtually identical; no variation or improvisation occurs within the performance of one song. In the accompanying recording, only three renditions of the strophe are provided. The phrase structure of the Kiowa Peyote song can be interpreted in at least two ways. In the first interpretation, which focuses on rhythm, the strophe is composed of two large phrases each comprising a series of motivic rhythmic units. Unit A, lasting seven eighth notes, has the rhythm 1–1–1–1–2–1. It repeats several times at the opening of each phrase. At the end of each phrase appears a longer unit, B, lasting fourteen eighth notes, with the rhythm 1–1–1–1–2–2–2–2–2, including the *he ne yo we* closing formula, and it is followed by a two-eighth rest. Bar lines in the transcription indicate these units and their variants. Accordingly, the form of the strophe may be diagrammed as

A A A A1 B [:A2 A A A1 A A1 A A A1 B:].

This is slightly more elaborate than, but fundamentally identical to, the arrangement in the Arapaho Wolf Dance song. The second interpretation takes into account pitch patterns as well as rhythmic motifs. The melody of the final A–A–A1–B is essentially the melody of the opening A–A–A1–B, transposed down an octave. In this hearing, then, there are *three* phrases: the first in a higher octave, the second intermediate in pitch, and the third in the lower octave. Considering the different lengths of these phrases and the subtle pitch variations, the form is clearly asymmetrical, as we have defined it. Thus in many respects, the Kiowa Peyote song is quite different from the Arapaho Wolf Dance song, but it shares the overall strophic form with asymmetrical repetition.

Ishi's Flint Song

Ishi, the last member of the Yahi Yana people, has become an icon in Native American studies. The Yana and Yahi Yana lived in the southern Cascade foothills of California in the vicinity of Lassen Peak. Following some twenty years of brutal attacks by Euramerican settlers on Yana and Yahi Yana communities, Ishi survived with a small family group in relative isolation from about 1860 until 1911. After the last four members of his family died in 1911, Ishi lived alone for some months, but then came out of hiding and was taken to live at the University of California Museum of Anthropology in San Francisco. During his years at the museum, Ishi served as a research consultant, documenting many aspects of Yahi and Yana culture, including music. He died at the museum in 1916 (Johnson 1978; Kroeber 1960; Nettl 1965).

Ishi performed sixty-three songs for Alfred L. Kroeber and Thomas T. Waterman, who recorded them on wax cylinders; these recordings are now archived in the California Collection of the Phoebe A. Hearst Museum of Anthropology, University of California–Berkeley. All of Ishi's songs are short, between five and eight seconds, and in each case the tune and text are both repeated many times, either precisely or with slight alterations. The melodies range from a major third to a diminished fifth and the scales normally include three or four pitches. The scales use intervals compatible with the European diatonic scale. The poor quality of the recordings makes it difficult to describe the singing style. Rhythmically, the songs consist largely of two note lengths, and the text settings are syllabic or neumatic, with two pitches per syllable. Given the extreme brevity of these songs, a discussion of meter seems inappropriate, but units of two and three beats often occur in the same song.

In terms of form, most of Ishi's songs consist of two phrases; the second phrase is a variation of the first. The two phrases constitute a strophe that is repeated many times during the performance of the song. The second phrase may be varied in one of several ways. It may involve slight alterations in the melody or rhythm, it may extend or reduce the phrase, or it may present the material of the first phrase in inversion. Since the second phrase of the strophe involves variation of the first, these songs provide another illustration of asymmetrical repetition as a design element. The Flint Song (figure 8.4, track 3◐) conforms to the above description in terms of tone material and rhythm, and it employs a strophic form featuring asymmetrical repetition. Similar to the design of the Arapaho Wolf Dance song and the Kiowa Peyote song, the second half is longer than the first. But by contrast, the second half of the Flint Song appears to be a simple variation and extended repetition of the first phrase, in which the third quarter note is D instead of C, and the fifth quarter note, C, is replaced by a gesture CAC that lasts three quarter notes. The alterations are subtle, but they are made to both content and duration, so in the miniature context of this song, they mark a significant differentiation between the two halves of the strophe. Other songs in Ishi's repertory also provide miniature versions of strophic forms with asymmetrical repetition. For example, the design of the Maidu Doctor's Song (figure 8.5) contains two gestures of three or four tones each, which are arranged as follows: AABAB.

Figure 8.4.   Ishi's Flint Song.

Figure 8.5.   Ishi's Maidu Doctor's Song.

Ye - ni - ni   wo - ki - ma   wo - ki - ma   ye - ni - ni   wo - ki - ma

Chickasaw Friendship Dance Song

The Chickasaw originally lived in the Southeastern United States, primarily in northern Mississippi; the federal government forcibly removed them during the 1830s to what is now Oklahoma. They speak a Muskogean language that is closely related to Choctaw, and they share certain cultural similarities with the Choctaw, Muskogee (Creek), and other Native Southeastern peoples, particularly in the domains of music and ceremonial life. Before the twentieth century, the Chickasaw performed seasonal ceremonies that involved an extensive repertory of songs and dances, but they discontinued some of these ceremonies after their removal to Oklahoma. In the early twentieth century, they held nighttime social dances at private homes, eventually discontinuing these events as well. Then in 1992, the Chickasaw Nation formed a dance troupe in order "to educate tribal members as well as non-Indian audiences on the songs and dances of Southeast people" (Brightman and Wallace 2004: 494). The dance troupe published a compact disc recording titled *Chickasaw Social Songs and Stomp Dances* in 1994, produced by Gary White Deer. The Friendship Dance song analyzed here comes from that recording.

The Friendship Dance is also performed by the Muskogee and Cherokee, and its song is similar to the Yuchi Starting Dance song, although Yuchi choreography, use, and meaning of the dance differ (Jackson 2003: 301). No published descriptions of the Chickasaw or Muskogee Friendship Dance exist, but Charlotte Heth describes the Cherokee Friendship Dance as follows.

> The men participants line up beside the leader, back to the fire, facing east. The women dancers are in another line closer to the fire, slightly behind and between the men, also facing east. After the men sing the introductory section and Song I, the leader signals the group

with his rattle, and the women fall in alternately behind the men, the shell shakers foremost and the others following. All join hands and circle the fire counterclockwise in a normal walk throughout the first repetition.

On the second repetition of Song I, the single shake of the shackles begins in unison with the drum when one is used. There is a pause in the dancing between songs at each refrain and at the beginnings of each new song. The leader introduces the new material using only his rattle tremolo as accompaniment. When the chorus echoes the new material, the dancing begins anew and continues in a counterclockwise circle or spiral, depending on the number of dancers around the fire (Heth 1975: 81).[7]

Since the authors have not seen a performance of the Chickasaw Friendship Dance, it is not possible to compare Chickasaw choreography to Heth's description. However, on the basis of our transcription and recording (figure 8.6, track 4⊙), Heth's transcription of the Cherokee song, and a recording of the Muskogee version,[8] it is possible to compare the musical performances. The Cherokee, Muskogee, and Chickasaw Friendship Dance songs are similar to one another in many respects. In each case, a male singer leads the performance with brief solo phrases; male dancers constitute a chorus that responds to the leader during antiphonal sections or sings together with the leader in unison sections. The alternation of solo, antiphonal, and unison passages creates textural richness and variety in this genre. The song leader uses a degree of vocal tension to project more effectively in call-and-response passages and to perform special vocal ornaments, such as pulsations on accented tones. The chorus uses a relatively relaxed and open method of vocal production. The contrast in vocal quality between the leader and chorus produces interesting effects of timbre within the song. The song lyrics consist entirely of vocables. The song leader uses a handheld container rattle made from a gourd, turtle carapace, or coconut shell to signal articulations in the form, to support the melody through a steady pulse, and to guide changes in tempo. A drummer, playing a wooden or ceramic water drum, further supports the underlying pulse once the dancing begins. Women dancers provide an additional layer of accompaniment with the

---

7. The term *shackles* refers to the leg rattles worn by women dancers; in the early twenty-first century, most ceremonial ground participants no longer use this term, and Heth's use of it here reflects Cherokee usage from the 1970s.

8. The Muskogee version of this song is labeled "Peace Song" on the recording (Isaacs 1995).

Figure 8.6.   Chickasaw Friendship Dance song.

(1) The actual starting pitch is about C♮ but the pitch begins to rise about a half step here.

container rattles, called shells, which they wear strapped to their lower legs. The leg rattles are made of turtle carapaces or evaporated milk cans filled with small pebbles, and the women who dance wearing these rattles are known as shell-shakers.

An analysis of the Chickasaw Friendship Dance song reveals the subtleties of its form and design. The performance begins with a through-composed introduction, includes three separate strophic songs, each of which features asymmetrical repetition, and ends with a song in iterative form. The performance thus constitutes a song set, as opposed to an individual song, and the

Figure 8.6.   (Continued)

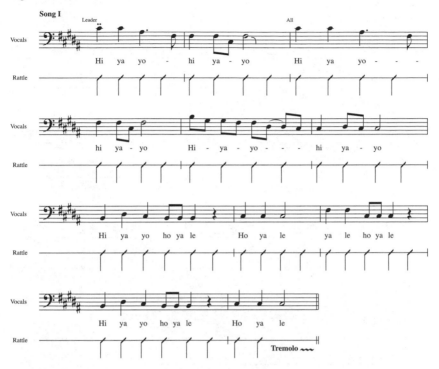

different sections are connected to one another by a short transition phrase.[9] The introduction is brief but intricate. It begins with a four-note call-and-response pattern sung by the leader and chorus on an indefinite pitch in the men's highest vocal range. Then the leader sings an unmetered solo phrase with a melody that descends in undulating major seconds and minor thirds over the course of an octave. Next the leader and chorus sing six phrases in unison; a steady pulse is supported by a handheld rattle, but the beat groupings change frequently so that the six phrases are asymmetrical in length. The introduction ends with an unmetered call-and-response phrase that leads into the first strophic song; this phrase, labeled "Transition" in figure 8.6, articulates each new section in the performance.

In the three strophic songs that follow, the leader sings the first phrase of the song as a solo; that phrase is then repeated by the leader and chorus together as they continue to sing the strophe in unison. Song 1 includes a total

9. In reference to Cherokee music, Heth calls the song set a song cycle (1975: 132); she calls the transition phrase a refrain (1975: 80).

Figure 8.6.   (Continued)

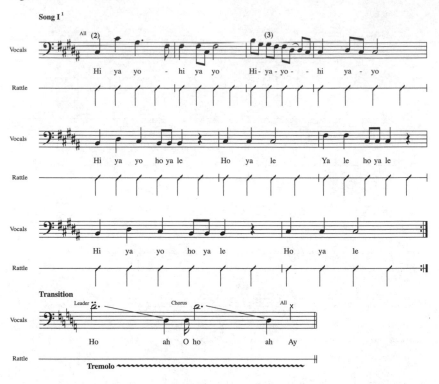

(2) The shell shakers enter here and the tempo accelerates.
(3) The drum enters here and maintains a steady pulse with the rattle, except during transitions, when the drum stops.

of eight phrases and features an undulating melodic contour with a descending inflection. The melody maintains a steady pulse, although beat groupings change frequently. The strophe repeats three times; after the initial rendition, however, the opening solo phrase is omitted, and thus the form employs asymmetrical repetition. It is worth pointing out that this is our first example of the omission of an entire phrase from the strophe upon repetition; the entrance of the shell shakers and drum in the second statement of the strophe reinforces the asymmetry. The transition phrase raises the tonal center of the performance by a half step. The incremental raising of the pitch builds excitement during the course of the song set as a whole.[10] Song 2 involves the same

10. Heth also observed a gradual raising of the pitch in the Cherokee Friendship Dance, which she described as "a gradual upward drift from the beginning to the end of a form without modulation" (1975: 172).

Figure 8.6. (Continued)

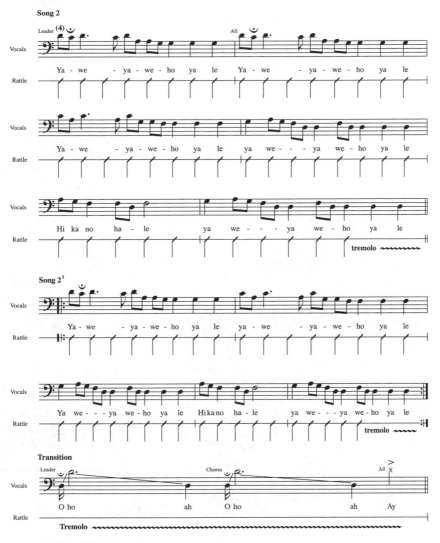

(4) Pitch begins slightly flatter than written.

principles of form and asymmetrical repetition as in song 1, although details of melody, rhythm, and beat groupings differ, and the strophe is repeated only twice. For song 3, the repeats have been transcribed because each one extends the song by two new phrases at the end of the strophe. This represents another method of creating asymmetry within the performance. The closing song uses iterative form, consisting of several short motifs that may or may not be repeated consecutively, and the song as a whole does not repeat. In this regard,

Figure 8.6. (Continued)

song 4 resembles Stomp Dance songs, although it does not belong to that genre.[11] The form of this performance as a whole is diagramed as follows.

11. The authors wish to thank Jason Baird Jackson for clarifying this point. For further information on the Stomp Dance, see Heth 1975. Heth states that in performance, the Cherokee end the Friendship Dance with a Stomp Dance (1975: 80, 132), which appears to differ from Chickasaw and Muskogee practice.

Figure 8.6.   (Continued)

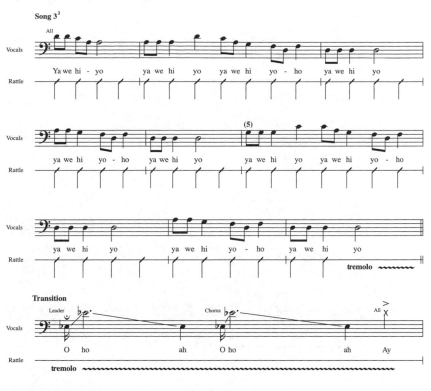

Song 3[2]

(5) Pitch begins to rise here.

Introduction Transition A A1 A1 A1 Transition B B1 B1
Transition C C1 C2 Transition D
(A = Song 1; B = Song 2; C = Song 3; D = Closing Song)

Each performance of the Friendship Dance includes the standard introduction, individual strophic songs linked together by the transition phrase,
and the closing song. However, no two performances are exactly the same,
even when led by the same singer. This is because several individual strophic
songs belong to the Friendship Dance genre. What appears as song 1 in this
transcription is performed first to mark the genre in Cherokee, Muskogee,
and Chickasaw performances of the Friendship Dance. But after song 1, the
leader may sing any of the strophic songs belonging to the Friendship Dance
in the order of his choice and with as many repetitions as he chooses. The
chorus does not know in advance which songs the leader will sing, and
therefore the solo phrase that starts the first round of a strophic song has the

Figure 8.6. (Continued)

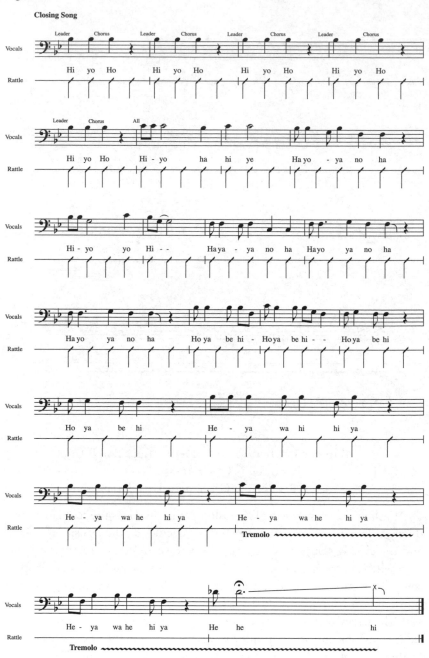

practical purpose of cueing the singers. Song leaders display their knowledge of the genre and express their individual artistry through their choices, and the repertory remains fresh and engaging for the participants because of the element of surprise inherent in this approach to the performance of communal dance songs.

Strophic Form, Asymmetrical Repetition, and American Indian Music

Beyond the four case studies presented here, songs in strophic form featuring asymmetrical repetition are also found in the music of many other Native North Americans. In the Southwestern United States, for example, this kind of form is heard among the Akimel O'odham (Pima) (Herzog 1936: 304), Tohono O'odham (Papago) (Haefer 1977: 15), and Southern Athabascans (cf. McCullough-Brabson and Help 2001). There are other genres among Woodlands tribes that employ song sets with elaborate strophic forms similar to that of the Chickasaw Friendship Dance. Furthermore, other forms that incorporate asymmetrical repetition also appear in North American Indian songs. For example, Pueblo ceremonial songs often involve long, variegated forms with an overall repetition scheme diagramed as AA BB A (La Vigna 1980). Iroquois Eagle Dance songs feature a five-part form diagramed as A A B A B (Kurath 1964: 6). Ghost Dance songs, which originated in the Great Basin region and diffused among Plains tribes, employ a kind of form that combines a paired-phrase pattern with asymmetrical repetition, such as AA BB CC BB CC (Herzog 1935; Vander 1986: 17). What, if anything, is the significance of this widely distributed characteristic of musical form? It is possible, of course, that the various songs we have described as employing asymmetrical repetition bear no relationship to one another, and indeed, are similar only by coincidence. However, it also seems possible that these similarities reveal systematic aspects of form related to larger cultural and social systems. Specifically, it seems possible to connect these similarities to certain underlying concepts of time and place, to widespread intertribal musical performance, and to deep historical connections among geographically distant communities.

Concepts of time and place have important implications for musical form in Native North America. The ways in which Native peoples have traditionally perceived and reckoned time involve both cyclical and linear concepts (Krech 2006: 572). In the realms of spirituality and ritual, Native Americans tend to think of time as cyclical, tied to recurrences in natural phenomena such as seasonal changes or phases of the sun and moon. At the same time, Native peoples conceptualize personal and tribal histories as linear, and prior to European contact, they developed a wide variety of material objects to preserve sequential records (Krech 2006: 572). Regarding the sense of place, American Indians traditionally express a profound connectedness to specific geographic locations. Connections to place are institutionalized through myth, legend, and sacred history, and are sanctified from generation to generation by ceremonial performance. Native artists express traditional concepts of time and emplacement visually with patterns such as circular or spiraling designs and images of "containment and surroundment" (Toelken 2003: 37). This imagery is also embedded in the form and design of Native American songs. Strophic forms express circularity and recurrence, since the strophe can be repeated indefinitely, containing and surrounding the participants in song. When songs accompany dance, this imagery is reinforced by the choreography, as dancers circle the arena or ceremonial ground. Yet strict repetition could become tedious for performers and listeners alike; the subtle variations introduced through asymmetrical repetition generate a feeling of vitality and vigor. In addition, since they involve sequentially varied repetitions, Native American strophic songs may reflect the commingling of cyclical and linear concepts of time by advancing through a series of cyclical movements, thus tracing a spiral in aural imagery.

Scholars of American Indian music have generally perceived intertribal performance as a twentieth-century phenomenon, associated primarily with powwows. However, recent interpretations of Native history suggest that intertribal performance on a regional level has been a widespread phenomenon for centuries. Each of the songs presented in our four case studies was or is typically performed in a regional intertribal venue. Songs in strophic form have the practical function of facilitating participation in multilingual, multitribal performance contexts, in which everyone present is expected to participate. Strophic songs enable those who are unfamiliar with the music to join in as the repetitions unfold. Asymmetrical repetition also has a practical function. In genres such as the Arapaho Wolf Dance song or the Chickasaw Friendship Dance, the leader introduces the strophe as a solo to let the other singers know which song he has chosen; thus asymmetrical repetition provides a cueing device.

The distinctiveness of American Indian strophic-form songs featuring asymmetrical repetition, and the many variants of this form in a widely distributed group of repertories suggests deep historical connections that transcend geographic boundaries and distances. This is especially true when we consider the virtual absence of this approach to strophic form outside of Native America, such as in European folk music. Our analysis suggests that Native American music history before the arrival of Europeans must have been far more complex than what has been imagined previously.

Archaeologists have come to portray precontact Native America as much more densely populated than was previously believed, with a series of substantial urban cultures supported by developed agriculture (Mann 2005). Furthermore, it is well documented that Native Americans—whether as individuals, small parties, or entire nations—have a long history of travel for purposes of trade, visiting, and migration. We can thus imagine North America in the precontact era as a continent filled with prolific composers contributing to dynamic and inspirational communal performances, creating and exchanging specific songs as well as ways of thinking about music and musical design along active trade routes and among extensive social networks. This view of American Indian music history may help to explain the wide geographic distribution—and the diversity—of strophic forms with asymmetrical repetition.

The case studies presented here encourage listeners to think more deeply and broadly about American Indian music and music history. We have attempted to use musical analysis to demonstrate some of the intricate details of form and design in Native American songs, to suggest ways in which comparative analysis may reflect widely shared concepts and values, and to illuminate general historical processes.

References

Anonymous. [n.d.] *Songs of the Redman*. Lawton, OK: American Indian Soundchiefs.

Brady, Erika. 1999. *A Spiral Way: How the Phonograph Changed Ethnography*. Jackson: University Press of Mississippi.

Brightman, Robert A., and Pamela S. Wallace. 2004. "Chickasaw." In *Handbook of North American Indians*, vol. 14, *Southeast*, ed. Raymond D. Fogelson, 478–495. Washington, DC: Smithsonian Institution.

Browner, Tara. 2002. *Heartbeat of the People: Music and Dance of the Northern Pow-wow*. Urbana and Chicago: University of Illinois Press.

Densmore, Frances. 1936. *Cheyenne and Arapaho Music*. Southwest Museum Papers Number 10. Los Angeles: Southwest Museum.

Fowler, Loretta. 2001. "Arapaho." In *Handbook of North American Indians*, vol. 13, *Plains, Part 2*, ed. Raymond J. DeMallie, 840–862. Washington, DC: Smithsonian Institution.

Giglio, Virginia. 1994. *Southern Cheyenne Women's Songs*. Norman and London: University of Oklahoma Press.

Haefer, J. Richard. 1977. *Papago Music and Dance*. Tsaile, AZ: Navajo Community College Press.

Herzog, George. 1935. "Plains Ghost Dance and Great Basin Music." *American Anthropologist* 37: 403–419.

———. 1936. "A Comparison of Pueblo and Pima Musical Styles." *Journal of American Folklore* 49: 283–417.

Heth, Charlotte Anne Wilson. 1975. "The Stomp Dance Music of the Oklahoma Cherokee: A Study of Contemporary Practice with Special Reference to the Illinois District Council Ground." Ph.D. diss., University of California, Los Angeles.

Isaacs, Tony. 1995. *Tallahassee Ceremonial Ground Music of the Mvskokee Nation.* Audio cassette recording IH 3007. Taos, NM: Indian House.

Jackson, Jason Baird. 2003. *Yuchi Ceremonial Life: Performance, Meaning, and Tradition in a Contemporary American Indian Community.* Lincoln and London: University of Nebraska Press.

Johnson, Jerald Jay. 1978. "Yana." *Handbook of North American Indians,* vol. 8, *California,* ed. Robert F. Heizer, 361–369. Washington, DC: Smithsonian Institution.

Krech, Shepard, III. 2006. "Bringing Linear Time Back In." *Ethnohistory* 53(3): 567–593.

Kroeber, Theodora. 1960. *Ishi in Two Worlds.* Berkeley: University of California Press.

Kurath, Gertrude P. 1964. *Iroquois Music and Dance: Ceremonial Arts of Two Seneca Longhouses.* Bureau of American Ethnology Bulletin 187. Washington, DC: Smithsonian Institution.

La Vigna, Maria. 1980. "Okushare: Music for a Winter Ceremony: The Turtle Dance Songs of San Juan Pueblo." *Selected Reports in Ethnomusicology* 3(2): 77–99.

Levine, Victoria Lindsay, ed. 2002. *Writing American Indian Music: Historic Transcriptions, Notations, and Arrangements.* Music of the United States of America, vol. 11. Middletown, WI: A-R Editions for the American Musicological Society.

Levy, Jerrold E. 2001. "Kiowa." In *Handbook of North American Indians,* vol. 13, *Plains, Part 2,* ed. Raymond J. DeMallie, 907–925. Washington, DC: Smithsonian Institution.

List, George. 1985. "Hopi Melodic Concepts." *Journal of the American Musicological Society* 38(1): 143–152.

Mann, Charles C. 2005. *1491: New Revelations for the Americas before Columbus.* New York: Vintage Books.

McAllester, David P. 1949. *Peyote Music.* New York: Viking Fund Publications in Anthropology, No. 13.

McCullough-Brabson, Ellen, and Marilyn Help. 2001. *We'll Be in Your Mountains, We'll Be in Your Songs: A Navajo Woman Sings.* Albuquerque: University of New Mexico Press.

Nettl, Bruno. 1953. "Observations on Meaningless Peyote Song Texts." *Journal of American Folklore* 66: 161–164.

———. 1965. "The Songs of Ishi: Musical Style of the Yahi Indians." *Musical Quarterly* 51: 460–477.

Pantaleoni, Hewitt. 1987. "One of Densmore's Rhythms Reconsidered." *Ethnomusicology* 31(1): 35–55.

Snyder, Bob. 2000. *Music and Memory: An Introduction.* Cambridge: MIT Press.

Tenzer, Michael. 2006. "Introduction: Analysis, Categorization, and Theory of Musics of the World." In *Analytical Studies in World Music,* ed. Michael Tenzer, 3–38. New York: Oxford University Press.

Toelken, Barre. 2003. *The Anguish of Snails: Native American Folklore in the West.* Folklife of the West, vol. 2. Logan: Utah State University Press.

Vander, Judith. 1986. *Ghost Dance Songs and Religion of a Wind River Shoshone Woman.* Monograph Series in Ethnomusicology, no. 4. Los Angeles: University of California Program in Ethnomusicology.

White, Phillip. 2000. *Peyotism and the Native American Church: An Annotated Bibliography.* Westport, CT: Greenwood Press.

White Deer, Gary. 1994. *Chickasaw Social Songs and Stomp Dances.* Ada, OK: Chickasaw Nation Cultural Resources. CD recording.`

CHAPTER 9

Musical Form and Style in Murriny Patha Djanba Songs at Wadeye (Northern Territory, Australia)

Linda Barwick

Photo: Djanba dancers perform in a circumcision ceremony at Wadeye, 1992. Photograph by Mark Crocombe.

One of the most stunning performances I ever witnessed was a *djanba* ceremony at Peppimenarti near Wadeye in Australia's Northern Territory in 1998. A group of about forty people, wearing colorful clothes and beautifully painted up with traditional designs, processed toward the building in which a ceremony was shortly to take place to confer a bravery award on a young man who had saved his friend from a crocodile attack. The core of the group was a small ensemble of singers, senior men and women accompanying their songs on resonant ironwood clapsticks. As the melodies repeatedly descended and plateaued, separate groups of male and female dancers alternately surged toward the stage and ebbed back to surround the singers, their footfalls timed by the clapsticks. The combination of energy, grace, and group synchrony was breathtaking.

Before long I was drawn into an extended engagement with the *djanba* performers and their families, into grappling to learn a little of the notoriously difficult Murriny Patha language,[1] and into a major project to document the songs and their history. This chapter is about the musical form of these *djanba* songs—public dance songs from Australia's northwest Northern Territory— and how they fit into the musical landscape of traditional Australian Indigenous song styles.

As several commentators have noted (Nettl 1964; Blum 1992), ethnomusicologists characterize musical style to allow comparison—between different genres, different repertories, or different composers. Two methodological challenges of particular importance to the discipline arise in definition and understanding of style across linguistic and cultural boundaries. These relate to analytical frameworks on the one hand and social meaning on the other. Diversity in musical elements and organizational principles in the selected musical repertories may mitigate against the development of appropriate common analytical terms and frameworks that can operate across them: many ethnomusicologists prefer to describe the internal logic of particular musical practices and traditions, and are wary of imposing *a priori* categories developed to describe exotic musical cultures. Secondly, in a comparative analysis it may be difficult to do justice to fine-grained differences of social meanings and

---

1. The sound system used in Murriny Patha is set out in the appendix. Note that the final *y* in *Murriny* is not pronounced as a separate syllable. Rather, it signifies that the preceding *n* is to be pronounced as a palatal nasal, like the sound in the middle of the English word *onion*, or in the Spanish word *señor*. In addition to the efforts of our Wadeye collaborators to teach us about the songs and their significance, I have relied on the ongoing assistance of my linguist collaborators Michael Walsh and Joe Blythe, together with the published work of Chester Street (1987).

performance practice, two key concerns of ethnomusicology's "study of music in culture" (Merriam 1963; Blum 1992).

Nevertheless, musical cultures do not exist in a vacuum. Whether through formal or informal contexts for sharing and displaying music face to face, or through globalized media of music commoditization, musicians are not only aware of the musical traditions of their neighbors or exotic others, but frequently react to them, sometimes intensifying the contrasting elements of their own musical practices in order to mark off their own identity, sometimes drawing inspiration from encounters with novel musical practices to generate innovation within their own traditions. Musical style is as much a social fact as it is an analytical concept. In the case of *djanba,* encounters and exchanges with other musical styles have been of profound importance in its genesis and development.

It goes without saying that we cannot access these social meanings of musical style merely by describing the features of musical style. As Stephanie Ross remarks,

> . . . the significance of any given feature is contextually limned. We cannot correctly interpret it unless we know the options that were available to the artist, the repertoire from which it was selected. . . . The work of previous artists, present conventions, available materials and techniques, and the interests and skills of practising artists are all determinants of style. . . . [O]ne factor that should shape our account of general style and its temporal evolution is our background knowledge of the context of creation—what was available to each artist at the time. (Ross 2003)

While her observation pertains to critical assessment of general style[2] in the visual arts, it applies equally well to the study of style in Western music, as acknowledged by such critics as Meyer and Levinson (Meyer 1989; Levinson 1990). In ethnomusicology, as in the study of past musical cultures, the knowledge of context required to interpret stylistic features depends on the analyst's understanding of performance practice as well as the circumstances surrounding the creation of the piece of music (Blum 1992).

The stylistics of *djanba* in relation to its context of creation and use will come into focus here through close attention to one song. Its composer shaped the song to conform to the established conventions of the *djanba* genre and to distinguish it from songs belonging to other genres within the community of

---

2. *General style* is the style of a repertory, an era or a society, as opposed to *individual style* of an artist or a work.

Wadeye, while allowing it to continue to interoperate with these genres in a ceremonial context.

There are numerous relevant ways to compare *djanba* style with that of two related genres, *junba* from the Kimberley region, some hundreds of kilometers to the southwest of Wadeye, and *lirrga,* another dance song genre from Wadeye. My discussion of *djanba* will draw on recordings, interviews, and discussions assembled and annotated by the Murriny Patha Song Project,[3] a collaboration between elders in the Wadeye community and a research team including linguists and ethnomusicologists. For *lirrga* and *junba,* I will rely on two previous projects in which I participated in the 1990s.[4]

The three examples chosen for comparative analysis originated in a common social and musical milieu. A conventional framework of public dance song performances applied and continues to apply across linguistic and cultural boundaries throughout northern Australia. In both ceremonial and informal performance contexts, different song genres are frequently performed together, and even where a single song genre is presented, the audience almost always includes members of other groups, who may even have commissioned the performance.

The most fundamental common convention is the organization of the performance around the presentation of a number of song items—stretches of singing with instrumental accompaniment during which dance and other ceremonial action takes place—interspersed with periods of informal discussion or silence. Each song item typically presents a single song topic. Selection and ordering of the items to be performed is the responsibility of the lead singer. Further common conventions apply to the internal structuring of the song items, which will be further discussed below.

These common formal conventions provide a technical framework for the stylistic comparison, thus answering the first of the methodological challenges raised above. The second challenge—establishing and interpreting the social meanings of sung performance—is addressed through description of the social situations in which the songs are performed, together with statements about

3. Funded by the Australian Research Council 2004–2008, DP0450131, "Preserving Australia's Endangered Heritages: Murrinh-Patha Song at Wadeye," investigators Allan Marett, Michael Walsh, Nicholas Reid, and Lysbeth Ford, with coinvestigators Linda Barwick and Joe Blythe.

4. Both funded by the Australian Research Council and undertaken in collaboration with Allan Marett: the ARC Large Grants "An Ethnomusicological Study of Lirrga, a Genre of Australian Aboriginal Song from NW Australia" (2001–2003), and "Public Performance Genres of the Northern and Eastern Kimberleys" (1997–1999).

style and social meaning of individual songs from knowledgeable performers and composers.

In order to understand the context of creation of the *djanba* song example, we therefore need to understand something of the social history of Wadeye and the landscape of traditional Australian Indigenous song styles.

Social History of Djanba

The Murriny Patha *djanba* song genre was created around 1960 in the community of Port Keats (now known as Wadeye), in Australia's Northern Territory by Robert Dungoi Kolumboort, a man of the Dimirnin clan in whose traditional estate the community is situated. While Robert Kolumboort is credited with initiating the repertory, he died before the mid-1960s, and most of the songs in the present repertory were composed by others, including his two brothers Harry Luke Palada Kolumboort and Lawrence Kolumboort. The latter is the composer and main performer of the *djanba* song that forms the focus of this chapter.

The known *djanba* repertory consists of 106 songs in the Murriny Patha language, one of the healthier Australian languages today, with about 2500 speakers, most living in Wadeye. Most of the songs concern the activities of the Dimirnin clan's ancestors, whose spirits inhabit Kunybinyi,[5] an area near Wadeye.[6] From here they emerge at night to visit their kin and teach them new songs and dances. Many *djanba* songs reproduce the utterances of the ancestors during these song-giving events.

The songs are used to enable seven Murriny Patha speaking clans to participate in circumcision ceremonies and *burnim rag* (mortuary ceremonies performed some months or years after death). The ceremonies all involve reciprocal relations between three larger clan alliance groups, or "mobs," each of which created for this purpose a new repertory of songs "in language" (that is, in the patrilineally inherited spoken language of the song composer). *Djanba* was created by and for the Murriny Patha speaking clans, whose

5. Since in the Murriny Patha orthography used here (see the appendix and note 1) the digraph *ny* indicates a single palatal nasal phoneme, the *y* in the middle of the word *Kunybinyi* is not pronounced as a separate syllable.

6. A small number of songs composed by members of the neighboring Yek Nangu clan concern that clan's spirit ancestors, known as *tidha,* who perform the same sort of activities as do *djanba;* that is, visiting their clanspeople at night to teach them new songs and dances.

traditional estates include the community of Wadeye itself and areas to the west and south, *lirrga* by clans (speakers of Marri Ngarr and Ngen'giwumirri) whose traditional country lies inland, to the east of Wadeye, and the *walakandha wangga* by clans speaking various small coastal languages to the north of Wadeye (Magati-ge, Marri Tjavin-Marri Ammu, Emmi-Mendhe) (Marett 2005; Furlan 2005).[7] These sister repertories enable social cohesion between these three broad groupings in Wadeye and celebrate the relevant clan's relations to the country and the totemic beings that inhabit it.

The patrilineal clan (Falkenberg 1962; Stanner [1963] 1989) has been reported as a primary form of social organization in the Daly region since anthropologists first began working there in the 1930s. By this social system, ownership of land and everything that springs from it—plants and animals as well as cultural products like songs, language, and stories—is handed down from father to son. Both sons and daughters identify with their clan country and its stories, but only the sons pass on the ownership to their children, while a woman's children carry on their father's clan and its property (Rumsey 1990). In larger communities such as Wadeye, whose current population is about 2000 (Taylor 2004), many different clans now have to coexist (Furlan 2005; Ivory 2005; McCormack 2006). Marett describes the genesis of *walakandha wangga* (one of *djanba*'s sister traditions):

> From the point of view of social history, the main impetus for the invention of the Walakandha *wangga* was changing circumstances at the Port Keats (Wadeye) mission [in the 1950s] . . . [which] brought together in the one place a number of groups who had been in serious dispute in the preceding decades. . . . In order to provide a greater degree of social cohesion, the three principal factions decided to develop a ceremonial system whereby the factions were obliged to perform for each other at *burnim-rag,* circumcision ceremonies, and other ceremonies such as funerals. At that time, three completely new repertories of song—*djanba,* the Muyil *lirrga,* and the Walakandha *wangga*—were created. Thus, if members of the *djanba*-owning group . . . needed ceremony performed for them, they could call on one of the other two groups, either the Walakandha "*wangga* mob," or the Muyil "*lirrga* mob." Similarly if members of the *lirrga* mob . . .

---

7. Today Murriny Patha is the lingua franca at Wadeye and the first language of everyone under 50. All other languages are now severely endangered, with use limited to people of the grandparent generation, although younger people maintain an affiliation to their ancestral language (Ford and Klesch 2003).

needed ceremony performed, they could call on either the *djanba* mob or the *wangga* mob, and if members of the *wangga* mob . . . required ceremony, they could call on either the *djanba* or the *lirrga* mob. (Marett 2007)

In Wadeye, as in many other Australian Aboriginal communities, the community's residence pattern reflects the geographical orientation of the relevant group. Thus, when I first visited Wadeye, families belonging to the *wangga* mob, whose traditional country lies to the north of Wadeye, were clustered in the northern part of the community, while the *lirrga* mob, whose traditional country lies inland, to the east of Wadeye, tended to live on the eastern side of the community. The *djanba* mob, whose traditional country lies to the southwest as well as including Wadeye itself, were clustered on the southern side of town. The three new repertories created in Wadeye in the early '60s were each inspired by other repertories that lay in the same direction as their traditional country, though even further afield (see figure 9.1). The Walakandha *wangga* was modeled on *wangga* repertories of Wadjiginy and

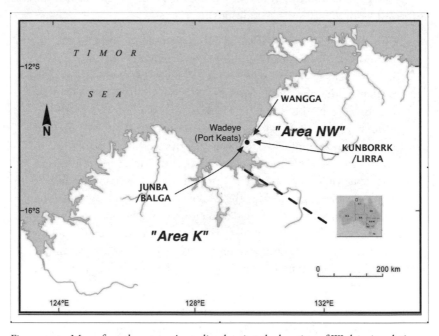

Figure 9.1. Map of northwestern Australia, showing the location of Wadeye in relation to the three external musical styles: *wangga*, *kunborrk/lirra*, and *junba/balga*. The dotted line indicates the approximate location of the divide between the musical stylistic areas "Area K" and "Area NW" defined by Alice Moyle (1974).

Emmi-Mendhe songmen from the community of Belyuen, to the north on the Cox Peninsula (Marett 2007), while the Muyil *lirrga* repertory was based on *kunborrk* songs from the Southern Arnhem Land community of Beswick, far to the east (Barwick 2006; Ford 2006). *Djanba* was inspired by and modeled on Kimberley music. The relationship of *djanba* to Kimberley style music such as *junba* and *balga* has previously been noted by Furlan (2005) and by Marett, who states, "The models for [*djanba*] were public Kimberley song genres such as *junba* and *balga,* which had previously been encountered by [Murriny Patha] men working in cattle stations in the Kimberley" (2005: 25).[8]

While there seems little doubt that Murriny Patha composers did indeed consciously reference Kimberley music in creating their new repertory, analysis shows that there was no thorough-going adoption of Kimberley musical conventions. Rather, the Murriny Patha composers adopted certain stylistic elements in preference to others. To understand what these were, and why they were preferred, we need to consider the broad characteristics of Kimberley musical style.

Mapping Musical Style

If musical styles are associated with places, it is through human action and interaction in those places. This is not the occasion to pursue an investigation of this dynamic, beyond noting that referring to other places through quotation or nuanced imitation of characteristic features of associated music is one of the resources frequently used by musical creators worldwide, from Turkish references in the music of Mozart and other European composers of the eighteenth and nineteenth centuries (Pirker 2007)[9] to the use of Central African music structure in Herbie Hancock's "Watermelon Man" (Feld 1996).

Following her wide-ranging fieldwork in the 1960s and '70s to record as much as then possible of the public Indigenous music of northern Australia, the ethnomusicologist Alice Moyle proposed a taxonomy of northern Australian musical style (Moyle 1974). Adapting the linguistic/cultural groupings proposed by Capell and used to classify the collections of the Australian Institute of Aboriginal Studies (Capell 1963), Moyle analyzed the geographic distribution of particular musical features of traditional Aboriginal music,

8. There are also secret song genres that have come into the Wadeye region from the Kimberley region, but these cannot be recorded or discussed.

9. An example is Mozart's *Violin Concerto in A major* (K. 219).

considering such factors as instrument use, performance practice, and musical form, and found that the distribution of musical stylistic features into "musical regions" broadly corresponded to the linguistic areas identified by Capell. The two areas that are relevant for this paper are Area NW (including the western part of the Top End of the Northern Territory, in which the community of Wadeye is situated) and Area K (the northernmost region of Western Australia, known as the Kimberley) (see figure 9.1).

The most obvious marker of difference in musical style between the public dance songs of these two regions is the presence or absence of the didjeridu in the sound-making ensemble. The didjeridu[10] is a wooden trumpet, commonly constructed from a tree branch of the ironwood or woolly-butt trees (types of Eucalyptus) hollowed out by termites. The instrument may be further hollowed out, and is then decorated and sealed, with the frequent addition of beeswax to provide a mouthpiece at the proximal end. It is played using circular breathing to provide a continuous drone, embellished by various techniques including humming or the singing of syllables to produce a variety of rhythmic and timbral effects (Jones 1963, 1967). In traditional practice, didjeridu is only ever played by men (Barwick 1996), and indeed only men perform the songs in public, although women may compose songs (which they pass on to their husbands or other close relatives for public performance) and are frequently very knowledgeable about the song texts and their significance. Both men and women participate in dancing, which is an integral part of ceremonial performances but not required in informal contexts. In Area NW, the principal genres of public didjeridu-accompanied songs include *wangga* and *kunborrk* (also known as *lirra* or *lirrga*).

Moyle's definition of the general characteristics of Area NW includes (amongst others that are irrelevant for this discussion) the following elements:

1. Didjeridu-accompanied items of comparatively long duration (one or two minutes)
2. A relatively wide melodic range
3. Several vocal descents or sections within a single song item
4. Continuous didjeridu accompaniments which give tonal coherence to the vocal sections of each item
5. Assistant singers combine unisonally with the leading singer. (Moyle 1967)

10. The word *didjeridu* does not occur in any Aboriginal language; it seems to derive from the syllables sung into the instrument (Jones 1967). In Aboriginal English and Kriol, the word *bambu* is preferred. Each language has its own word for the instrument: in Marri Ngarr, it is *karnbi,* and in Murriny Patha, *marluk.*

For Area K, she does not provide a comparable list of characteristics, but two may be extracted: (1) the frequent presence of women singers in Area K (which she contrasts with the men-only performance ensemble of Area NW); and (2) the repetition "throughout the duration of each song item of the same sequence of songwords," a structural feature that is shared with song styles from Central and Western desert areas (Moyle 1968). Moyle (1967) notes that songs originating in Area NW and Area K were not infrequently also performed in the neighboring area, but their exotic origin was well known (see further discussion below). As can be seen from figure 9.1, although Wadeye lies within Area NW, it is close to Area K. Wadeye was an important staging place on the traditional coastal route for trading or exchange of ceremonial objects between the Kimberley and the rest of northern Australia (Falkenberg 1962). Songs too were part of this exchange.

While various features of *djanba* point to its classification as belonging to Area K, thus supporting statements that point to Kimberley music as its stylistic model, musical analysis reveals that in musical form it is actually closer to the superficially dissimilar didjeridu-accompanied genres of Area NW. To illustrate this point, I will frame my analysis of one *djanba* song with relation to briefer discussions of two other songs recorded at roughly the same time, one Kimberley *junba* song and one didjeridu-accompanied *lirrga* song (the latter also composed in Wadeye), which exemplify the two structural models to which *djanba* relates.

Djanba and Kimberley Music

On first listening, *djanba* does indeed resemble Kimberley music, most notably in its use of a mixed ensemble of men and women, which strongly distinguishes it from the men-only ensemble used for the didjeridu-accompanied songs of Area NW. A Kimberley origin is also suggested by the genre name *djanba* itself, which is shared with that of a Kimberley ritual complex centered on song-giving spirits (Meggitt 1955; Muecke 2005; Rowse 1987; Swain 1993), and there are references in the Murriny Patha *djanba* song texts to Kimberley ritual paraphernalia such as the paperbark headcap referred to in Murrriny Patha songs as *kadjawula*.[11]

Despite these features, from a Kimberley perspective Murriny Patha *djanba* is not viewed as Kimberley-style music. In 1976, Kimberley elder Jack

---

11. The everyday Murriny Patha word is *muturu.* The use of special vocabulary in song is a feature of Australian music found across the continent (Koch and Turpin 2008; Dixon 1980; Walsh 2007).

Sullivan, in a conversation with Bruce Shaw about ceremonial traditions of the eastern Kimberley, referred to the popularity of the Murriny Patha *djanba* repertory, commenting, "Now it is everywhere. They made it up out Legune way and Port Keats somewhere, a dance like this didjeridu corroboree but without the didjeridu" (Sullivan 1983). Clearly, for Sullivan the first point of comparison for Murriny Patha *djanba* is not the native Kimberley genres *junba* and *balga,* but rather the "didjeridu corroboree"[12]—*wangga* and *lirrga* dance songs that have been adopted by many Kimberley communities within living memory (Moyle 1968; Marett 2005), traded there as part of the *wurnan* ceremonial exchange (Redmond 2001). A similar analogy was made by Pannikin Manbi, a member of Kununurra's expatriate Murriny Patha community and holder of his own set of *djanba* songs. As Moyle reports, "the djanba series . . . was said to be new. It had been found at Port Keats by one of the singers, and was described as being 'like wongga' (a popular dance song type in the northwest, accompanied by didjeridu) or 'like Rock-and-Roll'" (Moyle 1977: 12). The assertions by Kimberley authorities of fundamental similarity between Murriny Patha *djanba* songs and the didjeridu-accompanied genres of Area NW are borne out when one considers the musical form of *djanba.* Analysis will show that in this important respect *djanba* indeed resembles the didjeridu-accompanied dance songs of the Daly region (and much rock-and-roll) far more than it does Kimberley musical styles such as *junba,* however similar the styles may appear in other respects.

Three Examples

Let us now turn to the particulars of the three examples to be discussed.

- The *djanba* example, Djanba 23 (*Kunybinyi tjingarru,* "Sorry for Kunybinyi") was composed in Murriny Patha language by songman Lawrence Kolumboort (1939–2006). The performance analyzed here was recorded at Wadeye on April 10, 1997, by Mark Crocombe, for the Wadeye Aboriginal Languages Centre. ◐
- The *junba* example, Junba 01 (*Gurreiga narai binjirri,* "Brolga Preening") was composed by Ngarinyin-Miwa songman Scotty Nyalgodi Martin, who now lives near Gibb River in the northern Kimberley. It was recorded by me at Bijili, near Gibb River, on May 15, 1999. ◐

12. *Corroboree* is an Australian English term for an Aboriginal dance song; the word probably derives from a southeastern Australian language (Moyle 1968).

- The *lirrga* example, Lirrga PL08 (*Muli kanybubi,* "Mermaid Women") was composed in Marri Ngarr by songman Pius Luckan (d. 1998), a Wadeye resident whose traditional country lies to the east of the community. It was recorded by Allan Marett at Wadeye on October 1, 1998. ◐

The validity of comparing the musical features of these three examples is suggested by certain nonmusical (but musically consequential) features that they share. They are composed works of known authorship, sung by an ensemble led by the composer. Each is made up of a small number of translatable text phrases, which repeat regularly within the song item and indeed across different performances. The works are intended to accompany dance and other ceremonial actions in public performances that invoke significant beings or places associated with the composer's ancestors and tied to his social identity.

Text

All Australian music is primarily vocal: there are no Indigenous genres of purely instrumental music (Moyle 1967; Barwick and Marett 2003). Therefore no discussion of musical form can avoid song text, yet understanding and comparison of text is no trivial matter, because of the great linguistic diversity across the continent and the use of specialized vocabulary and forms in song (Walsh 2007). We have worked closely with composers, singers, and linguists over many years in order to transcribe, translate, and understand the significance of the text content of these songs. In these examples, the text is regularly repeated, so that it is possible to distill the lexical meaning of the song into two or three phrases. In some cases I reproduce linguistic interlinear glossing (provided by my linguistic collaborators), which follows standard conventions adopted by Australianist linguistics.

In Djanba 23, the text (figure 9.2) appeals to deceased ancestors to show the composer (and by extension, his patrilineal kin) the location of their residence at Bathuk, a particularly important and sacred focal site (*nguguminggi*) within the Dimirnin clan area Kunybinyi. As is often the case for *djanba* songs, the inspiration stemmed from a real event. Here, Lawrence Kolumboort and other senior men were attempting to visit Bathuk with a number of non-Aboriginal people. The vehicle in which they were traveling got a flat tire, which was interpreted as an action by the ancestors to protect their important spiritual site from outsiders, who are traditionally forbidden to visit the focal clan sites.

The question "Can you show us where Bathuk is?" can be interpreted in multiple ways. By implication, it is the question asked by the non-Aboriginal people who requested the visit to Bathuk. Lawrence Kolumboort explained to

Djanba 23

Text phrase A

(aa) **Kunybinyi** **Kunybinyi** **tjingarru** **-ye**

(ah)   place_name   place_name   poor_thing   -Dub

"Poor old Kunybinyi [we can't find it]"

Text phrase B

(aa) **Bathuk**   **mani**   **na-ngarru-ngkarda-nu-ngime**   **-ya**

(ah)   place_name   be_able   2plS.19.Fut-1daucnsibexIO-point_out-Fut-paucf   -Dub

"Can you show us where Bathuk is?"

Abbreviations for the linguistic gloss:

-Dub = dubitative particle
2plS = second person plural subject
19 = Murriny Patha verb class 19
Fut = future
1daucnsibexIO = first-person exclusive dual or paucal nonsibling indirect object
paucf = paucal feminine

Figure 9.2.   Song text of Djanba 23 "Kunybinyi tjingarru." Text transcription, gloss, and translation by Joe Blythe for the Murriny Patha song project.

Allan Marett in 1998 that it was his own wife who had asked him this question (perhaps on behalf of their children), and that later Lawrence himself had a dream in which he was asking the *djanba* ancestors the same question. In any case, the paucal feminine ending "-ngime" (referring to a small group of people including at least one woman) suggests that the party asking to have the site pointed out included one or more women. Traditionally, women too are forbidden to visit the focal clan sites, so the song text may imply that this was one reason for the ancestors' displeasure and the party's failure to find the place.

The text of Junba 01 (figure 9.3) also refers to culturally crucial information, here belonging to Ngarinyin people from the northern Kimberley. The composer, Scotty Nyalgodi Martin, explained to us that *gurreiga,* the ancestral brolga, first taught Ngarinyin people to dance. The brolga (*Grus rubicunda*) is a large Australian crane with a long beak and elaborate mating ritual behavior including frequent bobbing of the head and dance-like movements. The song's text (figure 9.3) makes a parallel between the preening actions of the brolga and the bobbing motions of the paperbark headcap *ngadarri* worn by *junba* dancers, which resembles the brolga's long beak.

Junba 01

Text phrase A

gurreiga   narai   binjirri

brolga   preening

Text phrase B

ngadarri   jagud   binjirri

headcap   dancing

Figure 9.3.   Song text of Junba 01 "Gurreiga narai binjirri." Text transcription and translation by Sally Treloyn and Linda Barwick.

The creative source of Marri Ngarr songs, in the country to the east of Wadeye, is invoked in Lirrga PL08 (figure 9.4), in which the singer calls out to the song-giving mermaids who appeared to him while he slept by a lily-covered billabong (waterhole) and gave him the song. The water lily and the mermaids are both important totems of the composer's Darrin-pirr clan (Falkenberg 1962). The totems and the songs are owned by the composer and his patrilineal kin, and used in ceremonies that emphasize this identity.

Analytical Framework

Studies of musical form in both Western and non-Western musics analyze the temporal sequencing of musical elements. It is held that repetition and contrast of sound elements are fundamental to our perception of sound as "musical": "repetition and contrast are the two twin principles of musical form" (Parry and Hubert 1954). Focusing on such presumed universals of human musical perception—such as repetition, contrast, beat, and meter—is therefore one way to meet the challenge of comparing music from different cultures.[13] In studies of song, strophic form, "in which all stanzas of the text are sung to the same music" (Tilmouth 2008), is commonly distinguished from through-composed forms (Jacobs 1977), in which there is no regular repetition of musical material. A third formal type, cyclic form, refers to music that "is always continuously reverting rather than progressing in structure, such that it continually approaches its beginning" (Goldsworthy 2005). In ethnomusicology, the

13. My thanks to John Roeder (pers. comm.) for suggesting this wording.

Lirrga PL08

Text phrase A

aa   muli   kanybubi kanybubi

SW female mermaid   mermaid

"Mermaid women, mermaids!"

Text phrase B

wuyi   = ga   niwiny   = ga   yi   = ngi

country = FOC 3DU.PRO = FOC FAR.DEIC = now

"Their country is there now"

Text phrase C

kangarkirr bugim + mi   kwang

water lily   white   + face 3SG.S.R.stand

"Where the white-faced water lily stands"

Abbreviations for the linguistic gloss:

SW = song word
FOC = focus marker
3DU.PRO = third-person dual pronoun
FAR.DEIC = deictic meaning "far"
3SG.S.R = third-person singular subject, realis mood

Figure 9.4.   Song text of Lirrga PL08 "Muli kanybubi." Text transcription, gloss, and translation by Lysbeth Ford for the Murriny Patha song project.

term is often applied to music based around an ostinato (such as in sub-Saharan African music) or in which different components cycle independently, such as the *raga* of northern India.

In this chapter I adopt the broadest definition of *strophic*, to refer to the regular repetition of the same sung melody within a single item. Unlike strophic songs in many other parts of the world, in these songs the text does not change from one stanza to the next, rather the musical item is made up of a number of repetitions of the same text set to the same melody (a minimum of two stanzas). Although it could be argued that this type of strophic form is a special instance of cyclic form, in that the same text and its accompanying melody is repeated (or *cycled*) several times, I prefer the term *strophic* because of its emphasis on the binding of text to melody to form a single unit.

In traditional Australian song, all three forms commonly occur: strophic forms are characteristic of didjeridu-accompanied musics of northwestern northern Australia, while cyclic form is fundamental to the organization of the song lines of central Australia and the Kimberley. Although it will not be discussed here, through-composed form may be found in the didjeridu-accompanied manikay styles of Central and Northeastern Arnhem Land, in which a tripartite form is normal, with improvised elements in the central didjeridu-accompanied section (Knopoff 1992). I will draw on this terminology in the course of my analysis.

Musical notation, like textual transcription and translation, is not used in transmission or performance; these works are orally transmitted. I use standard Western music-notational conventions here, with some special annotations designed to highlight features relevant for my argument. The transformation of sound into visual symbols here should be regarded more as a map designed to highlight salient features (which could always be more faithfully described) than as a normative document.

In all three examples, repeated phrases of text are regularly set to the same rhythm. There are some small discrepancies in rhythmic performance between tokens of the text (for example, a short-long sequence notated as eighth note followed by a quarter note may be performed with varying degrees of precision) but the syllables are always regularly placed in relation to the recurring beat (performed by paired clapsticks, sometimes also with handclapping accompaniment), and the duration of the text phrase is always a whole number of beats as measured by the percussion. The tempo of the beating is quite closely maintained across performances of the same song; tempo, together with the subdivision of the beat by the vocal rhythm, indicates rhythmic mode, an important organizational principle found throughout music from northern Australia. In any one repertory, a small number of tempi are used, each associated with a characteristic vocal rhythm and a different dance style (for *lirrga*, see Barwick 2003; for an extended discussion of rhythmic mode in *wangga*, see Marett 2005).

It is less clear whether beats in these songs are grouped metrically. Because this is dance music, the left-right alternation of dancers' feet in synchrony with the clapstick beat may be argued to provide a duple meter, but dancers need not lead with the same foot, and the larger structures of the dance follow the text structure. In the transcriptions, therefore, bar lines simply indicate text phrases.

The melodic dimension of this music lends itself less readily to standard Western notation. Although unison performance is the ideal, pitches and intervals are not absolute: different singers, or the same singer in different renditions, may perform slightly different versions of what is recognizably the same portion of a melody. There is frequent use of glissando and with group singing some smudging of melodic contours, as performers within the ensemble may slightly anticipate, delay, or ornament movement to the next pitch. Furthermore, there tends to be a gradual fall in relative pitch across the course of a sung item (this may amount to as much as a semitone over the course of an item lasting a minute and a half). Nevertheless, in the setting of text to melody, we can identify recurrent pitch contours involving consistent melodic movement between important pitches, especially the octave, fifth, and third above the final pitch (in the terminology adopted by Australianists the final is usually called the "tonic"). For convenience of comparison and discussion in this analysis, I have not attempted to notate small deviations in intonation or relative pitch, and I have transposed the examples to have a common final. I adopt a shorthand notation using C for the final "tonic," capital letters for notes in the octave above it and lowercase letters for notes in the upper octave (if needed). A summary melodic contour might be notated, for example,

e-c, c-G, A-E, F-C,

indicating a four-section descending melody, the first section covering the pitch area from the tenth to the octave above the tonic, the second section from the octave to the fifth above the tonic, the third section from the sixth to the third above the tonic, and the third section from the fourth above the tonic to the tonic itself. Boundaries of melodic sections are defined by breaths.

The separate treatment of melody and rhythm is required by certain features of Australian music, especially music in central Australian and Kimberley styles, in which the setting of text to melody is highly variable (this will become clearer in the course of the analysis) (Barwick 1989; Turpin 2007a; Treloyn 2006). In order to facilitate comparison across genres, I have maintained this approach throughout.

Analysis

Djanba Example: Djanba 23

Djanba is exemplified by the song *Kunybinyi tjingarru* ("Sorry for Kunybinyi"), classified as Djanba 23 in the Murriny Patha Song Project's database. As mentioned above, the song was composed by Lawrence Kolumboort (1939–2006), the youngest brother of the initiators and major composers of the Murriny Patha *djanba* repertory, probably some time in the 1970s. The Murriny Patha song database holds recordings of forty-six different performances of the song between 1988 and 2002. Most performances were led by the composer, with a few led by his backup singers Felix Bunduck (1938–2008), Kevin Bunduck (1942–1994), and Leo Melpi (1940–).

Djanba songs are strophic. Song items consist of between two and six presentations of the song stanza (three is the norm, with longer items occurring only in ceremonial performances). The song stanza presents the two text phrases in the configuration AAAABBAAA. Taking into account the varying number of stanzas per item, the forty-six performances of Djanba 23 represent a total of 149 instances of this song stanza. In the performance discussed here (song 9 on Wadeye Aboriginal Sound Archive tape 569B), a small mixed-sex singing ensemble of elders, led by the senior composer Lawrence Kolumboort, performed in a documentation session for the Wadeye Aboriginal Languages Centre on April 10, 1997.

In each stanza, each text phrase is rhythmicized nearly identically, as given below in figure 9.5. The anacrusis "aa" is optional (indicated by bracketing). The core text of the first text phrase (A) covers seven clapstick beats (see discussion below for information on the addition of beats after the core text). When there is more than one syllable per beat, the vocal rhythm produces a triple subdivision. The first syllable of each word is consistently short (notated as an eighth note), with lengthening at the last syllable, which usually extends over two clapstick beats.

The second text phrase (B) covers eight clapstick beats. Here too an optional anacrusis precedes the core text, and the last syllable is extended over two clapstick beats. The text transcription shows the subdivision of the eight-syllable verb complex into its constituent morphemes (separated by hyphens), and if we examine the rhythmic setting (figure 9.5) we can see that the one-syllable morphemes are set to a short value (eighth note) with the two-syllable morphemes being set to short-long. This tendency to highlight linguistic boundaries by shortening at the front (or "left") and lengthening at the end

Figure 9.5.   Rhythmic setting of Djanba 23 song text. Text transcription by Joe Blythe; rhythmic transcription by Linda Barwick.

Text phrase A

(aa) **Kunybinyi   Kunybinyi   tjingarru   -ye**

Text phrase B

(aa) **Bathuk   mani   na-ngarru-ngkarda-nu-ngime   -ya**

(or "right")—which we can see in this example at the level of morpheme, word, and phrase—is a prosodic feature of natural speech that is conventionalized in rhythmic settings of text in song throughout Aboriginal Australia, and may serve to increase intelligibility of text (Barwick, Birch, and Evans 2007; Marett 1992; Turpin 2007). These two text phrases are arranged to form a sung stanza AAAABBAAA in almost every rendition of the text.[14]

Whatever the constitution of the text structure, *Djanba* melodies are always presented in two parts:

- Part 1: an opening performed by men alone, which typically descends over the men's entire melodic range
- Part 2: a second descent, often smaller in melodic range, which can be subdivided into three sections:
  - 2A: a descending section performed only by men
  - 2B: a transitional section continuing the descent, in which the women join in an octave higher as the descent nears the tonic
  - 2C: a final section entirely on the tonic, led by the women an octave above. This part is usually more precise in its rhythm than the preceding parts. The men usually cease singing at some point during this section

The actual melodic shape and range varies from one *djanba* song to the next, but for a given song text, each rendition of the text is set to its conventional melody in almost exactly the same way: the text stanza with its fixed melody is repeated several times in the course of each song item, and the same song typically recurs several times in the course of a performance. The broad outlines of the melodic contour used for this particular song, Djanba 23, are as follows ("MS" stands for "melodic section"):

Part 1

MS1, MS1 (Two identical descents B–A–G–B♭–A–G–E–D–C)

Part 2

MS2A: A descent B–A–G–B♭–A–G–E, with the women joining in an octave higher part way through (a–g–e–d)

14. The sole contrary example was a performance led by the secondary singer while the main singer was otherwise occupied, probably with other aspects of the accompanying ritual. In this instance (AF2001-21-s16) the stanza AABBAAA was presented three times. The main singer LK rejoined the singing ensemble toward the end of this item, and can be heard forcefully leading the correct performance AAAABBAAA in the following item (AF2001-21-s17).

MS2B: Continuation of the descent E–D–C (women and male song
   leader an octave higher e–d–c)

MS2C: Repetition of the tonic, led by the women on c, with the men
   on C, dropping out about halfway through

Figure 9.6 schematizes the "melodic layout" (Pritam 1980) of the text
phrases of the song against this melodic structure to form the complete stanza
(see also the musical transcription of stanza 2, in figure 9.7). In the recorded
musical example, you can hear that the stanza is presented three times to form
the complete item, with the only significant deviation being the song leader's
lowering of the pitch of the first three syllables of the third stanza ("aa Kuny-
bi–") by about a tone and a half to A♭. This feature functions as a cueing
device, signaling to the rest of the ensemble that this will be the last stanza in
the item. The backup singers maintain the usual pitch (B) of these syllables,
resulting in a momentary dissonance.

Looking more closely at the fitting of the text lines to the descent (see
figure 9.7), we can see that in each case MS1 divides into B–A–G over the first
text phrase, and B♭–A–G–E–D–C[15] over the second phrase, so that each
phrase comprises a simple descent within the larger terraced descent, with a
rise in pitch at the beginning of the second text phrase. In MS2A, we see a
similar pattern, with the first text phrase covering B–A–G and the second
B♭–A–G–E, during which the women enter an octave higher.[16] The descent
to the tonic note is completed with the return to text phrase A in MS2B, covering the range E–D–C. Unusually, the male song leader Lawrence Kolumboort (LK) joins the women for section 2B and the first phrase of MS2C
(usually he sings an octave lower, with the other men). The final section MS2C
is performed entirely on the tonic c by the women (and LK) and an octave
lower by the men, with the women completing the section, performing the
final text phrase alone.

In figure 9.6 I have indicated by the annotation "+ 2" that two additional
clapstick beats are placed at the end of each rendition of MS1. This is the usual
practice, but on occasion, particularly when the item is led by a less experienced singer, the number of additional beats may be 1 or 3. In any event, the
addition of the beats here is significant. Structurally, the extra silence articulates

---

15. In different renditions of this song, the initial unaccented G may be performed
as A or B♭, and because of this instability I omit the pitch from the melodic contour
analysis. Here its performance on G, the final pitch of the preceding phrase, serves to
stitch together the two halves of the descent.

16. The transcribed performance is actually unusual in the Djanba 23 corpus: in
other performances women join in only at MS2B rather than during MS2A.

MS1	aa Kunybinyi Kunybinyi tjingarruya	(A)
	Kunybinyi Kunybinyi tjingarruye + 2	(A)
MS1 (repeat)	Kunybinyi Kunybinyi tjingarruye	(A)
	Kunybinyi Kunybinyi tjingarruye + 2	(A)
MS2A	aa Bathuk mani nangarrungkardanungimeya	(B)
	aa Bathuk mani nangarrungkardanungimeya	(B)
MS2B	Kunybinyi Kunybinyi tjingarruye	(A)
MS2C	Kunybinyi Kunybinyi tjingarruye	(A)
	Kunybinyi Kunybinyi tjingarruye – 1	(A)

Figure 9.6.   Layout of the text phrases of one stanza of djanba 23 across melodic sections.

the section boundary, and in this case balances the durations of MS1 and MS2A (7 + 9 = 8 + 8). In the three repetitions of text phrase A performed by the women in MS2B and MS2C, the rhythmic performance is notably more emphatic and the unison more precise than in the men-only renditions of the phrase. The seven-beat setting of A is used for the first two lines sung by the women, but the third is truncated to six beats, with the final syllable shortened to an eighth note, after which the song leader LK cues the start of the next stanza (see figure 9.7, which transcribes the second stanza of the item).

This song constitutes the only instance of the AAAABBAAA stanzaic text-repetition pattern in the *djanba* corpus of 106 songs. It is just one of a wide variety of stanzaic text-repetition patterns found in the djanba repertory, but for any given song text one and only one stanzaic text-repetition pattern is used. Figure 9.8 summarizes the patterns found, the most common being AABBB.

It is also important to consider how the melody of this song relates to the many different melodies used in the *djanba* corpus. The pitch contour of the melody outlined above for Djanba 23 is unique to that song text, but some of its features, such as the binary division of the song into a first part sung entirely by the men, and a longer second part initiated by the men but finished by the women, are maintained throughout the corpus.

Junba Example: Junba 01

The next musical example, a brolga song from Scotty Nyalgodi Martin's *jadmi junba* repertory, exemplifies structural features typical of Kimberley music.

Turning first to text rhythm (figure 9.9), we can see that the two text phrases are set identically, supporting the poetic parallelism that implicitly

Figure 9.7. Transcription of stanza 2 of song item WASA569B-s09, sung by Lawrence Kolumboort and others at Wadeye, recorded by Mark Crocombe for Wadeye Aboriginal Languages Centre, 10 April 1997. Transcription by Linda Barwick and Corin Bone.

compares the preening action of the brolga to the bobbing motion of the dancers' paperbark headcaps as they dance.

The rhythmic setting exhibits some similar features to the *djanba* example just discussed, with short durations marking the beginning of significant linguistic units and progressively longer durations toward the end of the phrase. The beating pattern here is differentiated between the clapsticks played by the lead singer and the handclaps of the rest of the singing ensemble, which proceed at half the rate of the clapsticks. The alternation of clapstick plus handclap (indicated by the symbol "⊗") with clapstick alone (indicated by "x") yields a duple meter, with each text phrase corresponding to three complete

AAA	2
AAAA	5
AAAAA	2
A x 5, A x 6 in third stanza	5
AAAAAA	4
AAAABB	2
AAAABBB	2
AABB	10
AABBA	2
AABBAA	2
AABBB	10
AABBBB	3
AABCC	12
AABCCC	4
AABCD	5
AABCDD	2
ABABAB	2
ABABABAB	4
ABABABABAB	2
ABABCDCDCD	2
Other	25
TOTAL	**106**

Figure 9.8.   Stanzaic text-repetition patterns in the djanba corpus. Asymmetrical text-repetition patterns (those with unequal repetitions of the text lines) are italicized.

measures of compound duple meter.[17] As will be discussed below, the percussion accompaniment is suspended for a short period within the song item.

Melodically, this *junba* is constructed very differently from the *djanba* example. The melody for this particular rendition of the text has three descents, the first and third being longer and nearly identical, while the second is shorter in both duration and melodic range, and includes different pitches. Consideration of all performances of the text (Treloyn 2006) reveals cyclic form, with optional repeats of a two-descent sequence (long descent plus short descent) for as long as necessary to allow the completion of the danced activity it accompanies. The first long descent is optionally repeated and the item ends with a long descent, to yield the structural pattern (long) ‖: long + short: ‖ + long (Treloyn 2006). The three-descent item discussed here represents the minimal realization of this melodic form.

17. As previously stated, bar lines in the musical transcription (figure 9.11) mark off text phrases.

Figure 9.9.   Rhythmic setting of Junba 01 song text. Text transcription by Sally Treloyn and Linda Barwick; rhythmic transcription by Sally Treloyn, reproduced with her permission.

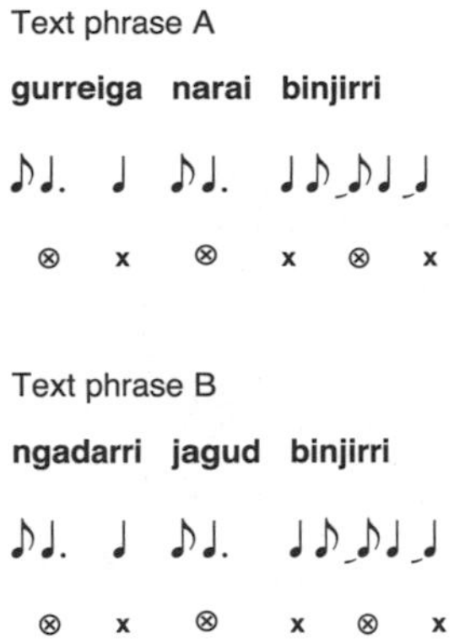

Text phrase A

gurreiga   narai   binjirri

Text phrase B

ngadarri   jagud   binjirri

Treloyn has published extensive analyses of the underlying melodic structures of this *junba* series (Treloyn 2006, 2007a, 2007b), which I will summarize here. The composer Scotty Nyalgodi Martin divides the melody into three registers, termed *arrangun* (head), *balaga* (middle), and *alya* (low). There is some overlap between these, but *arrangun* refers to the octave above the tonic (e–c), *balaga* to the pitch area between c–E, and *alya* to the area F–C. The melodic sections within the long descent are identified as follows (based on Treloyn 2006):

Large Descent (LD)
MS1 e–c (A) (*arrangun*)
MS2A c–A–G (c) (*balaga*)
MS2B c–G–c–G–F–E (*balaga*)
MS3A A–F–G– F–E E–C—(*balaga–alya*) (women enter an octave higher e–c)
MS3B C/c (*alya–biyo–biyo*)

To facilitate comparison with the *djanba* example, I have subdivided Treloyn's MS3 into two: the main descent (MS3A) and the extended repetition of the tonic (MS3B), which, as in *djanba,* is mainly carried by the women. This section carried by the women is called *biyo–biyo* "pulling," and explained as pulling the dancers forward toward the singers (Treloyn 2006, 2007b).

The small descent lacks the section in *arrangun* "head" register, and also negotiates the descent differently:

Small Descent (SD)

MS4A c–A–F (*balaga*)

MS4B A–G–F–E (*balaga*)

MS5A F–E–C (*alya*) (the percussion accompaniment is suspended for this section)

MS5B C/c (*alya–biyo–biyo*) (women)

The setting of the text to this melody for the whole item is set out below in figure 9.10 (see also the full musical transcription in figure 9.11).

The long descent (LD), which occurs in first and third positions, matches to the text phrases AABBAABB, with the first half (AABB) performed by the men over the descending part of the melody, and the second half performed as level movement, led by the women on the octave above the tonic (with some decoration with the second above). The shorter second descent is similarly subdivided, with half (here only three rather than four text phrases—AAB) performed over the descending part of the melody, and the second half (BAA) on level movement, again led by the women. It is outside the scope of this discussion to delve further into the intricacies of this musical system, but Treloyn's work shows that the relation of text to melody is not fixed, and that with song texts of different rhythmic duration (about half the repertory) the melody is expanded or contracted to fit: this song text is particularly regular in its construction, having identical rhythm in both phrases and using the most common meter. In other songs, the text phrases and melodic sections do not necessarily match as neatly as in this example.

The musical form is neither strophic nor through-composed, but rather cyclic. There are two interlocking cycles at play: the text unit AABB cycles 3.5 times in the course of a single (two-descent, LD plus SD) melodic cycle. Several other features of this example are also typical of Kimberley music. The rhythmic duration of the text line is strictly maintained (thus constituting what Catherine Ellis calls an "isorhythm" or "the regular repetition (with culturally acceptable deviations) of the one [syllabic] rhythmic pattern throughout a musical item irrespective of the melodic contour of that item" (Ellis 1968, 1984). The rhythmic setting of the text line is fixed ("isoperiodic"): by contrast with the *djanba* example, there are no additional beats inserted. The durations of the descending and level movement (tonic repetition) parts of the melody are balanced. Lastly, the strict alternation of doubled text phrases AABB appears in every song throughout the *junba* repertory

LD	MS1	gurreiga narai binjirri	(A)
	MS2A	gurreiga narai binjirri	(A)
	MS2B	ngadarri jagud binjirri	(B)
	MS3A	ngadarri jagud binjirri	(B)
	MS3B	gurreiga narai binjirri	(A)
		gurreiga narai binjirri	(A)
		ngadarri jagud binjirri	(B)
		ngadarri jagud binjirri	(B)
SD	MS4A	gurreiga narai binjirri	(A)
	MS4B	gurreiga narai binjirri	(A)
	MS5A	ngadarri jagud binjirri	(B)
	MS5B	ngadarri jagud binjirri	(B)
		gurreiga narai binjirri	(A)
		gurreiga narai binjirri	(A)
LD	MS1	gurreiga narai binjirri	(A)
	MS2A	gurreiga narai binjirri	(A)
	MS2B	ngadarri jagud binjirri	(B)
	MS3A	ngadarri jagud binjirri	(B)
	MS3B	gurreiga narai binjirri	(A)
		gurreiga narai binjirri	(A)
		ngadarri jagud binjirri	(B)
		ngadarri jagud binjirri	(B)

Figure 9.10. The layout of the text phrases of Junba 01 across melodic sections within the whole item.

(although other texts have one or both phrases of different duration); in other words, there is no variety of text-repetition patterns as found in the *djanba* repertory, although the duration and rhythmic composition of text phrases varies considerably between song texts. Indeed, the AABB text pattern is predominant in all repertories of Kimberley song, and also shared by much central Australian style song.[18] The two forms of the melodic descent defined here recur throughout Scotty Martin's *jadmi junba* corpus: in other

18. In the case of Central Australian style, the text sequence AABB is strictly maintained throughout the item, not just within the descent, as in Kimberley style. In Central Australian music, a descent can start anywhere within the text, while in Kimberley style each descent must begin anew with AABB (Treloyn 2006).

Figure 9.11. Transcription of song item LB1999, I(ii), sung by Scotty Nyalgodi Martin (male leader) and Maisie Jodpa (female leader), at Bijili near Gibb River, Western Australia, recorded by Linda Barwick for the Kimberleys song project, May 15, 1999. Transcription by Sally Treloyn and reproduced with her permission; edited by Linda Barwick.

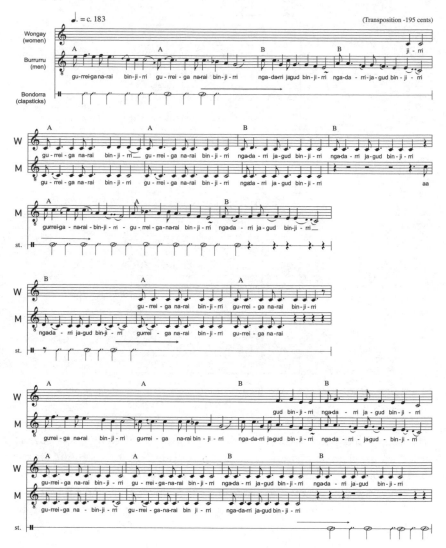

words, there is little variety in melodic range or contour between items across the repertory, although the number of text phrases set to each descent varies considerably according to the duration of the text phrases in a given song text.

In short, although the *djanba* and *junba* examples use the same sound-making components (a mixed-sex singing ensemble with percussion accompaniment by clapsticks and handclapping) and display a similar division of labor within the singing ensemble (alternation of men's and women's singing through the item, with the men's parts being primarily descending and the women's primarily on level movement), the ways in which the melody is fitted to the song text are quite different, with the *djanba* song displaying strophic form, breaking strict isoperiodicity and also diverging from the doubled AABB text form typical of the Kimberley. Further differences emerge when considering the whole corpus of each song genre: in *djanba* there is a great variety of stanzaic text-repetition patterns, melodic contour, and melodic range, while in *junba* a single text-repetition pattern AABB is used throughout, and the same two melodic contours recur across the whole corpus.

Lirrga Example: Lirrga PLo8

The third example, the Muyil *lirrga* song PLo8 *Muli Kanybubi,* "Mermaid Women," displays musical features typical of public didjeridu-accompanied songs of Area NW (Western Arnhem Land and Daly regions of the northwest Northern Territory). Like Djanba 23, this song is clearly strophic in form, with text, rhythm, and melody being repeated three times in the course of the item (in other renditions the number of presentations of the stanza varies between two and six). The stanzaic text-repetition pattern is AABC (figure 9.12).

As in the previous examples, we can see that the text rhythm reinforces linguistic boundaries by short values at the front, and progressively longer values at the end of the phrase and the text itself. The final note is prolonged into the instrumental section (didjeridu and clapsticks) that follows each presentation of the stanza, and its exact duration may vary somewhat (although in this particular performance it is fairly stable).

In Lirrga PLo8, the three stanzas of text are framed by the drone of the didjeridu, whose fundamental lies an octave lower than the melody's final note. To apply the terminology developed in Marett's work on *wangga* (2005), each stanza constitutes a "vocal section," while the instrumental introduction, interludes between stanzas and terminating parts of the item constitute "instrumental sections." Within the item the following sections can be identified:

IS = instrumental section (clapsticks and didjeridu on C an octave lower than voice)

Figure 9.12.   Text rhythm of Lirrga PL08.

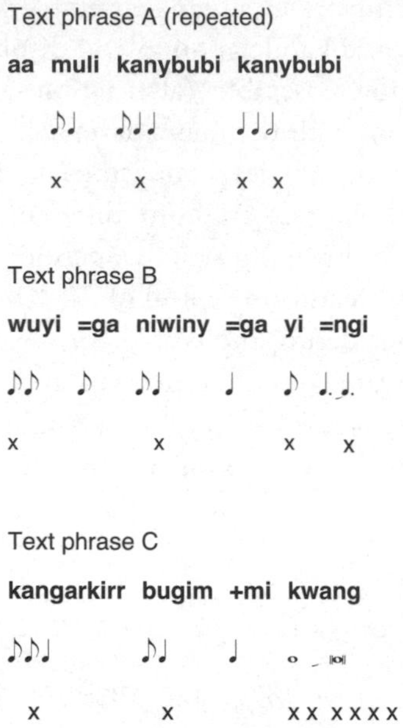

Text phrase A (repeated)

aa muli kanybubi kanybubi

Text phrase B

wuyi =ga niwiny =ga yi =ngi

Text phrase C

kangarkirr bugim +mi kwang

VS = vocal section (clapsticks, didjeridu and voice)
MS1 = descent G–D (repeated)
MS2A = descent G–D
MS2B = alternation D–C

The whole item's structure can be diagrammed as in figure 9.13. See figure 9.14 for a full transcription of one stanza of this song item.

The AABC text form in this example is just one of a number of stanzaic text-repetition patterns found in the Muyil *lirrga* repertory. Others include AAB, AABB, ABA, ABAB, ABABABC, ABAC, ABC, and ABCD (Barwick 2006). As is true of *djanba,* there is very little sharing of melody, even between songs having the same stanzaic repetition pattern: typically each Muyil *lirrga* song text has its own unique associated melody.

This song, from one of the repertories created in the same period and for the same purposes as Murriny Patha *djanba,* thus shares some important characteristics with it. Musical form is strophic, different songs use a variety of different text-repetition patterns within the stanza, and strict isoperiodicity of the text phrase is not maintained, with the final note being of variable duration. Also like *djanba,* melodies across the corpus exhibit a wide variety of melodic contours and melodic ranges.

344

IS	—	
VS		
MS1	muli kanybubi kanybubi	(A)
MS1	muli kanybubi kanybubi	(A)
MS2A	wuyiga niwinyga yingi	(B)
MS2B	kangarkirr bugimi kwang	(C)
IS	—	
VS		
MS1	muli kanybubi kanybubi	(A)
MS1	muli kanybubi kanybubi	(A)
MS2A	wuyiga niwinyga yingi	(B)
MS2B	kangarkirr bugimi kwang	(C)
IS	—	
VS		
MS1	muli kanybubi kanybubi	(A)
MS1	muli kanybubi kanybubi	(A)
MS2A	wuyiga niwinyga yingi	(B)
MS2B	kangarkirr bugimi kwang	(C)
IS	—	

Figure 9.13.   Layout of the text of Lirrga PL08 across melodic sections within the song item.

Conclusion

Let us now turn to synthesizing the results of the preceding analyses with respect to musical form. Figure 9.15 summarizes the relationship of textual and melodic structures in the three items analyzed. The strophic structure of *djanba* and *lirrga* is reflected in the coterminous textual and melodic structures. The *junba* example shows a complex relationship between text and melody, with noncoterminous, independently cycling textual and melodic structures.

Extracting the key features identified from this musical analysis (figure 9.16), we can see that only in instrumentation and its internal alternations does *djanba* resemble its imputed Kimberley model, *junba*. In other dimensions (the presence or absence of strict isorhythm, the text-repetition pattern,

Figure 9.14.   Transcription of stanza 1 of song item MarettDT98–12-s24, sung by Pius Luckan, Clement Tchinburur, Johnny Nummar and Benedict Tchinburur (didjeridu) at Wadeye, recorded by Allan Marett for the Marri Ngarr song project, October 3, 1998. Transcription by Linda Barwick and Corin Bone. The complete item presents three stanzas.

musical form, melodic variety, and dance gender), *djanba* is much more similar to its sister repertory, *lirrga*.

Another commonality among *djanba, junba,* and *lirrga* emerges when we consider the dance. As mentioned above in the discussions of Djanba 23 and Junba 01, the sections of the melody in which the women perform are particularly rhythmically precise. In both *djanba* and *junba* dancing, a clear distinction is made between the parts of the melody sung by the men alone (predominantly descending), and sections sung by the women (including the final part of the descent, but mainly consisting of level repetition of the tonic).

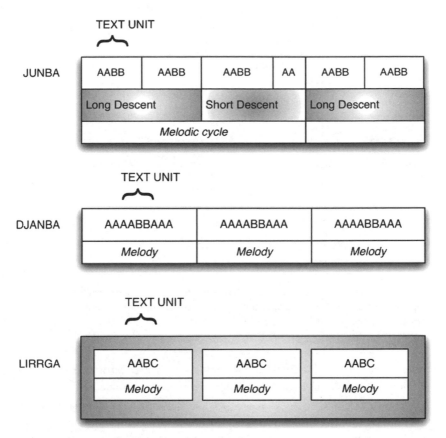

Figure 9.15.   Comparison of rhythmic and melodic form in Junba 01, Djanba 23, and Lirrga PL08.

During the men's part of the melody, the dancers tend to perform less em-phatic movements while staying in one place or retreating, often enacting aspects of the content of the text. During the women's part of the melody, the dancers move forward with exaggerated rhythmic stamping toward the singing ensemble or other focal area in the dance ground (in *djanba burnim rag* cere-monies, this will be the hole in the ground in which the belongings of the deceased are burned). As already noted, in *junba* this women's section of the melody is called *biyo-biyo* "pulling" (Treloyn 2007b): it is as if the dancers are animated by and pulled toward the singing ensemble by the voices of the women. I observed a similar effect on my first encounter with *djanba:* in the procession, the rhythmically marked and energetic surging of the dancers toward the stage took place as soon as the women's voices entered the texture,

	Junba	Djanba	Lirrga
Instrumentation	Voice and clapsticks	Voice and clapsticks	Voice, clapsticks and didjeridu
Alternating elements	Men and women	Men and women	Men and didjeridu
Isorhythm	Yes	No	No
Text repetition	Doubled AABB	Varies	Varies
Form	Cyclic	Strophic	Strophic
Melodic variety	No	Yes	Yes
Dance gender	Men only	Men and women	Men and women

Figure 9.16.   Shared stylistic features between Junba, Djanba, and Lirrga.

	– TRAVELING	+ TRAVELING
– RHYTHMIC	*Djanba* descent (men)	*Wangga/lirrga* vocal section (men)
+ RHYTHMIC	*Wangga/lirrga* drone (instrumental section)	*Djanba* drone (women)

Figure 9.17.   The matching of dance stylistic features (greater or lesser rhythmic emphasis, and presence or absence of travelling movement) to musical form in *djanba* compared to *wangga* and *lirrga* as performed at Wadeye.

while the ebbing back to rejoin the singing group, which advanced at a steady walking pace, took place during the men's section of the melody.

A similar contrast between less structured movement and emphatic rhythmic movement is made in dancing of the didjeridu-accompanied genres *lirrga* and *wangga*, but in this case, it occurs between the men's singing in the vocal sections (the sung stanzas) and the didjeridu in the instrumental section (for *wangga*, see Marett and Page 1995). Structurally, the women's drone in the final section of each *djanba* stanza seems to equate to the didjeridu's drone in the instrumental sections of *lirrga*. There is one significant difference however: in both *wangga* and *lirrga* dancing, traveling movements by both men and women take place during the descending melody of the vocal section, while the rhythmically marked stamping movements by the men, and vigorous arm movements by the women, are performed more or less on the spot during the instrumental drone sections. The traveling feature of the dance movement is thus reversed in *djanba* compared to *wangga* and *lirrga* (figure 9.17).

The similarities between *djanba* and *lirrga* that we have identified in this analysis arise from the common context in which the two genres are performed. Musical style is just one of several dimensions in which the song genres are consciously differentiated by their creators: others include dance style, dancers' body design, and text content (use of a particular language, as well as specific references to clan places, ancestors, and associated beings). This "constructive fostering of variegation" (Evans 2010) is a major driver of cultural change in language as well as music. It is especially relevant in the context of Wadeye community and its struggles to embrace cultural difference and establish formal mechanisms for managing it within ceremony.

Djanba needs to be different enough from its sister repertories *wangga* and *lirrga* to allow it to be instantly recognizable from a distance, as the group approaches the ceremonial ground. For this purpose, the use of the sound components of Kimberley music is particularly effective, because the *djanba* group always approaches from the southwesterly direction, the same direction in which the Kimberley lies. At the same time, *djanba* needs to be structured similarly to *wangga* and *lirrga* in order to allow the parallel ceremonial actions, of separating the boys from their mothers and bringing them to be circumcised, or containing the negative energy of the deceased by encircling and eventually effacing the hole in which their belongings are burned. And for this purpose, *djanba* composers have maintained similar underlying musical forms and dance practices as *wangga* and *lirrga*.

Because of the geographical isolation of Australia from the rest of Oceania and Southeast Asia, traditional Australian Aboriginal musical styles, like Aboriginal languages, appear not to bear any close genetic relationship to other song styles in the Asia-Pacific region, although (as with language) there is some evidence of loan forms from trading contacts with Southeast Asian fishermen who visited Australia's northern coasts over several centuries before being banned by the British in the early years of the twentieth century (Macknight 1976). Various ethnomusicologists, including Trevor Jones, Alice Moyle, and Allan Marett, have mentioned the possibility of Macassan influence on the traditional musical forms of northern Australia, with Marett suggesting that the widespread use of rhythmic mode may be one parallel tying northern Australian music to pan-Asian musical systems (Marett 2005). No doubt European colonization of Australia since 1788 has affected the practice of indigenous musical cultures in many dimensions, many of them devastating. But there is considerable evidence from the time of first European contact that Aboriginal people soon created their own songs on European models.

I believe that Pannikin Manbi's statement likening *djanba* and *wangga* to "Rock-and-Roll" relates to the use of strophic form common to all three styles. While I would not go so far as to propose direct influence, it is certainly likely that the composition of the first *djanba* songs in the early 1960s took place in environments of contact with modern institutions such as cattle stations, mission settlements, and government ration stations where radio, vinyl records, and perhaps live performances of popular and folk music in English would have been available, as well as perhaps the most widespread strophic forms of all, Christian hymns (Furlan 2005). Thanks to global mass media, the stylistic models accessible to Aboriginal composers today are even more varied (I have recently observed that Bollywood films are very popular in northwestern Arnhem Land communities, for example). Nevertheless, the long-standing, geographically referenced, and highly articulated systems linking clans, songs, cultural practices, and land in relatively isolated communities such as Wadeye has meant that musicians remain keenly aware of traditional musical style and its uses.

Acknowledgments

The research for this paper was funded by the Australian Research Council (Grant DP0450131). My first debt of gratitude is owed to the performers who have shared their songs here: for *djanba,* Lawrence Kolumboort and his family, and Felix Bunduck and Elizabeth Cumaiyi were particularly closely involved in initiating the research project; for *junba,* Scotty Nyalgodi Martin and Maisie Jodpa; for *lirrga,* Pius Luckan, Clement Tchinburur, Johnny Nummar, and Benedict Tchinburur. Mark Crocombe at the Wadeye Aboriginal Languages Centre and the Kanamkek Yile Ngala Museum gave permission for use of his recordings and photographs, and has also supported our research in many practical ways over the years. I am also very grateful for the collaboration of my linguist coresearchers Joe Blythe (Murriny Patha language), Michael Walsh (Murriny Patha language), and Lysbeth Ford (Marri Ngarr language), and fellow ethnomusicologists Allan Marett (*wangga, lirrga,* and *djanba*) and Sally Treloyn (*junba*) have also generously shared their recordings, transcriptions, and insights.

Appendix

Orthography Adopted by the Murriny Patha Song Project

Murriny Patha has four vowels for which there is no phonemic length distinction. The four vowels are listed in figure 9.18.

For the consonants, there are six places of articulation and a voicing contrast for the stops (figure 9.19). However, in nasal-stop clusters, the contrast is essentially neutralized. In these environments, rather than choose a particular series, we represent the stops as voiced or voiceless, as we hear them on a word-by-word basis. We recognize that certain speakers' pronunciations of the same word may on occasion differ. To represent the alveolar nasal/ voiced velar stop cluster, we use an apostrophe /n'g/ to avoid confusion with the velar nasal /ng/.

VOWELS	+ FRONT	– FRONT
+ HIGH	i	u
– HIGH	e	a

Figure 9.18.   Murriny Patha vowels.

Consonants	Bilabial	Dental	Alveolar	Retroflex	Palatal	Velar
Voiceless stop	p	th	t	rt	tj	k
Voiced stop	b	dh	d	rd	dj	g
Nasal	m	nh	n	rn	ny	ng
Lateral			l	rl		
Flap/trill			rr			
Glides	w		r		y	

Figure 9.19.   Murriny Patha consonants.

The orthography in figure 9.19 differs from the one in use at the Our Lady of the Sacred Heart school in Wadeye (Street 1987), which has a single laminal series and uses voiceless stops in nasal clusters.

Discography

Barwick, Linda, and Nyalgodi Scotty Martin. 2003. *Jadmi Junba: Public Dance Songs by Nyalgodi Scotty Martin, Recorded by Linda Barwick.* Sydney: Undercover Music RRR135. Audio compact disc of research recordings with accompanying scholarly booklet.

Barwick, Linda, ed. 2010a. *Lirrga ma Muyil.* Songs by Pius Luckan and Clement Tchinburur, recorded by Allan Marett. Sydney: University of Sydney. Audio compact disc of research recordings for Wadeye community release.

Barwick, Linda, ed. 2010b. *Nanthi thanpa: djanba at Kuy 2001.* Songs by Lawrence Kolumboort and others, recorded by Allan Marett and Linda Barwick. Sydney: University of Sydney. Audio compact disc of research recordings for Wadeye community release.

Jones, Trevor. 1963. *The Art of the Didjeridu.* New York: Wattle Ethnic Series No. 2. LP recording.

Moyle, Alice M. 1967. *Songs from the Northern Territory.* Canberra: Australian Institute of Aboriginal and Torres Strait Islander Studies. Five LP disc recordings rereleased on audio compact disc 1997.

Moyle, Alice M. 1977. *Songs from the Kimberleys.* Canberra: Australian Institute of Aboriginal and Torres Strait Islander Studies. First published 1968.

References

Barwick, Linda. 1989. "Creative (Ir)regularities: The Intermeshing of Text and Melody in Performance of Central Australian Song." *Australian Aboriginal Studies* 1: 12–28.

———. 1996. "Gender 'Taboos' and Didjeridus." In *The Didjeridu: from Arnhem Land to Internet*, ed. Karl Neuenfeldt, 89–98. Sydney: John Libbey in association with Perfect Beat Publications.

———. 2003. "Tempo Bands, Metre and Rhythmic Mode in Marri Ngarr 'Church Lirrga' Songs." *Australasian Music Research* 7: 67–83.

———. 2006. "Marri Ngarr Lirrga Songs: A Musicological Analysis of Song Pairs in Performance." *Musicology Australia* 28: 1–25.

Barwick, Linda, Bruce Birch, and Nicholas Evans. 2007. "Iwaidja Jurtbirrk Songs: Bringing Language and Music Together." *Australian Aboriginal Studies* 2: 6–34.

Barwick, Linda, and Allan Marett. 2003. "Aboriginal Traditions." In *Currency Companion to Music and Dance in Australia,* ed. Aline Scott-Maxwell and John Whiteoak, 26–27. Sydney: Currency Press.

Blum, Steven. 1992. "Analysis of Musical Style." In *Ethnomusicology. I: An Introduction,* ed. Helen Myers, 165–218. New York: Macmillan.

Capell, Arthur. 1963. *Linguistic Survey of Australia.* Sydney: Australian Institute of Aboriginal Studies.

Dixon, Robert M.W. 1980. *The Languages of Australia.* Cambridge: Cambridge University Press.

Ellis, Catherine. 1968. "Rhythmic Analysis of Aboriginal Syllabic Songs." *Miscellanea Musicologica* 3: 21–49.

———. 1984. "Time Consciousness of Aboriginal Performers." In *Problems and Solutions: Occasional Essays in Musicology Presented to Alice M. Moyle,* ed. Jamie C. Kassler and Jill Stubington, 149–185. Marrickville, New South Wales: Hale & Iremonger.

Evans, Nicholas. 2010. *Dying Words: Endangered Languages and What They Have to Tell Us.* Chichester, UK: Wiley-Blackwell.

Falkenberg, Johannes. 1962. *Kin and Totem: Group Relations of Australian Aborigines in the Port Keats District.* Oslo: Oslo University Press.

Feld, Steven. 1996. "Pygmy Pop: a Genealogy of Schizophonic Mimesis." *Yearbook for Traditional Music* 28: 1–35.

Ford, Lysbeth. 2006. "Marri Ngarr Lirrga Songs: A Linguistic Analysis." *Musicology Australia* 28: 26–58.

Ford, Lysbeth, and Maree Klesch. 2003. "'It Won't Matter Soon, We'll All Be Dead': Endangered Languages and Action Research." *Ngoonjook: Journal of Australian Indigenous Issues* 23: 27–43.

Furlan, Alberto. 2005. "Songs of Continuity and Change: The Reproduction of Aboriginal Culture through Traditional and Popular Music." Ph.D. diss., University of Sydney.

Goldsworthy, David. 2005. "Cyclic Properties of Indonesian Music." *Journal of Musicological Research* 24(3): 309–333.

Ivory, Bill. 2005. "Indigenous Governance and Leadership: A Case Study from the Thamarrurr (Port Keats) Region in the Northern Territory." In *ICGP & WA and Australian Government Partners Workshop.* Perth, Western Australia: Australian National University Centre for Australian Economic Policy Research, Occasional Paper No. 8.

Jacobs, Arthur. 1977. *The New Penguin Dictionary of Music.* 4th ed. Harmondsworth, Middlesex: Penguin Books.

Jones, Trevor. 1967. "The Didjeridu." *Studies in Music* 1: 23–55.

Knopoff, Steven. 1992. "Yuta Manikay: Juxtaposition of Ancestral and Contemporary Elements in the Performances of Yolngu Clan Songs." *Yearbook for Traditional Music* 24: 138–153.

Koch, Grace, and Myfany Turpin. 2008. "The Language of Central Australian Aboriginal Songs." In *Morphology and Language History: In Honour of Harold Koch,* ed. Claire Bowern, Bethwyn Evans, and Luisa Miceli, 167–184. Amsterdam: John Benjamins.

Levinson, Jerrold. 1990. *Music, Art and Metaphysics.* Ithaca, NY: Cornell University Press.

Macknight, Campbell. 1976. *The Voyage to Marege: Macassan Trepangers in Northern Australia.* Melbourne: Melbourne University Press.

Marett, Allan. 1992. "Variability and Stability in Wangga Songs of Northwest Australia." In *Music and Dance in Aboriginal Australia and the South Pacific: The Effects of Documentation on the Living Tradition,* ed. A.M. Moyle, 194–213. Sydney: Oceania Publications, University of Sydney.

———. 2005. *Songs, Dreamings and Ghosts*: The Wangga of North Australia. Middletown, CT: Wesleyan University Press.

———. 2007. "Simplifying Musical Practice in Order to Enhance Local Identity: The Case of Rhythmic Modes in the Walakandha Wangga (Wadeye, Northern Territory)." *Australian Aboriginal Studies* 2: 63–75.

Marett, Allan, and JoAnne Page. 1995. "Interrelationships between Music and Dance in a Wangga from Northwest Australia." In *The Essence of Singing and the Substance of Song: Recent Responses to the Aboriginal Performing Arts and Other Essays for Catherine Ellis,* ed. Linda Barwick, Allan Marett, and Guy Tunstill, 27–38. Sydney: Oceania Publications, University of Sydney.

McCormack, Dominic. 2006. "The Substance of Australia's First Men." Paper presented at the National Mental Health and Homelessness Advisory Committee of St. Vincent de Paul Society, July 20, Darwin, Australia.

Meggitt, Mervyn J. 1955. "Djanba among the Walbiri." *Australia Anthropos* 50: 375–403.

Merriam, Alan P. 1963. "Purposes of Ethnomusicology, an Anthropological View." *Ethnomusicology* 7(3): 206–213.

Meyer, Leonard. 1989. *Style and Music: Theory, History and Ideology.* Philadelphia: University of Pennsylvania Press.

Moyle, Alice M. 1967. *Songs from the Northern Territory.* Companion Booklet for Five 12-inch LP Discs (Cat No. I.A.S. M-001/5). Canberra: Australian Institute of Aboriginal Studies.

———. 1968. *Songs from the Kimberleys.* Companion Booklet for a 12-inch LP Disc (Cat. No. AIAS/13). Canberra: Australian Institute of Aboriginal Studies.

———. 1974. "North Australian Music: A Taxonomic Approach to the Study of Aboriginal Song Performances." Ph.D. diss., Monash University.

———. 1977. *Songs from the Kimberleys.* Canberra: Australian Institute of Aboriginal and Torres Strait Islander Studies.

Muecke, Stephen. 2005. "Boxer Deconstructionist." In *Dislocating the Frontier: Essaying the Mystique of the Outback,* ed. Deborah Bird Rose and Richard Davis, 165–175. Canberra: ANU E Press.

Nettl, Bruno. 1964. *Theory and Method in Ethnomusicology.* New York: Free Press.

Parry, C., and H. Hubert. 1954. "Form." In *Grove Dictionary of Music and Musicians,* ed. E. Blom. London: Macmillan.

Pirker, Michael. 2007. "Janissary Music." In *Grove Music Online. Oxford Music Online,* http://www.oxfordmusiconline.com/subscriber/article/grove/music/14133 (accessed December 31, 2009).

Pritam, Prabhu. 1980. "Aspects of Musical Structure in Australian Aboriginal Songs of the South-West of the Western Desert." *Studies in Music* 14: 9–44.

Redmond, Anthony. 2001. "Places that Move." In *Emplaced Myth: Space, Narrative, and Knowledge in Aboriginal Australia and Papua New Guinea,* ed. Alan Rumsey and James F. Weiner, 120–138. Honolulu: University of Hawaii Press.

Ross, Stephanie. 2003. "Style in Art." In *The Oxford Handbook of Aesthetics,* ed. Jerrold Levinson, 228–244. Oxford: Oxford University Press.

Rowse, Tim. 1987. "'Were You Ever Savages?' Aboriginal Insiders and Pastoralists' Patronage." *Oceania* 58: 81–99.

Rumsey, Alan. 1990. "Wording, Meaning and Linguistic Ideology." *American Anthropologist* 92: 346–361.

Stanner, William E.H. [1963] 1989. *On Aboriginal Religion.* Oceania Monograph 11. Sydney: University of Sydney.

Street, Chester. 1987. *An Introduction to the Language and Culture of the Murrinh-Patha.* Darwin, Northern Territory: Summer Institute of Linguistics, Australian Aborigines Branch.

Sullivan, Jack. 1983. *Banggaiyerri: The Story of Jack Sullivan as Told to Bruce Shaw.* Canberra: Australian Institute of Aboriginal Studies.

Swain, Tony. 1993. *A Place for Strangers: Towards a History of Australian Aboriginal Being.* Cambridge: Cambridge University Press.

Taylor, John. 2004. "Demography of the Thamarrurr Region." In *Social Indicators for Aboriginal Governance: Insights from the Thamarrurr Region, Northern Territory,* ed. John Taylor, 17–37. Canberra: Centre for Aboriginal Economic Policy Research, Australian National University.

Tilmouth, Michael. 2008. "Strophic." In *Grove Music Online. Oxford Music Online,* http://www.oxfordmusiconline.com/subscriber/article/grove/music/26981 (accessed December 31, 2009).

Treloyn, Sally. 2006. "Songs that Pull: Composition/Performance through Musical Analysis." *Context: A Journal of Music Research* 31: 151–164.

———. 2007a. "Flesh with Country: Juxtaposition and Minimal Contrast in the Construction and Melodic Treatment of Jadmi Song Texts." *Australian Aboriginal Studies* 2: 90–99.

———. 2007b. "'When Everybody There Together. . . . Then I Call That One': Song Order in the Kimberley." *Context: A Journal of Music Research* 32: 105–121.

Turpin, Myfany. 2007. "Artfully Hidden: Text and Rhythm in a Central Australian Aboriginal Song Series." *Musicology Australia* 29: 93–108.

Walsh, Michael. 2007. "Australian Aboriginal Song Language: So Many Questions, So Little to Work With." *Australian Aboriginal Studies* 2: 128–144.

PART II

Cross-Cultural Analytical Comparisons

CHAPTER 10

Integrating Music

Personal and Global Transformations

Michael Tenzer

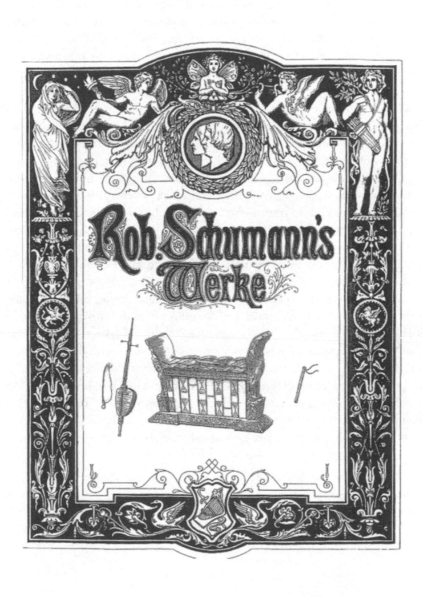

The Problem of Integration

Jared Diamond's *Guns, Germs, and Steel*, a memorable book of the late 1990s, begins with a question.[1] It is asked by Yali, a New Guinean civil servant who had never left his island's shores and whom Diamond, an evolutionary biologist, had long employed as a field research associate. The intelligent but unassuming Yali asked, "Why is it that you white people developed so much cargo (Yali's word for material goods) and brought it to New Guinea, but we black people had little cargo of our own?" (Diamond 1999: 4) Diamond devotes the book to an answer, scanning 30,000 years of human history across the planet. He concludes that more than anything else it was god-given and favorable environmental conditions—not innate superiority—that led to the ascendancy of what we today call the Western world. Reading the book, one becomes sensitive to the distinction between dominance and value. Diamond is cleverly provoking his English-language readers who, despite their likely liberal educations, and despite the recent progress in human rights, may harbor prideful prejudice that European-based culture is innately superior. The West may well dominate, Diamond ultimately explains to Yali—and to us—but it is not better. It just figured out how to run with its good luck.

This chapter also departs from a question, formulated not by Yali, nor across the world in Bali, where I often go to make music. It was posed to me in Vancouver, as I sat down to a restaurant meal, by an equally intelligent and unassuming research associate, my colleague the music theorist William Benjamin. Bill knows that I love many kinds of music from all over the world and claim to hold them in equal regard in my heart and mind. That is in line with bedrock ethnomusicology dogma—to each culture its own magnificent beauties, the better to wonder at. But he challenged me on this, specifically with reference to Balinese music and Western art music, which he knows I love too, when he asked, "Do you really think that stuff (Balinese music) is as *good* as classical music? Do you really get comparable rewards from it?" After all, he went on, "classical music comes from a time and culture that allowed it to be composed expressly for listening and contemplation, and to develop whole systems and approaches to this over the generations." Bill knows that Balinese music comes from a tradition that until recently was mainly devotional and functional and more communal, designed to fill a certain, mainly

1. Sincere thanks to William Benjamin, Judith Becker, and Steven Blum for their comments on a draft of this article, and for permission to reproduce them in the appendix. Thanks also to Ellen Koskoff, Robert Morris, Ralph Locke, Steve Larson, Brenda Romero, Alfred Ladzepko, Gage Averill, and numerous others who gave constructive feedback at colloquia where the paper was presented in its original form.

religious, requirement. Thus in his view Western music is especially enriched, and superior in that vital way. He casts no aspersions on Balinese music by saying that it rewards aesthetic contemplation less. It just wasn't made for that.

The belief that Western art music is inherently of deeper value than other musics surely persists among many admirers and practitioners of that tradition all over the world. In the broader community of academic humanists, even the most brilliant and prestigious, it lingers heavily (I know this from personal experience with poets, philosophers, and scientists). Some such believers may nowadays be furtive, but if we are to speak candidly we should acknowledge that this is a natural enough point of orientation. Anyone might well assume that their own music is best, and one often hears not only Western classical music lovers but also purist Indian music connoisseurs or jazz buffs assert such superiority. On the other hand, of course, many proudly shun such views. Indeed, in these days of cultural multiplicity and reluctance to pass value judgments, it is somewhat preposterous to speak in this way about music or any other aspect of culture. It is an anachronistic echo from our parochial pasts and something scholars have supposedly left behind.

But have we? I think these questions were put to bed too early by frustrated progressives who tranquilized it with twentieth-century mantras like *It's all relative, Cultures are separate but equal,* and *How dare you compare.* Exemplary is Judith Becker's 1986 article entitled precisely "Is Western Art Music Superior?" Becker, a superb ethnomusicologist fed up with the coarse remarks and prejudices of her colleagues, decided to tackle the problem once and for all. She took three common reasons cited for Western music's superiority—naturalness (i.e., its supposed relation to the overtone series), complexity (i.e., of form, counterpoint, or inner coherence), and meaningfulness (i.e., expressivity and richness of reference and signification)—and showed how absurd it is to think that these properties are exclusively Western, once one views any given music rationally and on its own terms. Becker's formulations were inspired by her negative experiences in the halls of American academe, but I take them to be iconic and assume that their equivalent could be encountered in some form at the heart of any cultural milieu powerful enough to inspire loyalty and identity in its adherents.

In my view Becker's cool rhetoric sidesteps what is of the essence by appealing to fact and logic, however necessary that may also be. And the last sentence of her article—"*Music systems are simply incommensurable* [emphasis added]"—seems to me a cop-out. For though we are interested in determining music's deepest intrinsic qualities, we are also vitally interested in our own perceptions of them; we have long ceased the charade of pretending that music has a value or meaning apart from its perceivers. Even supposing we could rank and compare musical systems along some Diamondesque scale of complexity and advancement, that would still not measure value or meaning, nor would it allow us to take on a contentious issue such as "superiority." None of this matters as much as our subjective inner experiences, and Becker overlooks these questions. I contend that orthodox twentieth-century relativism of the kind Becker promulgates is partly disingenuous because although it teaches and preaches tolerance, it does not acknowledge or suggest how we might measure and compare our diverse *inner* relationships to many kinds of music. Yet this is something we cannot help but do, inchoately but powerfully, in our private worlds.

Something elemental is at issue. We instinctively shrink from the dangers of claiming superiority for some art over others, as if it were race or religion. Debilitating intolerance of those kinds provoked the growth of relativism in the first place. Yet even in terms of such a charged subject, it is imperative to distinguish between fact and experience. Even for a bigot or a zealot, acknowledging an *experience* of superiority would be preferable to hiding or being in denial about it, and could open the door to change or understanding. With music the stakes are not so high, perhaps, yet music comprises a central and tenacious aspect of our identities, and the analogy is clear: musical awareness and self-knowledge make growth possible.

A quarter-century after Becker, therefore, I propose that we not shun the question of Western music's higher value anymore, but rather use it as a tool to introspect. For one thing, today we have much more faith in our inner subjectivities than we do in external ones like the so-called musical object or shared cultural belief systems. Nowhere is the notion of the autonomous musical work more alive than in our minds and fantasies about music, where our favorite musics are our favorite vehicles of contemplation. Today the question "Is Western Art music superior?'" goes to the heart of our distinctive selves. It challenges us to be attentive to and to order our experiences, and so to transform ourselves musically in the midst of a world that is also transforming musically.

With this in mind, I return to Bill Benjamin for a moment. As I see it, that night in the restaurant he was challenging me, a man of comparable training, education, class, and background, to see if I really *felt* that Balinese music was equal to Western music *in my own experience,* and, if so, to please help him understand how that could be, because he didn't really believe it could for the reasons he gave. It was a variation on the classic desert island question: which music would I take with me? He was saying, "C'mon, admit it. Isn't Western music preferable to all others *for people like us?*" He was looking for explicit support or refutation for his position and hoped I was courageous enough to admit what my core musical values are, whatever they are.

This is a challenge for an ethnomusicologist like me, but in a way we are all ethnomusicologists since we are relativists and study tolerance. But what of our own values and attachments to certain ways of being musical? To say we love it all is like saying we love none. Do we in fact each have core musical values arising from one music-cultural context central to our identities, or do our values fluctuate to accommodate each new music we encounter? To what do our musical values attach—the structures of the music, our experiences and the associations we have with that music (what one could call a "comfort factor"), or something else? How are we to hone an awareness of this in a time when each of us lives with the equivalent of an inner iPod of multiple music experiences and diverse playlists, whose often stark juxtapositions may sow confusion more than enlightenment? "Life is random," quoth the iPod marketers, and they often seem distressingly right.

There are many paths to musical experience, in all roughly congruent with ways to lead our lives. Some will find the idea of an inner struggle over the question of comparative musical value preposterous. Why probe? Why decide? Relax, or enter alertly, into shuffle mode; there is no conflict, only beauty. These are the "healthy-minded" identified by William James, who by nature hold that

> ... the world can be handled according to many systems of ideas, and is so handled by different men, and will each time give some characteristic kind of profit, for which he cares, to the handler, while at the same time some other kind of profit has to be omitted or postponed ... [and] ... the world be so complex as to consist of many interpenetrating spheres of reality, which we can thus approach in alternation by using different conceptions and assuming different attitudes, just as mathematicians handle the same numerical and spatial facts by geometry, by analytical geometry, by algebra, by the calculus, or by quarternions, and each time come out right. (2002 [1902]: 138)

But for one not so disposed, such equanimity seems oblivious to the very possibility of attainment and growth coveted by others, for whom

> ... the normal evolution of character chiefly consist(s) in the straightening out and unifying of the inner self. The higher and lower feelings, the useful and the erring impulses, begin by being a competitive chaos within us—they must end by forming a stable system of functions in right subordination. (ibid: 190)

I believe that when I can hold two different musics in my mind still enough to examine them closely and to weigh the similarities in the differences and sensations they elicit, I have made a concrete step toward reconciling the musics and their roles in my experience, and thus reconciling into "right subordination" aspects of myself that were hitherto unintegrated. If I ultimately conclude that Western music is most valuable to me, it is more than a decision about what I like or prefer. It is a decision about myself—am I especially attached to Western music's sonic ingenuities, colors, architectures, and their associative meaning and symbolism? Or have I accepted Bali into my inner system to the point where my qualitative responses to gamelan music are no less deep than my responses to Western music? To generalize further, how fully can I assimilate other musical ways of being? Am I fated to always prioritize my native values? This is the problem of *integrating music* alluded to in my title. I feel safe assuming that others may relate to this problem, whether or not Western music is a component of the equation (it could apply to a Nigerian musician living in Seoul and coming to terms with Korean music or a sitarist drawn to free jazz).

In what follows, I perform this act of reflection and discernment to the best of my ability, under the premise that integration and reconciliation are valuable goals. I am trying to become an integrated self, organizing and making sense of the personal and global transformations I live through. This means, according to the particular challenge I will now take up, that there must be ways to compare my responses to Balinese and Western musics according to some fixed compass. But how? Of course comparison of any kind is inherently difficult. It is hard enough to compare two pieces by Elliott Carter to one another, let alone to another post-1950 Euro-American work, and even more so to one by Mozart, or to something from Iran or Central Africa. Even so, experience teaches that the best path to making headway on such questions is through the scrutiny of perceptions that can be had only through close listening and analysis. Methodology will be allowed to develop in stages below, and the chips shall fall where they may.

Personal Transformations

Two comparative analyses follow. The first is between a pair of closely related works of Balinese music. They are from the same weighty repertoire of sacred compositions and share the same complex, culturally standardized formal plan. I want to investigate what kinds of differences there are between two such works, because in my inner dialogue about Balinese music there remains the persistent unresolved issue—no longer possible to ignore after Bill Benjamin's question, and embodied in a comparison of two pieces such as these— of whether Balinese compositions are individuated and to what degree, or whether they tend toward the cookie-cut. I take *individuated* to be a positive value, for I distinguish carefully among the toys in my mental sandbox, and if they were too similar I might confuse them or lose interest in one or the other. So I stay within the framework of gamelan and attend to this issue first, to see just exactly what sort of individual character Balinese pieces within specific genre categories have.

Using the results of that comparison, I will further compare some aspects of the Balinese pieces with portions of the first movement of Robert Schumann's Opus 47 *Piano Quartet in E♭ Major* from 1842. Schumann presumably would have relied on Goethe for knowledge of anything even generically Asian, and I wager that today there are more toes on my feet than Balinese who know Robert Schumann's music. So why this East-West connection, and why to this Schumann piece? Well, it is one of my very favorites, and I know it by heart. It has nothing overtly to do with Bali, not even by coincidence. And that is exactly the kind of comparison I am interested in justifying. Because inside, *I* relate the two musics together strongly. They both have high—in fact, the highest—prestige value for music within their respective cultures, though for different reasons. They both get frequent play on my inner iPod. I have an inkling that they are congruent in transcendent ways, despite all the potential for mistranslation from one time and culture and medium to another.

Moreover, my instinct says they are roughly equivalent in scope and impact. It wouldn't do, for example, to compare the Balinese pieces to Beethoven's *Eroica,* which would be too big and omnivorous, nor to a Chopin *Nocturne,* which would be too small and intimate. The Piano Quartet is "just right": elaborately arranged, serious and ambitious, and exemplary of the ethos of chamber music, qualities I also associate with the tightly rehearsed music of Balinese repertoires. So, even though I know that this is a shotgun wedding, and that I am groping and guessing, I wager that taking these specific pieces out of the worlds of their respective contexts and juxtaposing them will stimulate new ideas leading to a useful comparison I present this to you as an article of faith. *Useful* is defined in terms of helping me to integrate my experiences of these musics. Perhaps my investigation will help me understand whether I experience one more deeply than the other, or not, and whether that experience is something I must own entirely, or whether it is based on something "out there" in the music itself.

Two Lelambatan

The two Balinese works I consider are called *Lokarya* and *Tabuh Gari.*[2] Both come from the genre *lelambatan,* a major category of sacred compositions dating from the past several centuries, played at temple ceremonies or state

2. *Lokarya* is an original composition by composer Wayan Sinti in strict classical lelambatan style (see below). Its title is a shortening of the names Wayan Lotring, Nyoman Kaler, and Gusti Madé Putu Griya, three prominent mid-twentieth-century

occasions.[3] They still are, but today *lelambatan* have also become center-pieces of popular secular gamelan competitions. *Lelambatan* are complex, up to thirty minutes long, and considered by Balinese to be profound. Until the late twentieth century, they were performed in an austere, pared-down style constructed mainly from a series of gong cycles arranged around a central cycle called the *pengawak* (figure 10.1) which has the broadest gong pattern and weightiest connotations. In general, the tempo is quick at the outset, slows for the *pengawak* cycle, and then quickens approaching the end, but there is a great deal of local tempo change. The cycles are fleshed out with austere, fixed melodies of minimal rhythmic variety composed using a five-tone scale to fall within a range of two octaves (ten available tones), and played on metallophones. My analysis zeroes in on the *pengawak* sections of these works, each lasting about 2:45. ◐

The two *pengawaks'* central, "core" melodies are represented in figure 10.2's comparative transcription with stemless quarter, half, and double-whole notes all equivalent to half notes in duration. The open note heads signify points of greater metric stress arriving every eight, or, in the case of the double whole notes and zeroes, still greater stress every thirty-two beats. This hierarchy expands through the sequence of powers of two from 1 to 256 to regulate meter throughout the cycle. Since the two pieces share exactly the same form, they can be precisely vertically aligned on the page, enabling quick comparison of their core melodies and other features. They are notated using C#–D–E–G#–A, an approximation of the Balinese *pélog* scale (note that E–G# and A–C# intervals are scalar adjacencies). The interlocking rhythms of the two lap-held, double-skinned conical drums are beamed across a staff with two sets of two lines separated by a larger space. The upper line of each set shows an unpitched left-hand slap, the two lower lines represent a pair of deep pitches played with a mallet held in the right hand.[4]

In old style *lelambatan*, the melody is elaborated flatly in certain conven-tional ways on various other instruments and underpinned with simple drum

---

Balinese musicians to whom Sinti wished to pay homage. *Tabuh Gari* was composed by Wayan Beratha, but it is in large part a modern arrangement of preexisting material. For more on Beratha and Sinti, see Tenzer 2000, chapters 8 and 9

3. See further Tenzer 2000: 358–363.

4. Figure 10.2 does not show every part in the texture, only the ones most essential to the structure. Among those omitted are a small choir of bamboo flutes and a *rebab* (bowed spike fiddle), prominent throughout the *Lokarya* recording, that embellish the core melody in their own idioms.

rhythms that mainly serve to herald the arrival of upcoming strokes on gongs of various sizes. In recent years, more intricate ways of elaborating core melodies and drum patterns have evolved and it is through this process that the music has sprouted rich details that give it critical mass for comparison with Schumann. It is in this more composed-out—but still highly constrained—style that both *Lokarya* and *Tabuh Gari* were created for competitions in 1993 and 1978, respectively.

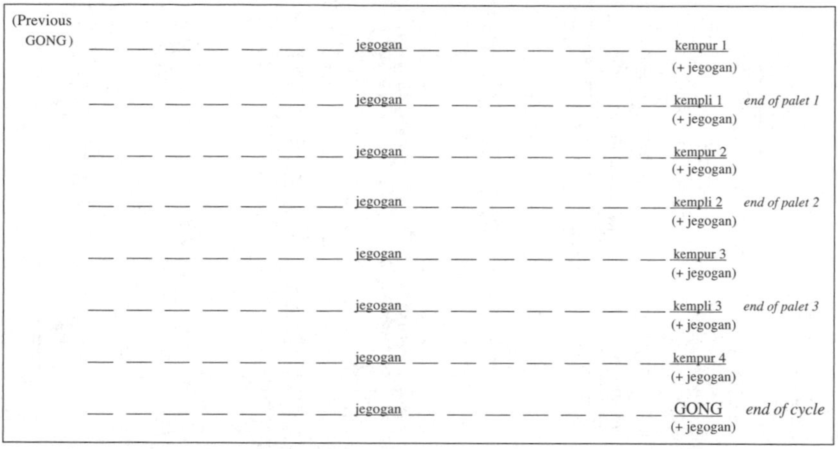

Figure 10.1.   Schematic of *pengawak* in *tabuh empat* form. Each dash represents 2 beats (= one "core melody" tone).

The length of the melody and the pattern of gong strokes marking the *pengawak* section are strictly determined by tradition. In both *Lokarya* and *Tabuh Gari,* a gong pattern called *tabuh empat* is specified (figure 10.1). All *pengawak* in *tabuh empat* form have the following ten structural features:

- The 256 total beats are separated into four sections, called *palet,* of 64 beats each.
- The first three *palet* conclude with a stroke of the small gong *kempli.*
- The last *palet* concludes with the large gong.
- Each *palet* is bisected by a stroke of the medium-sized gong called *kempur.*
- Each quarter-*palet* concludes with a melodic bass tone on the instrument *jegogan* that matches the tone of the core melody at that point.
- The core melody is played by mid-range instruments called *calung.* For each *palet,* the melody consists of a series of thirty-two tones, each of two beats' duration, except for the first *palet,* in which the first four or five tones are dropped. Underscores in figure 10.1 represent the two-beat *calung* tones.
- The large group of metallophones, gong-chime instruments, and bamboo flutes not performing these basic structural and melodic

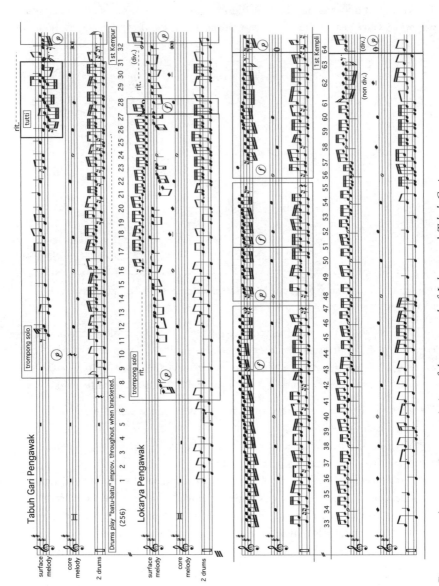

Figure 10.2.   A comparative transcription of the *pengawak* of *Lokarya* and *Tabuh Gari*.

366

Figure 10.2. (Continued)

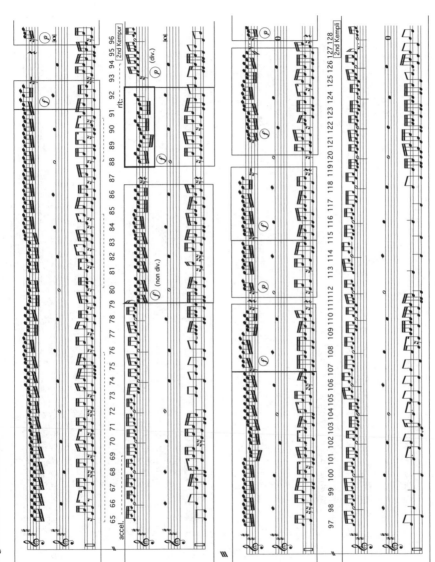

Figure 10.2. (Continued)

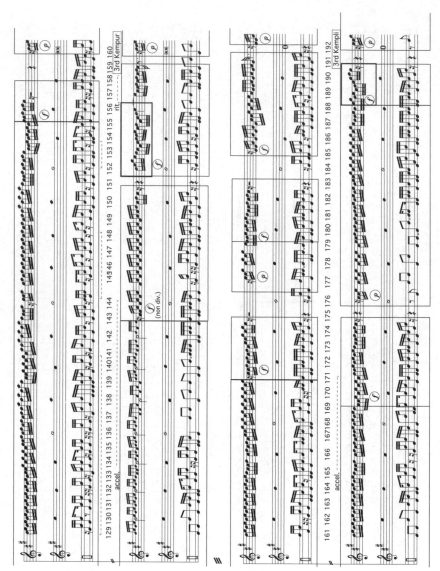

Figure 10.2. (Continued)

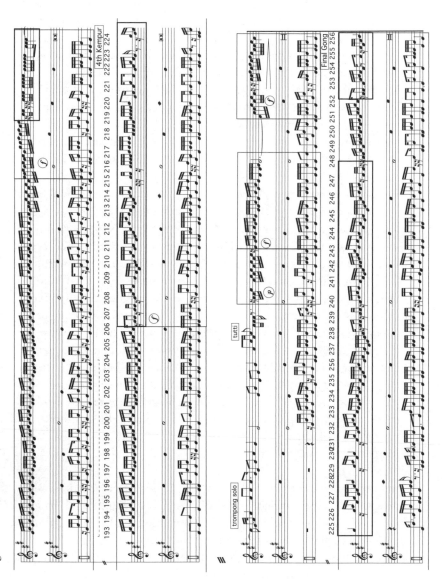

markers are elaborating the melody. Elaboration proceeds in states of either soft or loud dynamic, simple or complex melodic or drumming pattern, and in tutti or partial texture. In a few places, an instrument of small gongs called *trompong* is foregrounded while the other elaborating instruments rest. Actually it is always present, but it emerges on the recordings at the beginnings of both pieces, beats 225–240 in *Tabuh Gari,* plus other brief connectors (not all shown in the transcription). The flutes are also prominent, especially throughout *Lokarya.*

• Movement among dynamic states is built into the music and meticulously rehearsed and memorized. The changes are decisive and sharply juxtaposed, almost always set off with a brief break (a notated rest in the transcription) in the elaboration's rhythmic continuity, and cued by special drum rhythms. Crucial to the analysis, boxes have been drawn around these time spans of constant dynamics.

• A normative and simple elaboration style called *norot* is used well over 75 percent of the time on all elaborating instruments except the *trompong* and flutes. Shown in its basic form on the "surface melody" staves of figure 10.2, it is a continuous pattern of alternation between scale-tone neighbors at a rate equivalent to sixteenth notes. Interruptions of this flow are significant. The lower tone in each pair of tones matches the operative core melody tone at that moment, though the *norot* does not move to match *all* core tones; the ones it skips are heard as passing or neighbor tones within the core melody itself. When *norot* does shift to align with a new core melody tone, a double-note figure is inserted as a pick-up.[5] Occasional substitution of different elaboration types for *norot* is musically weighted and can occur more and more as the cycle progresses. The transcription highlights these as boxes within the boxes delineating dynamic change and pauses in the continuity of the surface melody.

• Many tempo changes mark the form.

As a performer and student of this music, I have never lacked for stimulation or pleasure. Negotiating the span of such a long melody, with its many structural nodes and interlocking melodic elaborations and drum rhythms, is a deep musical challenge. So is memorizing and attuning oneself to the subtle beauty of the comparatively featureless core melody, and learning to feel the tension and release of its moods in a Balinese way.

---

5. See, for example, the double C♯ leading to beat 38 or the double D leading to beat 40 in the surface melody staff of *Tabuh Gari,* and innumerable similar places.

Yet clearly, the compositional constraints in this genre are severe. They are far more severe than I would ever impose on myself when I compose music and, I think it fair to say, quite a bit more severe than the limits Schumann experienced. In fact, I have always been unable to rid myself of a certain skepticism about Balinese claims to appreciate and evaluate individual compositions in this genre on terms refined enough to justify the awarding of things like the prestigious composition prizes they have. For decades I have listened as Balinese expert juries and thoughtful musicians discuss and compare endlessly, distinguishing among works in terms of their "refined and balanced sense of melody," "ebbing and flowing and wave-like undulations," "tasteful drumming patterns," "depth of expression," and so forth, or the lack of any of these. Over many years I attended rehearsals and performances and listened to dozens of recordings of this music.[6] I studied hard, but I still could not hear the differences they claimed to hear so naturally, and besides, according to my own standards, any two Schumann chamber works (to take the example at hand) seemed to me hugely more distinctive. Thus, deep in this music of sacred origin, where I am assured the soul of Balinese music resides, I could only weakly recognize or identify individuality. Were the Balinese posturing and telling me what they thought I wanted to hear? Was I fated to always remain an outsider and never hear gamelan as deeply as I might? Was this my problem, theirs, or the music's? *Was* Western music more individuated than this, or wasn't it, and was the question itself even a fair one? The riddle of this intimate dilemma brought home to me with uncommon precision the feeling of being caught between two cultures.

I had long since accepted this unease as permanent when I had an unexpected breakthrough. The young Balinese musician directing the gamelan at my university, Wayan Sudirana, and some friends and I were talking about this very issue. Sudirana admitted that when he was younger he shared my inability to critically distinguish among *lelambatan* the way other Balinese claim to, and he said he felt puzzled and worried, like me, that he was an inadequate listener. Just to have him confess that was reassuring, and teased me with the promise of cross-cultural empathy. But, he went on, as an adult he at last felt himself developing sensitivity to what Balinese call the *bayu* of the music—which he defined as its energy, breath, organicism, flow. "*Bayu* is behind the notes," he said. "The composer puts *bayu* in the music just like he/

6. I was able to closely monitor the complete three-month rehearsal-to-performance trajectory for Balinese gamelan competitions in 1982, 1987, and 1989, and to a lesser but still significant extent in 1985, 1991 and 1992, and spoke at length throughout these periods with musicians and jurors.

she chooses the notes and rhythms. And I discovered that every *lelambatan* has a *bayu* all its own" (Sudirana, pers. comm., February 2005). Now in some ways that remained for me a cryptic idea, but since elements like tempo, dynamics, and orchestration are so carefully composed and rehearsed in this music, I also glimpsed how I could translate *bayu* into something concrete and susceptible to comparison (by adding the boxes to the transcription) that could possibly help me out of my quandary.

Of course I well knew what *bayu* was before Sudirana mentioned it. I considered it to be a dimension of musical macrorhythm expressed through the changes in tempo, dynamic, and texture—all aspects that until then I had assumed behaved as conventionally as the gong structure does. I took it for granted that these features always changed in much the same ways at the same points in relation to the gongs in each piece of this type, which would, if so, mitigate further against individuality. But I had never really stopped to analyze closely, an unfortunate reflection, perhaps, of a practiced overemphasis on the more standard analytical foci: pitch, rhythm patterning, and form. On the one hand, there was great appeal in Sudirana's point, because his definition of *bayu* as energy or flow goes hand-in-glove with Balinese musical values of community and togetherness. On the other hand, I flashed on the idea that Schumann's music has no shortage of its own *bayu*. But then I reflected: what if Balinese music in fact locates its very individuality in *bayu,* because their system of oral transmission, memorization, and group learning nurtures special sensitivity to *bayu*-like modes of expression? Is *bayu* the medium through which composition and ensemble virtuosity integrate to forge each piece's distinct identity? It occurred to me that this might serve the same individuating function as things in Schumann like piquant modulations and harmonic colors, expansive cantabile melodies, multilayered patterns of tension and release, and other compositional nonpareils of the European tradition.

Figure 10.2 reveals that *Tabuh Gari* and *Lokarya* in fact have richly distinctive *bayu*. In the passage linking beats 32 and 64 (second half of the first *palet*), for example, *Tabuh Gari* abruptly shifts twice from *piano* to *forte* and back again. Such coordinated rapid change is stylistically modern and suggests a Balinese self-image of possessing sufficient power and competence to master the challenges of modernity. The dynamic contrasts are forcefully articulated and offset by intervening rests of differing lengths. Even the sixteenth-note rest at beat 43 achieves musical and visual importance as the musicians inhale together, raise their mallet arms in an explicitly choreographed unison motion during the tiny pause, and restrike their instruments at full volume. *Lokarya,* by contrast, sustains a *piano* dynamic throughout this segment. The down-stemmed (mainly) half notes shown correspond to an orchestration technique whereby a group of four middle-register metallophones that would normally join in the *norot* play this variant of the core melody instead. *Norot* still dominates the sound; however, this change plus the textural steady-state are sufficient to reference the older, premodern way of playing *lelambatan,* and hence evoke a putative purer and more sacred time in the Bali of centuries past. As the music unfolds through the remaining three *palet, Tabuh Gari's* rate of dynamic and texture change varies within a narrower band than *Lokarya's,* for the latter accrues momentum for change as it proceeds until, by the end, disruption—and the evocation of the modern—occurs more than at any point in the former.

The process of making the transcription opened me to new levels of appreciation and perception that had remained inaccessible for the many years I have been studying gamelan. The shock of that realization—that after so long I can still add significant new dimensions to my appreciation of Balinese music— suggests that while *lelambatan* are formulaic in some parameters, they are still full of irregular nooks, crannies, and paths to explore. One need only glance back and forth between *Tabuh Gari* and *Lokarya* to see these differences in force throughout. Lelembatan music may be understood by Balinese as sacred, but it is not impersonal, just as so much of J. S. Bach's music was created with devotional intent but is nevertheless a repository of many of its creator's most inspired ideas. And though I can't now claim empirically that these examples of gamelan music are as individually nuanced as two comparable European works, my new sensitivity to *bayu* is reassuring evidence that there is ever more depth to be discovered, which may be all I need to respond to Bill Benjamin's question.

Nodes of Comparison

Carrying along my awareness of these nooks and crannies as I now turn to the Schumann Piano Quartet, I first need to further articulate a context for comparing it with *lelambatan.* This is a key juncture in the progress of my thinking. One naturally and sensibly shies from leaping between any kinds of systems to compare one's apples with the other's oranges. There is too big a difference between them. I would feel unsafe, fearing that perhaps, as Judith Becker wrote, musical systems really are incommensurable. But sometimes conventional wisdom should be overridden. Could I juxtapose, for example, a certain unexpected harmony in Schumann with a particular turn in a Balinese drum rhythm and ask myself to compare their effects? Can I transform the disjunctive experiences I have of these two musics, as shaped by my socially constructed apprehensions of them as belonging to distinct worlds, and turn them into a conjunctive experience in which I subsume them under the common label "music"? This requires a certain blind trust in one's personal phenomenology, a willingness to feel the feelings and ask what the connections are.

To find the proper focus for comparison, I opt to rely on familiar levels of musical action: foreground, middleground, and background. Balinese and Western music are both sufficiently hierarchically structured to make distinguishing between these levels possible. In the backgrounds we find the most culturally generalized modes of musical behavior. Large-scale form dwells there; and both theorists of Western art music like Heinrich Schenker and Balinese thinkers and writers on music such as Nyoman Rembang (1984/1985) have shown that in their respective systems ultimately there is little variety in that realm. I have noticed, however, an interesting difference between Balinese and Western background levels. In a Schenkerian view of Western music, we know what the fundamental tonal structure will be, but we don't know how and exactly when the *Urlinie*—the structural stepwise descent through the scale to the tonic tone—will be revealed in the course of the piece. In Balinese music like *lelambatan,* it is exactly the reverse: we cannot know what a composition's important tonal scaffolding will be, but whatever it will be, we know precisely when to expect its arrivals, because these will always coincide with important gong strokes, which are predetermined. Thus I elect not to make my entry into the comparison through the background, for I shall consider Balinese and Western background structures to be equivalently weighted in terms of individuation and significance.

In the foreground we find facades of untranslatable musical behaviors. These are the day-to-day vocabularies of music—scale and melody, elaboration styles, harmonic vocabularies, surface rhythms, drum patterns, and so on. Beginning by comparing the musics at this level would be like comparing the words in spoken languages without considering grammar or syntax; we might find some superficial resemblances like homonyms, but what good would it do when it is structural aspects like synonyms and antonyms that we need? And the languages make no sense to us unless we can parse sentences and paragraphs to conceive the structural gist of the ideas they convey, which is the linguistic analog of a musical middleground. Indeed, it is said for Western music that the middleground is where the most significant action takes place, where essential structure and compositional specificity coalesce, where we make the strongest cognitive and associative connections. Seeking efficiency and mindful of the precariousness of the ensuing exercise, I therefore find that the middleground is the best place to begin.

Comparison with Schumann's Piano Quartet

I choose two cases in point out of a great many that could be taken. The first compares the opening *palet* of *Tabuh Gari* with the slow introduction and opening theme of the Schumann (mm. 1–36; figure 10.3), and the second compares the end of the Piano Quartet's exposition (mm. 88–119; figure 10.4) with the final *palet* of *Lokarya*.

After the final gong of the section preceding the *pengawak, Tabuh Gari's* own *pengawak,* like those in most compositions in the genre, begins with a caesura equivalent (but not equal) to eight beats of silence, and clearly understood by Balinese as "subtracting" from the strict sixty-four-beat length of the first *palet.* This silence is punctuated first by the drums and then by a solo melodic instrument, the *trompong.* After beat 26, more instruments enter, completing a tutti. This leads to a cadence of three sixteenths on the note [A], the last of which lands on beat 31. Beat 32 is the first kempur stroke, an important gong marker signifying the middle of the *palet,* and subsequently the music gets underway with the steady, tutti presence of the full gamelan's melodic elaborations. On the way to beat 64, the next big formal mark, dynamic contrasts and interruptions to the tutti shape the *bayu,* while the core melody describes an arch going straight from [A] up to [G♯] (beat 44) and then receding to its starting point ([A]) windingly between beats 44 and 64. In this, the first fourth of the cycle, the music has already shown many complexly related layers of form, dynamics, melody, and texture.

Remarkably, there is something similar going on in the Piano Quartet. Up to m. 12 we are given a slow, sparse introductory passage, surprisingly parallel to *Tabuh Gari's* opening thirty-two beats. The moment at which Schumann takes up his *allegro* at mm. 13–14 is like beat 32 in the *lelambatan,* in the sense that the engine is felt to be moving into gear, and when Schumann's motive at mm. 13–14 reappears transformed, issuing from the highest reaches of the cello at mm. 36–37, it is rather like the return to the starting pitch [A] at beat 64 in *Tabuh Gari.*

But otherwise the Quartet doesn't seem like *Tabuh Gari* at all. For starters, the flesh of the skeletal ascending arpeggio of mm. 1–12 in the Schumann touches on E♭, F, G, A♭, A, B♭, C, and D♭; this is already more pitch classes than are present in the entire *lelambatan* repertoire. After m. 12 the sequencing and development of the motive at mm. 17, 21, 26, and 30 divides the passage into phrase groups that are in one sense all the same because they derive from minimal thematic material. Yet they are different due to their distinctive orchestration, harmony, pitch level, and supple alternating lengths of four and five bars. In gamelan such middleground elasticity occurs among the elements of *bayu,* like dynamics and orchestration, but the inflexible background rhythmic structure restricts any sense of loosening or distorting the music from firm foursquare, duple metric moorings. On the other hand, gamelan's freedom from anything like Schumann's rigorous allegiance to melodic motive liberates the music, making it unbeholden to the nagging constraints of a returning melodic idea.

Figure 10.3.   Schumann: Piano Quartet in E♭ Major, Op. 47, first movement, mm. 1–36.

Finally, although in general the harmonies between mm. 12 and 36 are unremarkable for nineteenth-century European music and thus in an abstract way equivalent to the conventional succession of core melody tones in *Tabuh Gari,* they are perhaps more susceptible to nuance. Consider, for example, the A♭ augmented chord-with-added-seventh on the downbeat of

Figure 10.3. (Continued)

Figure 10.4. Schumann: Piano Quartet in E♭ Major, Op. 47, first movement, mm. 88–119.

Figure 10.4.   (Continued)

m. 33. The piano's left-hand E natural and G, doubled in the violin and viola, are appoggiaturas that delay by one beat a resolution to the F of an F minor chord, a resolution itself deceptive since it gives us a luscious, leaning predominant instead of the stable tonic chord, which does not come until two bars later. This inner voice E–F motion is both prefigured and echoed in the right hand of the piano, for a total of three passes (circled in figure 10.3). Meanwhile the phrasing liquidates the previously established four-bar unit, and moreover chops the downbeat note from the dotted-half established at mm. 14, 18, and 27 to the quarter notes at 31 and 33, which highlights the dramatic changes to the characteristic contour of the ensuing eighth notes. I don't know if gamelan has this kind of layered, synesthetic sound-color-warmth sensation that moment gives, a sensation I experience as an essence of Western tonality's power.

Here is the second comparison. In *Lokarya,* approaching the final gong at beat 256 from all the way back at beat 206, Sinti, the composer, breaks definitively with the foregoing texture of predominantly *norot* elaboration. He introduces a sharply contrasting style of snaking melody, interrupted with disjunctures of style and rhythm, and unpredictably split into subphrases at 215, 220, 223, 225, 228, 230, 238, 247, and 252. Coordinated with this, the drumming abandons its default explicit coordination with the metric structure and instead intensifies the melodic changes by tracking their phrase rhythms closely. This is like a roller-coaster ride in which the twists are exciting and unpredictable, even though safe arrival at the gong's landing platform is known to be just ahead at a specific point in time.

In *Lokarya,* that final gong is as inevitable as sunset. In Schumann, we similarly know that we are going to arrive at a strong dominant cadence at the end of the exposition, and we know some of the main thematic signposts we will pass on the way. Like in *Lokarya,* we have no idea precisely what paths we will take to get to this goal, but unlike *Lokarya,* neither do we know when we will arrive or from how far away. For example, the modulation to the dominant is already all but assured at m. 88, when B♭'s own dominant, F, is confirmed. There follows a series of upward-slipping modulations by half step through the tonalities of B and C (a tension-building strategy) at mm. 92 and 96, and an interruption of texture at 103–107 leading up by thirds through dominants of G, B♭, and D. At 107 the modulation goes up by half step once more to the dominant of E♭ minor, but the motion is unexpectedly hushed and sustained, repeating the same phrase and harmony at 107 and 109. Time has slowed, and we feel something about to give way.

In m. 111, an arrival on a local tonic of C♭ major, inverted so that its third (E♭) is in the bass, is reinterpreted as a Neapolitan chord, that is, it is heard as the flattened second degree of B♭, the key of the dominant. The E♭ in the bass acts as a pre-dominant to the stable cadence on B♭ in m. 117. After traversing such a circuitous route, one feels a soft surface yielding to free fall and swift, safe rescue. The fall begins in a surreal slow motion because of the surprising augmentation of the theme in the previously unexplored alto range of the viola and piano, but then the diminished seventh harmony in m. 114 thrusts sharply ahead to the dissonant, cadential 6/4 chord (a tonic chord with the dominant note in the bass) in the next bar. The analogy I'll use is that of a three-dimensional maze with a trap door in the remotest corner opening onto a chute of suddenly increasing slope that leads instantly to the exit.

Finally, I want to contrast in a more general way two levels of rhythm that seem to me especially significant. In the Schumann quartet, as in nearly all tonal music, the harmonic rhythm—the domineering, lumbering pace of chordal colors on the move—exerts a powerful force on affective response. Changes of speed in harmonic rhythm really do feel like a quickening or slowing of the pulse or heart, which is the closest analogy we have in bodily experience. In *Tabuh Gari* and *Lokarya,* there is no counterpart to this flexibility save for literal tempo change, but instead there is the constant shattering ofmusical phrases into tiny subcutaneous micropulsations ticking along relentlessly even through extreme tempo fluctuations.[7] Each micropulsation has a strongly identifiable color and character due to the sum total of each instrument's special behavior at each subdivision of the beat. Not all of these recombinations are represented in figure 10.2 because not all instruments are shown; in particular, the *reyong*, a set of twelve tuned gongs played by four musicians, is at all times kaleidoscopically and improvisationally varying the basic *norot* patterning. The snowflake-like particles of Balinese music are never the same, always recombining the same five tones, repertoire of melodic patterns, and handful of drumstroke possibilities in familiar but endlessly varying groups, like the recombining bases of the genome. In Schumann, our attention is not drawn to such a teeming and vital pulsation.

Heartbeats, snowflakes, roller coasters, and three-dimensional mazes— who would want to choose among them? They are crude, barely serviceable metaphors. Would I take Schumann's suspenseful, measured heartbeat of a music, leading me inexorably through mazes and halls of mirrors where shapes change and things are hardly what they seem? Or is it preferable to hurtle through the pointillist scenery in *Tabuh Gari* and *Lokarya?* Having narrowed the discussion down to these impoverished formulations, it is a choice that feels onerous indeed.

Global Transformations

It is important to reemphasize the inseparability of analyst and analysis. Marion Guck writes,

> Analyses necessarily bear the traces of the personal sensibilities, experiences, and inclinations of their authors, or their public personae. At the same time, analysts use the vocabularies, concepts and methods we've learned or chosen. Our personal inclinations and commitments shade into our interpersonal and cultural backgrounds and commitments. An analysis celebrates the personal significance of the music that it takes as its subject and it engages in intersubjective social relationships, including those of our disciplines. (2006: 197)

7. Taruskin (1997) describes Steve Reich's music as having a "'subtactile pulse': a strongly articulated, rock-steady rhythmic unit that lies beneath the level of the 'felt beat,' or tactus, the beat that conductors show or that we normally walk or waltz or exercise to."

In the course of writing this essay, I have found Guck's invoked notions of the "traces," "concepts," "inclinations," and "significance" (et cetera) to be unstable at best, owing to the cultural disjuncture that stimulated the venture. Attempting to answer Bill Benjamin's question, I was uncomfortable with different things on different days—"The West is best," or "No, it's Bali," and "It's impossible to decide," or "I'm too wishy-washy to decide," and "Judith Becker was right after all." As for musical value, it is good, after years of avoiding the issue, to have finally tried to measure it, but I feel the values constantly jumping back and forth between the music and me. My perceptions are fleeting, my contemplation wracked. To the extent that I can juxtapose the two musics on a given day and find them separate but equal, I may have succeeded in an act of personal and cross-cultural integration. On some days, when I cannot find any gamelan experience to rival the complex poignancy of Schumann's quartet, then I am faced with two possibilities: either the Schumann is inherently deeper or I myself am still in transition from an earlier, more culturally centered self. On days when gamelan seems to me the acme of humankind's musical invention I feel grateful to know it, savoring the awareness that this cross-cultural pilgrimage would not have been possible in any earlier era.

But you did not read this far to have me chicken out of making a choice. So I return to the appoggiatura chord in m. 33 of the Schumann, now taking it to stand for all such multidimensional, multiprocessual convergences in Western music. Let me continue to focus on it as an evocative sonic event, setting aside the whole realm of extramusical meaning. Let us assume with regard to such referentiality that all musics have equal potential. But just as sound process, that chord has a subtle hold on me. Balinese music gives me many sublime sensations that Western music doesn't, but ultimately I cannot suppress a voice in me saying that those things touch me in a less compelling way. Why? Because m. 33 evokes multiple lines, protagonists, and rates of motion that feel richer and more evocative than anything else in terms of a particularly Euro-American sense of freedom and potential that is central to my class and educational background and identity. I have tried to show that this multidimensionality is objectively *in* the one music and not the other, so it is not simply a matter of cultural conditioning or preference—though one *does* need cultural conditioning to understand this. But now that I have confessed this publicly, what are the consequences?

Following the writing of those last thoughts was a long moment of reflection. I felt strangely upset. Did I cross the line separating insight from overindulgence? My decision has qualities of a pyrrhic victory and might even be seen as cruel to the poor musics themselves, as if I had deliberately instigated a duel between two loved ones just for sport. Rather than facilitating inner integration, I may have wedged myself apart.

Expanding Outward

To rescue something from the ashes of my indiscretion, and to claim that it may amount to something of interest or use to you, dear readers, I can place my search for musical value in a wider context. My judgment reveals that I reserve pride of place for things that, like the Schumann chord, seem to move in many directions simultaneously at different rates. This is not just due to the way they suggest a compelling realm of layered time, but also to how they evoke a narrative of freedom, potential, and democratic individuality, capable even of bending and warping its dimensions and time structure even though the final goal (tonal resolution) cannot be avoided. Balinese music, unshakable from its formal trajectory and strict patterns of gong strokes and beat counts once it has set forth, would seem to be opposed to this. To me, the one music reflects an imaginary more empowered self, the other a more powerless self, swept up in inevitabilities. (I do not claim that others, and in this case especially Balinese, would see it this way, nor that their views of such things as "freedom," "empowerment," "powerless," "inevitability," etc. would be imbued with the same connotations I impute to them. Balinese musicians experience all of these things in their own ways through their music; indeed, my analysis of *bayu* supports this.)

I don't believe, however, that my views of Balinese and Western music are really at such an impasse. That would be to say, with Judith Becker, that they are incommensurable. I reject that. A longer view, such as the one offered by epistemologist Karl Popper, exhorts us to assume that communication is *always* possible between different cultures, so long as they approach each other openly and do not have unrealistic expectations about how quickly understanding can grow. He rejects outright the notion of a cultural "framework" that is incommensurable with others.

Popper writes of Herodotus, himself writing of King Darius the First of Persia, who called to court the Greeks and the Callatians living in his kingdom. The former cremated their dead relatives and the latter, being cannibals, consumed them. Communicating through an interpreter, each group expressed horror at the other, as we may feel particular horror toward the Callatians. Since Darius did not act to restrain either group, "there can be little doubt that both parties were deeply shaken by the experience, and that they learned something new." Herodotus himself drew a further lesson from the encounter, "that we should look with tolerance and even respect upon customs or conventional laws that differ from our own" (Popper 1994: 36–37).

Popper avers that one need not have agreement or reconciliation for encounter to be fruitful; even mere confrontation can result in the changing of a mind, especially if one is wise like Herodotus. Indeed, the very linkages between musical structures and fundamental values I have been making could not have emerged solely from within either of the musical systems under consideration; they could result only from the perspective granted by cross-cultural encounter. So, rather than bemoan my inability to make the Piano Quartet reconcile with the *lelambatan,* I should accept their incompatibilities and consider that they may not forever appear to me thus. I should savor the small ways in which I *have* been able to bring the two systems into dialog and reflect that the empowerment and powerlessness I find embedded in these musics are not antinomies, but rather complementary components of a universal tension that regulates human experience of the beautiful and the valuable.

Evidently my decades of immersion in Balinese music have so far not caused me to neutralize my native values, however different my musical experiences have been from what they probably would have been in previous generations. But in terms of a perspective like that taken in *Guns, Germs, and Steel,* my values are just a statistic anyway. Like Jared Diamond, I need to seek out the broadest historical patterns. Scanning, I see musics and their makers worldwide moving in several directions at once. The diffusion of Western art music in the twentieth century represents both the best of Western values, such as the ascendance of Western ideals of human rights, and the culture's underside of colonialism and exploitation. It is of course exactly to the point that the very practice of ethnomusicology emerged from the dominance of Western modernity, opening pathways for practitioners like me to engage with other cultural systems. Fuller hybridity and integration can be expected eventually, but the built-in power asymmetry between the West and the rest, plus bona fide cultural differences of all kinds, have put a check on the processes of change and assimilation. What feel like radical encounters and shifts in us as individuals are surface manifestations of slower change happening at deeper levels. In this regard I disagree with Leonard Meyer's depiction of contemporary culture as a Brownian cloud full of tempest but moving nowhere (Meyer 1994: 349). We are integrating, but at a pace that is glacial compared to the pace of everyday life and the vividness of our ongoing awareness of who we have become in our lives.

But back to the best of Western values and their dominance: if much of humanity is evolving toward greater individual autonomy and power, European music forms part of the soundtrack for this evolution; maybe it even led the way. For some, Western art music's day is done, and the ethos of African and African-derived musics, with its balance between communality and individual expression, has the hold on global consciousness now, or at least they provide its alter ego. Howsoever, music is evolving, and the evolution gestates somewhere distinct from the actual music making—namely, in our imaginations. Anthropologist Arjun Appadurai (1996: 22) describes imagination as having an enhanced function in the twenty-first century, serving as a social space at the cutting edge of human development. It is here, perhaps, as we work in our own ways through and with music toward (but not necessarily achieving) the equanimity of James's "healthy-minded," that we may draw within audible range of "the keynote of the universe sounding in our ears" (James op. cit: 55).

I have been speculating about the kinds of connections and comparisons we may draw in the future. Late nineteenth-century European musicologists saw their landscape through such a tinted lens of nationalism that many considered Verdi and Wagner to be speaking in entirely different musical tongues, perhaps proportionately as far apart as I set Schumann and the gamelan (Childs 1991: 7). With time we have learned to compare and contrast German and Italian music instead of segregating them. Here I envision a late twenty-first-century musicology that finds coherence and congruence in things that today seem incompatible.

More than thirty years ago, I took two distinct musical systems into my mind's crucible, allowed them to mingle, and here tested the depth of my responses to find that the music of my own culture came out ahead by a slim margin. All over, no matter what kind of music engages them, people conceal their own versions of this laboratory. Then they go out and make more music, planting memes in hope of replication.

My imagination is host to what it perceives as two conflicting symbolic systems, one indebted to the European fantasy of the ennobled individual, the other to a deterministic universe where individual agency is subsumed into the exemplary center represented by the gong. Having taken root over decades of musical encounter and contemplation, I do not know if these symbolic worlds are now immobile in me, if they will change further in my lifetime, or if they must lodge in other minds and bodies before they can come into a new relationship. May I report back to you once again in thirty more years?

Appendix

Written responses from Judith Becker, William Benjamin, and Steven Blum to an earlier but substantially identical version of this chapter are reproduced below for the diversity of perspective they bring.
Judith Becker:

> [Your article is] relevant, I think, to those few persons in this world who are SERIOUSLY involved with someone else's music. (Maybe not so few.) I would want to claim that it is no surprise that you

ended up, after all, with Schumann. You have made the point that the Piano Quartet is about identity. And that is also your, and my, identity, in some ways. That is what we look for in music, above all else. And I think this applies to all of our various genres, from rap to Bach. That is what music is for, I think, for us. The lelambatan examples are for very different things. The original lelambatan, as you well know, are not for people at all, but for the "unseen" audience of spirits and deities. The fact that the composed lelambatan can somewhat more easily be compared with Schumann doesn't change the fact that the lelambatan form is not about personal identity. That is not what traditional Balinese work is about. So, even if your examples are not purely traditional, that is their source, and that makes them, to my mind, not comparable to Schumann. I would still stick with my original premise that music systems are incommensurable.

William Benjamin (after reading Becker's comment):

I think I agree with Judith, that musics can be incommensurable. My life's work has turned out to be about one question: what are the conditions under which it is possible to create a music (a musical culture) in which music serves as an end in itself, or—to put it less formalistically and less *l'art pour l'art* (which is not my thing)—in which it is possible to derive a complete experience from music on its own. I don't think most of the world's music is meant to be meaningful apart from words, dance, ritual, religion, story, theatre, etc., but the Schumann quartet is. I don't know about Balinese music. Judith seems to be saying that even the secular, recently composed Balinese orchestral music is religious/ritualistic in some sense. I know that the same argument can be made about a lot of Bach, so things get complicated. I leave it to you, who have spent your life with this music, to report on the extent to which it provides you with a complete experience, as a listener when you strip away your relationships with Balinese musicians, your memories of experience in that society, your political commitments, etc. etc.

In my view, if the Balinese piece were to mean as much (or more) to someone, qua music, than the Schumann, it would be because he/she found it fascinating to imagine that music and to feel it as if emanating from his/her body. That's at root what I find so fascinating about the Schumann, not anything formal or expressive in a semiotic sense, and thus not anything intellectual. It wouldn't astound me that the Balinese piece could provide the same richness for someone who had lived with it for a long time. But there's plenty of important music around, that I have lived with for a long time, that doesn't live inside me in this way, and I think we all know what that is. I am concerned about the loss of the capacity to imagine music with great force in our society, except in the popular sphere.

Stephen Blum (after reading both Benjamin and Becker's comments):

I can't accept Judith's premise that "music systems are incommensurable," given that so many musicians are engaged with more than one system (however we decide to distinguish "systems") and can hardly avoid making comparisons of various sorts. We know that systems are subject to change, and it seems reasonable to assume that changes can result from comparisons not unlike the one you've undertaken here. Your paper is centered on your own experience and doesn't claim to go beyond that in the ways I'd call destructive (e.g., by denying that a Balinese or a Persian could possibly attain a condition of full engagement with a unique sound and syntactic world fully comparable to the engagements we record for ourselves).

I'll admit that there are the historical issues of (1) concert music as something of a substitute for religious ceremony, and (2) the obvious, oft commented upon affinity between the freedom of Western composers to experiment/explore etc. and the intellectual freedom that was crucial to the development of Western philosophy, science, technology. I don't want to leap from that commonplace to stereotypes of "non-Western" composers as "prisoners of tradition," not least because interrogation of "tradition" is an especially valuable way of exercising the hard-won freedom we enjoy. You and I can probably agree that more discussion of how contemporary composers and performers (in all parts of the world) understand themselves as interrogating traditions is needed at our meetings and in our publications.

References

Appadurai, Arjun. 1996. *Modernity at Large: Cultural Dimensions of Globalization.* Minneapolis: University of Minnesota Press.
Becker, Judith. 1986. "Is Western Art Music Superior?" *Musical Quarterly* 72(3): 341–359.
Childs, John Brown. 1991. "Rethinking the Classical: Giuseppe Verdi and Other European Advocates of Cultural Diversity." *New Observations* 86: 6–9.
Diamond, Jared. [1997] 1999. *Guns, Germs, and Steel.* New York: W. W. Norton.

Guck, Marion A. 2006. "Analysis as Interpretation: Interaction, Intentionality, Invention." *Music Theory Spectrum* 28(2): 191–210.

James, William. [1902] 2002. *The Varieties of Religious Experience: A Study in Human Nature.* New York: Modern Library.

Meyer, Leonard. [1967] 1994. *Music, The Arts, and Ideas: Patterns and Predictions in Twentieth-Century Culture.* Chicago: University of Chicago Press.

Popper, Karl. 1994. *The Myth of the Framework: In Defense of Science and Rationality.* London: Routledge.

Rembang, Nyoman. 1984/1985. *Hasil Pendokumentasian Notasi Gending-Gending Lelambatan Klasik Pegongan Daerah Bali.* Denpasar: Proyek Pengembangan Kesenian Bali, Departemen Pendidikan dan Kebudayaan.

Taruskin, Richard. 1997. "A Sturdy Musical Bridge to the 21st Century." *New York Times,* 24, New York edition, sec. Arts and Leisure.

Tenzer, Michael. 2000. *Gamelan Gong Kebyar: The Art of Twentieth Century Balinese Music.* Chicago: University of Chicago Press.

CHAPTER II

Combining Sounds to Reinvent the World

World Music, Sociology, and Musical Analysis

SIMHA AROM AND DENIS-CONSTANT MARTIN
(TRANSLATED BY FRANK KANE)

Frontispiece: Cover art for the MELT2000 compact disc *Tribal Ethno Dance Cha(p)tter One, Drum 'n Metal*. Reproduced by permission of Robert Trunz.

In recent decades, the soundscape of many countries has been flooded by music marketed and referred to in the press as "world music."[1] Radio and television stations play recordings evoking distant lands, whether collected in regions presumably considered "exotic" by the inhabitants of the "North" countries,[2] or simply manufactured in a studio. These recordings have conquered a significant share of the commercial music market;[3] some are heard in supermarkets, elevators, and parking lots. Specialized festivals devoted to the genre are held in Europe, North America, Japan, and even in countries such as Burkina Faso, Trinidad and Tobago, and South Africa.

A significant trend of musical production and distribution in the late twentieth century, this music has been studied and analyzed by social scientists, chiefly communication specialists and sociologists.[4] However, it has drawn little interest from musicologists; consequently, there have no been

1. An initial version of this text was published in Italian with the title "Commercio, esotismo e creazione nella 'World Music,' un approcio sociologico et musicologico," in *L'érédità di Diego Carpitella, Etnomusicologia, antropologia e ricerca storica nel Salento et nell'area mediterranea*, ed. Maurizio Agamennone and Gino L. Di MIitri (Nardo, Italy: Besa, 2003), 277–299 The original French text was published as "Combiner les sons pour réinventer le monde, la *World Music*, sociologie et analyse musicale" *L'Homme* 177–178 (2006): 155–178. We would like to thank Sara Le Menestrel for her comments on the original French text of this article that led to the development of its conclusion, and the Centre for International Research and Studies (CERI, Sciences-Po Paris, CNRS) for funding this translation.

Editors' note: The original French text uses the French plural term *musiques du monde* and the singular English form *world music* interchangeably. The authors' subject here is world music as commonly understood in France and elsewhere in Western Europe, that is, a loose collection of popular, heavily marketed synthetic music genres adapting and combining traditional musics from many parts of the world. This usage is fundamentally distinct from the North American vernacular, in which world music more commonly signifies the totality of music in the world.

2. Editors' note: The terms "North" and "South" here and below are not endorsed by the authors but are employed as one of various possible binary oppositions that are popularly invoked for classifying music, musicians, and audiences, carrying the connotations from French speakers that "developed" and "undeveloped" do for English readers; see footnote 21 below.

3. In France, 7–15 percent of all CD sales at the end of the 1990s, in other words, more than jazz (including blues, gospel and soul music) and about as much as classical music (Aubert 1997: 154; Lefeuvre 1999: 62; Daffos 1999: 223). Over the same period, world music accounted for 30 percent of the airtime on FIP, a French station broadcasting music nonstop (Simporé 1999: 248).

4. See chapter references.

studies dealing specifically with its musical characteristics and the manner in which musics of various origins, forms, and structures are combined to develop original products. Thus, while the economic and social dimensions of world music have been attentively considered, it is still not well defined from a strictly musical standpoint. A range of innovations developed over the past thirty years remains poorly understood, and the work of social sciences devoted to them is likewise burdened because the fog that surrounds their object has not been dissipated.

This observation leads us to the question: what is world music really? Can it be defined and categorized with established techniques of musical analysis? Is it rather a commercial label that covers musical products that have nothing in common? Or is it possible, given this commercial rubric, to discover specific traits defining particular types of musical production?

This text will try to answer these questions by combining sociological and musicological approaches. The vastness of the field of world music and the enormous quantities of recordings and videos sold in this category make a comprehensive account impossible. We therefore decided to work with a limited sample, postulating that it could be considered representative of world music productions.[5]

First, we will briefly trace the history of the appearance of world music on the commercial music market, then we will propose an initial typology based on selections made using discographies and publications on the subject (Azoulay 1997; Broughton et al. 1994; Fnac/Géo ca. 2000), and lastly, we will consider types of discourse built around this music and the representations of the world that they suggest.

The second part of the chapter presents Simha Arom's systematic "blind" analysis of seven world music recordings. This reveals characteristic traits of the pieces in the sample and clarifies some of the mechanisms of their construction.

Brief History of an Ill-Defined Genre

While musical creation has always been nourished by cross-pollination and blending, these processes intensified after the major voyages and discoveries

---

5. We refer to music classified below as "synthetic music," that is, original products designed for the world music market, and distinct from "recycled" music, that is, existing or having existed outside of the world music universe but commercially included in it.

of the late fifteenth century, the subsequent conquests accompanied by slave trading leading to colonization. At the end of the nineteenth century, the invention of sound recordings, and in the twentieth century, the development of radio and then television to transmit these recordings and the immense development of the record and video market totally transformed the conditions in which borrowing and mixing occurs, and also the means to carry them out.

Disjunctions and New Conjunctions

Before the invention of sound recording, most musical exchange required direct contact between human beings. Even when music or song texts could be circulated in print, aspects like timbre and style remained in the oral tradition, and transmission depended upon meetings among flesh-and-blood individuals with voices. Recordings—first acoustical, then electroacoustical, and finally audiovisual—introduced a technological mediation allowing for remote exposure to other forms of music. This accelerated the pace of circulation and made music a commodity fully integrated within an increasingly globalized commercial economy. Ongoing research into sound-capture and -processing techniques led to constant improvements in the quality of recordings and to the development of tools that make possible a vast range of ways to alter and manipulate recorded sound.[6] By the end of the century, recording studios concocting mass-market music became havens for "kluge" virtuosos who exploited new technological resources (especially computers, samplers, and all sorts of electronic sound producing and transforming devices) to fashion customized musics.

Such technological intermediations led to the phenomena of "disjunction" (Appadurai 1990) and "schizophonia" (Feld 1995). Both terms refer to a separation of sounds from the people, societies, and cultures in which they arose. But this separation also favored their circulation on a wider scale and so bred new conjunctions, the making of new mixtures. So these mediations and their consequences made the advent of world music possible.

---

6. To cite only a few of these tools: synthesizers can produce new electronic sounds, samplers reproduce natural sounds, and the use of the two together allows for the mixing of all imaginable types of recorded or electronically produced sounds (with regard to the Australian *didjeridu,* for example, see Gebesmair and Smudits 2001: 52–53). All of the techniques that we refer to as electroacoustic (for the sake of brevity) offer musicians and sound engineers an almost infinite sound palette.

Invention of a Label

World music's roots extend to the 1960s when pop groups such as the Kinks and the Beatles[7] began using the Indian sitar. From a certain perspective this was hardly radical, because the Indian "color" printed on the fabric of English pop music could be seen as just another example of the exoticism that had been influencing various musics since at least the beginning of the century. During the 1950s in France, for example, songs with Oriental or Latin American flavors enjoyed a degree of success,[8] but were often parodies[9] and did not appear to be linked to any particular type of ideological discourse. The successful export of reggae from Jamaica in the 1970s indicated that a real change was taking place. Bob Marley & the Wailers and Burning Spear quickly became popular in Europe, North America, and Japan—throughout the world in fact—and, this time, the music's trendiness was inseparable from a myth of rebellion and from a loose set of ideas associating a rejection of consumer societies and bourgeois conventions with dance rhythms and tropical landscapes (Constant 1982). Next it was the turn of African urban music, beginning with the unexpected success of Manu Dibango's "Soul Makossa" (1973) and then the discovery outside of Africa of "afro-beat" stars King Sunny Ade and Fela Anikulapo Kuti. To this point, the introduction and marketing of "third world" artists' music internationally was haphazard, with no concerted commercial strategy.

In 1982, the first WOMAD (World of Music, Arts and Dance Festival) was held in Somerset, Great Britain. In its wake a label was created to publish recordings of artists from the world of rock, such as Peter Gabriel, David Byrne, and Pete Townshend, playing with musicians from Bali, India, and Jamaica (Feld 1995). In 1986, the American Paul Simon recorded with South Africans the album *Graceland*, which won a Grammy Award. At this stage, it was clear that a new market had opened up and that there were audiences ready to consume music of the "South," in its original forms or crossed with Euro-American rock and pop. Several producers distributing these types of music looked for a way to bring a degree of homogeneity to their product.

---

7. The Kinks, *See My Friends*, 1965; The Beatles, *Norwegian Wood*, 1965.

8. Artists such as Dario Moreno, born in Izmir, Turkey, but of Mexican origin, made this a specialty; Los Machucambos (composed of a Costa Rican, an Italian and a Spaniard) presented "South American" music reinvented for European audiences.

9. F. Bonifay and F. Barcellini, *Le facteur de Santa Cruz*, 1957; J. Plante and Ch. Aznavour, *Un Mexicain basané*, 1962; D. Moreno, *Si tu vas à Rio*, 1958; and J. Constantin and M. Persane, *Le Pacha*, 1958); J. Belin, L. Missir, and F. Andreoli, the *Cha cha des thons*, 1958; or A. Canfora and J. Bingler, *Fais-moi du couscous chéri*, 1960 . . .

They finally agreed on the term *world music,* which was later translated into French as "musiques du monde." This term quickly became standard, both commercially (it was adopted by the Grammy Awards and became a category in the classifications proposed by the magazine *Billboard*) and in academic studies (Frith 1989). What does it cover?

A Tentative Inventory

Based on the types of recordings presented in specialized documents (Azoulay 1997; Broughton et al. 1994; *Les musiques du monde en question* 1999) or in the press, it seems possible to group the music proposed under the heading *world music* into two large categories, themselves divided into two subcategories.

Recovery

Some genres now sold as world music actually existed well before the term was coined; they were "recycled" to take advantage of the developing market for commercial popular music.

In some cases, it was simply a matter of *reissuing* recordings of orally transmitted, "traditional"[10] music from around the world (including Europe), including non-Western classical or ritual musics from India, Pakistan, Indonesia, Japan, China, Arab-Andalusian, or other repertoires. Many of these were initially collected by ethnomusicologists.

In other cases, *reclassifications* of music emerged from spontaneous blending processes or local creations predating world music, especially those forms stemming from the conquest of the Americas (with the exception of African-American musics from the United States: jazz, blues, gospel, and derived forms, which still constitute a separate commercial category): cajun and zydeco in North America; tango, chamame, samba, foro, cumbia, mariachi, and so on in Latin America; and calypso, compas, merengue, beguine, zouk, reggae, son, charanga, and so on in the Antilles. The reclassification as world music has also been applied to forms of music that appeared in cities in the nineteenth and twentieth centuries, or even earlier, in Europe (flamenco, fado, rebetiko, brass bands in the Balkans, but not including the type of pop songs labeled *variétés* in French); the urban dance music of Africa blending "traditional" forms and Creole-American innovations — continental or island

---

10. "Orality" and "traditionality" belong to a body of terminology that has led to much debate that we do not broach in this chapter. With regard to tradition in music, see, in particular, Schlanger 1995.

(mbalax, morna, highlife, rumba, soukous, Ethiopian singing, taarab, sega, mbaqanga, African rap, and reggae); music referred to as "Arab" coming from the Maghreb, the Machrek, and the Middle East (Oran, Algerois chaâbi, Constantine, maalouf styles, Kabyle music, Egyptian and Lebanese songs); music from Asia (such as Indian songs or Indonesian pop); forms of music created by émigré populations (klezmer, rai, bhangra, salsa); and also non-Western film music (Arab, Indian).

Synthetic Musics

World music also includes original products: musics whose conception and realization were stimulated by the existence of a particular demand and means of distribution. These were made possible thanks to the existence of new recording, processing and sound reproduction tools. The music synthesizes diverse elements, often leading to entire new compositions, assembled from multiple sources using electroacoustic techniques.

One type of synthesis involves remodeling "traditional" music by layering it with "modern" rhythms (pop or rock) using electric and acoustic instruments, resulting in *modernized and reinvented traditions*. In this way, "new" Celtic (Breton and Irish in particular), Gypsy, Corsican, and Basque music appeared. The Australian group Yothu Yindi popularized an updated version of Aboriginal music around the world. CDs with descriptions such as *Sufi Pop* or *Oriental Hip Hop* can now be found in record stores. In South Africa, Pops Mohammed remixes forms of Xhosa music, while Zap Mama, a group based in Brussels, created *a cappella* vocal harmonies from songs of several regions of Africa.

Through *musical engineering* syntheses of another kind are developed by musicians or producers of CDs, concerts, or festivals. They may organize encounters between artists from very different spheres (Ry Cooder and Ali Farka Touré; Michael Brook and Nusrat Fateh Ali Khan). Other instances are concocted in studios where live musicians can be mixed with recordings of "traditional" music, although sound designers can also simply rework various recordings to make them into truly synthetic products (Massive Attack with Nusrat Fateh Ali Khan; Deep Forest with all sorts of music).

Visions of the World in Music: Contradictory Images

World music is a brand invented to sell, and there are unquestionably large sums of money involved.[11] But to reduce it to this would be an oversimplification.

11. The analysis in this section is developed in Martin 2002.

While the desire for profits is undeniably part of the strategy underlying its launching, the discourse that accompanies it suggests that for many customers and probably also for some producers (quite apart from any cynicism or greed that may be imputed to their motives), the love of world music is closely linked with humanist and humanitarian concerns.

Generosity

Some of the first mass gatherings at which world music took form were events organized to mobilize and collect funds for worthy causes such as the struggle against apartheid or famine (Garofalo 1992: 15–66). Thereafter, world music was accompanied by discourses in favor of brotherhood between peoples and world solidarity. One of the first world music CD guides described it as a "force for understanding and good will in an increasingly dark world."[12] In an introduction to a conference organized at her request at the Grande Halle de la Villette in Paris, Catherine Trautmann, French minister of culture at the time, repeated this refrain:

> Be they ethnic, traditional, folkloric, primitive, [or] world, these musics, urban or rural, classical or folk, religious or secular, certainly express the living and evolving part of a common heritage, a link that unites peoples across borders[; they] joyfully incarnate France as a country that is united, curious, open to traditions and creations wherever they are from. (*Les musiques du monde en question* 1999: 15–16)

More recently, an issue of a promotional publication distributed by a chain of stores specializing in cultural products was symptomatically titled: "It's ethnic, it's ethical!" Focused on a collection of world music recordings[13] including "original compositions based on meetings between musicians of sixteen countries . . . and Western composers, sent to these countries by Jean-Patrick Teyssaire, founder of Origins," the article stated:

> Among the countries facing severe environmental problems, we chose sixteen that have real musical identities. In each of these countries, "our" musicians worked with artists who bear this identity. The result is a universe of sound that is both exotic and familiar, homogeneous and mixed. (Lavarène 2001)

12. Peter Spencer, *World Beat: A Listener's Guide to Contemporary World Music on CD* (1992), cited in Taylor 1997: 19.

13. *Planète Verte* published by Origins.

This wording reflects the key points of the ideology underlying world music: meetings between human beings, mixing, exoticism, concern for the environment, and solidarity.

Exoticism

World music is certainly heir to the exotic musics that have long enchanted music lovers of Europe and North America. The texts that praise it claim that it generates emotion, charm, a state of awareness that is born of mysticism and spirituality and can induce trance.[14] In short, it conveys what the West is supposed to lack. It is sensual. Unlike earlier vogues, it bears witness to the identity of certain peoples, it abounds in their heritage (for Europe, the supposed heritage of the "Celts" and "Gypsies" is underscored), and thus brings regeneration. World music is said to combine generosity and fraternity with exoticism.

In this regard, it in no way represents a break with the fascination for the Other that has been for centuries a feature of Western societies in general, and France in particular. Exoticism implies criticism of one's self and of one's society based on a valorization of the Other, and the dream of an ideal society built on a romantic image of distant societies. As Tzvetan Todorov demonstrates, exoticism offers "praise in ignorance" (Todorov 1989: 298); it amounts to constructing the Other to be different, but not frighteningly so—a difference that makes the Other able to seduce and to be consumed.

Commerce

This musical exoticism that pretends to authenticity (of the music, of "encounter") is certainly a response to a demand. While Western societies were falling into an economic and moral crisis that Marc Augé (1994) diagnoses as a crisis of "overmodernity,"[15] Western rock and pop were becoming trite and lifeless; they no longer surprised dispirited listeners or made them dream. These crises

14. In particular, Fnac/Géo ca. 2000, which—with enthusiastic candor (but little musical rigor)—accumulates the most common clichés heard regarding world music; here, *exoticism* and *generosity* clearly become commercial arguments.

15. Overmodernity (*Surmodernité*) is characterized by three excesses (Augé 1994): time (everything goes faster), space (the feeling that distances are shrinking), and excess individualism (the individual is at the center of all social phenomena and all strategies). All are clearly at work within *world music*.

of morality and musical inspiration raised expectations that regeneration would come from elsewhere.[16] The 1980s saw burgeoning efforts to meet this demand, whether through travel, magazines, television programs and channels, food (Turgeon 2003), or furnishings. World music provided the background soundtrack for them, and opened up a field in which plundering and creation rubbed shoulders.

About the plundering: samplers, synthesizers and MIDI technology made possible the manipulation of all kinds of music in studios, unbeknownst to their creators, who did not receive any of the royalties that should have been paid to them. According to Steven Feld, musical sequences were taken from recordings of Pygmy music and included on pop music CDs that generated earnings of millions of dollars, without the Pygmies benefiting from this in the least (Feld 1996). In the same way, in 1992 Deep Forest pirated a song from the Solomon Islands for a CD of which over four million copies were sold, without its initial performer receiving a penny (Feld 2000). From Madonna to Manu Chao, whatever the performer's ideological orientation, it has become commonplace to freely use all sorts of recorded music, taking advantage of the loopholes in international law, which does little to protect artists belonging to societies in which the notion of artistic property was unknown until very recently.

Creation

On the other hand, the connections established or intensified by world music and the promotion and distribution networks it forged can also benefit inventive artists of the "North" as well as of the "South." Products labeled "world music" are hawked through commercial networks facilitating the music's dissemination. It thus participates, like jazz, reggae, rap, and other musics, in contemporary processes of exchange and innovation that bring genres into circulation for local appropriation throughout the world, where they are used for original local creations, many of which are then put in world circulation themselves.[17]

World music has thus allowed for a broader diffusion of certain ethnomusicological recordings and knowledge regarding the societies where they were made; it has promoted better understanding of present and past hybrid music forms; it has stimulated the invention of new genres that reflect the

16. A bit like the musical exoticism of the 1920s, symbolized by the jazz band and the *Revue nègre* (Martin and Roueff 2002).

17. Regarding rap, see Mitchell 2001.

experiences of immigrants (rai, bhangra); and it has provided means of creation to artists mixing genres and styles of very diverse origins.[18]

An Echo of the World

This overview suggests that world music as a social phenomenon is closely linked to the transformations of contemporary societies and, to a certain extent, expresses them. It thrives on the transnational flux that weaves around the world today (Badie and Smouts 1994), and it is sold on a market in which it satisfies a demand for exoticism of a new type caused by the dissatisfaction that many people experience living in the so-called developed societies of Europe, North America, and Asia. Under these conditions, world music raises questions that are at the heart of the changes that these societies are experiencing: What is difference? Is difference a right, and to what extent? How can differences coexist?

World music provides contradictory answers to these questions. On the one hand, it covers, when it doesn't facilitate them, practices that lead to the leveling of differences, to the reification and commercialization of the Other and its images; it has opened the door to new forms of piracy and despoilment. On the other hand, it has provided new means of expression and creation that show how the interaction between human beings, collaboration, and real knowledge of and respect for the Other lead to novelty and creation.

For this reason, world music, more than other forms of music, demands critical examination. It is important to distinguish recycling from creation; it is necessary to detect plundering and to denounce it; and it is equally essential to better understand the workings of the mixtures and fusions that have made world music successful and have led to undeniable esthetic achievements. It is at this point that a sociological analysis alone (even with economic and political dimensions) becomes insufficient. World music productions are the result of complex processes using sophisticated musical and electroacoustical techniques. The second part of this chapter will shed light some of these.

18. See, for example, Ray Lema, *Tout partout,* Paris, Buda, 1994 (CD 925932); le Viellistic Orchestra, *Archets infinis, miroirs du millénaire,* Casseuil, Alba Musica, 2000 (CD AL 0420); Annie Ebrel, Ricardo Del Fra, *Voulouz loar / Velluto di luna,* Rennes, Coop Breizh, 1998 (CD GWP 016); Lydia Domancich et al., Andouma, Paris, Gimini Music, 2000 (CD GM 1013).

How Can We Analyze World Music?

The analysis done by Simha Arom is based on a collection of seven pieces selected by Denis-Constant Martin. The choice focused on recordings considered—with inevitable subjectivity—representative of world music productions in the *synthetic music* category of the inventory proposed above. It did not seem necessary to include *recycled* music, for which there have already been important studies (Guilbault et al. 1993; Waterman 1990). We elected to investigate music that is invented or renewed by the mixing of various genres and/or the application, live or in studio, of electroacoustic processes to one or more of these genres. The pieces of this collection were rerecorded onto a CD given to Simha Arom without any indication of their origins.

Initial Approach

Arom listened to the recordings a first time to get a feel for them, then a second time to identify the instruments, voices, and processes used, and to note when changes occur (in theme, in motif, in timbre, from measured to unmeasured rhythm and vice versa) in order to identify and select units of comparison. This yielded a general idea of the construction of each piece and its formal organization.

These initial listenings were followed by many others, each one focusing on a different aspect: processes for linking and superimposing of the various units, scales, often complex rhythms, timbres. In a type of music in which clear forms are rarely detected immediately, the first step is to determine the exact times of reference points. The in-depth analysis then focused on describing as accurately as possible the events that occur between two given time points. With regard to analysis of rhythms in particular, it was necessary to rerecord the set of pieces at reduced speed in order to note the patterns (which would not always have been possible at actual speed). Listening at normal speed after the transcription confirmed that slowing down the playing speed did not lead to any perceptual distortions.

Description of the Set of Pieces

After many listenings, it was possible to propose descriptions of the music. Of the seven selections, two are purely instrumental (1 and 3);[19] the others are vocal and instrumental (2, 4, 5, and 7 are sung; 6 is "rapped," i.e., declaimed

19. The numbers refer to the pieces of the collection presented in appendix 1.

with strong rhythmic scansion). Piece 3 apparently uses no electroacoustic processes nor MIDI instruments. In 2 and 4, it is difficult to determine whether all of the instruments are "natural" or whether they are sampled and synthesized. It seems, however, that the accompaniment is exclusively synthetic in 5 and that the didjeridu in 7 has been processed electroacoustically. Lastly, in 1 and 6, "natural" and electroacoustical instruments coexist. The (possible) errors and uncertainties in this attempt to identify the types of instruments used are themselves interesting in that they show the extent to which it is difficult to understand, at first listening, how world music is built.

In the following analyses, the number of the piece is followed by its characterization in terms of "blind listening," and by an indication of its total duration in parentheses; for the most complex passages of pieces 2 and 3, there is a detailed presentation in appendices 2 and 3.

1: "Celtic" (?), non-Scottish (live) (3'28") ◑

The piece is composed of blocks of a rather simple form: AAB/AAB/ AAAAAA/mini-coda. Part A has forty-eight beats: two times a melodic-rhythmic sequence of eight beats [3.3.2 + 3.3.2], followed by two of sixteen beats [4 + 4 + 4 + 4]. Part B has thirty-two beats, organized in eight periods of four beats each. There is a major change in tempo, which becomes slower in B and coincides with the entry of a "blues/rock" electric guitar and a synthesizer.

2: "Minimalist" (structure evoking African music) (2'48") ◑

This piece is composed of two main parts. The first one is characterized by a rhythmic counterpoint that combines accents every three, seven, and twelve beats, and the complexity of this relationship leaves residues that force the musicians to "cheat" so that they can meet at a common junction point. The transitions are partly for this purpose. In the second part (which begins at 1:01), strictly regular accents (every three beats) are combined with accents in the main vocal part that fall on other beats and that are dephased, within a cycle of forty-eight beats divided into four periods—A, B, C, D—with respectively eleven, twelve, twelve, and thirteen beats, giving an impression of great ambiguity (see appendix 2). This cycle is repeated four times, with modifications of the instrumentation in periods B and D.

3: "Africa/Balkans" (5'02") ◑

This piece is marked by the use of rhythmic patterns resembling *aksak*.[20] One section of interest begins at 3:04: just before this, there is an acceleration

20. Regarding *aksak*, see Arom 2005.

of the tempo that brings in two linked rhythmic "themes." The first is, in fact, the so-called pan-African rhythmic pattern (*African standard pattern*): twelve brief durations grouped as 2.3/2.2.3. It is therefore not a real *aksak;* it is, however, perceived as such because it is based on the alternation of binary and ternary groups of durations in a very fast tempo. This pattern is repeated eight times. At 3:17 we have the second rhythmic theme, based on a succession of three different elements: first, a reprise of the preceding pattern, followed by a truncated segment of this one in 2/3/2/2—which is missing the concluding group of 3. This is an extremely subtle modification that has a disconcerting effect because of the rapidity of the tempo and the resemblance of this segment with the pattern that precedes it and also the one that follows it. The listener loses orientation within the flow of sound and the capacity to mentally organize it, because the segment of nine durations is immediately followed by a rotation of the first pattern as 3.2/3.2.2//3.2/.3.2.2//. The musicians offset it, and, in this form (2 × 12), repeat it three times (i.e., 3 × 24). The whole thing is very finely performed and ingeniously constructed. The brief segment with only nine durations, inserted between the patterns based on even numbers (12 and multiples of 12 durations), creates an out-of-phase effect. The sequence has a total of ninety-three durations—an odd number obtained through the juxtaposition of binary and ternary groups—whence the impression of hearing an *aksak,* although that is not really what it is (see appendix 3).

4: Africa (East or South? War Cry?), manipulations without synthesizers (2'52") ◐

The melody of this song, limited to three notes, is rudimentary. It is structured in periods of twenty beats, grouped asymmetrically into 16 + 4.

5: African techno (from Zaire or the Congo?) (4'28") ◐

This piece is in the form ABCD / ABED. It is based on periodic units of eight beats each. The beat remains absolutely stable.

6: Some kind of rap (Finnish or Turkish?) (4'11") ◐

The piece begins with an unmeasured dialogue between two plucked string instruments reminiscent of a *maqam.* At 1:20, with a voice that "raps," a measured section begins. The accompaniment blends acoustic and electro-acoustic instruments.

7: Singing and didjeridu; text from the "Song of Songs," sung in Hebrew (4'40") ◐

This last piece presents a real *aksak* on 5 brief durations, grouped in 2 + 3, with dephasing (2 + 3 / 2 + 3 / 2 + 3 / 2 + 3 + 3); these groupings follow one another and alternate. This piece is reminiscent of Burundian lullabies, and it is possible that the *aksak* were originally part of them, because they are known to exist in Africa. However, an *aksak* is by definition a reiterative pattern, and the dephasing heard here suggests that there was some arrangement. At some points, the vocals split into three parts, and the harmony produced is very refined.

Formal Organization and Composition Processes

The study of this set of pieces allows us to identify characteristic types of formal organization and to demonstrate that world music pieces can use ingenious composition processes.

Listening to these seven pieces revealed three types of forms:

a. Simple forms in which the periodicity of the various segments is more or less regular (1, 4, 5)
b. Complex forms (compared with the simple forms) that alternate segments of varying periodicity (2, 3, 7)
c. Forms called "arbitrary," for want of a more precise term, in which we observe an absence of synchronization between the soloist and the accompaniment (6, "rapped" part; 7, partially). In some cases, the periods are not completed and the musical segments are difficult to distinguish.

Based on this set of pieces, it is thus impossible to give a definition founded on general parameters of what would be a characteristic "world music form." Of the seven pieces, there are three types of forms. Diversity prevails: there is no matrix.

World music thus seems to be different from most other genres of commercial contemporary music in that it cannot be characterized formally other than by its heterogeneity. What distinguishes it is its tendency to use preexisting materials, traditional and/or modern, natural or reworked electroacoustically.

Attentive analysis of the body of pieces reveals the presence, within this formal diversity, of interesting compositional processes, such as the following:

• Rhythmic *ostinati*
• Dephasing that creates perceptual ambiguity
  –Dephasing of cycles, but within the framework of an overall symmetry [**2**: 11 + 12 + 12 + 13] = 48 (3 × 12)
  –Dephasing of the accompanying elements [**2**: "flutes"]
• *Aksak*

–Regular [**7**: 2 + 3]

–Dephased [**3**: 2 + 3/2 + 2 + 3 becomes 2 + 3/2 + 2, then again 2 + 3/2 +
2 + 3]

• Polyrhythms [**2**: 3 in one drum against 7 in the other, with a junction
point every 21 (3 × 7)]

These processes are not original except in the way in which they are associated. All of the elements they use already exist elsewhere, but the manners
in which they are combined in the horizontal (melodic) and vertical (simultaneous) dimensions are new.

In the horizontal dimension, there is an alternation of highly contrasted
sequences or ones that overlap each other. During certain transitions, it
becomes impossible to exactly distinguish where one stops and another one
begins; however, that which precedes the transition and that which follows it
are identifiable and clearly constructed. These alternations and overlappings
create wonderful contrasts or "feints."

In the vertical dimension, we find remarkable simultaneous combinations: for example, the sequence in piece 2 that creates ambiguity
(see appendix 2). In music, this process importantly produces tension, and
thus attracts and maintains attention. The analysis of this piece demonstrates
the cogency of its underlying thought or constructive idea.

Typology

The value of the formal organization and the composition processes lies essentially in the combinatory mechanisms that they use, and it seems to us that
however tentative, a typology of world music structure can be based only on
the types of combinations of preexisting elements used, grouped in terms
of whether they are played by "natural" instruments or electroacoustically
processed (figure 11.1).

"Combining" and Creating

This set of pieces, here hypothesized provisionally as representative of all world
music production, is characterized not by the invention of original formulae,
but by combinatory methods. Except for reprised and recycled music, which
is older than the name *world music,* the new syntheses collected under this
heading use diverse possibilities of mixing and association between "traditional" music (orally transmitted rural or "popular" urban) and electroacoustic

Association between Traditional Music	OTHER TRADITIONAL MUSIC		• Live playing (concert or studio) ► 3
			• Live playing + prerecorded elements ► 4, 7
(VOICE, NATURAL INSTRUMENTS; REPERTOIRES FROM A TRADITION)			• Live playing and/or prerecorded elements treated in studio with electroacoustic processes • Musically perfect synchronization between the superimposed parts ► 2, 4
	INSTRUMENTS AND ELECTRO- ACOUSTIC PROCESSES		• Live playing (concert or studio) • Musically perfect synchronization ► 1
AND . . .			• Live playing + instruments and electroacoustic processes • Musically perfect synchronization ► 5
			• Live playing + instruments and electroacoustic processes • Approximate synchronization ► 6 and partly 7
MODALITIES OF MIXTURES ON . . .	THE HORIZONTAL DIMENSION: ALTERNATIONS BETWEEN . . .	Traditional music AND	• Other traditional music ► 2, 3, 4 • Instruments and electroacoustic processes ► 1, 6, 7
	THE VERTICAL DIMENSION: SUPERPOSITIONS OF. . .		• Traditional music ► 3, 4 • Instruments and electroacoustic processes ► 1, 2, 4, 5, 6, 7

Figure 11.1. Draft typology of *world music* from the set of pieces studied ("synthetic music").

techniques. "Forest Gate" (piece 2) distinguishes itself with its succession of sampled, transformed songs, forming a coherent musical construction; "Liqa" (piece 3) is remarkable for the virtuosity with which it associates elements in both the horizontal and vertical dimensions. "Forest Gate" intrigues by the ambiguity that it maintains; "Liqa," clever and complex, stirs curiosity because it constantly leaves the impression that not everything that is happening can be grasped on first listening; "Fair & Ruddy" (piece 7) contains sophisticated harmonic effects.

Combining seems to be the main *modus operandi* of world music: there is a crafty, sleight-of-hand aspect to the way that it is designed (by artist-musicians, sound engineers, artistic directors, and commercial agents, inseparably) that produces combination in the way heterogeneous musical elements are associated. Combining is a direct response to the commercial concerns that led to giving certain musical practices the name *world music*, and to the ideology of mixture, meeting, and merger. The musicological analysis specifies and confirms the conclusions of the sociological approach.

It is therefore the meaning that these schemes, combinations, and combinatory mechanisms can have in the contemporary world that interests us. A first observation: they correspond to the "new New Worlds," which, according to Georges Balandier (2001), are opening to all forms of contemporary exploration. They are deployed in a borderless "great planetary system." Music, as a nonlinguistic sound phenomenon, has always provided a privileged means of contact and exchange between human beings who do not know each other and lack the means to communicate. It was for this reason that it played a decisive role in the creolization processes set in motion by colonization and slavery, in the Americas and in Africa especially. Today, as already underscored, cultural contacts without physical meeting often arise between individuals who are bearers of different practices, conceptions, and values. Yet pervasive inequalities in the world's social organization remain, as does the persistent violence that scorns and kills people everywhere. Though the absolute negation (ending with the social assassination analyzed by Orlando Patterson [1982]) of the Other that underlays slavery, and which, behind more human pretexts, nourished colonialism, is now condemned by national and international law, hostility to the Other can still reappear in the form of torture, genocide, and war.

The exploration of the worlds of music thus continues in a universe in which technical mediation has become an essential means of knowledge, while humanist ideologies, concerned to preserve the diversity of "differences," the rights of minorities, and indeed of peoples considered to be "first," have spread widely in some sections of the world's population. Law has evolved in the direction of recognition of the equality of human beings. The exploration is spurred by greed and the need to encounter the unknown that probably impelled the great voyagers of yesteryear, but, blown by generous winds, it now drifts and surfs on electroacoustic waves. What can be brought back from such expeditions? For some, booty: a heap of jumbled—combined—sounds in the treasure chest that people are trying to sell (use of the word *piracy* is used to refer to certain types of commercial exchanges of music is not a coincidence). But, on the one hand, in the holds of world music, we find more than just loot from random pillaging. On the other, for those who buy it—in whatever form—it means much more than that, something quite different.

Behind any exploration there is a need for knowledge, a desire for the Other. Technical mediation offers a vehicle more accessible than the journey to assuage this need—even a journey to nearby neighborhoods where immigrants perpetuate the music of their countries of origin. Paradoxically, it seems a better guarantor of the authenticity considered indispensable for escaping the dissatisfactions of modernity, urbanity, and material comfort, because the neighbor from abroad is always suspected of having been contaminated by his new environment. For some journeys of exploration and encounter, the vehicle of technical mediation might be an airplane or a Jeep in the bush. Here it appears to be the means of access to a reconstructed Other modeling a vibrant counter-society of mysticism, "traditions," social harmony, and an immediate relationship with nature.

Thanks to technical mediation, the field of world exploration is open to invention. We recognize here the two original meanings of the word *invention:* finding/discovering and imagining/creating. The inventing of the world in music allows us to find and imagine the Other in the same movement; it is also the search for the unprecedented and offers possibilities for its realization. Mediation, in a network with no limits, favors the multiplication of inventions and their infinite combinations. "Modern" music and "traditional" music, "classical" and "folk" music, music of the "North" as well as of the "South,"[21] music of the present and even of a mythical past are associated in diverse organizations. As established on the basis of the set of pieces studied in this article, we have a more precise idea of their typology.

The combinations of world music play a part in the edification of an imagination with a triple power: to explore the world, to get to know the "new New Worlds" in a spirit of playfulness and curiosity thanks to the most recent technologies; and to have the feeling of embracing and controlling all of these worlds through practices of mixing, association, and uninterrupted peregrinations. We feel we are moving away from, or probably rather forgetting about— in the ephemeral and extraordinary temporality of these practices—the aspects that disenchant people the most.

This power should not be underestimated under the pretext that it is imaginary, because this is a power of creation: musical creation, and the creation of the world in a time in which it is to be reconstructed and reformed.

---

21. These terms and the categories that they claim to designate are, from an analytical standpoint, at least debatable, perhaps even fallacious; they are relevant here only because they act as accepted points of reference in the discourse and the mental constructions of world music.

The combinations enabled by technical mediations are instruments of these two inseparable types of creation, as long as they are grasped in their dynamic reality and not taken as merely static, individual products launched on the market. Seen thus, the combinations trace sketches and carry out experiments with results that vary in success and inventiveness. The intertwined logics of music commoditization and esthetic pursuit engender both sterile patchworks and works in progress full of potential, and sometimes even works of polished achievement. Creolized musics, born of the direct confrontations of human beings in abominable situations of injustice and brutality, went through long and complex phases of evolution and transformation of which few traces remain, and along the way probably abandoned attempts that were fruitless or unsatisfactory with respect to the needs of their time. Similarly, world music, born of technical mediation and circulation through international networks of music commoditized for audio recordings, videos, and stages, results in combinations that are provisional, unstable, and display uncertain forces of invention.

Confronted with a phenomenon of incredible diversity and uncontainable fluidity, musical analysis, within the framework of a general anthropology of music, is necessary to better determine what passes through it and what happens. Musical analysis reveals the functioning of the combinatory mechanisms and identifies the elements that are combined with quantified accuracy. If needed, it thus constitutes useful proof for the denunciation of misappropriations and despoilments.[22] It certainly cannot have the predictive function of announcing what will be fruitful or not, and still less what will or will not be commercially successful, or provide recipes for fabrication. It can however, without making any other claims, reveal the complexity or the simplicity of the processes used (as here with regard to pieces 2 and 3);[23] it lays a foundation on which, *a posteriori,* it will be possible to more finely study the relationship between success, the begetting of new forms of music, and the combinatory mechanisms used. Based on musical analysis, work on symbolism can at last begin, taking into consideration the social representations attached (by a group, at time t and in place p) to the various mixed elements, and the understood

22. The law must define these offenses, and decide to judge them and punish them; this is not the case at the moment, unfortunately, but we must hope that this situation will change (Mundy 2000, particularly p. 17; see also the document, including texts in Italian and English, published in EM 2003).

23. It may be necessary to specify that these two pieces use radically different processes and that the observation of great inventiveness in the combinatory mechanisms does not mean, for the authors of this article, that they put them on the same level in terms of the perfectly subjective listening pleasure that they derive from one or the other.

significations in the equilibria or hierarchies established by diverse elements' combination.

That work is obviously not achieved in this essay. To do so would require investigations that we did not carry out, and the results of which could not have been presented in a brief text. Our purpose was thus simply to point out the social and musical importance of the phenomenon known as *world music* in the contemporary world. We tried to show that, beyond the rejection of some people, who argue that this music is adulterated and hybrid in order to deny it any esthetic value and to judge that it is not worth being seriously studied, and beyond the enthusiastic proclamations of others, who hear in it a "world sound" rustling with generosity, humanity, and cultural intercomprehension, sincerely or because this ideological noise masks the jingling coins of the merchants, beyond the scorn and rapture, both deaf to what is to be heard in world music, we must, as with any human phenomenon, try to analyze it, understand it, and find adequate methods to do so.

Appendix 1

Corpus

The information from the booklets regarding the instruments and the sources of the musical material used are indicated in brackets.

1. "Call to the Dance" (Dan Ar Braz), Dan Ar Braz and the Héritage des Celtes, excerpt from *Zénith,* Sony 1998 (CD 491811.2) [live recording during a concert; amplified natural instruments (flutes, whistle, bagpipes, *uillean pipes, bombard* (oboe of Brittany), *gaïta,* harp, guitars, keyboards, accordion, violin, percussion) reworked in real time with electroacoustic processes].

2. "Forest Gate" (Norbert Galo), Aman, excerpt from *Lhã,* Vox Terrae 1999 (CD VT 99012) [programmed synthesizer; *tarka* (recorder, with terminal mouthpiece, played in the Bolivian and Chilean Andes); *anata* (same type of flute as the preceding one, played in the Northwest of Argentina, Peru, and in Bolivia); percussion; voice; sampling of Inuit and Burundian voices].

3. "Liqa" (Bijan Cemirani and Henri Agnel), excerpt from *Gulistan, Jardin des Roses,* L'empreinte digitale, 2000 (CD ED 13127) [*kemençe,* short-necked bowed spike fiddle from Turkey; *lyra,* short-necked bowed spike fiddle from Greece; rebec; percussions (*zarb, daf, reqq*); the booklet mentions the "musical universes of Iran and Azerbaidjan"].

4. "Sfebe Sendoda" (Dizu Plaatjies and Mzwandile Qotoyi), excerpt from *Tribal Ethno Dance Cha(p)tter One*, Drum 'n Metal, MELT, 2000 (CD BW 092) [concertina; percussions, including *congas, bata* (two-skin hourglass drum from Cuba), bells; voice; percussion effects; according to the booklet: "ethnic music recorded in the field in a rural area, often made with rudimentary equipment, and then improved in a modern recording studio by contemporary musicians who add their own styles and feelings"].

5. "Millè" (Mory Kante), excerpt from *Tatebola*, Misslin, 1996 (CD DME 18) [voice; violins; viola; cello; large *ngoni* (or *nkoni*, lute played among the Mandinka of West Africa); small *nkoni;* balafon; drums, including *djembe;* programmed effects]

6. "Bundan Sonrasi" (words: Aziza A; music: Boris Meinhold; arrangement: Boris Meinhold, Turgay Ayaydinli, Andreas Advocado; singing: Aziza A), excerpt from *Kendi Dünyam* ("Oriental Hip Hop, Berlin-Istanbul"), Doublemoon, 2001 (CD DM 0014) [guitars; bass guitar; keyboards; violins; cello; percussions; *kanun;* voice; recorded in Berlin and Istanbul].

7. "Fair & Ruddy" (Meira Asher), excerpt from *Dissected*, Crammed Discs, 1997 (CD Cram 094) [singing: Meira Asher; didjeridu: Gil Hendelman; "words based on chapter 5 of the Song of Songs; music based on three lullabies from Burundi"].

Appendix 2

Detailed Analysis of Piece 2 from 1'01" to 2'28" (Dephasing Processes that Produce Perceptual Ambiguity)

	11 Beats	12 Beats	12 Beats	13 Beats
Period A = 48				
• hand clapping on	4 and 10	5 and 11	5 and 11	5 and 11
• "sanza" on	3, 6, and 9	1, 4, 7, and 10	1, 4, 7, and 10	1, 4, 7, 10, and 13
Period B = 48				
• hand clapping on	4 and 10	5 and 11	5 and 11	5 and 11
• "sanza" on	3, 6, and 9	1, 4, 7, and 10	1, 4, 7, and 10	1, 4, 7, 10, and 13
• response of flutes on	3 and 4	4 and 5	4 and 5	4 and 5
Period C = 48				
• hand clapping on	4 and 10	5 and 11	5 and 11	5 and 11
• "sanza" on	3, 6, and 9	1, 4, 7, and 10	1, 4, 7, and 10	1, 4, 7, 10, and 13
• response of flutes on	3 and 4	4 and 5	4 and 5	4 and 5
Period D = 48				
• hand clapping on	4 and 10	5 and 11	5 and 11	5 and 11
• "sanza" on	3, 6, and 9	1, 4, 7, and 10	1, 4, 7, and 10	1, 4, 7, and 10
• response of flutes on	3 and 4	4 and 5	4 and 5	4 and 5
• high flutes echoing singing on	3 and 4	4 and 5	4 and 5	4 and 5

Appendix 3

Piece 3: Out of Phase "Double Aksak"

Rhythmic Pattern 1 (at 3'04")	2.3 / 2.2.3 //	12 values [× 8]
Rhythmic Pattern 2 (at 3'17")	a. 2.3 / 2.2.3 //	12 values
	b. 2 / 3 / 2 / 2 //	9 values
	c. 3.2 / 3.2.2 // 3.2 / 3.2.2 //	2 × 12 [× 3] = 72 values

References

Appadurai, Arjun. 1990. "Disjuncture and Difference in the Global Cultural Economy." *Public Culture* 2(2): 1–24.

Arom, Simha. 2005. "L'aksak: principes et typologie." *Cahiers de musiques traditionnelles* 17: 11–48.

Aubert, Laurent. 1997. "Le grand bazar: de la rencontre des cultures à l'appropriation de l'exotique." In *Pom pom pom pom. Musiques et Caetera,* ed. François Borel et al., 141–164. Neufchâtel, Switzerland: Musée d'ethnographie de Neufchâtel.

———. 2001. *La musique de l'autre: les nouveaux défis de l'ethnomusicologie.* Geneva: Georg, Ateliers d'ethnomusicologie.

Augé, Marc. 1994. *Le sens des autres: actualité de l'anthropologie.* Paris: Fayard.

Azoulay, Éliane. 1997. *Musiques du monde.* Paris: Bayart.

Badie, Bertrand, and Marie-Claude Smouts. 1994. *Le retournement du monde: sociologie de la scène internationale.* Paris: Presses de la Fondation nationale des sciences politiques et Dalloz.

Balandier, Georges. 2001. *Le grand système.* Paris: Fayard.

Broughton, Simon, Mark Ellingham, Dave Muddyman, and Richard Trillo, eds. 1994. *World Music: The Rough Guide.* London: Rough Guides.

Constant, Denis. 1982. *Aux sources du reggae: musique, société et politique en Jamaïque.* Marseille: Parenthèses.

Daffos, Dominique. 1999. "Les disquaires et les musiques du monde." *Internationale de l'imaginaire* 11: 219–223.

EM. 2003. "World Music: Globalizzazione, identità musicali, diritti, profitti." *EM: Annuario degli Archivi di Etnomusicologia dell'Accademia Nazionale di Santa Cecilia,* I, 77–95.

Erlmann, Veit. 1994. "Africa Civilised, Africa Uncivilised: Local Culture, World-System and South Africa." *South African Journal of Musicology* 14: 1–13.

Feld, Steven. 1995. "From Schizophonia to Schismogenesis: The Discourses and Practice of World Music and World Beat." In *The Traffic in Culture, Refiguring Art and Anthropology,* ed. Georges E. Marcus and Fred R. Myers, 96–126. Berkeley and Los Angeles: University of California Press.

———. 1996. "Pygmy Pop: A Genealogy of Schizophonic Mimesis." *Yearbook for Traditional Music* 28: 1–35.

————. 2000. "A Sweet Lullaby for World Music." *Public Culture* 12(1): 145–171.

Fnac/Géo. [ca. 2000]. *Le guide des musiques du monde, la discothèque idéale en 250 CD*. Paris: Prélude et Fugue.

Frith, Simon, ed. 1989. *World Music, Politics and Social Changes*. Manchester: Manchester University Press.

Garofalo, Reebee, ed. 1992. *Rockin' the Boat: Mass Music and Mass Movements*. Boston: South End Press.

Gebesmair, Andreas, and Alfred Smudits, eds. 2001. *Global Repertoires: Popular Music Within and Beyond the Transnational Music Industry*. Aldershot, UK: Ashgate.

Gruzinski, Serge. 1996. "Découverte, conquête et communication dans l'Amérique ibérique: avant les mots, au delà des mots." In *Transferts culturels et métissages Amérique/Europe, XVIe–XXe siècle*, ed. Laurier Turgeon, Denis Delâge, and Réal Ouellet, 141–154. Québec: Presses de l'Université Laval.

————. 1999. *La Pensée Métisse*. Paris: Fayard.

Guilbault, Jocelyn, with Gage Averill, Édouard Benoit, and Gregory Rabess. 1993. *Zouk: World Music in the West Indies*. Chicago: University of Chicago Press.

Hayward, Philip, ed. 1999. *Widening the Horizon: Exoticism in Post-War Popular Music*. London: John Libbey/Perfect Music Publications.

Krümm, Philippe. 1999. "Les musiques traditionnelles d'en France et leurs métissages Actuels." *Internationale de l'imaginaire* 11: 29–35.

Lavarène, Franck de. 2001. "C'est ethnique, c'est éthique!" *Contact* 369: 20–21.

Lefeuvre, Gildas. 1999. "Les musiques du monde et leurs publics." *Internationale de l'imaginaire* 11: 61–68. Paris: Maison des cultures du monde (Babel no. 387).

Les musiques du monde en question. 1999. *Internationale de l'imaginaire* 11. Paris: Maison des cultures du monde (Babel no. 387).

Martin, Denis-Constant. 2002. "Les 'Musiques du Monde': Imaginaires Contradictoires de la Globalisation." In *Sur la Piste des OPNI (Objets Politiques non Identifiés)*, 398–430. Paris: Karthala.

Martin, Denis-Constant, and Olivier Roueff. 2002. *La France du jazz: musique, modernité et identité dans la première moitié du 20ème siècle*. Marseille: Parenthèses.

Mitchell, Tony. 1996. *Popular Music and Local Identity: Rock, Pop and Rap in Europe and Oceania*. London: Leicester University Press.

Mitchell, Tony, ed. 2001. *Global Noise: Rap and Hip-Hop outside the USA*. Middletown, CT: Wesleyan University Press.

Mundy, Simon. 2000. *Musique et mondialisation: quelques questions et quelques réponses*. Paris: UNESCO, Conseil International de la Musique (Roneographic report).

Patterson, Orlando. 1982. *Slavery and Social Death: A Comparative Study*. Cambridge, MA: Harvard University Press.

Pennewaert, Eddy, ed. 2000. *Musiques du monde, produits de consommation*. Brussels: Colophon.

Plisson, Michel. 1999. "Les musiques d'Amérique Latine et leurs réseaux communautaires en France." *Internationale de l'imaginaire* 11: 123–134.

Schlanger, Judith. 1995. "Tradition et nouveauté." In *Ndroje Balendro, musiques, terrains et disciplines: textes offerts à Simha Arom*, ed. Vincent Dehoux et al. Paris: Peeters, 179–185.

Simporé, Bintou. 1999. "Des radios et des musiques du monde." *Internationale de l'imaginaire* 11: 241–251.

Taylor, Timothy D. 1997. *Global Pop, World Music, World Markets.* New York: Routledge.

Tenaille, Frank. 1999. "Historique: les musiques du monde en France." *Internationale de l'imaginaire* 11: 23–26.

Todorov, Tzvetan. 1989. *Nous et les autres, la réflexion française sur la diversité Humaine.* Paris: Le Seuil.

Turgeon, Laurier. 2003. "La cuisine: manger le monde dans les restaurants étrangers de Québec." In *Patrimoines Métissés, Contextes Coloniaux et Post-Coloniaux,* 161–187. Paris: Éditions de la Maison des Sciences de l'Homme.

Turgeon, Laurier, Denis Delâge, and Réal Ouellet, eds. 1996. *Transferts culturels et métissages Amérique/Europe, XVIe–XXe siècle.* Québec: Presses de l'Université Laval.

Waterman, Christopher Alan. 1990. *Jùjú: A Social History and Ethnography of an African Popular Music.* Chicago: University of Chicago Press.

A Cross-Cultural Topology of Musical Time

Afterword to the Present Book and to Analytical Studies in World Music (2006)

Michael Tenzer

Typology and Topology

Here at the combined conclusion of this volume plus its companion-predecessor *Analytical Studies in World Music* (Tenzer 2006; hereafter *ASWM*), not to strive for a synthetic overview would be to miss a rare opportunity to inquire into a range of features ordering all music.[1] As linguists gather a cross section of languages to search for universals, so we have selected repertoire in the two books to maximize historical and geographic diversity. There has been no intent to define music or to canonize any subset of it, rather to sample broadly. Naturally, the process of choosing leaves room for expansion and improvement, as both past and future unsuspected musical bloodlines and provenances may emerge or be discovered at any time. Many *sui generis* musical regions and families were bypassed because space was limited. Insider knowledge was prerequisite for joining the project, but more experts write analysis for some musics than for others. Nonetheless, this is a start. With all

---

1. This study is indebted to formulations of contemporary theorists of musical rhythm to the extent that it would be unwieldy to trace and reference the origins of the many concepts and tools marshaled. So as not to impede the flow, and to preserve something of the character of a primer in lieu of a scholarly argument, the decision was taken to eschew citations altogether. Suggested readings are listed at the end. Most are concerned with rhythm and its properties. For discussion of the ontology of musical rhythm as it pertains to categorizations both different and related to that of the present essay, see Tenzer 2011. Molino 2009, Nettl 2001, and Rowell 1983 explore music's ontology more generally.

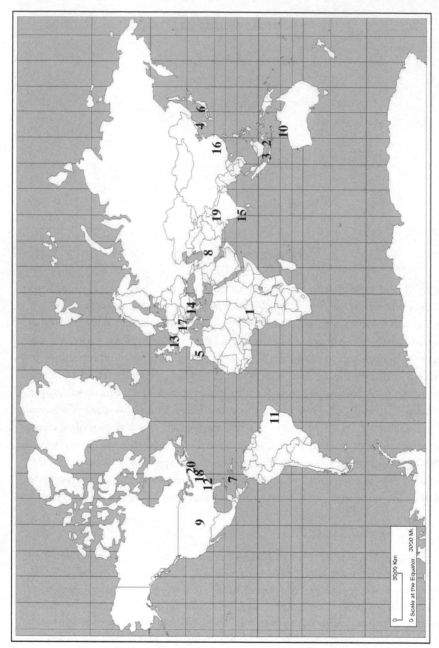

Frontispiece: Regions of the world represented by the selections studied in the present volume and in Tenzer (2006), numbered as in figure A.1, column 2.

populated continents at least minimally represented there is variety enough to support organizing and testing the corpus as a database for typological study. Yet since the evidence available in this collection is still insufficient to enable more than a quite provisional typology, it is better to think of what follows as a *topology*—a conceptual map of kinds of musical structure, still coarse for the moment, organized according to relations among the structures themselves rather than their geographic or cultural origins.

"Typological study," of which this effort partakes nevertheless, suggests comparison and a unified perspective on diverse phenomena. It is a worthy effort if the purpose is clear. Yet such a venture may be jarring in its conception for those who love and practice music analysis. The chasm between the microcosm of a given musical instance—that is, the realm of the analyst—and the mere outlines of musical features at many orders of magnitude removed, beyond even the limits of a cultural perspective (except, of course, that of this writer's), is vast by any reckoning, and perhaps the gap is unbridgeable for the present. Analysis is lifeless without particularity, but typology is inevitably concerned with bird's-eye features seemingly more relevant to disciplines (neurobiology, cognitive science, anthropology, etc.) that do not address why a given piece inspires its own fascinating and engaging musical experience.

Perhaps at the global order of magnitude the phenomena linking musics together are solely hardwired, reflect evolutionary and cultural needs, or are constrained by limits on perception, memory, and fine motor skills. Alan Lomax suggested as much in the 1970s when he described his Cantometrics system for comparison as concerned not with "songs" but with "singing." It should be clear that leaving such issues aside for the moment is a gesture of respect for them (although some of these issues, largely invisible here, were foundational in the individual analyses from which the corpus is drawn). But can we ultimately find continuity between the particular and the universal in musical experience?

One way to proceed surely hinges upon insight into music and time. While musico-temporal structure may be perceived in different ways depending on its contexts of production and reception, it is important to strive for analytical language able to bridge these modalities. Consistent with *ASWM,* the present focus is on the nature and variety of musical time flows. Many writers have investigated this topic, but almost always in the context of a culturally delimited repertoire. The current aim is to gloss the processes and relationships generating the flows evident in the global corpus at hand. Of the many dimensions of musical time, I focus on a few of the most important to see how these are evoked and given a particular balance by the structure of each selection. The broad tripartite classification explained on pages 25–32 of *ASWM* and used to group chapters therein (part I: *sectional periodicity,* part II:

isoperiodicity, and part III: *linear composition*[2]) serves as a springboard for the ideas developed here.

Three motivations for this venture stand out: a creative urge to tell about the musics as I have learned to hear them in relation to one another; a utopian wish to reconcile and share disparate musical experiences; and fascination with diverse and ingenious constructions of musical architecture. Naturally the perspective I take can only complement—and will never diminish—each music's profound individuality. But this is not an exercise in the anthropology of time. It is a snapshot of one editor-analyst's ongoing engagement with features of musical time described in this body of contributors' work. Perhaps we can later learn to extend downward from the glosses to reconnect with individual works in greater detail "on the ground," integrating the many other layers of significance that a time-based perspective seems naturally to want to accommodate. For the present it is enough to observe, note, and take inventory, and rely on the books' chapter-length analyses to provide their particular varieties of detail separately.

The expertise of the assembled authors is assumed to validate the cultural relevance of the data supporting my analysis. The repertoire items vary widely in length, texture, the fixity of structural identities, and social contexts and functions, but all such factors are set aside—or, rather, taken as having neutralized one another—to zero in on strategies of temporal organization. Cultures have multiple approaches to time that do not neatly sum up in any single musical example or concept.[3] Thus while the selections may represent their cultures, they are not intended to stand for them: they are individual expressions irreducible to norms, mere instances among many and presumably diverse others. Ultimately we stand a better chance of producing a more thorough typology with this culture-blind approach.

More significantly, like time in all realms, each instance of musical time is always multiple, with layered, contradictory qualities. Its complexity (however defined) need not vary proportionally with any other musical or social parameter. Time is experience, which takes shape and shape-shifts once it enters the imagination. In both experience and reflection upon experience, days can be as concentrated as moments, private experiences as rich

2. These broad categories have mainly given way to more focused terminology below. *Isoperiodicity* is described using the terms *cycle* and *ostinato cycle,* and the word *linear* has been dropped to avoid its connotations of teleology and progress.

3. It is simplistic to say, for example, that "Balinese time is circular" or "Western time is linear." Although it may seem like splitting hairs to substitute (as I do below) similar formulations such as "cyclical" and "transformative," the latter two at least have the virtue of suggesting temporal experience rather than spatial geometry.

as public ones, simple materials are apt to generate intricacy, and intricacy can cross a perceptual threshold back to simplicity.[4] Familiarity may greatly clarify such unstable perception; here is where expert knowledge provides the compass we need.

The following discussion condenses and interprets the collected analyses, reorienting them to the purpose at hand, which often supplements the authors' original purposes. After an exposition of analytic parameters and terms, the twenty repertoire selections in the corpus are then categorized and described with reference to this lexicon of time organization and temporality types. In chapters where multiple selections were analyzed, only one was chosen for inclusion here.[5] The categories proposed describe only the music in the corpus; no universal completeness is presumed. Detail may be added in the future with the accretion of more examples.

I stress the qualitative nature of this project. It is intended to inspire interpretations about which the artistically inclined may argue, not dispense case-closers.

I. Pure Parameters and Their Continua

Sections I.1, I.2, and I.3 review common concepts of musical temporality in a theoretical vein: *time organization* (mental constructions of time through which we cognize musical rhythm); *configuration* (how we understand musical events to be grouped); and *formal continuity* (the overarching quality of temporal process). Each topic concludes with one or more focus questions that guide later discussion of the corpus. Closely related terms are given in parentheses. Section I.4 considers overlaps between categories and other contingencies.

I.1. Time Organization (Figure A.1, Column 5)

Keywords: unmeasured rhythm, pulsation (beat), meter (metric periodicity), cycle, ostinato cycle; open and closed time.

---

4. One musical example: it should be intuitively clear that for insiders to each culture, one of Anton Webern's terse *Five Pieces for Orchestra*, lasting less than a minute, may present as rich a temporal experience as a nightlong vocalization of an epic poem from the Sulu archipelago.

5. For example, Blum and Buchanan/Folse in Tenzer 2006 and Nettl/Levine and Barwick here (see figure A.1 for selections). The choices were subjectively made. The music on which the comparative analyses in Tenzer and Arom/Martin were based (this volume) was also excluded.

1. Temporal Category	2. Author (volume[a] and chapter)	3. Origin and Genre	4. Selection Title	5. Time Organization	6. Place of Articulation	7. Formal Continuity
A. "Pure" ostinato-cyclic	1. Fürniss (ASWM 5)	Central African song	*Dikòbò dámù dá sòmbé*	Ostinato cycle	Cycle boundaries	Cyclic
B. Cyclic—discursive	2. Tenzer (ASWM 6)	Balinese gamelan	*Oleg Tumulilingan*	Ostinato cycle and expansions	Metacycle boundaries	Through-composed with cycles
	3. Sutton/Vetter (ASWM 7)	Javanese gamelan	*Ladrang Pangkur*			
C. "Pure" hybrid (transformative/ sectional/cyclic)	4. Hesselink (ACCSWM 7)	Korean *p'ungmul*	*P'an Kut*	Succession of ostinato cycles	Metacycle boundaries	Sectional
D. Sectional with ostinato cycle basis	5. Manuel (ASWM 3)	Spanish *flamenco*	*A Quién le Contaré Yo*	Ostinato cycle layer, metered layer	Metacycle boundaries	Sectional
	6. Terauchi (ACCSWM 1)	Japanese *gagaku*	*Etenraku*			
	7. Moore/Sayre (ASWM 4)	Cuban *batá*	*Obatalá*			
E. Sectional with nonmetric (pulsed, unmeasured rhythm) basis	8. Blum (ASWM 1)	Xorasani *navā'i*	*Sāqi-nāme of Qomrı*	Unmetered/ measured/cyclic	Configured group boundaries	Sectional/cyclic
	9. Levine/Nettl (ACCSWM 8)	*Arapaho* song	*Wolf Dance Song*			
	10. Barwick (ACCSWM 9)	Murriny Patha *djanba*	*Kunyibinyi Tjingarru*			
F. Sectional—cyclic	11. Stanyek/Oliveira (ACCSWM 3)	Brazilian *samba pagode*	*Sorriso Aberto*	Metered/cyclic	Configured group boundaries	Cyclic
	12. Ziporyn/Tenzer (ACCSWM 4)	American *jazz*	*I Should Care*			
	13. Leach (ACCSWM 2)	French medieval *balade*	*De Petit Po*			

Figure A.I.   The corpus and its parameters.

				Metered/cyclic	Configured group boundaries	Through-composed
G. Sectional—metered	14. Buchanan/Folse (ASWM 2)	Bulgarian *horo*	*Georgi, le Lyubile*		Configured group boundaries	Through-composed with sectional articulations
	15. Morris (ASWM 9)	S. Indian *varnam*	*Valachi Vacchi*			
H. Transformative—sectional	16. Stock (ASWM 8)	Chinese *huju*	*Jin Yuan Seeks Her Son*	Metered	Configured group boundaries	through-composed with sectional articulations
	17. Benjamin (ASWM 10)	European piano concerto	*Concerto 17 in G Major, K. 453, I*			
I. Open transformative	18. Roeder (ASWM 11)	American chamber music	*Enchanted Preludes*	Multiply-pulsed free rhythm/ *unmeasured* rhythm	Configured group boundaries	Through-composed with sectional articulations
	19. Widdess (ACCSWM 5)	North Indian *ālāp*	*rāg Pūriyā-Kalyān*			
J. "Pure" transformative	20. Bunk (ACCSWM 6)	American "timbre-and-form"	*Phoneme (3)*	*Unmeasured* rhythm	(Weakly) configured group boundaries	Through-composed with weak sectional articulations

[a] *ASWM = Analytical Studies in World Music* (Tenzer 2006); *ACCSWM = Analytical and Cross-Cultural Studies in World Music* (current volume)

Figure A.1. (Continued)

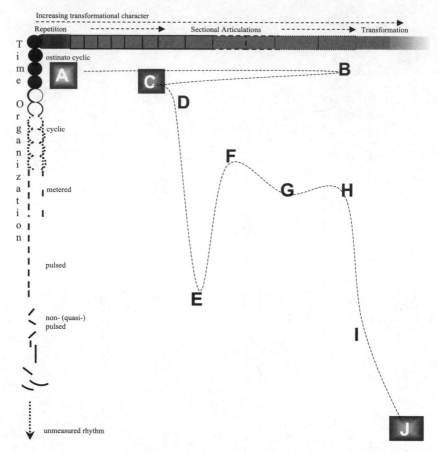

Figure A.2.   A cross-cultural topology of musical time in this corpus, based on the temporal categories in column I of figure A.1.

The five terms *unmeasured rhythm, pulsation, meter, cycle,* and *ostinato cycle* describe a continuum of diachronic frameworks along which time is perceived as increasingly regulated and constrained by equidistant pulsations (beats) and by repetition of content. The frameworks enable us to create a mental construct of how time is organized, a construct naturally shaped by cultural and individual agency. Moving along the continuum, our minds increasingly rely on two cognitive universals: the neural capacity to entrain and synchronize different streams of pulsation,[6] and the ability to compare two sound events in terms of relations such as difference, similarity, and repetition.

6. In general, we can entrain pulsations that repeat durations of between 100 and 1500 microseconds.

These stimulate the listener to predict the recurrence of similar events at similar temporal intervals. This quality of predictability, which becomes more intense in each subsequent type of organization, is inherent to what we call musical *periodicity*.[7]

- When the timing of sound events is largely unpredictable because they are too fast, slow, multilayered, or otherwise complex, their rhythm is *unmeasured*.[8]
- When time intervals between events are related by simple proportions without exhibiting higher-order regularity, we feel them to be calibrated by a stream of equidistant *pulsations*. Such a stream organizes perception of the timing and duration of local events, and through it we are more able to anticipate when (and only a bit of what) near-future events will occur.
- When events *do* suggest higher-order regularity, we can track two or more synchronized streams as long as the pulsations' durations are related by sufficiently elementary ratios. This is the framework of *meter*. This multidimensional perceptual field allows more long-range prediction of content. A time span has *metric periodicity* if one can predict when (i.e., at what regular time intervals and rates coinciding with the pulsations) events will recur and, in a general way, what they will be.
- A *cycle* is a metric time span whose specific content and periodicity repeat in coordination, possibly with variation in either.[9] Events that appear at equivalent positions in different statements of a cycle play equivalent roles in the musical processes of the cycle.[10]

7. Note the distinction between this usage of *period* and that in European art music, where the term connotes a balanced antecedent-consequent phrase pair. Note also that the use of *meter* to mean "notated time signature" is avoided throughout.

8. A special case of unpredictability arises from concurrent pulsation streams not coordinated by simple ratios. See the discussion of ASWM's chapter II under "I. Open Transformative" on pages 437–438 below.

9. Cycles with unmeasured (hence unmetered) rhythm occur but none are in this corpus. Cycles with only a single pulsation stream are probably not possible because the repetition itself marks a second level of periodicity.

10. As with the Thelonious Monk selection, the *iŭmsae II* pattern in Hesselink's analysis of Korean drumming (both in this volume), certain kinds of gamelan music, plus other examples, a cultural expectation for immediate repetition can suffice to qualify a time span as a cycle or ostinato cycle, even if it does not actually repeat in a given instance.

• An *ostinato cycle* is a cycle with a duration that approximates the psychological present, usually repeated many times. Ostinato cycles are brief, such that our attention grasps the entirety.

In the first three types, in which content need not repeat, time organization may be said to be *open,* whereas in the last two, which involve cyclic recurrence, it is *closed.* But as befits a continuum it is important to see the progression through the five categories as gradual. Moving from simple pulsation to meter to cycle, both time organization and content gradually bring repetition to the fore. But repetition and its lack are elusive to pin down: they are manifestations of sameness and difference, a duality permanently underlying all experience. Experience is multidimensional and repetition always coexists with change. What we observe moving through the continuum is the emergence of the former and the gradual (but never full) retreat of the latter.

For example, in unmeasured rhythm we might understand repetition simply as the continuation of something already begun, without expectation of specific timing for change. Only when change comes can we measure the distinctiveness of what was before. With simple pulsation, timing plays a role, and we begin to cognize relationships of sameness between events because by entraining them we regularize and compare them. In meter we may expect still more, such as a certain *kind* of event—say, the arrival of a new harmony—at predictable moments. In a cyclic recurrence we would expect not only a harmony change but a particular harmony; and in an ostinato cycle a brief series of such changes fuse into an insistent unit.

In some textures we can perceive multiple, interacting types of time organization, possibly dislodging the sense of directed progression from type to type depicted here. Rhythm configurations interpretable in terms of open frameworks—unmeasured, pulsed, or metered—may extend over and be parsed in terms of shorter cycles that are present simultaneously. Such layers, if in different meters or pulsation rates (tempi), are perceived as independent in proportion to the complexity of the ratios of their pulsation speeds.

Focus: Toward which of the five kinds of time organization does a music tend, and to what extent does it move among or layer them?

I.2. Configuration (Figure A.1, Column 6)

Keywords: configuration, mark, group, identity, variation, section, metacycle.

A series of sounds may be *marked* by contrasts in rhythm, tone color (including pitch, harmony, timbre, etc.), or loudness; it may contain recognizable patterns and repetitions that have beginnings and endings. Marks and patterns configure sound series into *groups* (such as motives and phrases).

Groups have multifaceted *identities* determined by listener expectation, cultural norm, compositional theory, performance practice, and other codes. We perceive them as arranged hierarchically, so that groups can nest in larger groups, or be segmented into smaller groups.

Group is a general term that denotes the mere presence of marks, but says nothing about repetitiveness or transformation. Naturally, the music in a group can repeat that of a previous group, with or without *variation* in content and duration. Groups are thus linked, via the concept of repetition, to cycles, and are often synchronized with them but should not be confused with them. Groups are defined by marks and by repeated or varied content, not consistency of duration.

I.2A. LARGE GROUP TYPES: SECTION, METACYCLE

- *Sections* are groups that are so long and distinctive that the changes from one to the next are perceived as the most important formal divisions of the music. As with groups, sensations of cadence or "reset" prevail at section boundaries, but not necessarily repetition/periodicity.
- *Metacycles* are a special case of sections in cyclic and ostinato cyclic contexts. They emerge when a configuration pattern spans two or more cycles, beginning and ending at their boundaries.

I.2B. PROCESSES THAT ARTICULATE SECTIONS AND METACYCLES

The following processes, deriving from the basic types of mark mentioned above, are among those at work in the corpus. Not all are operative in any given music.

- *Melodic (or textual) articulation:* An idiomatic melodic ending, beginning, or return, possibly aligned with a textual boundary, such as the end of a strophe or refrain.
- *Harmonic articulation:* A harmonic arrival of significance within its particular system.
- *Modal shift:* Articulation via shift from one pitch mode to another.
- *Instrument change:* Change of instrumentation, orchestration, predominant timbre, or featured instrument.
- *Structural tempo change:* In other words, not merely an inflection.
- *Change of time organization:* Movement among different kinds of time organization (as above).
- Others such as registral shift, dynamic contrast, and so on.

When groups transform, we use memory to check the identity of an unfolding group against those previously heard. Acculturated listeners track a group's transformation, follow which dimensions are intrinsic to its identity, and can perceive which of its dimensions are preserved, varied, or jettisoned.

Focus: Which configuration techniques are present, and how do they form sections and/or metacycles?

I.3. Formal Continuity (Figure A.1, Column 7)

Keywords: stasis (repetition, cyclicity), transformation (through-composition), rupture (alternation), sectionality.

Musical time may be *static* in some aspects (e.g., harmony or sectional content) and simultaneously *transformative* in others (e.g., timbre or density of events), and then suddenly *rupture* into something new. The relative predominance of these qualities is always fluctuating and contextual. In evaluating this balance we consider the nature of the events themselves, their durations and proportions with respect to one another and to sections or wholes, and the degree of contrast or continuity between them. These terms are meant to be value-neutral and not to connote "progress" or "timelessness" or other culturally coded terms; indeed, any music can be static *or* transformational and at the same time be experienced viscerally (or not) as dynamic, engaging, calm, dramatic, spiritual, vulgar, and so on.

Prolonged stasis and continual transformation are really only ideals, since *repetition* can only approach the limit of actual stasis, and its lack can merely suggest continuous change. In their "pure" forms, we can imagine stasis as ‖:A:‖, that is, a continual repetition of an unvarying group, and transformation as A → B (the arrow can be read as "leads to"), that is, the presentation of a distinctive group (or section) followed by a contrasting one. That the "pure" states are hypothetical may be seen by reflecting that they are in permanent dialog: our proclivity to anticipate the future can give a directedness to unvarying repetition, while change that constantly thwarts expectation can make time seem undirected.

For example, repetition with incremental variation (A → A' → A", etc.) generates different stasis than a single exact iteration (A → A), yet even the latter contains transformative aspects because the iteration is heard in the fresh context of coming *after* its initial statement. A chain of strongly contrasting groups (A → B → C, etc.) is differently transformative than an incremental one (A → A' → A", etc.), but the latter of this pair also suggests stasis (as stated). The engine of the ambiguity lies equally in the formulation A → A,' which denotes both change and stasis, and in the fact that different such processes may be occurring simultaneously in different synchronic dimensions.

Definitive *alternation* between qualities creates hybrids. Perhaps the most forceful ("purest") action of this sort is the change from one kind of repetition to another, as in ‖:A:‖ → ‖:B:‖. Sometimes repetition gives way to transformation (‖:A:‖ → B → C), or vice versa (A → B → ‖:C:‖), or switches from one kind (or rate) of repetition or transformation to another (A → A' → B → C). An A → B transformation suggests rupture to the extent that the articulating moment is clearly marked, and the segments before and after are relatively stable and contrasting. Alternation happens in an instant but its effect ripples ahead in anticipation and back through memory.

A music's *sectionality* is the aspect of its form that emerges through these and other related processes of forming sections (or metacycles). For the present we are concerned with those comprising relatively larger proportions of the whole. In the corpus we identify *cyclical, sectional,* and *through-composed* (i.e., consistently transformational at the sectional level) formal continuities.

Focus: To what extent is each of the three temporal qualities present, and how does sectionality shape them?

I.4. Ambiguities and Overlaps

Understanding the relationship between the formal continuities just introduced, their three associated qualities (stasis, transformation, rupture), and time organization requires the practical reconciliation of contrasts and the overlapping of nominally distinct categories. The following conundrums—conceptual, cultural, and cognitive—may help disabuse those for whom the illusion persists that the categories described thus far are discrete.

CONCEPTUAL

Repetition may be only a mental framework in some situations. If what recurs is a conceptual referent or model (as it is for many kinds of improvisation and variation), sound may be manifest externally as transformative, sometimes radically so. Only in some cases (repeating rhythms, cyclical harmonic progressions, etc.) are these kinds of time organization materialized. Thus, for example, the conditions specified above for *ostinato cycles*—brevity and repetition—might, if the repetition is only in the mind of the performer, suggest (mere) meter to a listener. As stated, the boundaries between the kinds of time organization are easily blurred.

Duration and scale further blur our perceptions of cycle and meter. How long is too long for a cycle to be understood or felt as a recurring structure? As such structures extend in duration, our awareness may focus on local events with noncyclic properties; the cyclic enclosure receding out of immediate sensory experience and into conceptual awareness.

Irregularity is another conceptual gray area. In meters where all pulse streams are merely isochronous (i.e., relatively featureless), meter may be felt as a regulating, calibrating action, not an actual rhythmic entity. But at what point does a distinctive metric periodicity of (for example) seven pulses organized 2 + 2 + 3 become perceived as an actual pattern in the musical flow, and at what point does it cause the flow to be heard as an ostinato cycle? Context, of course, is all.

CULTURAL

Cultural and historical patterns are always shifting, but people of all eras and places acculturate to particular ways of listening. Human communities of the past, more mutually isolated and exposed to fewer kinds of rhythm, perhaps recognized correspondingly fewer rhythms as musical. What was reported as cacophony in earlier cross-cultural encounters might well be called sublime today, but can ever be misheard in cultural terms. What may sound like unmeasured rhythm to one may relate to pulse for another, or be generated by a performer in relation to an internal, unstated pulse or cycle. The organization of densely layered, intensely cyclic music (as in many sub-Saharan instances) can be impenetrable to the outsider's ear. And the ability to perceive long-range harmonic relationships such as in European classical music clearly requires extensive training.

COGNITIVE

Cognition as shaped by human evolution acutely shapes perception. Age, experience, and training all play roles in refining innate capacities. Bodily impulse to entrain is strong. It may cause listeners or performers to group sounds in terms of a pulsation (breath, pulse, heartbeat) even when none is meant. Or, in the case of some kinds of complexity (e.g., Roeder, *ASWM* 11) *not* to perceive pulsation even though it is a necessary calibrator for performers. Each musical instance is its own special case; separation of concepts is equal parts necessity and convenience. This, again, is why analysis thrives on particulars rather than generalities.

II. Orientation in the Repertoire through Analysis of Sections

In figure A.1 the corpus has been sorted into ten temporality categories, named in the leftmost column of each row. Figure A.2 displays the categories as a topology. Most of these ten evolve into one another as if moving from the most cyclically constrained to the freest and most aperiodic—as if from a concentrated, strictly bounded field to an unbounded, transformational, quasi-free liberty of movement. We must distinguish the categories themselves—intended as a higher-order system of temporalities with its own useful anatomy—from the subjective musical *experiences* they provide. Within each category the items from the corpus (if more than one) are ordered to illustrate a certain gradation within the category. But in figure A.2, categories B and E lurch out in another direction, as will be explained. Each category is treated separately below; the corpus is referenced by chapter number (*ASWM* or *ACCSWM* [the current volume]) and author. The focus questions introduced above comprise core concerns and are repeated here for convenience:

- *Toward which of the five kinds of time organization does a music tend, and to what extent does it move among or layer them?*
- *Which configuration techniques are present, and how do they form sections and/or metacycles?*
- *To what extent is each of the three temporal qualities (stasis, transformation and rupture) present, and how does sectionality shape them?*

THE EXTREMES

Consistent with I.3 above,[11] three items in the corpus are seen as approaching the "pure" states of stasis and transformation and the "pure hybrid" of rupture more closely than any others. They are, respectively, the Aka Pygmy song *Dìkòbò dámù dá sòmbé,* the "timbre-and-form" music of the BSC's *Phoneme (3);* and the Korean *p'ungmul p'an kut* (categories A, J, and C, boxed and shaded in figure A.2).

A. "PURE" OSTINATO CYCLIC: I. FÜRNISS (ASWM, CH. 5)

Dìkòbò dámù dá sòmbé never departs from a twelve-pulsation (thirty-six-subdivision) ostinato cycle in which, by definition, each position in the pulse stream is considered structurally equivalent to its counterparts in subsequent cycles. The unchanging identity of the four constituent melodic parts, as understood by the musicians, generates the music's static aspects. Given the Aka's flexible approach to the actual realization of the four parts, each ostinato cycle may in fact sound partly transformed and can also be experienced in terms of this change. The flow is nonetheless ‖:A:‖ because although there is some variation, it is limited compared to other ostinato cyclic music (see category B). Nevertheless, the four contrapuntal parts are in constant fluctuating motion; there is no default state. In this performance

---

11. . . . and with *ASWM*'s three supercategories isoperiodicity, sectionality, and linear composition.

each group begins with, and lasts as long as, an ostinato cycle. Sections are thus marked by those same boundaries, and there are no metacycles (see Fürniss figure 5.2).

B. CYCLIC—DISCURSIVE: 2. TENZER (ASWM, CII. 6);

3. SUTTON/VETTER (ASWM, CH. 7)

The term *discursive cyclicity* suggests a transformative temporality anchored by a permanent cycle. How is this possible? These analyses depict a cycle that, as it repeats over and over, draws a basic melodic structure through a series of transformations in elaboration and (particularly striking) radical tempo changes that create a through-composed whole. This disturbs neither the identity of the underlying melody nor the duration of the cycle as measured in number of pulsations—however much the pulsations may slow down or accelerate.

In the Balinese gamelan example, the initial melody is brief, configured with an unchanging sequence of skeletal tones—literally stated among the many sound layers—and marked with a fixed pattern of gong strokes. The Javanese example is also made that way, except that the duration of its initial melody exceeds the psychological present (lasting nineteen seconds, from 0:07 to 0:26), so that strictly speaking it is a cycle and not an ostinato cycle. But for this category the distinction recedes in importance. What matters is that essential features of the initial structure recur unchanged (as in all cyclic music) but the duration of the cycle constantly varies, constructing an idiosyncratically elastic temporality. These strong affinities, combined with the appearance of a true ostinato cycle in the Balinese example (and the fact of their existence in other Javanese examples), explain their coexistence within a single category, and the location of the category in the topology.

In both examples a series of metacycles occurs at irregular intervals of two or more cycles, articulated by changing melodic elaborations and tempi. The interaction here among stasis, transformation, and rupture is perhaps the most balanced in the corpus. But their unique integration in this music interrupts the flow of the temporal categories in column 1 of figure A.1; hence the shifting of "B" all the way to the right (under "transformation") in figure A.2. To have placed the music farther down in column one (perhaps near G) would have prioritized the transformational aspects of the music over the cyclic ones and insufficiently weighted the deep structural anchor the cycle provides. Here, at its designated position, the specific nature of the transformation is clarified by stressing its debt to the cycle.

My analysis of Balinese music shows a mainly nonrepetitive overall structure with a few elements of large-scale formal return (or at least parallelisms; see Tenzer figure 6.6). But Sutton/Vetter's Javanese selection goes further, ending at a tempo vastly slower than that with which the music began, exploring melodic permutations distantly related to the basic melody, with exponentially greater rhythmic density; and even interpolating small segments in unmeasured rhythm that nearly undermine the cyclic frame (see Sutton/ Vetter figure 7.1). The selection begins as a rushing stream of cyclic regularity but is overtaken by an enormous, diffuse deceleration, descending through several levels of formal expansion and rhythmic multiplication. For both pieces, an appropriate representation of the overall form could be A → A' → A", and so on, with each letter corresponding to a cycle.

C. "PURE" HYBRID (TRANSFORMATIONAL/SECTIONAL/CYCLIC): 4.
HESSELINK (ACCSWM, CH. 7).

In the Korean *p'an kut,* a series of ostinato cycles unfolds. Their rhythms strongly contrasted to an acculturated ear, most are reinforced through unvaried repetition, and they occur without transitions between them. A few progress to the next ostinato after only a single statement, nonetheless retaining cyclic character in this context. Instrumental layers closely reinforce one another and the clarity of the structure. The temporal process thus comprises passage through a series of static spans, with each repeating ostinato cycle ultimately leading to rupture. The flow could be described as ‖:A:‖→‖:B:‖→. . .→‖:n:‖, each ‖:x:‖ corresponding to a metacycle comprising all the repetitions of each ostinato cycle. Since in this music transformation *equals* rupture and occurs exclusively at metacycle boundaries, stasis is juxtaposed with transformation more bluntly here than in any other selection in the corpus (see Hesselink figure 7.4).

D. SECTIONAL WITH OSTINATO CYCLE BASIS: 5. MANUEL (ASWM, CH. 3); 6.
TERAUCHI (ACCSWM, CH. 1); 7. MOORE/SAYRE (ASWM, CH. 4).

Categories D to F are mainly concerned with song and the setting of texts, or at least with succinct and self-contained melodies. Selections in D are related to those in B in that all have an ostinato cycle layer regulating other musical action: the repeating *compás* pattern in Manuel's chapter on *flamenco,* the *haya yo-hyôshi* drum-and-gong layer in Terauchi's discussion of *gagaku,* and the implicit *clave* of Moore/Sayre's Cuban *batá* analysis. Layered above each we find metacycles delineated by various means. In *flamenco* they form at the junctions of the strophic *copla* (sung verses) and the *falseta* (guitar interludes) with which they alternate (see Manuel figure 3.2). In *gagaku* it is the borders between three 8-"measure" melodies, each immediately repeated, and then returning together later in a fixed order (see Terauchi figure 1.17). In *batá* sections form when a series of drum patterns and songs shifts one to the next, sometimes the two layers in tandem, sometimes not (see Moore/Sayre figure 4.6).

Of these three selections it is the *flamenco* that has the most static conception in its upper layers (i.e., apart from the *compás*). Although there is plenty of melodic variation and slight through-composed change in the harmony (a few mild chordal tributaries and a different final cadence) the alternation between voice and guitar preserves a binary A → B → A' → B' and so on sectionality (each letter is one section). *Gagaku* is more transformative because it comprises exactly three distinct melodies, the third of which undergoes a modal shift: ‖:A:‖→‖:B:‖→‖:C:‖ etc. (see Terauchi figure 1.17). The *batá* selection has the most transformative construction because it uses five different drum patterns layered with seven songs, none of which recurs after it is replaced by another (i.e., ‖:a:‖→‖:b:‖→…→‖:e:‖ concurrently with ‖:A:‖→‖:B:‖→…→‖:G:‖). Moreover a trajectory of growing drum complexity overlays the whole.

E. SECTIONAL WITH NONMETRIC (PULSED OR UNMEASURED RHYTHM)
BASIS: 8. BLUM (ASWM, CH. 1; SĀQI-NĀME OF QOMRI); 9.
NETTL/LEVINE (ACCSWM, CH. 8; ARAPAHO WOLF DANCE SONG);
10. BARWICK (ACCSWM, CH. 9; KUNYIBINYI TJINGARRU).

This category is positioned between D and F to bridge the ostinati girding the former and the expanded cycles in the latter. Here is repetition (or near-repetition) of medium-sized internal structures. The selections' time organization includes cycles, single-stream pulsation, and in some spots unmeasured rhythm—hence the category's anomalous position in figure A.2. The difference between D and E in *how* sections are articulated is that in the latter it is only the grouping configurations of the melodic elements themselves that form boundaries. There is no repeating pattern allowing for the proportional segmentation of time. In these examples melodic grouping depends in turn upon the structuring of text (or vocable), but there is considerable freedom and irregularity in how text, melody, and pulsation work together.

Both pulse and unmeasured rhythm inform the structure of the Xorasani *Navā'i* analyzed by Blum, distinguishing it from the *flamenco* treated by Manuel. Both have an A → B → A' → B' sectionality (see Blum figure 1.10b), but where the guitar and vocal sections in *flamenco* are calibrated by the repeating *compás,* in the *Navā'i* irregularly accented strummed phrases with changing pulsation on the two-string *dotār* alternate repeatedly with *a capella* vocals declaimed in mainly unmeasured rhythm. In a slightly more intricate sectionality, the Arapaho song in Nettl/Levine's analysis is organized as ‖:A ‖: → B→A':‖:‖ (see Nettl/Levine figure 8.2). The highly irregular rhythms comprise an initial motive, followed by a transitional passage and the motive's varied restatement in a lower register. Though a steady drum pulsation underlies the whole, none of the beats are stressed and the idea of a shared pulse between the parts is difficult to substantiate. Barwick's analysis of *Kunyibinyi Tjingarru's* form as repeated AAAABBAAA reduces for current purposes to ‖:A → B → A':‖ (the second A is prime since it is shorter than the first; see Barwick figure 9.15). Here there is a clear alignment of clapstick and singers, and consequently an easily perceptible number of beats in each vocal phrase. But the sequence of durations (7, 9, 7, 9, 8, 8, 7, 7, and 6 beats) is too inconsistent for meter to be present.

Unlike in Xorasani song, the music and text in the Arapaho and Murriny Patha songs repeat verbatim, and are hence cyclic at that level. The irregular internal structure in both songs acquires metric periodicity only through this repetition. In this way they come to bear a resemblance to the expanded, fully metricized cyclic structures in F. The clear alignment of pulsation and vocal rhythm explains why the Barwick selection is placed last here, bumping up against the wall of that category.

F. SECTIONAL—CYCLIC: 11. STANYEK/OLIVEIRA (ACCSWM, CH. 3); 12. ZIPORYN/TENZER (ACCSWM, CH. 4); 13. LEACH (ACCSWM, CH. 2).

Temporality in this category is distinguished by the presence of relatively extended cycles of fixed length and identity that comprise the complete extent of the musical action. There is nothing outside the cyclic structure, either synchronically or diachronically; and although metacycles are possible, there are none in this sample. While all the music in the previous two categories had clear sectionality and often literal recurrence of melodies, it only approximated fully metricized cyclicity. In D, the smallest unit of repetition was the ostinato cycle, but other kinds of groupings were layered with it. In E, ostinato cycles vanished, ceding control to these larger, irregular groups, which correspond to lines of poetry or text repetitions. In F, each text strophe is coterminous with a cycle, analogous to these processes in E. But in F's comparatively extended cycles the irregularity reorganizes into hierarchically arranged internal sections.

Stasis is naturally evident at the level of the repeating cycle. Internally, there is transformation as we move through the variously contrasted sections internal to the cycle. In Stanyek and Oliveira's chapter the song *Sorriso Aberto's* full cyclic span is 98 two-beat metric units (measures) with internal divisions of 28 + 24 + 18 + 28. The two outer units are identical, the second a slightly truncated version of the same, but the third one is different; the sectionality is thus ‖:A → A' → B → A:‖. The song *I Should Care* has 32 four-beat measures divided 8 + 8 + 8 + 8 with sectionality ‖:A → B → A → C:‖.[12] Leach describes 56 three-beat units (i.e., "perfections") in her analysis of *De Petit Po*, organized into 18 + 18 + (13 + 7) with sectionality ‖:A → A' → (B → C):‖ (see Stanyek/Oliveira figure 3.2, Ziporyn/Tenzer figure 4.1, and Leach figure 2.4). The three selections are ordered within the category in this way because *Sorriso Aberto* has the most internal repetition, hence is the most static overall, while *De Petit Po* is both sectionally irregular and most internally through-composed. The asymmetrical syllable counts of the text lines and their melismatic treatment intensify this, making this music most transformative of the three. Note that in *pagode* and the medieval *balade* it is the texts themselves that mandate an action of strophic return. Without them, as in *I Should Care* (of course the song has words, but they are not sung in Thelonious Monk's performance) it is evident that each cycle has its own harmonic closure and *could* stand alone without repetition. Figure A.3 graphs a generalized comparison of categories D, E, and F.

G. SECTIONAL—METERED: 14. BUCHANAN/FOLSE (ASWM, CH. 2; GEORGI LE, LYUBILE); 15. MORRIS (ASWM, CH. 9).

This is music with metric time organization during which there are instances of internal repetition mixed with through-composed sections.[13] In these two pieces sections are built up from metric units ("measures," per the transcriptions), with melodic articulations aligned with beginnings and endings of these—just as melodies began and ended with the boundaries of a series of ostinato cycles in category D. But if sections repeat, they do so only once before moving on, sometimes (as in *Georgi le, Lyubile*) returning with a fully parallel structure that diverges only at the moment of cadence, or (as in the South Indian *varnam*) reappearing again later in the manner of a refrain, or simply cosmetically altered with subtle new filigree. Despite the temporary state of cyclicity such recurrences contribute, the music is not repetitive at any large scale. Melody develops throughout, traversing a long course to conclude somewhere quite different from the point of origin. The overall quality is more transformational than any category since B.

Buchanan and Folse's analysis of the song *Georgi le, Lyubile* describes two large sections of similar proportions, each further subdivided. The first contains four interior groups, the initial two of which immediately repeat verbatim, while the second two immediately repeat with modified ending cadences. The second large section contains a paired group with a modified second

12. See the chapter analysis for why this music can be treated as cyclic and metered even though in the performance analyzed there is neither a cyclic repetition nor a steady pulse. If treated as unmeasured rhythm, it could be argued that this music should appear in category E or I; if metric (not cyclic), in category G.

13. In *ASWM* the *horo* analyzed by Buchanan and Folse was classified under "Sectional Periodicities" and the music analyzed by Morris under "Linear Composition in Periodic Contexts." Their regrouping here is rationalized in these paragraphs. Note that the metric unit referred to here in relation to Morris's chapter is actually the 8-beat South Indian Adi *tāla*. It is commonplace to classify *tāla* as cycles both because of the importance of cyclicity in Indian culture and the recurring hand gestures that mark them. Here, however, I classify *tāla* as meters because repetition of the sounding music is neither expected nor required in many cases, and in particular this case.

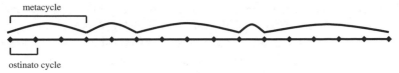

(a) Category D. An ostinato cycle layer, grouped by configuration in other layers into metacycles (i.e., beginning and ending at ostinato cycle boundaries) of irregular duration.

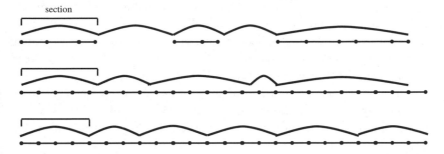

(b) Category E. Pulsation (or unmeasured rhythm) grouped by configuration into sections of irregular duration.
      Top: irregular pulsation alternating with unmeasured rhythm (e.g., Blum, #8).
      Middle: regular pulsation not aligned with rhythm (e.g., Nettl/Levine, #9).
      Bottom: regular pulsation aligned with rhythm (e.g., Barwick, #10).

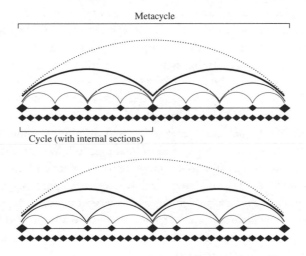

(c) Category F. Cycles of consistent length with hierarchically organized interior sections that begin and end at cycle boundaries (potential metacycle shown with dotted line).

Figure A.3.   Time organization and sectionality in categories D, E, and F of figure A.1

ending that repeats as a pair right away, followed by two longer phrases that are through-composed. With repeating pairs separated by commas, the whole is (6, 6 + 6, 6 + 4, 4' + 4, 4') + (‖:4, 4':‖ + 8 + 8) measures. Thus the song expands in group length and eschews exact repetition more and more as it proceeds (see Buchanana/Folse figure 2.19).

The twenty-nine metric units (*tāla*) in the South Indian *varnam* analyzed by Morris also split into two large sections, apportioned 13 + 16 as follows: (4 + 4 + (2 + 3)) + (3 + 3 + 3 + 5 + 2). The two initial four-*tāla* units further divide into an aabb internal structure, while all components in the second section begin with a refrain (the *carana*) lasting one metric unit. Thus there is a strong and growing transforming trajectory culminating in the through-composed five-*tāla* unit that begins at the twenty-third *tāla* (see Morris figure 9.4).

In both of these pieces sectional articulations are marked not only with new melody but usually also change of mode. Painted in broad strokes their sectionality is A → B, but those sections subdivide into a wealth of smaller parts as described.

H. TRANSFORMATIVE—SECTIONAL: 16. STOCK (ASWM, CH. 8); 17. BENJAMIN (ASWM, CH. 10).

These musics comprise extended forms with metric time organization, shaped by variety of lower-level periodicities and clear sectionality at a high level. Except for some very local events, nothing that recurs completes itself in the same way it does the first time it is heard. This integrated mixture of varied repetition, changing group lengths, and through-composition weakens the potential for cyclicity and greatly strengthens transformational quality to an intensity similar to that of the music in category B, below which this category is placed in figure A.2. In the Shanghai opera excerpt analyzed by Stock, the three consecutive large sections addressed (out of eight that comprise the complete opera scene) are of unequal length and articulated from one another by changes of mode, meter, register, tempo, and dramatic action. Within each, changing group durations and a call-and-response between singer and instruments create a constantly evolving and irregular flow (see Stock figures 8.2 and 8.7). Benjamin's analysis of the first movement of the Mozart concerto K. 453 shows the music to have six large sections of irregular length, distinguished by harmonic motion, opposition of piano and orchestra, thematic function, and many other features (Benjamin figure 10.2).

High-level sectionality can be represented as A → B → C for the Shanghai opera excerpt and A → B → A' → C → B' → A" for the Mozart movement, but these skeletal formulations, significant as they are for even expert listeners, give no inkling of the constant transformational momentum working at lower levels. (The variants of A and B in Benjamin's analysis retain a certain identity with their original versions, for example, but are thoroughly transformed by other processes at work.) Indeed, here in this category, for the first time in the topology, the notion of *grouping ambiguity* emerges. In categories A through F cycles exert control over section boundaries, and while they may have irregular internal structure there can never be doubt about where they start and stop. Their complete absence in this category means there can be many ways to interpret groups' beginning and ending points, especially in terms of how they link hierarchically at several levels of periodicity. In Benjamin's analysis especially the notion of *elision*—the overlapping of one group ending with another's beginning—can render metric periodicities unstable, their identities elusive.

I. OPEN TRANSFORMATIVE: 18. ROEDER (ASWM, CH. 11); 19. WIDDESS (ACCSWM, CH. 5).

Here are two kinds of specialized art music in which the gap between how the performer (or composer) and even an acculturated listener perceive the time organization can potentially be large. Both present long-range rhythmic trajectories that are intense and complex to parse in terms of a pulse, except for the dedicated and adept. The general classification scheme I am using hews to experts' perceptions, but this particular music exhibits an especially conceptual relationship between pulsation and rhythm. The music makers are pushing at the limits of what our entrainment capacities allow, and the authors of these chapters try to explain that perspective. But even experienced listeners may not feel the pulsations. So which experts should we heed? Perhaps the more salient factor justifying the chosen position in the topology is the music's complex and nearly unperiodic rhythmic surface, which is apparent to all.

The stark contrast between these two examples softens when viewed from the vantage point of this position in the topology. The Elliott Carter piece analyzed by Roeder is actually notated with straightforward time signatures allowing the performers to coordinate, but the musical patterns presented suggest a much more complex scheme of pulse streams and tempi unrelated by simple ratios. Similarly, sitarist Mukherjee, in Widdess's account, may possibly have referenced an inner pulse. But what most will experience, and what is perhaps intended in both cases, is a rhythm intricate enough to verge on the perceptually unmeasured, and such intricacy's frequent handmaiden, constant transformation. There are nonetheless emphatic articulations in these musics and with these one experiences ruptures among more and less intense qualities of change. Sections arise from the internal logic and shaping of configured patterns and not from any expectation of when changes should occur (except, in the case of the *ālāp*, a cultural understanding that a greater range of pitches will come into play as the music unfolds.)

Roeder's analysis of Carter's tightly scripted music as having eight sections (A → B → . . . H; *ASWM*, pp. 388–390) shows how the varied construction of local climaxes and nadirs defines sectionality in a new way at each moment of articulation. Widdess's figure 5.10 shows the A → B → C sectionality emerging from the slow climb through low, middle, and high registers. Without pulse, section junctures are not ambiguous in relationship to any periodic frame, as they were in the previous category—they emerge from the patterning of the configured sounds themselves.

J. "PURE" TRANSFORMATIVE: 20. BUNK (ACCSWM, CH. 6).

As if in the far reaches of the musical cosmos, *Phoneme (3)* evolves continually in a sparse unmeasured rhythm with only local, very approximate repetition of fragments, challenging our capacity to group events and edging provocatively close to a horizon of stasis as a result. Indeed the music's performers describe the stillness they value in it. Throughout, section-like components are articulated with varying degrees of intensity and clarity by ad hoc configurations, each further divided into smaller parts. Part of the delicacy of sectional change comes from the always changing layer formations. At the level of the three large sections identified in the chapter, the flow could be described as A → B → C, but with numerous subsections (see Bunk figure 6.2).

* * * *

The foregoing categorization is incomplete, though hopefully not fatally, and I have been mindful of its limitations. Further into the universe of music than we have been able to go, and beyond that at the borders of music and sound, must lie a range of other temporalities that we cannot name until we have isolated and felt them. Back in the very first sentence I spoke of "all music," aware that *music* is just a word, an evolving construct redefined each time we interact in a state of awareness with sound and time. Sound and our impermanent bodies are the media we have for experiencing time, and in so doing we cannot suppress the mimetic urgency of musical transformation and stasis, with whatever philosophical, aesthetic or spiritual dimensions they may have for the body and soul in one's particular historical or cultural position. Composer François-Bernard Mâche advised me to ask my students to always reflect that every musical utterance is a meditation on death, simply because its time will end. What he slyly didn't say is that each one is a celebration of life, and the varieties of music a catalog of ways to live.

Related Reading

Arom, Simha. 1991. *African Polyphony and Polyrhythm: Musical Structure and Methodology.* Cambridge: Cambridge University Press.

Bar-Yosef, Amatzia. 2007. "A Cross-Cultural Structural Analogy between Pitch and Time Organizations." *Music Perception* 24(3): 265–280.

Barry, Barbara. 1990. *Musical Time: The Sense of Order.* New York: Pendragon Press.

Benjamin, William. 1984. "A Theory of Musical Meter." *Music Perception* 1(4): 355–413.

Clayton, Martin. 1996. "Free Rhythm: Ethnomusicology and the Study of Music without Metre." *Bulletin of the School of Oriental and African Studies* 59(2): 323–332.

Hasty, Christopher. 1997. *Meter as Rhythm.* New York: Oxford University Press.

Kramer, Jonathan D. 1988. *The Time of Music: New Meanings, New Temporalities, New Listening Strategies.* New York: Schirmer.

London, Justin. 2004. *Hearing in Time: Psychological Aspects of Musical Meter.* New York: Oxford University Press.

Molino, Jean. 2009. *Le Singe Musicien: Essais de Sémiologie et d'anthropologie de la Musique.* Paris: Broché.

Nettl, Bruno. 2001. "Music." In *Grove Music Online. Oxford Music Online,* http://www.oxfordmusiconline.com/subscriber/article/grove/music/40476 (accessed November 24, 2010).

Parncutt, Richard. 1994. "A Perceptual Model of Pulse Salience and Metrical Accent in Musical Rhythms." *Music Perception* 11(4): 409–464.

Pressing, Jeff. 1993. "Relations Between Musical and Scientific Properties of Time." *Contemporary Music Review* 7(2): 105–122.

Rahn, John. 1993. "Repetition." *Contemporary Music Review* 7(2): 49–57.

Rowell, Lewis. 1992. *Music and Musical Thought in Early India.* Chicago: University of Chicago Press.

———. 1983. *Thinking About Music: An Introduction to the Philosophy of Music.* Amherst: University of Massachusetts

Temperley, David. 2001. *The Cognition of Basic Musical Structures.* Cambridge, MA: MIT Press.

Tenzer, Michael. 2011. "Generalized Representations of Musical Time and Periodic Structures." *Ethnomusicology* 55/3: 369–386.

———. 2000. *Gamelan Gong Kebyar: The Art of 20th Century Balinese Music.* Chicago: University of Chicago Press.

Tenzer, Michael, ed. 2006. *Analytical Studies in World Music.* New York: Oxford University Press.

Zuckerkandl, Victor. 1956. *Sound and Symbol: Music and the External World.* Trans. Willard R. Trask. New York: Pantheon Books.

Simha Arom is an ethnomusicologist and emeritus director of research at the Centre National de la Recherche Scientifique (Paris). His work is principally concerned with the musical systematics of Central African polyphony, and more broadly with temporal organization, modelized structure, and cognitive aspects of oral tradition musics. Many composers—among them Luciano Berio, György Ligeti, and Steve Reich—have used musical processes in their works that he first brought to light.

Sound and silence are allies in the minimal yet intricate music of Lou Bunk. Lou earned a Ph.D. in composition and theory from Brandeis University and lives in Somerville, Massachusetts, where he chairs the Somerville Arts Council and coproduces the concert series Opensound. He composes acoustic and electroacoustic music that is programmed locally and internationally. He is an assistant professor of music at Franklin Pierce University in New Hampshire, where he teaches electronic music (www.loubunk.com).

Linda Barwick is an ethnomusicologist based at the University of Sydney. She has undertaken fieldwork in Australia, Italy, and the Philippines and is particularly interested in uses of digital technologies for extending access to research results by cultural heritage communities. Her publications include multimedia CDs accompanied by extensive scholarly notes, produced in collaboration with Indigenous singers and their communities. She is the director of PARADISEC, the Pacific and Regional Archive for Digital Sources in Endangered Cultures.

Nathan Hesselink (n.hesselink@ubc.ca) is a researcher-performer of South Korean percussion traditions. He received his Ph.D. in ethnomusicology from the University of London, SOAS, and was a postdoctoral research fellow at the University of California, Berkeley. His publications include *P'ungmul: South Korean Drumming and Dance* (University of Chicago Press, 2006) and *Music and Politics on the Korean Peninsula* (guest editor, *World of Music* 49.3). He is currently an associate professor of ethnomusicology at the University of British Columbia.

Elizabeth Eva Leach (elizabetheva.leach@music.ox.ac.uk) is a university lecturer in music at the University of Oxford and has published widely on the music and poetry of Guillaume de Machaut. Her monograph, *Guillaume de Machaut: Secretary, Poet, Musician,* will be published by Cornell University Press in 2011.

Victoria Lindsay Levine (vlevine@coloradocollege.edu.) serves as a professor of music at Colorado College, where she teaches ethnomusicology and comparative music theory. Specializing in Native North American musical cultures, Levine has published research on the music of Woodlands peoples of Oklahoma, especially the Choctaw and Yuchi, and on the history of transcriptions, notations, and arrangements of American Indian music. Levine also works with archival recordings of Spanish New Mexican music and is an avid performer of Balinese gamelan.

Denis-Constant Martin (denisconstant.martin.monsite.orange.fr) is a senior research fellow at Sciences Po Bordeaux (CEAN, University of Bordeaux), where he teaches political anthropology. His research focuses on comparative studies of the relationship between culture and politics, and on the sociology of popular music. He has published about a hundred articles in academic journals and more than fifteen books or edited volumes, including *Coon Carnival, New Year in Cape Town, Past and Present* (Cape Town, David Philip, 1999); *Sur la Piste des OPNI (Objets politiques non identifiés)* (Paris, CERI/KARTHALA, 2002); and *Quand le Rap Sort de sa Bulle, Sociologie Politique d'un Succès* (Paris, Mélanie Séteun/IRMA, 2010).

Bruno Nettl (b-nettl@illinois.edu), educated at Indiana University, has devoted his career mainly to teaching ethnomusicology at the University of Illinois, where he is now a professor emeritus of music and anthropology.

With fieldwork experience among the Blackfoot and Arapaho peoples, and in Iran and India, he is the author of several books, including *Blackfoot Musical Thought: Comparative Perspectives* (1989), *The Study of Ethnomusicology: 31 Issues and Concepts* (2005), and *Nettl's Elephant: On the History of Ethnomusicology* (2010).

Dr. Terauchi Naoko is a professor of Japanese performing arts at Kobe University, Japan. Her publications include *Gagaku no rizumu kôzô* (The Rhythmic Structure of *Gagaku*, 1996), "The Western Impact on Traditional Music: 'Reform' and 'Universalization' in the Modern Period of Japan" (*Journal of Chinese Ritual, Theatre and Folklore* 141, 2003), and "Beyond the Court: A Challenge to the *Gagaku* Tradition in the 'Reconstruction Project' of the National Theatre" in *Performing Japan: Contemporary Expressions of Cultural Identity* (2008).

Dr. Fabio Oliveira is a percussion soloist who directs the Percussion and Drum-set Programs at the Federal University of Goiás, in Brazil. As an avid performer of contemporary classical music as well as traditional Brazilian Samba and Pagode, he's performed in the Americas, Europe, and Asia. Dr. Oliveira has recorded for Tzadik and New World Records, and he can also be heard on Mode Records in upcoming DVDs featuring the percussion music of Roger Reynolds and Karlheinz Stockhausen performing alongside Steven Schick and redfishbluefish. He earned a B.M. from the São Paulo State University in Brazil, an M.M. at University of Massachusetts–Amherst, and a.D.M.A. at University of California–San Diego.

John Roeder, coeditor of this volume, is a professor in the School of Music at the University of British Columbia. He specializes in the theory and analysis of music outside the classical Western canon, focusing especially on rhythmic and pitch processes in recent art music. Grants from the Social Sciences and Humanities Research Council of Canada have supported his research into graphical representations of music, musical transformations, the preservation of digital art, and musical periodicity.

Jason Stanyek has published on subjects ranging from Brazilian hip hop to Pan-African jazz, from intercultural free improvisation to capoeira. He is a member of the advisory board of *Critical Studies in Improvisation* and the multimedia reviews editor of the *Journal for the Society of American Music.* Currently he is a member of an international research team for a major collaborative project entitled "Improvisation, Community, and Social Practice." Also highly active as a performer and composer, he has released two CDs as a guitarist with the improvisation quartet O'Keefe, Stanyek, Walton, White-head and served as an assistant conductor for the premiere recording of Anthony Davis's opera *Tania*.

Michael Tenzer (www.michaeltenzer.com), coeditor of this volume, is a professor in the School of Music at the University of British Columbia. He is the editor of *Analytical Studies in World Music* (Oxford University Press, 2006) and author of *Gamelan Gong Kebyar: The Art of Twentieth Century Balinese Music* (University of Chicago Press, 2000), as well as other articles and books. In 2009 New World Records released *Let Others Name You,* a CD of his intercultural compositions for diverse ensembles.

Richard Widdess is a professor of musicology in the Department of Music, School of Oriental and African Studies (SOAS), University of London. He specializes in the musicology of South Asia, with reference to the history and theory of Indian classical music, and the religious music traditions of the Kathmandu Valley. He also has research interests in the analysis of performance, music cognition, and orality in music and language.

Evan Ziporyn (www.ziporyn.com) is an award-winning composer, clarinetist, founding member of the Bang on a Can All-Stars, and Kenan Sahin distinguished professor at the Massachusetts Institute of Technology. He has performed and recorded his own and others' music with the world's most prominent creative musicians, including Brian Eno, Ornette Coleman, Thurston Moore, Meredith Monk, Steve Reich, Paul Simon, and many others. His decades of involvement with the Balinese gamelan tradition have resulted in a series of cross-cultural compositions, including *A House in Bali* (2009), an opera for singers, dancers, gamelan, and chamber ensemble.

Numbers in boldface direct the reader to definitions or initial descriptions